This exciting new book is essential for understanding sexuality and gender in the 21st century. Topics range widely, from sexting to sexual assault. Many chapters are deeply personal, but with broader social implications. This book will stimulate animated conversation and deep thinking; it is one of the most important books on gender and sexuality in the past thirty years.

Tom Digby, *Professor of Philosophy, Springfield College, and author of* Love and War: How Militarism Shapes Sexuality and Romance

This sparkling book challenges us to pursue fresh critical thinking on feminist issues of exploitation and empowerment, pointing out how we can use constructive dissent rather than destructive disagreement—a great addition to the canon.

Loretta Ross, *Former National Coordinator, SisterSong Women of Color Reproductive Justice Collective*

In our insanely fast-paced, Twitter-trigger world, discussion of sexuality and gender too often consists solely of snarky knee-jerk statements that do nothing to contest dominant thinking. These essays, on the other hand, invite us to think and rethink about power, and for the best reason of all: so that we can equalize it. If you care about gender, sex, and politics, this book is for you.

Leora Tanenbaum, *author of* I Am Not a Slut: Slut-Shaming in the Age of the Internet

This is a must-read for the academic and practical alike and should be in every college sociology and psychology course. The first chapter "Hollaback!" is an eye-opener and makes me want to join the movement. The book goes on to unveil many truths we must all face.

Kristin Beck, *former US Navy SEAL, and Candidate for US Congress 2016*

Forty years after the sex wars first captured popular imagination, Shira Tarrant makes it brilliantly clear that sex wars matter anew. In this edgy collection of truth-tellers, contributors invite readers to open their minds, hearts, and conversations. They redefine sexual literacy and challenge the very notion of taboo. Bridging theory, practice, and competing perspectives, the book unsettles and entices. As with the best in gender studies, it's sure to hit a nerve.

Deborah Siegel, *PhD, author of* Sisterhood, Interrupted: From Radical Women to Grrls Gone Wild

GENDER, SEX, AND POLITICS

Gender, Sex, and Politics: In the Streets and Between the Sheets in the 21st Century includes twenty-seven chapters organized into five parts: Gender, Sexuality, and Social Control; Pornography; Sex and Social Media; Dating, Desire, and the Politics of Hooking Up; and Issues in Sexual Pleasure and Safety. This anthology presents these topics using a point-counterpoint-different point framework. Its arguments and perspectives do not pit writers against each other in a binary pro/con debate format. Instead, a variety of views are juxtaposed to encourage critical thinking and robust conversation. This framework enables readers to assess the strengths and shortcomings of conflicting ideas. The chapters are organized in a way that will challenge cherished beliefs and hone both academic and personal insight. *Gender, Sex, and Politics* is ideal for sparking debates in introduction to women's and gender studies, sexuality, and gender courses.

Shira Tarrant, PhD, is Professor of Women's, Gender, and Sexuality Studies at California State University, Long Beach. She has written and edited several books including *Men and Feminism* (Seal Press), *When Sex Became Gender* (Routledge), and *Men Speak Out: Views on Gender, Sex, and Power* (Routledge). Read more at http://shiratarrant.com.

Titles of Related Interest from Routledge

Men Speak Out: Views on Gender, Sex, and Power, Second Edition
Edited by Shira Tarrant

Women, Science, and Technology: A Reader in Feminist Science Studies,
Third Edition
Edited by Mary Wyer, Mary Barbercheck, Donna Cookmeyer, Hatice Ozturk, and Marta Wayne

Reproduction and Society: Interdisciplinary Readings
Edited by Carole Joffe and Jennifer Reich

Gender Circuits: Bodies and Identities in a Technological Age,
Second Edition
By Eve Shapiro

Pursuing Intersectionality, Unsettling Dominant Imaginaries
By Vivian M. May

Threshold Concepts in Women's and Gender Studies: Ways of Seeing,
Thinking, and Knowing
By Christie Launius, and Holly Hassel

GENDER, SEX, AND POLITICS

In the Streets and Between the Sheets in
the 21st Century

Edited by Shira Tarrant

NEW YORK AND LONDON

First published 2016
by Routledge
711 Third Avenue, New York, NY 10017

and by Routledge
2 Park Square, Milton Park, Abingdon, Oxon, OX14 4RN

Routledge is an imprint of the Taylor & Francis Group, an informa business

© 2016 Taylor & Francis

Library of Congress Cataloging in Publication Data
Gender, sex, and politics : in the streets and between the sheets in the
   21st century / edited by Shira Tarrant.
      pages cm
   Includes bibliographical references and index.
   1. Sex—United States.   2. Social control—United States.   3. Social
media—United States.   4. Feminism—United States.   I. Tarrant, Shira,
1963–
HQ18.U5G463 2015
306.70973—dc23
2015002725

ISBN: 978-0-415-73783-8 (hbk)
ISBN: 978-0-415-73784-5 (pbk)
ISBN: 978-1-315-81779-8 (ebk)

Typeset in Adobe Caslon
by ApexCoVantage, LLC

CONTENTS

PREFACE

Sexting, hookups, abortion, and porn are familiar topics for most students in a college classroom. These are the sorts of things that students—and, really, all of us—daydream about (dating), cope with (street harassment), and get angry over (sexual assault). What may be newer for some readers of *Gender, Sex, and Politics*, though, is the opportunity to think critically and to talk out loud about these issues. This book introduces controversial, and sometimes contentious, subjects with which the contemporary landscape of gender and sexual politics is infused. The perspectives in this book may be challenging for readers. Sometimes, the authors' views challenge each other.

To that end, this anthology is organized using a point-counterpoint-different point framework. Its arguments and perspectives do not pit writers against each other in a binary pro/con debate format. Instead, a variety of views are juxtaposed to encourage critical thinking and robust conversation. This framework enables readers to assess the strengths and shortcomings of conflicting ideas. The chapters are organized in a way that will challenge cherished beliefs and hone both academic and personal insight.

This book is designed to appeal to curious readers, students and professors, activists and organizers. In doing so, *Gender, Sex, and Politics* includes twenty-seven chapters organized into five sections: Gender, Sexuality and Social Control; Pornography; Sex and Social Media; Dating, Desire, and the Politics of Hooking Up; and Issues in Sexual Pleasure and Safety. Included throughout the chapters are sidebars that define key terms, provide quantitative data to further the discussions, and present counter-evidence to the debates. Organized with the intention that readers (and educators) will select from this combined material as each sees fit, the essays in this anthology—which are forthright accounts of contemporary gender and sexuality—highlight the personal struggles, political viewpoints, academic scholarship, and engaged concerns the authors bring to bear in their writing. The chapters are not included on the basis of meeting a political litmus test but, rather, on the basis of how deeply the topics encourage people to think. I hope that this book provokes discussion and that readers will relate to, argue about, agree and disagree with, expand on, and improve upon the ideas presented here. Ultimately, I hope points of both agreement and disagreement, review of well-worn paths, and new topics and perspectives will enable the reader to engage with these issues more powerfully.

This anthology includes subjects and concerns that impact many, yet few discuss. Among many of my activist-educator friends and colleagues, female ejaculation and pornography is dinnertime conversation. But it's easy to forget that talking about these topics is not routine. Usually, I'm reminded of that in the classroom with my students who want to learn more information—not just from cable news polemics. They want to talk about sex and gender politics, debate the issues, learn how to discern between reliable and questionable data, and they are excited to have the chance. It was this enthusiasm, and the need to talk openly about various issues and perspectives regarding sex and gender, that spawned my idea for this book. The point is not to agree (although I have my preferences). My hope is that *Gender, Sex, and Politics* provides tools for increasing understanding and articulating questions about issues that matter in deeply personal and political ways. I hope this book is a beginning to future conversations.

ACKNOWLEDGMENTS

Thank you to my current and former students who provided research assistance and brainstorming sessions about the ideas in this book. My appreciation goes to Mandy Acklen, Cassie Comley, Elizabeth Juarez, Amber Melvin, Nia Pines, and Jessica Ross for their research and editorial assistance. I appreciate your insight about the issues in this collection that prompted many lively (and sometimes irreverent) conversations. Thank you to the Routledge crew: Samantha Barbaro, Margaret Moore, Steve Rutter, and the marketing and editing teams that made this book possible. Comments and suggestions from reviewers helped refine this collection as the project took shape:

Gene Kelly	Lafayette College
Robyn Epstein	University of Maryland, Baltimore County
Mishuana Goeman	University of California, Los Angeles
Becca Cragin	Bowling Green State University
Carol Conaway	University of New Hampshire
Tanya Bakhru	San Jose State University
Catherine Orr	Beloit College
Meredith Worthen	University of Oklahoma
Melissa Meade	Colby Sawyer College
Lorena Russell	University of North Carolina, Asheville
Jill Gillespie	Denison University
Michelle Scatton-Tessier	University of North Carolina, Wilmington
Julie Berebitsky	Sewanee University
Ausra Buzenas	Indiana University Northwest
Ellie Schemenauer	University of Wisconsin-Whitewater

| Kimberly Welch | University of Redlands |
| Brian Jara | West Virginia University |

A timely writing retreat with Lynn Comella helped me finish the book with needed warmth and support (#PalmSprings). As always, my love goes to my family. Emilie Tarrant and Roman Rozenblyum: Your love back makes everything possible.

INTRODUCTION

Shira Tarrant

I don't agree with every viewpoint in this book. And neither will you.

The point of *Gender, Sex, and Politics* is to promote post-oppositional critical awareness of gender, sex, and politics. Oppositional politics involves the unproductive practice of pitting people against each other, getting mired in binary us/them thinking; the risk is that progressive movements can implode from antagonism. There is a difference, though, between constructive dissent and destructive disagreement. As AnaLouise Keating says, "I've been concerned by the limitations in oppositional politics, oppositional forms of thinking, and the oppositional interactions I've seen in classrooms, at conferences, and among various politicized academic groups."[1] To this, I say a hearty *Yes*!

Embracing post-oppositional politics requires that we create the skills for truly listening to each other, especially when there is good reason to disagree, get angry, or feel defensive. The chapters in this collection challenge readers to do so by boldly addressing subjects such as sexting, pornography, abortion, and street harassment. There is a chapter about dating while fat, one about inappropriate sex questions that strangers ask people with disabilities, and another about the problem of sexual violence on campus. The writers in this collection will ask you to think about rough sex, anal sex, hooking up, and transgender experiences. Reading about these topics can be new, exciting, uncomfortable, or even embarrassing. Some chapters in this collection are controversial and inspiring. Readers might even find some chapters offensive while other readers will find the topics are old hat. So why do I hope that you will read them? Because we live in a cultural climate that is immersed in sex and opinion, but often provides little factual information to provide foundations for reasoned debate. We all have desires and political perspectives but when we talk about sex and gender politics—if we discuss these things at all—we often tend to stick with like-minded people. When we stumble across folks with whom we disagree, the conversations easily become fights on the streets, in the bars, or at our family dinner tables. These disagreements can be unproductive and beleaguering.

Gender, Sex, and Politics: In the Streets and Between the Sheets in the 21st Century provides opportunities to think through various perspectives and ideas that we may take for granted or assume to be true. These chapters encourage us to examine our assumptions and presuppositions and come to better informed understanding about the politics of sex and gender. I hope this book serves as a catalyst for open conversations across communities, even—and especially— when we disagree.

The freedom to think and believe what we want, and the freedom to express these thoughts and opinions, is at the heart of liberty and democracy. But democratic liberty is flawed when we are coerced or under-informed, and it is improved when we have data that hones the accuracy of our opinions. Without liberty *and* information there is the danger of a huge pressure to conform to popular opinion. This pressure to conform, or to go along with the crowd, is the antithesis of liberty. To that end—and particularly instructive for conversations about sexuality and sexual politics—are four specific reasons why it is necessary for our collective well-being that we have cultural and legal freedom of opinion and the freedom to express these opinions: First, what happens if we silence somebody's opinion and it turns out they were right? To deny this possibility is to presume that we are perfect. And, of course, nobody is perfect. Second, what if we silence somebody else's opinion and they are wrong? Even the most flawed perspectives may—and often do—contain a kernel of truth. The opinions we hold on a subject are hardly ever the *entire* truth, and we benefit by hearing contrary perspectives. "It is only through the collision of adverse opinions," writes John Stuart Mill, "that the remainder of the truth has any chance of being supplied."[2]

Third, what if somebody has an opinion we don't agree with . . . and it turns out they are right? It is important that people with opposing opinions have the freedom to express them. If we don't openly discuss issues and contested ideas, we will lose any understanding of the rational basis, the facts and data, on which knowledge is grounded. When that happens, opinions simply become dogma or prejudice. Finally, if we don't have the freedom to state our opinions—and the freedom to disagree—ideas lose their efficacy. Silencing people prevents the growth of any real and heartfelt conviction.

Liberty, knowledge, creativity, and strength of character do not come from being told what to do or from following the crowd. Each comes from having the freedom to have our own thoughts and opinions. Otherwise, we end up trying to blend in, or expressing nothing strongly, or having no clear opinions about much of anything at all. And this strikes at the very heart of liberty.

This book includes points, counterpoints, and different points on sexual pleasure and safety. Slut-shaming, hookups, sexting, and porn are among the backdrops to sex in the 21st century. Legal incursions into women's most private reproductive decisions are currently severe. Sexual politics are a popular focus of public debate. Media stories, political pundits, and best-selling books co-opt, exploit, and highlight sexuality, especially among younger adults. Yet when it comes to hook-up culture, pornography, sex work, reproductive justice, and even sexual assault, the experts disagree about the data and desired outcomes.

This book brings together various perspectives about key issues in contemporary sexual politics. Juxtaposing chapters from activists, scholars, and thought-leaders in the field, *Gender, Sex, and Politics* promotes dialogue and debate about the issues. This collection encourages readers to consider why the sex wars matter and what is at stake. This book promises to help each of us identify our core values and to thereby improve our dialogue among those with opposing viewpoints. To that end, *Gender, Sex, and Politics* will inform and empower readers to be savvy about sexuality in a media-saturated culture that is filled with competing perspectives.

THE CHAPTERS

Navigating the sexual climate of the 21st century can be challenging. Accurate data is sometimes hard to come by, the debates are often contentious, and the information can certainly be confusing—or even incorrect. We are immersed in a hypersexualized world with marketers and media selling sex 24/7. Yet we often lack the opportunity to talk rationally about the issues. Statements from pundits and anonymous online comments vie for attention and invoke moral panic, making it even harder to sift the sexual facts from the ideological fictions. This is especially true for when so many are provided with high-speed Wi-Fi but low-level literacy when it comes to understanding sexual politics.

The chapters in this collection are written by experts, activists, and educators, all concerned with issues such as sexual harassment, reproductive rights, pornography, premarital sex, kink, and queer rights. Many authors critically interrogate the ways in which race, class, gender, and geography intersect with sexual politics. In some chapters, privilege goes unexamined, and I invite readers to interrogate what this means and how it impacts our understandings of sexual pleasure and safety. By considering a variety of perspectives in a point-counterpoint-different point framework, *Gender, Sex, and Politics* promotes critical thinking, encourages debates about the issues, and provides tools for readers to think carefully about what is at stake when it comes to contemporary policies, legislation, and cultural trends in the public arena.

The chapters in this collection are thematically organized into five parts, beginning with Gender, Sexuality, and Social Control. This first part investigates a variety of issues including street harassment, victim blaming, SlutWalks and racism, the war on reproductive justice, transgender politics, and the difficulty of discussing abortion from differing viewpoints. These authors explore various ways gender and sexuality are used as tools for social control from the bedroom to the streets; they raise questions about gender, race, and stereotypes, while suggesting ways we might inform ourselves, improve our politics, and fight back. The chapters in Part II, Pornography, include forthright perspectives on pleasure, desire, sexism, and subjugation. This section includes competing feminist debates about porn, Christian cures for addiction, and a first-person chapter written by a porn performer describing his experience. This part makes clear that while there are many competing perspectives, there are no easy answers.

In Part III, Sex and Social Media, the authors address the various impacts of Internet culture on policing sexuality, finding allied queer communities, online infidelity, and debates about sexting, selfies, and safety. Part IV is titled Dating, Desire, and the Politics of Hooking Up. This group of chapters includes first-person perspectives on sex and disabilities, dating while fat, debates about orgasm rates, why some people hook up, and why asexual people aren't hooking up at all. The final part is Issues in Sexual Pleasure and Safety. These chapters juxtapose conversations about consensual rough sex, nonconsensual assault, anal sex, premarital and nonmarital sex. The collection ends with a chapter about enthusiastic consent and encourages positive sexuality in a culture that often promotes shame and blame about our personal sexual decisions. At the end of each chapter there are questions for discussion and further consideration.

In the spirit of John Stuart Mill and Harriet Taylor Mill, I encourage each of us to respectfully think, discuss, and debate the issues in this book. Doing so promotes free speech, well-formed decisions, and rational perspectives on what are often emotionally laden issues. Discerning where we stand in the pursuit of sexual justice, sexual pleasure, and sexual safety requires that we understand competing arguments. It is important that we are able to consider various points of view with intelligence and respect, knowing when to discard perspectives that promote narrow-minded thinking, hate, and factual inaccuracy. In doing so, we strengthen our own resolve to work for a better future in the public realm and in our private lives. Dear Readers: I want you to take a strong stand about gender, sex, and politics. I want these opinions to be as smart and as well informed as possible. I want each of us to be free from the harm of prejudice, the danger of gendered abuse, and the constraints of ideologically biased laws. I hope the information in *Gender, Sex, and Politics* helps hone these skills in critical analysis and promotes collective well-being. The personal is, after all, quite political.

NOTES

1. Layli Maparyan and AnaLouise Keating, "The Promise of Post-Oppositional Politics: A Preliminary Conversation," *Feminist Wire*, April 7, 2014, http://thefeministwire.com/2014/04/post-oppositional-politics/.
2. John Stuart Mill, *On Liberty and The Subjection of Women*, ed. Alan Ryan (New York: Penguin Classics, [1859] 2007).

Part I

Gender, Sexuality, and Social Control

The first section of *Gender, Sex, and Politics* includes a series of essays that explore how gender and sexuality are used as tools of social control. These six essays focus on street harassment, reproductive justice, and transgender politics. Thematically connecting each of the topics in Part I are three central questions: How is sexuality used as a form of social control; whose bodies are regulated; and who does the regulating?

Catcalls on the street, abortion politics, and emerging debates about transgender identity can have a deeply personal impact. However, these issues are not only matters of individual struggle. It is important to think about how gender and sexuality are deployed as vehicles to control groups of people and curtail our freedom. The essays in this section raise questions about gender, race, and stereotypes, while suggesting ways of improving our politics and fighting back against injustice.

In chapter 1, "Hollaback! You Have the Power to End Street Harassment," Emily May and Samuel Carter describe how and why the global Hollaback! movement got started. As violence prevention educator Jackson Katz writes, we like to say the United States is the most free nation in the world. Yet the prevalence of street harassment and the threat of sexual violence mean that half the population does not feel free to simply walk down the street. We therefore need to think about street harassment in terms of its effect and impact in terms of social control. Comments from "You'd look good on me" to groping, flashing, and assault are a daily, global reality for women and LGBTQ individuals. Street harassment is one of the most pervasive forms of gender-based violence and one of the least legislated against. Street harassment is rarely reported, and it is culturally accepted as "the price you pay" for being a woman, or for being gay, or for being gender nonconforming. Street harassment is actually a form of social control that interferes with the basic right to walk down the street in safety and without harm.

In chapter 2, " 'But Look at What She Was Wearing!' Victim Blaming and Street Harassment," Kimberly Fairchild explains that blaming female survivors for their own sexual victimization is still highly present in society. Researchers consistently find that victim blame occurs in rape cases and that a strong source of that blame rests on perceptions of how provocative the woman appeared. Victim blaming also happens in less severe forms of sexual victimization, specifically street harassment. In two studies, female participants judged a sexy or non-sexy victim of street harassment. Both studies found a significant difference in who got blamed: The sexy victim was viewed to be more at fault for the harassment. This raises important questions about victim blaming in sexual assault and sexual harassment when it comes to seeking help and justice.

In chapter 3, Aura Bogado further takes up the issue of street harassment, sexual violence, and victim blaming by addressing the unexamined racism and white normative presumptions of the global SlutWalk movement. As Bogado explains in "SlutWalk: A Stroll Through White Supremacy," rape, slut-shaming, and reclaiming the term "slut" is highly impacted by the intersections of gender, race, and class. Ignoring the politics of racism exacerbates the problems of social control and sexual violence—including when this happens among seemingly progressive activist movements.

In chapter 4, "The Body Wars: Sexuality, Social Control, and What Texas Can Teach Us," Carrie Tilton-Jones writes about the summer of 2013, "when the eyes of the world turned to Texas as we rose up by the thousands to fight against one of the worst anti-abortion bills in recent memory." Tilton-Jones recounts Senator Wendy Davis's 11-hour filibuster, the sea of orange-clad protesters, the nail-biting down-to-the-wire finale. This chapter about grassroots political activism is instructive because it is part of a much larger struggle over gender and reproductive justice in Texas and beyond. As Tilton-Jones explains, the rhetoric around sexuality and reproduction—driven by an overwhelmingly white, male, conservative legislature—constitutes a fierce attempt to regulate and control anybody that does not look like them.

Continuing the conversation about reproductive justice, Caroline Heldman blends her personal story with a political dilemma in chapter 5, "The Abortion Debate: How Do We Talk With Each Other When We Disagree?" As Heldman acknowledges, the subject of abortion is so often fraught and difficult for people to talk about when we agree—let alone when we don't. This chapter suggests pragmatic solutions to the unproductive stalemates around abortion debates in order to maximize constructive solutions and to minimize the imposition of social beliefs on others. This chapter also attests to the fact that strongly held beliefs about abortion can radically change, as Heldman describes her deeply personal story of demonstrating against abortion as a child and seeking an abortion as an adult.

Part I ends with a chapter by Noah E. Lewis titled "Sex and the Body: A 21st-Century Understanding of Trans People." Lewis begins by asking, *How much would someone have to pay you to physically transition and live as the other sex for the rest of your life?* This question sets the stage for readers to carefully consider the personal, practical, political, and biological aspects of transgender issues.

HOLLABACK!

You Have the Power to End Street Harassment

Emily May and Samuel Carter

Summer was starting and it was hot. Like many other New Yorkers, we spent our days at tolerable jobs with our minds looking forward to happy hour at 5:30 p.m., barbeques on Friday, and trips to the beach the following morning. We were all fresh out of college or a graduate program, and eager to figure out just where we fit in this humongous metropolis. It was 2005. Insurgent attacks were growing in Iraq, Tony Blair had just won re-election in the UK, and Hurricane Katrina had yet to make landfall in New Orleans.

We were a group of seven friends—the kind that coalesces without much rhyme or reason. Some of us went to college together. A few were close friends of someone's cousin who recently moved to the city. Some of us were dating. But all of us were drawn to each other, finding ways to see some combination of the group once, twice, or three times a week.

And we talked. About a lot of things. The kind of free-wheeling conversations that are inspiring, frustrating, challenging, and disturbing. In a way, it was a kind of post-graduation reality check. All our freshly minted degrees were now bearing the weight of the workaday world, monthly rent checks, and a world beyond the lecture hall, where you needed more than a quote from Foucault to justify an argument. We were helping each other get by.

We talked about technology. We talked about Bush. We talked about these new things called blogs. We talked about how ridiculous it was that a recently upgraded cell phone came with a crappy camera embedded in it.

And we talked about the tremendous disparity between people around the world. Global inequalities laid bare by the middling War on Terror. We talked about racism and the very beginnings of the current wave of European oppression of North Africans and Muslims. And we talked about gender—a lot. We were three men and four women, all a bit queer, and we grappled every time we met up about our experiences and various social views on sex. We were upset and we were angry, and we had the time and energy, the space and community to explore these things. It was wonderful.

Gender was a particularly rich theme of our conversations, both because of who we were—and where we were. In New York City, people's experiences of daily life can be very diverse. Neighborhoods are wildly different, with their own cultures, styles, and demographic mix. Yet as we talked about our lives in our neighborhoods, and our commutes to work, and the parks and cafes where we went to sit and read, something profound emerged. The women of our group— Emily May, Lauren Spees, Kaja Tretjak, and Anna Weichselbraun—had a vastly different set of experiences in public space than the men, enduring a constant (and, sadly, predictable) barrage of foul comments, violations of personal space, and groping from strangers on the subway and the streets of the city.

For the men in our group—Elan Abrel, Sam Carter, and Colin Weatherby—hearing these stories from these friends with whom we had so much respect and affection—it was heartbreaking. And eye-opening, because this was a different way to imagine our city. In fact, it was a way to understand New York as two cities—one as experienced by women, the other by men. And this kind of visceral inequality, testified to by our friends across the table, shook us profoundly. The women found the men's reaction to their stories a bit quaint and naïve but they were also struck that these men, who had been living in this world for well over twenty years, could be so surprised by what was, for the women, a daily occurrence.

Stories were shared. The conversation continued. We kept circling back to this basic experiential difference between the sexes, but never coming to any real conclusions beyond "this sucks."

Then, in the last week of August, we heard about Thao Nguyen.

On August 19, 2005, Thao was riding the R train. She looked up only to discover a man, wearing all black and sitting across from her, making eyes at her. Then she noticed that he was exposing himself and masturbating. Thao did not avert her eyes and bury herself in a book. She did not get up and leave the train car. Instead, she took out her cell phone, and took a photo of the man. And when she got off the train, she tried to report the incident. In her words:

> I got off at 34th street and reported it to a token booth operator. She was very helpful and directed me to a policewoman. The policewoman wrote down my description of the man and I asked her if she wanted the picture but she didn't take it. She told me that she would radio other officers and they would be on the lookout for that man. I couldn't believe she didn't take the picture, it had a pretty clear view of this person.[1]

And then Thao took a second bold step. She shared her story on Flickr, where it quickly went viral. Gothamist picked it up first, then the *New York Daily News*, which ran the photo on the front page of their tabloid.

It was one of those stories that New Yorkers were all buzzing about. Gothamist was flooded with comments. Additional women came forward and recognized the man. Eventually, Dan Hoyt, the subject of Thao's snap turned himself in to the police.

But, perhaps most significant to our group, all of a sudden everyone in the city was talking about this incident. It felt like everyone either had a similar story of public masturbation, or they knew someone who did. Reading the Gothamist comments thread was like reading a summary of our debates (with some terribly sexist comments thrown in).

We sat around the table at a nondescript bar in Hell's Kitchen and we picked apart what had happened. Essentially, Thao had taken an action against her harasser using a digital tool that we all carry in our pockets, and then proceeded to share it with her broader community. It had sparked public debate. As we went through the timeline of the media story, we found ourselves revisiting familiar ground: use of this new personal technology, the power of the Internet and emerging social media, the rise of blogs, and, of course, gender.

At that moment we realized that it was completely within our power to keep this conversation alive in New York City. We could start a new site dedicated to sharing the kind of photos and stories that Thao Nguyen had, and make it open to everyone in New York to talk about. Looking back, without even realizing it, we had been talking about this project all summer long.

STREET HARASSMENT IN THE USA: MALE PRIVILEGE OF NOT KNOWING[2]

Joe Samalin

During a sexual violence prevention training with forty enlisted air force men ("airmen"), one young white man stood up and said that he had never thought about this issue before, until early one morning during an overseas deployment a few years ago. Let's call him Dan. As he awoke and poked his head out of his tent, Dan happened to see a friend, a female airman (females are called airmen, too), walking by at a fast clip, her head down. He wished her good morning, but she ignored him. Dan called out louder, and a third time, with no response. He then ran out of his tent and caught up to her, asking why she hadn't responded.

She seemed startled and Dan asked her if everything was ok. She explained that she was on her way to the chow hall for breakfast, and she hated the walk. It was a long one from her tent, and she got through it by keeping her head down and muscling through as best she could. Dan was completely stumped about what she meant. Rather than explain, she told him to walk with her, and he agreed.

As Dan described that walk to the chow hall, you could see he was viscerally reliving the experience. He said he didn't know what to expect or what the issue was. And yet as they walked, he became aware of a strange sensation. At first he couldn't put his finger on it but the feeling grew, and eventually he knew exactly what it was. It was the feeling of being watched. As they walked, every single tent they passed opened. Men's eyes were on them. Throughout the entire walk.

"Well, not on us," Dan explained. "On her."

Although the men were not looking at him, he said he physically felt their gaze and it was overwhelming. The men didn't say anything during the walk. Didn't catcall, didn't threaten. Dan said they didn't need to. By the time they got to the chow hall he was physically shaken. He had never known that this was her experience every single day going to breakfast.

It was that walk to breakfast that led him to eventually become an Air Force Victim Advocate for survivors of sexual assault on his base.

To this day the memory that airman shared remains one of the most powerful examples of a man coming to the realization about how we, as men, are expected, trained, taught, raised, socialized, bullied, threatened, and beaten into *not* seeing the epidemic levels of violence against women and girls all around us, let alone doing anything about it. This story he shared illustrated how powerful a look can be, how the public harassment of girls and women does not even have to be verbal to cause harm.

And yet even though we are socialized and taught to be silent bystanders, it is still our choice as men to actively engage in harassing women and girls. Or to not. It is our choice and our privilege as men to ignore that street harassment exists, and its effect on the women and girls in our lives and countless others we will never meet (and who deserve every bit of respect and safety as do our mothers, partners, daughters, and sisters).

A few years ago, right before International Anti-Street Harassment Week, I was working with my partner Bix, a mutual friend of ours, and others on a video modeling how men can challenge street harassment. As we filmed "Shit Men Say to Men Who Say Shit to Women on the Street" I had my own moment of truth.[3] My partner was harassed *during the video shoot*! And none of the men involved, myself included, even noticed. This is the inherent injustice: My male privilege allows me to ignore the reality of street harassment and other forms of gender-based violence, simply because I can.

> Helping men reach their own moment of recognition of the true scope, scale, and impact of street harassment is one of the most important first steps in engaging men to challenge it when they see it and to change the culture that allows it.

WE GOT TO WORK

We quickly identified the work to be done. Some of us had set up websites and registered domains before: check. Some were good with design: check. Marketing: check. Others had legal expertise and could put together a basic framework for the project: check.

We had a long conversation about the name, ultimately settling on Hollaback NYC. Our idea was to take the negative act of a "holla," which is slang for a "catcall," and encourage our contributors to turn it into a positive response, by giving a "holla back." After a couple of all-nighters, we were able to launch our first website: hollabacknyc.blogspot.com. It was simple, functional, and sassy.

On October 3, 2005, at 12:38 p.m., we put up our first post:

First Post!

Here's the skinny—next time you're out and about and some cocky ass on a power trip whistles, hoots, or hollas—Just Holla back! Whip out your digicam, cameraphone, 35mm (or sketchpad), and email us the photo. We'll post their ugly face for the whole world to see. If you can't pull out a camera, or you don't have one on you, just send us a story and we'll post that too.

We began to populate the site by soliciting stories from each other and from our friends. Here's Emily's first Hollaback from October 11, 2005, at 3:54 p.m.:

Trudging home from the subway I hear the words 'beautiful mommy' murmured. I look up to find a man (the one on the left) not staring into my eyes but rather sneering at my tits. I felt like poo, and it took all my willpower to grab my camera and run down the street after him to get this shot. A little scared, and very shaken, I scurried home holding my camera like radioactive material.

What Emily failed to mention is that she took the picture hiding behind a trash can. By the time she took it, the guys were halfway down the block.

WE PISSED PEOPLE OFF

The photos brought a lot of attention—and a lot of controversy—to the site. *The Village Voice* wrote a cover article about the project on April 18, 2006, titled, "The 21st-Century Peep Show: Big Brother's got you under surveillance. But so does little sister." They called what we were doing "sousveillance" (as compared to surveillance) and wrote, "sousveillance is looking from below, turning the lens on the higher-ups, altering the power dynamic." Our cell phone cameras became a cry of resistance.

This was, of course, very scary for folks. Changing up power structures usually is. Our first and favorite hate mail was from an audiologist named Ron. He wrote in an email from February 27, 2006: "Taking man-hating to new levels, huh? Then I saw all the dyke links on your website, and it all made sense. You hate men because you munch carpet, right?" Ron clearly missed that three of our founders were men, all of whom liked to munch carpet.

Trolls aside, the most common critique was "what if she's lying?" This question came in many different forms. Here it is in the *Village Voice* article:

> In legal circles, 'the types of solutions that are fashionable right now involve harnessing the wisdom of the crowds to solve legal problems,' Palfrey says. "But what if the wisdom of the crowd is wrong?"
>
> To the Holla Back group, these kinds of objections are exhausting. 'We're targeting a cultural institution, not persecuting one man,' Carter says. 'This is totally about the woman' and empowering her 'to do something practical about an issue.'[4]

This critique was about more than our project. If you watch the news, you'll be hard pressed to find coverage of a rape case that didn't question the victim's integrity—either because of her short skirt, her dark skin, or her failure to carry a boyfriend-on-arm at all hours of the night. And for those of us with questionable integrity what's a little lie? The media makes it sound like women are just running amok, making up stories about sexual assault for shits and giggles.

This is, of course, factually untrue. Researchers find that only 2 to 8 percent of sexual assault reports are false.[5] But the fear of being dragged through the mud by the media, a courtroom, the world, makes rape victims skittish about coming forward. According to the American Medical Association, it's "the most under-reported violent crime."

Street harassment is on the spectrum of gender-based violence. It's on the lower end of the spectrum, but it's important to note because people bring the same shit to the party. Victims of street harassment are seen as liars, and unsurprisingly, this has a hushing effect on victims. Being able to tell your story anonymously—with no risk of public shaming—was revolutionary. With each picture of a blurry sidewalk, a picture of gold cowboy boots being worn during the incident, or the harasser himself, the stories told on the site brought exposure into an otherwise unspoken part of our daily lives.

WITH SUCCESS CAME FAILURE

Over the next five years, the stories kept coming and interest in Hollaback! grew. We wrote op-eds, spoke at universities, spray painted T-shirts, and designed tote bags. We even successfully got anti-harassment ads in the New York City subways in coordination with New Yorkers for Safe Transit, a coalition we co-founded in 2008. Our work was featured by Good Morning America, NPR, CNN, and many, many others. By our count, we'd appeared in press articles over 450 times by 2010.

With international press came international interest. We started to receive posts from outside the United States, and some of our allies suggested that Hollaback! become the "Craigslist of street harassment" by posting stories from around the world. We discussed it, but deep in our hearts, we knew that although street harassment is a global issue, the power of our project lies in local leadership.

With this in mind, we designed a twenty-five-page startup packet with the hope that by sharing the experiences that contributed to Hollaback!'s success in New York, we could help other activists. But it didn't work. Of the thirty people who started Hollabacks in the first four years, only three remained by 2010. The limited support created a "sink or swim" effect, and far too many Hollabacks were left to sink. Those that remained were not officially affiliated, and collaborated only rarely and informally. Their blogs were independent, with different branding, logos, and messaging. Internally, we were acting like a movement. Externally, we looked like a mess.

To take on what the Centers for Disease Control recently identified as the "most pervasive form of gender-based violence," you need a strategy bigger than some loosely affiliated chapters and an out-of-date blog roll. You need a movement.

THE POWER OF NETWORKED LEADERSHIP

We set the goal of launching sites in five cities over the first year. We launched forty-five. Activists from around the world from radically different backgrounds were coming together to end street harassment. These volunteers were 44 percent LGBTQ, 33 percent people of color, and 75 percent under the age of 30. These are the leaders that we wanted to rule the world. And this became Hollaback!'s leadership model. We wanted to elevate people's voices that had historically been ignored in the conversation. Our job was not to be the boss, but to be a catalyst for action. Our job was to inspire and train these new leaders, but not to make them dependent on us. We realized they needed more support than just "Hey, here's a startup packet," but our gut instinct to let them localize, customize, and innovate our model without oversight still made sense.

The stakes were as high for them as for us. If we didn't speak up, and if we didn't lead, we were unnecessarily subjecting future generations to street harassment. Running a Hollaback! wasn't just an opportunity, it was an urgent necessity. And poised with the opportunity to make real change on this issue, our leaders are taking the public conversation about street harassment to the next level.

In March 2011, a prominent journalist and professor in Buenos Aires named Juan Terranova wrote an article on our Hollaback! site in Buenos Aires. He wasn't a fan, but instead of critiquing it from any reasonable academic or journalistic perspective, he went after our site leader, Inti Maria, and wrote, "I want to break her asshole with my cock."

His words reverberated across our network. A collective shock, rage, and concern about Inti Maria's safety lit our listserv on fire. Inti Maria left the country to gather her thoughts and ensure her safety, and we started a petition on Change.org to get him fired. Within a few weeks we had collected 3,500 signatures from 75 countries around the world. And still, the publication that he wrote for didn't budge. So we targeted their advertisers, Fiat and Lacoste. Within two days we gathered over 1,500 signatures, and both Fiat and Lacoste ended their advertising contracts. At that point, the main shareholder made the call. Terranova was fired, and both Terranova and the editor of the magazine wrote a front-page apology to Inti Maria.

In his apology, Terranova referred to Hollaback! as a "powerful, well-organized international organization." From our perspective, we felt about as far from "powerful" or "well-organized" as you can get. At this point, Emily had been on salary as executive director for two months, and we had no additional staff or an office. But as a badass collective of feminist activists with computers, Terranova was right. We were both powerful and well-organized.

Following the ordeal, Inti Maria wrote to the Hollaback! listserv:

> The other day I made a comparison to a friend between Hollaback! and a bee hive. I said I felt like a bee because we are organized, strong, active and when we get mad—we act together. He said, 'you are a strong bee,' haha. But the point is I feel strong because we are all strong together. Right now it feels like we're taking down the bear of institutionalized misogynism [sic] in the media!

What happened with Terranova reminded us that we were up against some pretty terrifying enemies. Before Terranova, we had all suffered through a range of hater comments calling us "fat," "ugly," or "just needing to get laid." They stung. But this was a whole new ballgame. The ordeal inspired the establishment of one of our core values: "I've Got Your Back." It reads:

Making revolution isn't always easy. It's scary to tell your story, and it's scary to lead a movement that challenges the status quo. When times get tough, we stand as a united front against the forces that try to pull us apart. We embrace others' perspectives, see debate as a learning opportunity, and we never, ever get holier-than-thou.

We had seen too many organizations and movements fail from internal drama. With Hollaback! we wanted to create a culture of support. Sure, dissent happens. Drama happens. But if we don't have each other's backs, no one else will either. As Inti Maria pointed out so aptly, we are weak bees independently, but together we can take down bears.

THE INFANCY OF A MOVEMENT

Social justice movements must continually modify strategies and change course. The Hollaback! that exists today probably looks dramatically different than the Hollaback! of two, five, or even ten years from now. And the leadership of the organization will have to adapt quickly to keep up.

Although each movement is unique, we've done some research to try and figure out how we fit in and what's ahead. We have found a lot of hope in the workplace harassment movement: It tackled sexual harassment (just in a different location than us), it wasn't too long ago, and, most importantly, it was pretty successful. We grew up knowing that workplace harassment wasn't OK, and that if it happened, there was some recourse we could take.

Like Hollaback!, the workplace harassment movement also was inspired by a powerful narrative. In 1975 in Ithaca, New York, Carmita Woods, a forty-four-year-old administrative assistant at Cornell, quit her job after becoming physically sick from the long-term stress of fighting off sexual advances. The perpetrator was a famous Nobel Prize winner. So famous in fact, that his name is omitted from all accounts of incidents. After being turned down for unemployment, Woods was outraged and found her way to a community oriented women's project on campus. They decided to hold a public speak-out in her honor.

Woods and the organizers, Karen Sauvigne and Susan Meyer, expected maybe a handful of women to show up. You can imagine their surprise when 275 women came to the speak-out. Through their tears and anger, attendees described workplace stories of being teased, grabbed, propositioned, and fired. Sauvigne and Meyer went on to found the Working Women's Institute, which has been credited by many in the movement to end gender-based violence for coining the term "sexual harassment."

Here's what we've learned, and what we can expect: Movements start by people sharing their stories and they grow with decentralized leadership. People start to pay attention with research. A tipping point is hit, usually

Photo 1.1 Graffiti Wall at Ohio University, Athens, Ohio

with a high-profile media story, à la Anita Hill, and then we see policies instituted.

At first, when we started Hollaback! we weren't sure anyone but us would care. To date, more than 7,000 stories have been shared across Hollaback!'s online platform, as well as through our free iPhone and Droid apps. We have leaders in over seventy cities around the world.

The movement to end street harassment isn't going anywhere. Question is: Are you ready to tell your story?

We're listening.

DISCUSSION QUESTIONS

• Why is addressing street harassment important in the fight against gender-based violence?
• Do you think there should be laws prohibiting street harassment? What are the pros and cons of such laws?
• Why do you think so many young leaders from around the world wanted to start a Hollaback! site? Is that something you would want to do in your town or city?

- Where is the line between a compliment and street harassment? How can we tell the difference?
- The chapter describes how it was eye opening for male friends to hear about women's street harassment experiences. If that's the case, then how can more men become involved in the conversation to end street harassment?
- Do you think it's important or vital to continually change or modify social justice movements? Explain your response.
- The authors share: "Internally, we were acting like a movement. Externally, we looked like a mess." How has this been a recurring issue in the history of social justice movements?

NOTES

1. Jen Chung, "Saw Something, Said Something," *Gothamist.com*, August 24, 2005, http://gothamist.com/2005/08/24/saw_something_said_something.php.
2. A previous version of this piece first appeared on *Stop Street Harassment*, February 3, 2014, at http://www.stopstreetharassment.org/2014/02/notknowing/.
3. To see the video, go to http://www.youtube.com/watch?v=5P4eVjwVd_U.
4. Kathryn Belgiorno, "The 21st-Century Peep Show," *Village Voice*, April 18, 2006, http://www.villagevoice.com/2006-04-18/news/the-21st-century-peep-show/full/.
5. Kimberly A. Lonsway, Joanne Archambault, and David Lisak, "False Reports: Moving Beyond the Issue to Successfully Investigate and Prosecute Non-Stranger Sexual Assault," *Voice* 3, no. 1 (2009): 1–11.

"BUT LOOK AT WHAT SHE WAS WEARING!"

Victim Blaming and Street Harassment

Kimberly Fairchild

In January 2011, a police officer in Toronto told a group of students at a safety forum: "I've been told I'm not supposed to say this, however, women should avoid dressing like sluts in order not to be victimized."[1] The aftermath of this comment resulted in the creation of "SlutWalk." The goal of this demonstration, as stated by co-founders of Toronto's SlutWalk,[2] is to take a stand against victim blaming. Regardless of how she dresses, a woman is never "asking for" harassment, assault, or violence. Since April 2011, global SlutWalks have been organized from Canada to Germany, and from the United States to South Africa. Around the world, there is a recognition that victim blaming is inappropriate, unfair, and cruel. However, beliefs such as the Toronto police officer's are not uncommon, and these are not only beliefs held by men. Female victims of sexually based assault and harassment are often judged on their appearance and clothing by both male and female perceivers.

VICTIM BLAMING AND RAPE

What qualities might a victim possess that could generate victim blaming in observers' minds? Several interesting studies on victim blaming and rape have focused on *victim attractiveness* and *victim dress* as two triggers that may result in observers blaming the victim.

Research suggests that victim attractiveness influences perceptions of responsibility in rape cases.[3] Marsha Jacobson and Paula Popovich presented participants with a rape case in which it was unclear if sexual assault occurred. The researchers manipulated the appearance of the victim to be attractive or unattractive. The results demonstrated a bias against the "beautiful is good" stereotype, such that the attractive victim was viewed as more careless than the unattractive victim. The results were marginally significant when participants were asked if the attractive victim was more responsible and provocative than the unattractive victim. The researchers conclude that especially in ambiguous cases, victim attractiveness will play a larger role in observers' minds. They even suggest that "the operative stereotype seems to lie more along the lines of 'beautiful gets raped' than 'beautiful is good.'"[4]

Contemporary work by Bill Thornton and Richard Ryckman disputes the idea that "beautiful gets raped" by demonstrating that the unattractive victim is blamed more for the sexual assault because she is viewed as more *provocative*. In previous research, participants demonstrated a belief that unattractive rape victims provoke the rapist. The participants seemed to reason that unattractive victims could not be raped unless they provoke it, whereas attractive victims are raped because their beauty instigated the assault.[5] Thornton and Ryckman's participants mirrored these research results by rating the unattractive victim as more at fault for the sexual assault because she presented a more provocative appearance.

Does "beautiful get raped" or does "ugly ask for it"? Many additional studies focusing on victim appearance and blame in rape cases have also demonstrated mixed results as to whether people believe that attractive or unattractive victims are more to blame.[6] It stands to reason that attractiveness alone is not the key variable, but rather provocative appearance and clothing may be significant elements in attributing victim blame.

A variety of studies show that victims' outfits are an integral piece of observers' decision-making about blame and responsibility for rape: A provocatively dressed rape victim receives more blame from male and female participants than a more conservatively dressed victim. These results hold for situations of acquaintance rape,[7] stranger rape,[8] and marital rape.[9] For example, Jane Workman and Elizabeth Freeburg investigated perceiver variables along with victim dress to understand blame and responsibility in rape that occurs in a dating or social situation. The researchers found that female victims wearing a short skirt were attributed more responsibility for the rape than victims in a moderate or long skirt. Skirt length was operationalized in this study as long (three inches below knee), moderate (at knee), and short (three inches above the knee) and presented to participants via black-and-white photographs with the target's face concealed. Provocative dress has also been manipulated in other studies without pictures, by instead using written description.[10] In his study, Mark Whatley focused on marital rape and provided participants with a written scenario that manipulated the sexiness of the victim's appearance. The sexy victim wore "an off-the-shoulder skin-tight red outfit" and accessories, while the non-sexy victim wore "a loose fitting beige blouse and pants" and accessories.[11] In line with the other research on victim's dress, Whatley found that the sexy victim was deemed more responsible and deserving of marital rape than the non-sexy victim.

The research on victim blaming and appearance strongly points to the victim's clothing as the key piece of evidence in the attribution of blame by observers.[12] A meta-analysis was conducted to tease out which attributes of the victim are most strongly related to victim blaming in rape cases, including the importance of the victim's character (morality), clothing, attractiveness, and relationship with attacker. The results of the meta-analysis clearly indicated that character and clothing are main factors by which observers assign blame to the victim in rape cases. Moreover, the findings for physical attractiveness and relationship with the attacker were inconsistent. Unfortunately, there is a confounded relationship between character and clothing. Participants are likely to view a woman in provocative, sexy clothes as less moral than a modestly dressed woman, whether or not morality actually influences clothing choice. What is clear from this literature is that a victim's clothing choices are more likely to influence victim blaming than her physical attractiveness.

In fact, clothing is of such importance to perceivers' interpretations of rape that researchers Jane Workman and Robin Orr state that the victim's clothing should not be presented in jury trials. Their "study provides evidence that details about a rape victim's clothing should not be presented to a jury because it may interact with belief in rape myths and lead to erroneous attributions about the cause of the crime."[13] The critical importance of this position is highlighted by a recent rape trial in Winnipeg, Manitoba, Canada. Justice Dewar ruled in the case that a rape had occurred, yet used evidence of the victim's clothing and behavior to reduce the punishment of the perpetrator from imprisonment to probation.[14] Dewar is quoted as stating in court that "sex was in the air" in part because the victim was wearing "a tube top with no bra, stiletto heels and lots of makeup."[15] In combination, the research and real-world evidence both demonstrate that women are judged based on their clothing choices, which can have terrible consequences for victims of sexual assault.

SEXUAL HARASSMENT AND ATTRACTIVENESS OF THE VICTIM

While victim blaming has been frequently studied in relation to rape and sexual assault, issues of victim blaming are less clearly studied in relation to sexual harassment. Sexual harassment research often mirrors the research on sexual assault by asking participants (observers) to make decisions based on cases. Sexual harassment researchers have frequently manipulated these cases by changing characteristics of the perpetrator and victim.[16] These researchers have investigated a myriad of factors including attractiveness, age, marital status, and power relationships.[17] Unfortunately, only a few studies have manipulated the attractiveness of the victim, and none have specifically focused on the victim's attire.

Many researchers investigating sexual harassment have manipulated the attractiveness of the perpetrator, but John Pryor and Jeanne Day are among the few that have actually looked at the effects of manipulating the attractiveness of the victim. In their study, Pryor and Day found that a sexy woman was less likely to be seen as harassed in comparison to an unsexy woman, who was clearly viewed as having been harassed. In other words, observers rated the behaviors as harassment when they occurred to an unsexy woman, but not when they occurred to the sexy woman. The authors speculate that the reason for this finding is that sexy women (by acting, dressing, and/or projecting sexuality) may be viewed as seeking male attention and thus may be thought to have provoked the harassing behavior. The researchers go on to suggest that such perceptions are the result of the common belief that sexual harassment is motivated by sexual interest. This suggestion would mean that the victim is assumed to be the cause of the sexually harassing behavior through her dress and actions. It should be noted that Pryor and Day did not directly assess victim blame; they only asked whether research participants considered the men's behavior mild or intense harassment. Ultimately, the harassment may be perceived as less harassing because a sexy woman is assumed to be seeking such attention. Pryor and Day state: "While being attractive or average vs. unattractive may be perceived as having little to do with a target's desires or intentions, how a woman dresses or uses makeup may serve as a basis of inferring her sexual intentions."[18]

Indeed, it may not be the attractiveness of the woman that predicts victim blame in sexual harassment situations, but as in the research on rape, her sexiness or provocative clothing is more predictive of blame. Research on job performance and appearance demonstrates that a woman's sexiness is detrimental to perceptions of her as competent in a high-status, masculine job.[19] As the authors note, altering one's physical attractiveness is accomplished with some difficulty, but accentuating one's sexiness is easily managed through dress, makeup, and demeanor. While this study did not assess the likelihood of sexy and unsexy targets being victims of sexual harassment, a natural conclusion when paired with Pryor and Day's observations is that sexy women in the workplace may be more likely to be blamed for inviting sexual harassment.

VICTIM BLAME AND STREET HARASSMENT

The current research investigates victim blaming in a street harassment situation. Street harassment is the sexual harassment of women in public places by strangers.[20] Recent research I conducted supports original findings from a project I conducted with Laurie Rudman in 2008. While this may be anecdotally obvious to most women or girls, this research provides quantitative evidence that women find catcalls, whistles, and stares unpleasant, yet street harassment frequently occurs in women's daily lives. Stranger (street) harassment is a form of sexual victimization, which sadly has become a "normal" part of many women's lives. This "normal" experience has documented consequences; men's street harassment of women is associated with negative outcomes such as self-objectification[21] and increased fear of victimization.[22] Street harassment is an under-investigated branch of sexual harassment, and additional research may demonstrate that street harassment is correlated with many of the negative outcomes of sexual harassment (i.e., depression, anxiety, decreased job/school performance).

While Laurie Rudman and I found that women report reacting passively to street harassment by ignoring and walking away from the harasser, there is a growing movement to fight back. Hollaback![23] is a movement co-founded by Emily May and Samuel Carter to increase awareness of street harassment and encourage women to "holler back." The Hollaback! movement originated in New York City, and has now become a global movement as women (along with men, genderqueer, and trans individuals) share their stories and experiences of street harassment. While the Hollaback! movement is growing, the 2007 investigation of sexual harassment on the NYC subway system by Manhattan Borough President Scott M. Stringer suggests that victims do not report their harassers.[24] In fact, Stringer's report found at least 86 percent of victims choose not to report the harassment to the police or transit officials. In addition, the onus should not be on victims alone to speak up against harassers. Bystanders and witnesses can play a crucial role in reducing incidents of street harassment by speaking up and reporting incidents that they observe. Stringer's report found that 44 percent of respondents had witnessed sexual harassment on public transit and 96 percent did not report the incident.

Why would victims and witnesses be reluctant to report incidences of street harassment? Stringer's information hints that apathy is not the issue: Part of the problem is a lack of availability of officials (i.e., police) and a lack of faith that the perpetrator will be apprehended. In addition, we can postulate that the ambiguity of street harassment situations may play a role. Yet another reason may be influential: Because victim-blaming, as wrong as it is, is part of our cultural milieu, victims and witnesses may worry that others will not believe their stories of harassment and/or downgrade the severity of the incident based on the victim's appearance or action at the time. Rudman and I even found that some victims already do this by blaming themselves (self-blame) for their experiences of street harassment. The questions, then, are *How can we better understand the dynamics of victim blaming and street harassment?* and based on this knowledge, *What can be done to change it?*

CURRENT RESEARCH ON STREET HARASSMENT
AND VICTIM BLAMING

The current research was designed to investigate if a woman's sexiness would influence an observer's perception of street harassment. It was hypothesized that participants would be more likely to blame the target woman for the street harassment if she was dressed and presented herself as sexy versus casual (nonsexy). Pryor and Day speculated that the reason that the sexy woman in their study was seen as less harassed than the unsexy woman is that sexy women, by acting, dressing, or projecting sexiness, are seeking male attention and may be thought to have provoked the harassing behavior (an unfortunate demonstration of victim blaming).

To conduct our study, a confederate was filmed giving an interview about her fashion preferences. The confederate wore a sexy outfit (tight top, mini skirt, and high heels) and makeup in one version, and a casual outfit (loose sweater, jeans, and sneakers) and no makeup in another version. During the interview, the confederate was catcalled off camera. The video ended before the confederate's reaction to the catcall could be recorded.

One hundred and forty female participants viewed one version of the recording and responded to a series of questions regarding the target's beliefs, experiences, and culpability. The hypothesis under investigation was whether participants will ascribe more blame to the sexy target than the casual target in a street harassment situation. The sexy version of the confederate was more likely to be blamed for the street harassment than the casual version.[25] It is important to note though that the ratings of blame (means) are extremely low. This suggests that overall our female participants did not assign much (if any) blame to the victim. However, the difference between the blame assigned to the sexy confederate and the casual confederate does support the hypothesis that sexy women will be more blamed than unsexy women. In addition, a significant difference was found in self-blame reactions; the sexy target was perceived to be more likely to self-blame than the casual target.[26] Finally, the sexy target was perceived to be more likely to experience more street harassment.[27] To summarize, our participants assigned more blame to the sexy confederate for being harassed, believed that she was also likely to blame herself for being harassed, and thought she is more likely to experience more street harassment in the future.

Even though the amount of victim blaming in our study was extremely low, the significant difference suggests that a woman's appearance may alter how a harassment situation is perceived. A sexy woman might elicit even slight feelings of blame from observers, which continues the cultural meme of blaming the victim for situations that are not at all her fault. It is important to note that the sexy version of our confederate was only rated as moderately sexy overall.[28] While our manipulation of the target's appearance did alter perceptions of her sexiness, the sexy target was not overly sexy to our participants. On reviewing the videos, it is apparent that the target's upper body and head were clearly visible, while her lower body and legs were not. If participants had been able to see the sexy target's mini-skirt and stilettos, sexy ratings may have been higher. Skirt length has been successfully used to manipulate provocativeness of clothing by researchers studying victim blame and rape.[29] If our sexy target had been "sexier," we hypothesize that ratings of blame would have been higher.

WHAT DOES THIS MEAN FOR VICTIMS?

For ten months, the women of Brooklyn, New York, were terrorized by a rapist, who committed ten attempted sexual assaults and one rape.[30] Between March 2011 and October 2011, the women of Brooklyn and the NYPD were on high alert for the attacker. According to the *Wall Street Journal*, the women of Brooklyn not only changed their behaviors to avoid the assailant, but individual NYPD officers were recommending that female Brooklynites change their clothing as well.[31] The NYPD officially denied telling women to dress more conservatively, but the *Wall Street Journal* interviewed a woman who was told by a male officer that her shorts were too short. The same officer addressed the woman in shorts and two women in dresses stating that "you're exactly the kind of girl this guy is targeting" and such clothes give the attacker "easy access."[32] When the woman in shorts shared her conversation with the police officer among friends and family, male friends and family members agreed that the police officer was wrong to make a comment, but they also believed that he had a valid point. This type of response and thinking is supported by the results of our study and is consistent with the research on victim blame and rape. Women are judged to be culpable for street harassment and sexual assault because of their sexy dress.

The Brooklyn attacker's assaults mostly involved groping and grabbing women on the street.[33] Such behaviors are at the severe end of the street harassment spectrum.[34] When women receive even small amounts of indirect victim blaming (such as warnings to dress differently) for being touched against their will, it is not surprising that female victims and observers of various forms of street harassment are reluctant to speak up.[35] Victim blaming need not be overwhelming to be a deterrent from seeking help and justice.

Research on what is called hindsight bias indicates that observers learning about an incident have the tendency to believe that the victim should have had the foresight (that they the observer have in hindsight) to see the event coming. In other words, study participants routinely causally link good (a promotion) and bad (a rape) outcomes to the behavior of the target, even when those good and bad outcomes came from the same exact behaviors. The same behaviors are viewed to cause two different events depending on the outcome the observer was given.[36] In conducting research on hindsight bias, Linda Carli and Jean Leonard highlight the importance of observers' understanding of a situation. Unlike the victim who could not foresee what would happen to her until it was too late, the observer is able to tie the antecedent events with the outcome and make a causal link. This unfortunately means it will be a challenge to eliminate victim blaming women for their experiences of street harassment, sexual harassment, and sexual assault. If observers causally link events leading up to harassment (or assault) with the harassment (or assault), then victims will likely be judged as culpable for the behaviors of the perpetrator.

Sadly, victim blaming is still a very real and present issue in our society. Researchers consistently find that victim blaming occurs in rape cases and that a strong source of that blame rests on perceptions of the provocativeness of the woman's appearance.[37] Current research demonstrates that victim blaming also occurs in less severe forms of sexual victimization, specifically street harassment. Street harassment victims who present a sexier appearance are viewed to be more at fault and more likely to self-blame. In other words, the woman was not only "asking for it," she knew that she was "asking for it." Bystanders and witnesses have a responsibility to help end harassment. The problem is that if we are apt to blame the victim then street harassment will continue to be considered typical, normal, and acceptable—despite all the negative consequences harassment entails.[38]

DISCUSSION QUESTIONS

• The author defines street harassment as the sexual harassment of women in public places by strangers. Are women the only ones affected by street harassment? Is street harassment always waged by strangers? What are your experiences with this?

• What (or who) is considered attractive or beautiful in American culture? Does being attractive excuse rape? Do only attractive people get raped?

• What role does gender play in this idea of attractive versus unattractive? What gender are the attractive people?

• What is the difference between sex and rape?

• Why does it seem easier for our culture to blame the victim rather than to hold the perpetrator accountable in street harassment?

• What do you think is the best response to street harassment? Have you ever witnessed street harassment of another person, and intervened (or wanted to) on their behalf?

• Do you think you've ever participated in street harassment? Why did you do it? Did you genuinely think that it was a compliment? How can you help share information on what street harassment is and why it's a problem?

NOTES

1. "Police Officer Apologises to Students After Saying They Could Avoid Sexual Assaults by Not 'Dressing Like Sluts,'" *Daily Mail Online*, www.dailymail.co.uk/news/article-1358453/Police-officer-tells-student-avoid-sexual-assaults-dressing-like-sluts.html.

2. Heather Jarvis, "SlutWalk Toronto," www.slutwalktoronto.com.

3. Marsha B. Jacobson and Paula M. Popovich, "Victim Attractiveness and Perceptions of Responsibility in an Ambiguous Rape Case," *Psychology of Women Quarterly* 8, no. 1 (September 1983): 100–104; Bill Thornton and Richard M. Ryckman, "The Influence of a Rape Victim's Physical Attractiveness on Observer's Attribution of Responsibility," *Human Relations* 36, no. 6 (January 1983): 549–562.

4. Jacobson and Popovich, "Victim Attractiveness," 103.

5. Clive Seligman, Julie Brickman, and David Koulack, "Rape and Physical Attractiveness: Assigning Responsibility to Victims," *Journal of Personality* 45, no. 4 (December 1977): 554–563.

6. Mark A. Whatley, "Victim Characteristics Influencing Attributions of Responsibility to Rape Victims: A Meta-Analysis," *Aggression and Violent Behavior* 1, no. 2 (Summer 1996): 81–95.

7. Linda Cassidy and Rose M. Hurrell, "The Influence of Victim's Attire on Adolescent's Judgment of Date Rape," *Adolescence* 30 (Summer 1995): 319–323; R. Thomas Dull and David J. Giacopassi, "Demographic Correlates of Sexual and Dating Attitudes: A Study of Date Rape," *Criminal Justice and Behavior* 14, no. 2 (June 1987): 175–193; Suresh Kanekar and Maharukh B. Kolsawalla, "Responsibility of a Rape Victim in Relation to her Respectability, Attractiveness, and Provocativeness," *Journal of Social Psychology* 112, (October 1980): 153–154; Jane E. Workman and Elizabeth W. Freeburg, "An Examination of Date Rape, Victim Dress, and Perceiver Variables within the Context of Attribution Theory," *Sex Roles* 41, no. 3/4 (August 1999): 262–277.

8. Ed M. Edmonds and Delwin D. Cahoon, "Attitudes Concerning Crimes Related to Clothing Worn by Female Victims," *Bulletin of the Psychonomic Society* 24 (September 1986): 444–446; Hubert S. Feild, "Rape Trials and Jurors' Decisions: A Psycholegal Analysis of the Effects of Victim, Defendant, and Case Characteristics," *Law and Human Behavior* 3, no. 4 (December 1979): 261–284; Jane E. Workman and Robin L. Orr, "Clothing, Sex of Subject, and Rape Myth Acceptance as Factors Affecting Attributions about an Incident of Acquaintance Rape," *Clothing and Textiles Research Journal* 14, no. 4 (September 1996): 276–284.

9. Mark A. Whatley, "The Effect of Participant Sex, Victim Dress, and Traditional Attitudes on Causal Judgments for Marital Rape Victims," *Journal of Family Violence* 20, no. 3 (June 2005): 191–200.

10. Whatley, "The Effect of Participant Sex," 191–200.

11. Ibid., 193.

12. Whatley, "Victim Characteristics," 81–95.

13. Workman and Orr, "Clothing, Sex of Subject, and Rape Myth Acceptance," 283.

14. Paul Thompson, "Judge Facing Calls to Resign After He Let Rapist Go Free Because Victim Sent Out 'Sex Was in the Air' Signals," *Daily Mail Online*, www.dailymail.co.uk/news/article-1361248/Judge-facing-calls-resign-let-rapist-free-victim-sent-sex-air-signals.html.

15. Ibid., N.

16. Douglas D. Baker, David E. Terpstra, and Kinley Larntz, "The Influence of Individual Characteristics and Severity of Harassing Behavior on Reactions to Sexual Harassment," *Sex Roles* 22, no. 5/6 (March 1990): 305–325; Lydia Cartar, Melanie Hicks, and Steve Slane, "Women's Reactions to Hypothetical Male Sexual Touch as a Function of Initiator Attractiveness and Level of Coercion," *Sex Roles* 35, no. 11/12 (December 1996): 737–750; John H. Golden III, Craig A. Johnson, and Rebecca A. Lopez, "Sexual Harassment in the Workplace: Exploring the Effects of Attractiveness on Perception of Harassment," *Sex Roles* 45, no. 11/12 (December 2001): 767–784; Roger C. Katz, Roseanne Hannon, and Leslie Whitten, "Effects of Gender and Situation on the Perception of Sexual Harassment," *Sex Roles* 34, no. 1/2 (January 1996): 35–42; Michela A. LaRocca and Jeffery D. Kromrey, "The Perception of Sexual Harassment in Higher Education: Impact of Gender and Attractiveness," *Sex Roles* 40, no. 11/12 (December 1999): 921–940; John B. Pryor, "The Layperson's Understanding of Sexual Harassment," *Sex Roles* 13, no. 5/6 (September 1985): 273–286; John B. Pryor and Jeanne D. Day, "Interpretations of Sexual Harassment: An Attributional Analysis," *Sex Roles* 18, no. 7/8 (April 1988): 405–417; David E. Terpstra and Douglas D. Baker, "A Framework for the Study of Sexual Harassment," *Basic and Applied Social Psychology* 7, no. 1 (January 1986): 17–34.

17. Interestingly, race is an understudied component of sexual harassment research. I could not locate any studies in which the race of the perpetrator and victim were varied. Racial discrimination is sometimes studied in conjunction with sexual harassment as an assessment of the climate of the workplace/school. The lack of attention to the race of the perpetrator and victim is surprising. In addition, there are few studies on rape and victim blaming that focus on the race of the victim. One of the few studies of rape and victim blaming that investigates issues of race finds that interracial (as opposed to intraracial) rape is more frequently judged to be "definitely" rape. (See William H. George and Lorraine J. Martinez, "Victim Blaming in Rape: Effects of Victim and Perpetrator Race, Type of Rape, and Participant Racism," *Psychology of Women Quarterly* 26 (2002): 110–119.) The lack of attention to race in relation to victim blaming, rape, and harassment is important to note.

18. Pryor and Day, "Interpretations of Sexual Harassment," 416.

19. Peter Glick, Sadie Larsen, Sadie, Catherine Johnson, and Heather Branstiter, "Evaluations of Sexy Women in Low- and High Status Jobs," *Psychology of Women Quarterly* 29, no. 4 (December 2005): 389–395.

20. Kimberly Fairchild and Laurie A. Rudman, "Everyday Stranger Harassment and Women's Objectification," *Social Justice Research* 21, no. 3 (September 2008): 338–357.

21. Fairchild and Rudman, "Everyday Stranger Harassment," 338–357.

22. Ross MacMillan, Annette Nierobisz, and Sandy Welsh, "Experiencing the Streets: Harassment and Perceptions of Safety among Women," *Journal of Research in Crime and Delinquency* 37 (August 2000): 306–322.

23. www.ihollaback.org.

24. Scott Stringer, "Hidden in Plain Sight: Sexual Harassment and Assault in the New York City Subway System," *New York Times*, July 2007, www.nytimes.com/packages/pdf/nyregion/city_room/20070726_hiddeninplainsight.pdf.

25. Sexy Condition (M = 1.66, SD = .99); Casual Condition (M = 1.29, SD = .38, t(138) = 3.03, p < .01).

26. t(138) = 2.23, p < .03.

27. t(138) = 3.24, p < .01.

28. 3.76 on a 6-point scale.

29. Workman and Orr, "Clothing, Sex of Subject, and Rape Myth Acceptance," 276–284; Workman and Freeburg, "An Examination of Date Rape," 262–277.

30. Sumathi Reddy, "A Thin Line on Skirts," *Wall Street Journal Online*, September 30, 2011, online.wsj.com/article/SB10001424052970204226204576601174240952328.html?mod=ITP_newyork_1.

31. Ibid.

32. Ibid.

33. Ibid.

34. Fairchild and Rudman, "Everyday Stranger Harassment," 338–357.

35. Stringer, "Hidden in Plain Sight."

36. See Linda L. Carli and Jean B. Leonard. "The Effect of Hindsight on Victim Derogation," *Journal of Social and Clinical Psychology* 8, no. 3 (1989): 331–343.

37. Whatley, "Victim Characteristics," 81–95.

38. Fairchild and Rudman, "Everyday Stranger Harassment," 338–357.

SLUTWALK

A Stroll Through White Supremacy[1]

Aura Bogado[2]

According to its website, SlutWalk was created by women who "are tired of being oppressed by slut-shaming; of being judged by [their] sexuality and feeling unsafe as a result." SlutWalk aims to "reclaim" the word "slut," by taking to the streets and demanding people begin to think about the way women are damaged by stereotyping. What's now grown into a Global North movement, SlutWalk has predictably captivated the media. One can read numerous blogs and articles, and examine diametrically opposed op-eds posted on both sides of the Atlantic—all authored by white women. With such a sensationalized event name, it makes sense that the event would gain attraction. What doesn't make sense is the racist way in which SlutWalk has chosen to present itself— the result of the group's white leadership, which has systematically silenced the voices of women of color. Women are left with little assurance that the word "slut" can even be reclaimed at all, and it would be absurd to imagine that SlutWalk's dramatized events will do anything to stop any kind of violence against women.

SlutWalk was conceived after a cop reportedly told a group of Toronto students that women "should avoid dressing like sluts in order not to be vic-timized" during a campus event to address sexual assault, which he was invited to. I understand the need to denounce this type of speech, particularly when uttered by a law enforcement officer. But what struck me was the fact that a group of students gathered with law enforcement to begin with. For people of color, our communities are plagued with police brutality, and inviting them into our spaces in order to somehow feel safer rarely crosses our minds. I've attended several workshops and panels on sexual violence and would never imagine seeing law enforcement in attendance. Groups like INCITE! have done a tremendous amount of work to address the way that systemic violence is directed against women in communities of color through "police violence, war and colonialism," as well as to address the type of interpersonal violence between individuals within a community, such as sexual assault and domestic violence. SlutWalk "want[s] Toronto Police Services to take serious steps to regain [their] trust;" our communities, meanwhile, never trusted the police to begin with. For a group of privileged students to stage such a massive event and dismiss the work that our communities have done to make sense out of the disproportionate accumulation of violence that we face is wholly unacceptable.

As Trymaine Lee has reported, black, poor and transgender women are being disproportionately and systematically branded as criminal "sex offenders" on an online database for engaging in "survival sex" in New Orleans. Under the cover of an obscure, slave-era legal term called "crimes against nature," police officers target those who engage in oral or anal sex-for-money. Those targeted for a second time are charged as felons (vaginal sex-for-money, meanwhile, is considered misdemeanor prostitution). Forty percent of those who appear on the sexual predator database are there because they were accused of committing a "crime against nature;" more than 80 percent of those are black women.

If SlutWalk truly wanted to bring attention to the systematic ways in which women are harmed by regressive and misogynistic thinking, they could have done the heavy lifting of reaching out and supporting black, poor, and transgender women in New Orleans, for whom the word "slut" carries a criminal sex offender record. Instead, they force us to keep bearing the multiple burdens that come with not only being a woman, but also being a working-class woman of color. Had SlutWalk organizers considered New Orleans—or perhaps any city in the Northern Hemisphere where undocumented women possess a very real fear that a call to the police for any reason will result in her own deportation—they might have thought twice about sinking so much time and energy into their event. They might have had to listen to women of color, and actually involve them in visioning for what an equitable future would look like. Instead, they decided to celebrate a term not everyone is comfortable even saying. While I will not pretend to speak for women targeted in New Orleans, I doubt that the mere idea of naming themselves "sluts" would be welcomed. SlutWalk has proven itself to be a maddening distraction from the systematic and interpersonal violence that women of color face daily.

On my Facebook feed yesterday, a prominent Boston-based white feminist complained that, although the BBC had interviewed her for one of its internationally highest rated programs, she "was on for like two seconds in the second hour which doesn't air in the US. Verrrrrrry [sic] frustrating." This woman had already participated in a 40-minute episode on a Canadian television program with four other white women, where they debated each other about SlutWalk. She was also a featured speaker at SlutWalk Boston, and her speech was posted online with full transcripts (as far as I know, not one person of color spoke at the event in question). The tremendous amount of entitlement implicit in her post felt suffocating. When I responded that two seconds of airtime was considerably longer than women of color had on the topic, she wrote that she agreed "with the larger critique," but felt compelled to correct me by adding that "there were a number of women of color on this program."

Her entitlement was coupled with the kind of lip service intended to keep women of color quiet, as well as a dose of correction to prove her superior ability to still be right—all typical of liberal white women who have never truly listened to begin with. Regardless of the fact that a scarce amount of women of color got international airtime on the BBC for the first time since SlutWalk was conceived several months ago, its organizers never reached out to women of color as equals to begin with; instead of making sure our voices participated in its visioning, we have been painted into a colored corner inside their white room. SlutWalk's next turn, I'm quite sure, will be our tokenization. I imagine that women of color will be coddled by white SlutWalk organizers, eager to save (white)face, into carrying their frontline banners and parroting their messages at a stage near you. I'm hoping my sisters won't fall for it; I know that I, for one, will stay home. This is not liberation—if anything, Slutwalk is an effective exercise in white supremacy.

There is no indication that SlutWalk will even strip the word "slut" from its hateful meaning. The n-word, for example, is still used to dehumanize black folks, regardless of how many black folks use it among themselves. Just moments before BART officer James Mehserle shot Oscar Grant to death in Oakland in 2009, video footage captured officers calling Grant a "bitch ass nigger." It didn't matter how many people claimed the n-word as theirs—it still marked the last hateful words Grant heard before a white officer violently killed him. Words are powerful—the connection between speech and thought is a strong one, and cannot be marched away to automatically give words new meaning. If I can't trust SlutWalk's white leadership to even reach out to women of color, how am I to trust that "reclaiming" the word will somehow benefit women? The answer is, I can't. In fact, "reclaiming" is defined as taking something back that was yours to begin with, and the word "slut" was never ours to begin with, so it would be impossible to reclaim it.

According to SlutWalk's website, the event is slated to be reproduced in Argentina sometime this year. It's the country I was born and raised in, among Spanish, Guaraní, and Portuguese speakers—and I can assure you that the word "slut" is not used by anyone there. This is not what we need. I do not want white English-speaking Global North women telling Spanish-speaking Global South women to "reclaim" a word that is foreign to our own vocabulary. To do so would be hegemonic, and would illustrate the ways in which Global North "feminists" have become a tool of cultural imperialism. I will be going back home in about a month, and want to do so without feeling the power of white women bearing down on me from 6,000 miles away. We've got our own issues to deal with in South America; we do not need to become poster children to try to make you feel better about yours.

Whether white supremacist hegemony was SlutWalk's intent or not is beyond my concern—because it has certainly been so in effect. This event will not stop the criminalization of black women in New Orleans, nor will it stop one woman from being potentially deported after she calls the police subsequent to being raped. SlutWalk completely ignores the way institutional violence is leveled against women of color. The event highlights its origins from a privileged position of relative power, replete with an entitlement of assumed safety that women of color would never even dream of. We do not come from communities in which it feels at all harmless to call ourselves "sluts." Aside from that, our skin color, not our style of dress, often signifies slut-hood to the white gaze.

If SlutWalk has proven anything, it is that liberal white women are perfectly comfortable parading their privilege, absorbing every speck of airtime celebrating their audacity, and ignoring women of color. Despite decades of work from women of color on the margins to assert an equitable space, SlutWalk has grown into an international movement that has effectively silenced the voices of women of color and re-centered the conversation to consist of a topic by, of, and for white women only. More than 30 years ago, Gloria Anzaldúa wrote, "I write to record what others erase when I speak." Unfortunately, SlutWalk's leadership obliterated Anzaldúa's voice, and the marvelous work she produced theorizing what it means to be a queer woman of color. They might do us all a favor now and stop erasing the rest of us for once.

DISCUSSION QUESTIONS

• What are the main goals of SlutWalk?
• Aura Bogado explains that SlutWalk is racist and white supremacist. What is the author's argument? Do you agree? Disagree? Discuss.
• Do you think there are benefits to reclaiming the word "slut"? Do you think there are problems with this goal? Explain.
• Aura Bogado writes that the word "slut" does not exist in the language in Argentina. Therefore, bringing SlutWalk to Argentina is problematic because you can't reclaim a word that doesn't exist. Do you agree? Do you think that addressing the concept of slut-shaming has cross-cultural value, even if the specific language to describe it is different?

NOTES

1. Editor's comment: This piece originally appeared on Tothecurb.com, May 13, 2011, and is reprinted here with permission of the author. To read the comments, disagreements, and robust dialog about the issues of SlutWalk and race, see http://tothecurb. wordpress.com/2011/05/13/slutwalk-a-stroll-through-white-supremacy/.

2. I had long ago decided to stop blogging for a couple of reasons. For one, I could not devote enough time to posting as regularly as I had in the past, but I also found more and more outlets with wider audiences that would publish my pieces. With so much dialogue surrounding SlutWalk lately, I wanted to insert the voice of a woman of color to add critical pressure from the margins; however, I found it difficult to find an outlet that would publish me. I first queried *The Guardian*, which had already printed a couple of pieces authored by white women about the event, and never heard anything back (they have, subsequently, posted more pieces about SlutWalk, all authored by white women). I then attempted to add this post on *HuffPo*, where I have contributed in the past—although they were nice enough to at least respond to me, they rejected my post. Rather than waste another week trying to find an outlet, I've taken the advice of people I love and trust and have revived my once-retired blog to post a piece that (oddly enough) explains some of the ways in which white women have constructed a conversation that women of color can't seem to participate in.

THE BODY WARS

Sexuality, Social Control, and What Texas Can Teach Us

Carrie Tilton-Jones

The eyes of the world turned to Texas as we rose up by the thousands to fight against Senate Bill 5 (SB 5), one of the worst anti-abortion bills in recent memory. State Senator Wendy Davis's epic eleven-hour filibuster, the sea of orange-clad protesters, the nail-biting down-to-the-wire finale, dirty tricks, and the vanquishing of cheaters with screenshots all made for a great story. Christy Hoppe of the *Dallas Morning News* called the tense last hours of the Senate debate, "a knife fight within the confines of Robert's Rules of Order."[1] Nearly 200,000 people worldwide watched the livestream, and President Obama tweeted about it.[2] It was a dramatic and moving night. But those of us who've been here fighting for years know that the battle over SB 5 and House Bill 2 (HB 2), its resurrected twin, was just one part of a much larger struggle.

The battle over SB 5/HB 2 got the most media attention of any state-level abortion debate, but we were not alone. In 2013, twenty-two U.S. states adopted seventy restrictions on abortion—more than in any other year save 2011.[3] Alarmingly, state legislatures around the country enacted more abortion restrictions from 2011 to 2013 than they did in the entire preceding decade.[4] According to the Guttmacher Institute's analysis, in 2000, just under one-third of U.S. women of childbearing age lived in the thirteen states considered hostile to abortion; but by 2013, both those numbers had doubled, with nearly 60 percent of U.S. women of childbearing age living in one of twenty-seven hostile states.[5] This is a disturbing national trend.

What does "hostile" mean in this context? It means that these states have severe restrictions on abortion procedures and providers. They force people seeking abortions to undergo ultrasounds—those in the early stages of pregnancy having to endure the invasive transvaginal ultrasound—and to look at images of the fetus, hear the heartbeat, and/or listen to detailed descriptions of the fetus before the procedure can be performed.[6] Various state governments have mandatory waiting periods and require multiple appointments, which makes accessing safe abortion care much harder for poor and working-class women who can't afford to take time off work and for rural women who have to travel long distances and pay transportation costs. State laws place absurd, medically unnecessary restrictions on medication abortion, commonly called the abortion pill, by mandating certain dosages, requiring extra appointments, banning its use after forty-nine days of pregnancy, and outlawing the use of telemedicine in prescribing it.[7] They place equally absurd and medically unnecessary restrictions on abortion providers. According to the Guttmacher Institute, "Most often, these restrictions require abortion providers to have admitting privileges at a local hospital, mandate transfer agreements with hospitals, or impose onerous structural requirements on clinics."[8] Most reasonable people can agree it is ridiculous for the state to regulate the temperature in abortion clinics or to mandate the exact width of the hallways. These sorts of requirements are not medically compelling and some are nearly impossible to put into practice. Changing the width of a hallway, for instance, basically means tearing down an entire building and starting new construction. This has nothing to do with actual medical safety and everything to do with trying to limit access to abortion.

In short, these restrictions make access to abortion, which is a Constitutional right as long as *Roe v. Wade* stands, far more difficult to obtain and largely dependent on one's economic status. These laws are intended to return the United states to a pre-*Roe* era, in which the rich can access safe abortion care through travel or social connections, the middle class is on shaky ground, and the poor take their chances with back alley providers, dangerous home remedies, and flea market pills from Mexico.

With these new abortion restrictions came deeply distressing conversations about gender, sexuality, consent, and responsibility. The 2012 Congressional elections saw so many Republicans making bizarre and horrifying statements about rape, you'd have thought they all received a memo advising them to drink heavily before interviews. Rep. Todd Akin, running for Senate in Missouri, takes the prize for the biggest bonehead with his assertion that pregnancy from rape is very rare because, "If it's a legitimate rape, the female body has ways to shut that whole thing down."[9] (Clearly Mr. Akin could use some medically accurate sex education.) The Steubenville, Ohio, rape case, which hit the news around the same time, showed how these victim-blaming ideas play out in real life. News anchors kept talking about how the high school athletes who had sexually assaulted a drunk teenager would have their young lives ruined by being labeled sex offenders, but failed to talk about the victim or note that the attackers could have avoided that stigma by not raping classmates at parties.

The big questions here are: Who gets to have sex? Who has cultural permission to be sexual? What is consent? Who is responsible for pregnancy? Who has to pay for all this—monetarily, emotionally, socially?

Texas is an instructive case study. Our colorful political culture tends to get media coverage because it's entertaining. Texas is full of big personalities, quotable lines, and fierce conflicts. But our struggles here are worth paying attention to because they are more than just good political theater. What happens in Texas has impact. We're a huge state with more than 26 million people—that's nearly 10 percent of the U.S. population.[10] Our members of Congress wield a proportional level of influence in the national legislature. Similarly, our governors and senators have a leg up in running for president; everyone assumes that candidates will win their home states, and winning Texas delivers thirty-eight electoral votes, a full 14 percent of the total one needs to win, more than any other state except California. So we tend to produce a fair number of presidential candidates, which gives us a big megaphone with which to influence the national conversation. It must also be said that people in equally conservative neighboring states often come here for abortions, so our policies affect them as well.

The politics and rhetoric around sexuality in Texas, and the contradictions that arise as our highly individualistic and increasingly diverse population struggles over public policy with the overwhelmingly straight, white, male, conservative legislature that governs it, are often confusing, frequently infuriating, and sometimes hilarious. Political fights over draconian abortion restrictions, mandatory focus on abstinence in sex education, marriage equality, massive cuts to public funding for family planning, and many other issues are all tied together by a common thread: that predominantly conservative, wealthy, straight, white, male legislators are fiercely attempting to regulate and control anybody that does not look like them.

In the last ten years, the Texas Legislature has adopted a wide variety of measures that make life harder for women, LGBTQ people, poor people, and people of color. To list just a few: The state legislature has drastically cut public funding for family planning clinics over several sessions, prohibited Planned Parenthood from receiving any remaining state family planning funding, mandated that patients seeking abortions have sonograms and receive false information linking abortion to breast cancer, cut $4 billion from our public schools (which actually motivated Sen. Wendy Davis' first filibuster in 2011), refused to expand Medicaid, and instituted one of the harshest voter ID laws in the country. They outlawed marriage equality with an amendment to the state constitution. And of course, SB 5/HB 2, the nightmare anti-abortion bill, ultimately passed, over the objections of not only protesters and pro-choice advocacy groups, but medical groups including the Texas Medical Association and the American College of Obstetricians and Gynecologists.

The impacts of all these policies are terrible, but those of Texas' anti-abortion and anti-contraception policies have been shattering. More than fifty reproductive health clinics all over the state have closed.[11] Nine abortion clinics have closed, and if HB 2 is not struck down by the federal courts, there will be only five clinics left for a state that is larger than many countries. Hundreds of thousands of women have lost access to reproductive health care—an estimated 200,000 in the last two years alone—and the state health department's own analysts predicted 24,000 additional unplanned births in 2014–2015, costing the state about $273 million.[12] It's difficult to quantify the impact on who has lost access to abortion; the data simply aren't there yet. It's hard to know what those folks will do if they can't get safe, legal abortions from legitimate medical providers. But already Dr. Lester Minto, who used to be one of the only two abortion providers in the Rio Grande Valley until HB 2 forced him to stop, says he sees between six and eight women a week who have taken Misoprostol they got at Mexican markets and experience complications as a result.[13]

Latina/Chicana women, especially those in South Texas, have been hit especially hard. The funding cuts forced 28 percent of state-funded family planning clinics in the Rio Grande Valley to close and many more raised their fees, reduced their services, cut their hours, or some combination thereof.[14] Many Latina/Chicana women already faced significant barriers to accessing quality reproductive health care, including high cost, lack of access to transportation, linguistic and cultural barriers, and, for some, fear that their undocumented immigration status would be discovered. Add the closing of trusted local community health care providers, the difficulty of finding new providers they can afford, and increased transportation costs to these existing burdens, and the prospects for women in the Valley seeking affordable reproductive health care are very grim indeed.

Several pro-choice groups, including Planned Parenthood and the Center for Reproductive Rights, sued the state to block the implementation of HB 2. In January 2014, the notoriously anti-abortion Fifth Circuit Court of Appeals reversed an earlier stay on the law, with the judges openly scoffing at the data showing that HB 2 had forced clinics to close. Judge Edith Jones grilled the pro-choice side particularly fiercely and demonstrated her profound misunderstanding of the obstacles low-income people in Texas face in seeking health care when she said that driving 150 miles on a "particularly uncongested highway" didn't seem like a big deal to her, especially since the speed limit is 75 miles per hour.[15] (One assumes that Judge Jones, who is paid more than $200,000 a year, has a reliable car, has no trouble paying for gas, and can take a day off work whenever she likes with no financial penalty.[16]) The case is expected to go to the U.S. Supreme Court, and predictions differ as to what the Court will ultimately decide.

Where the legislature has failed to take action is equally notable. Despite the fact that the U.S. Supreme Court overturned the state's anti-sodomy law in *Lawrence v. Texas* in 2003, the law remains on the books because the legislature never repealed it. In 2013, state senators Jose Rodriguez and Rodney Ellis authored a bill that would have done so, but it never got to the Senate floor for a vote. Several attempts have been made to add sexual orientation and gender identity to Texas' employment nondiscrimination law, but these, too, have gone nowhere. So have efforts to add queer youth to the state's Romeo and Juliet law, which protects young couples over the age of 14 and within three years of each other's ages from being prosecuted for consensual sexual activity with each other.[17] Queer youth can literally be arrested and jailed for having sex in Texas. And despite copious data showing that abstinence-only sex education simply doesn't work, and reports that abstinence-only curricula used in Texas public schools are riddled with factual errors, sexist stereotypes, and religious propaganda, the Texas legislature has failed to change state law requiring that abstinence be presented as "preferred choice of behavior . . . for unmarried persons of school age." Public schools continue to devote more attention to abstinence than to any other sexual behavior.[18] Despite Texas's high rates of unintended pregnancy and sexually transmitted infections, a bill that has been introduced every session since 2007 that would require sex education in Texas public schools to be medically accurate has also always died quietly without a vote. To be precise: It remains completely legal to lie to students in sex education classes.

Here's how hard lawmakers fight against quality sex education: In 2013, state Sen. Ken Paxton filed a bill that would have prevented any abortion provider or affiliated organization from providing sex education in Texas public schools. This bill was specifically targeted against Planned Parenthood. Terry Johnson, an Austin anti-abortion activist and mother of four, told the *Texas Observer* that she was upset over Planned Parenthood's lack of instruction on ethics and spirituality and "implied that Planned Parenthood was depriving middle schoolers of their childhood," asking, " 'Is there a condom for their innocence?' "[19]

That's a very telling question. Anti-abortion activists want to keep children pure, uninformed, and ignorant, leaving parents in control. That this ignorance endangers their children's health is less important. Instead, the message is that young people must be protected from sex because it is damaging. As Texan musician Butch Hancock once said, he learned from growing up in Lubbock that "sex is the most awful, filthy thing on earth, and you should save it for someone you love."[20]

So according to the state of Texas, who gets to have sex? Not very many people. Unmarried people should not have sex. Young people should not have sex. LGBTQ people should not have sex. Poor people should not have sex, or at least should not have access to medical care related to healthy sex. With the demographics of wealth being what they are in the United States, this means many people of color should not have sex. If you belong to one of these groups and you do have sex and face some unintended consequences, like an unwanted pregnancy or an STI, well, that's your problem. The legislature seemingly wants to make sexuality a luxury item instead of a basic human right.

This is about power. It is about control. It is about turning back the clock on the latter half of the twentieth century, when people of color, women,

LGBTQ folks, and poor people rose up to demand social equality; this is about taking the country back to the 1950s, when we Just Didn't Talk About These Things In Public. It is about reversing the changes brought about by the women's movement, the LGBTQ rights movement, the civil rights movement, and other social movements that have pushed us toward full human rights for all.

For some elected officials, these fights are strongly connected to religion. They bring their conservative, fundamentalist evangelical Christianity to the office and seek to inflict it on everyone through state power. Their worldview is captured disturbingly well by this conversation Rev. Beth Ellen Cooper had with legislative staff in state Rep. Steve Toth's office when she went to lobby for increased state funding for family planning:

> The staffer who was not meeting [with] me looked up and asked, 'Do you know anything about the history of birth control?'. . . I replied that I knew it helped equalize the status of women and allowed us greater self-determination. For the next ten minutes, I was subjected to what I can only call a sermon by these staffers. People should practice abstinence if they don't want children. Sex for its own sake is part of our sinful world. Single people should be celibate. My morality was questionable. And they 'just don't want to pay for other peoples' sinful behavior.'
>
> 'So,' I asked, 'You're telling me that as a mother of two children who doesn't want any more that I should either take my chances or never have sex with my partner again?' The staffers looked at each other.
>
> 'Well, we're married. We've been married a year and a half, and we've never been pregnant. People should take their own responsibility to make sure they don't,' she replied.[21]

These two staffers attend the same church as Rep. Toth, an ordained minister.[22] At least they were willing to speak with Rev. Cooper. Advocates who have gone to lobby days for Planned Parenthood and for the pro-LGBTQ group Equality Texas have reported that upon entering the offices of some religious conservative legislators staffers have told them that they were not welcome and asked them to leave.

There are plenty of Republican legislators who are not themselves motivated by religious conservatism, but they are nonetheless heavily influenced by it. These are the folks who advocated for the extremely restrictive law that requires all Texas voters to show current, state-issued photo identification before being allowed to cast their ballots. This law affects women, students, people of color, and poor people—in other words, the core of the Democratic Party constituency—the most. For them, these fights are about Republican control of the state, about raw political power. As the Texas Freedom Network puts it:

> Perhaps the greatest success of the religious-right movement in Texas has been its complete takeover of the state Republican Party. This effort

progressed steadily during the 1990s and was essentially complete by the end of Gov. George W. Bush's administration in 2000 . . .

Far-right dominance in the state GOP has been evident in the selection of delegates to national Republican Party conventions. In the 1990s, for example, religious-right activists sought to keep U.S. Senator Kay Bailey Hutchison from serving as a Texas delegate to the Republican National Convention [because she initially called herself pro-choice]. In addition, state party platforms have declared America a 'Christian nation,' called the constitutional principle of separation of church and state a 'myth,' and promoted discrimination against gay and lesbian Americans, efforts to limit access to contraception and calls to defund public education.[23]

Through extraordinarily effective and disciplined organizing, this relatively small portion of the population has used their control of the Republican Party of Texas to wield an influence far greater than their numbers merit. Less ideologically driven Republicans cannot win elections without their help. I was raised in a Republican household, and I remember hearing over and over that the religious right can't make you win elections on their own strength, but they sure make you lose. This is most obvious in Republican primaries. Texas has suffered extreme gerrymandering, so many races are effectively decided during primary, rather than during general, elections.[24] The far right has used this to their advantage. Over the last thirty years, nearly all the moderate Republican state legislators were defeated in their own party primaries by religious right-approved candidates. Sitting Lieutenant Governor David Dewhurst was the most recent official to face this problem when he suffered a surprise defeat by relative unknown Ted Cruz, who beat him out for the open U.S. Senate seat in 2012. The prospect of such an embarrassing defeat is an effective threat against any Republican legislator who might consider failing to toe the party line. So even if some Republican legislators want to vote against abortion restrictions or in favor of comprehensive sex education or LGBTQ rights, almost none of them are willing to risk their jobs to do so.

RESISTANCE STRATEGIES

I want to be clear that the overall picture in Texas is not entirely bleak. What is most interesting to me is the wide variety of resistance strategies that have emerged in Texas. All kinds of folks, from elected officials to grassroots activists, from weary policy wonks who know the Capitol like their own homes to new protesters who've never been in the building before, from doctors to doulas, are fighting back and finding ways to make change and support their communities.

People of color are hardest hit by all these policies, and they are frequently the ones taking the lead in responding in courageous, creative ways. Though Senator Davis has gotten the most media attention, blocking SB 5 was a team effort, and many of the legislators who led the fight against SB 5—and who have stood strong in other fights against anti-abortion legislation and fights for medically accurate sex education and public funding for family planning— are people of color. Sen. Davis's colleagues Sen. Sylvia Garcia and Sen. Juan Hinojosa, both Latino/a, and Sen. Royce West, who is African American, were vital to the effort. Strikingly, people seem to forget the crucial work of Senator Leticia Van de Putte, a Latina from San Antonio, on the day of the filibuster. Sen. Van de Putte was actually the whole reason the debate happened on the day it did. Her father was killed in a car wreck a few days before, and she went home to San Antonio, leaving the Democrats one vote down. Pro-SB 5 legislators believed they'd have enough votes to simply force its passage, and they scheduled the vote. But they underestimated the senator. With the encouragement and support of Carol West (wife of Sen. Royce West), this amazingly brave woman left her father's funeral to return to Austin and fight to block the bill.[25] When the filibuster was over and Senate Democrats were scrambling to fill the hours remaining until the midnight deadline, it was Sen. Van de Putte who exasperatedly asked, after being ignored by the chair and then told she would not be recognized because the Senate had moved on to another motion, "At what point must a female Senator raise her hand or her voice to be recognized over her male colleagues in the room?"[26] Sen. Van de Putte's blunt question crystallized the frustration we had all been feeling. It was this question that sparked the citizen filibuster (the fifteen minutes of yelling in the gallery that eventually ran out the clock and killed the bill).

Rep. Jessica Farrar, the Houston Latina leading the Democrats in the Texas House, was the main strategist on the House side, as well as a passionate speaker and vital source of information. Her pointed observation that ". . . in my nearly 20 years as a State Representative, I have never seen the Legislature work this hard to act in the interest of *born* children," was one of the most incisive comments on the whole mess, and it immediately went viral on Facebook.[27] On the day of the filibuster, she and her staff were incredibly generous with the activists who came to the capitol to protest, offering their office as a place to get food, water, a kind word, or just a relatively quiet place to rest. (Thanks again, y'all, for letting me take a much-needed nap on the couch!)

Other House members of color fought hard, too. Rep. Senfronia Thompson, who is African American, spoke powerfully during the floor debates, offered a multitude of amendments aimed at pointing out the worst deficiencies of the bill, and boldly hung a coat hanger—a longtime symbol of the unsafe measures desperate people turn to when abortion is not accessible—on the microphone while she spoke. (Thompson is also a supporter of marriage equality, and turned heads with her fiery 2005 floor speech during which she reminded her colleagues that, "When I was a small girl, white folks used to talk about 'protecting the institution of marriage' as well. What they meant was if people of my color tried to marry people of Mr. Chisum's color [Rep. Chisum, the bill sponsor, is white], you'd often find the people of my color hanging from a tree.")[28]

Other representatives of color, including Rep. Dawnna Dukes, Rep. Nicole Collier (African American), Rep. Mary Gonzalez, Rep. Armando Walle, and Rep. Naomi Gonzalez (Latino/a), were key players in the floor fight. These folks were joined by white colleagues such as Rep. Lon Burnam, who represents a lot of poor and working-class people who face difficulties accessing not only abortion but any affordable reproductive health care, because HB 2 forced their local clinics to close.

Legislators are often the most public face of policy battles, but local elected officials have also taken an active role in defending sexual health and freedom. County health officials can choose to prioritize reproductive health, as they have in Austin, and fund it as robustly as possible. Local school districts all over the state have pushed the limits of pro-abstinence state laws on sex education, adhering to the letter of the law while offering as much useful information as they can. Twenty-five percent of school districts in Texas have adopted this strategy, including those in Austin, Dallas, El Paso, and Houston.[29] Local folks can take action on LGBTQ rights, too. In 2012, Pflugerville, a small town just outside Austin, became the first school district in the state to offer domestic partner benefits, with a slightly embarrassed Austin following suit a year later.

Advocacy groups have also gotten more creative. Planned Parenthood organized activists to don *Mad Men*–inspired 1950s clothing, complete with hats and gloves, and protest silently in the House gallery during debate on SB 5, coordinated with press statements about how many of us really like the show, but we don't want to live in it. The House rules prohibit gallery visitors from being loud or disruptive, so this highly memorable visual protest was a smart, interesting way to work within the rules while making an impact. NARAL Pro-Choice Texas organized flash mobs of protesters wearing the now-iconic orange shirts bearing the slogan, "My Family Values Women." Rise Up/Levanta Texas, a new activist group, brought an important multilingual presence to just about every protest there was, with signs and shirts with slogans like, "¡Viva la mujer!" ("Long live women!" is an inexact but reasonable translation) and "Mi cuerpo, mi decision" ("My body, my decision"). The HB 2 fight also led to formation of the Stand With Texas Women coalition, an alliance of more than a dozen progressive groups working together to coordinate opposition activities. I represented the Austin chapter of NOW (the National Organization for Women) in the coalition, and while it wasn't perfect, the generosity and determination with which all the members shared information and worked together was wonderful and important. This coalition echoes the one forged around the fight against the anti-marriage equality constitutional amendment in 2006, and as has been true in many small victories on LGBTQ issues since, those linkages will serve the reproductive justice/rights community well in fights yet to come.

This can-do spirit is a hallmark of independent activist Kristian Caballero, who organized no fewer than three marches in 2013 on her own, with no formal organizational backing or affiliation. Caballero used her design skills and social networks to great advantage, and she mobilized thousands of people to take to the streets and show their opposition to SB 5/HB 2. It was stunning.

Caballero's successes show some of the power of social media, which was a huge influence in the SB 5/HB 2 fight and continues to be a vital tool for organizing and advocacy. The democratic nature of social media, with its ease of use and relatively low barriers to getting started, shifts the usual power dynamic and allows regular folks the opportunity for greater participation in public discourse. This is vital in our very large state. If you live in El Paso or Amarillo, both about eight hours from Austin by car, you might not be able to come to the Capitol in person with just a day or two of notice, but it's comparatively easy to share events and updates through social media. Activists and advocacy groups used Facebook to share details about the very quickly evolving situation—where to park and what room to go to if you could come to the Capitol, who to call and a suggested script for what to say if you couldn't be there in person. The Texas Capitol is notoriously difficult for disabled folks to navigate, and social media offered many far more accessible ways for them to participate. For example, disabled activist Virginia Pickel, who lives an hour outside of Austin and often couldn't tolerate the brutal summer heat or long waits in line, moderated a closed Facebook group, the #TXLege Ride and Accommodation Share page, where protesters driving in from all over the state could coordinate carpools and find crash space offered by locals who opened their homes by the dozens. Another disabled activist, who lives in downtown Austin near the Capitol but could not go there herself, used this page to offer her home as a way station where out-of-town activists could drop luggage, shower, catch a nap, or stay overnight. This, in turn, lowered costs and made it possible for more low- and middle-income people to attend protests.

Twitter was an especially vital platform, allowing updates and easy information sharing in real time. Activist journalist Andrea Grimes kept us informed with her excellent up-to-the-minute, on-the-ground analysis. Blogger Jessica Luther provided smart analysis, too, and also wrote up details of where to go and what to do for those who could come to the Capitol and, for those who couldn't, how to send food and drink to support the thousands of protesters. We got pizza, cookies, water, coffee, and soda from people all over the country and from as far away as Guatemala. Andrea, Jessica, and many others live-tweeted hearings and floor debates, and their personal experience gave depth to and demystified what can be very dry, complicated processes that are difficult to understand for those unfamiliar with the legislature.

The night of the filibuster, Twitter users communicated directly with senators and their staff members, providing arcane details of parliamentary procedure they could use to keep the debate going. And at the end of the night, it was the savvy Internet users whose tweeted screenshots of the altered timestamps on the Senate Website proved that the vote on SB 5 did not occur before the midnight deadline, thus exposing the leadership's deception.

Twitter conversation about how to keep the movement going sparked the founding of the Feminist Justice League (FJL), an online hub for reproductive justice organizing. It began with a discussion about how some folks had problems with the name and hashtag "Stand With Texas Women" because it excludes trans and genderqueer folks. It's also an ableist metaphor; plenty of people who can't physically stand did amazing work all summer. (Virginia Pickel often sported a cheeky sign that said, "Sit With Wendy," and tweeted with that phrase as a hashtag.) But everybody liked "Feminist Justice League." As the FJL website says, "it is trans-inclusive, ally-inclusive, and does not reduce women to an assumed reproductive capacity. It centers on justice, signaling our self-consciousness as one part of an intersectional social justice movement. This name suggests collective action, voluntary participation, a lack of hierarchy, and, of course, badassery and superhero powers."[30] The idea was contagious. There are now six FJL locals in Texas and seven more all over the country. Some are online only, some meet in person, but each one has its own page on the FJL site that includes Twitter and Facebook handles for the local chapter, links to area activist groups, information on local elected officials and voter registration, and an events calendar. The site, which is run by volunteers and paid for by donations, also includes pages describing concrete actions anyone can take, a Hall of Shame of anti-feminist lawmakers, and The Unruly Blog, to which anyone can submit a piece about their activist work. FJL's saucy attitude, positive energy, inclusiveness, and one-stop-shop information sharing are helping folks get involved and stay involved.

It's important to note that because social media is very friendly for mobile users and because many low-income people and people of color use their mobile phones as their primary source of Internet access, these mediums gave folks a voice in public discourse in ways they are usually denied by mainstream media. Stephanie Rand and Nancy Cardenas, Latina activists from the Rio Grande Valley, tweeted powerfully about the devastating impact HB 2 would have on their communities, as did Amanda Williams of the Lilith Fund and many, many others. Social media gave these folks, and thousands more who felt unheard, a way to use their voices to make an impact.

There is also amazing work being done to directly address community needs. Texas has two abortion funds, volunteer-run groups that help people who couldn't otherwise afford an abortion pay for the procedure. If you need help paying for an abortion, you can call their hotline and a volunteer will work directly with you and the most convenient clinic. The Texas Equal Access Fund handles the northern half of Texas and the Lilith Fund handles the southern half. Their volunteers are fiercely dedicated, and their fundraisers, from bowl-a-thons to roller disco parties, are some of the most creative and fun I've ever been to. If such events seem frivolous to you, please consider that the parties also serve as much-needed relaxation opportunities for their volunteers, who speak directly to desperate people who tell them stories of rape, relationship and family violence, homelessness, and skipping meals to save money for procedures. Believe me, abortion fund hotline volunteers deserve a drink or two.

Abortion funds focus on paying for the procedure itself, but that leaves many low-income people in smaller towns and rural areas scrambling for money to travel to the closest clinic, pay for child care, afford a hotel, etc. So teenager Lenzi Sheible worked with other activists to start Fund Texas Women, a new nonprofit that assists with those extra costs.

The abortion procedures can be stressful, and many clinics in Texas are besieged with anti-abortion protesters who harass and harangue people going in. Low-income folks can't always find someone to go with them, especially if they have to travel. So people seeking abortion are often in need of emotional support. Birth doulas, trained professionals who provide physical, emotional, and informational support to pregnant folks and their families during labor and childbirth,[31] are becoming more common, but abortion doulas are still relatively rare. Two organizations, the Bridge Collective in Austin and the Cicada Collective in North Texas, have volunteer doulas who will provide that emotional support before, during, and after the procedure, as well as help pregnant folks access accurate information. Bridge and Cicada both offer birth doula services along with rides to and from clinics.

Here in Austin, one group of women has decided to take their reproductive health into their own hands. Mamas of Color Rising (MOCR), a multiethnic collective of poor and working-class mothers who are women of color, is a community-based group in which members share leadership and work together, organizing themselves and other women around motherhood and caregiving issues. MOCR has set relatively small, concrete goals for themselves, based in the experiences and needs of members—and they have achieved their goals. After many members reported they had been treated rudely and insensitively by Medicaid-approved obstetricians (which are the only ones they could afford), they successfully lobbied to have Texas Medicaid cover the services of certified professional midwives (CPMs) for prenatal care and delivery. MOCR member Paula Rojas completed the arduous training to achieve her CPM status (while working two other jobs!) and can now provide the compassionate, culturally sensitive care everyone deserves and that her sister collective members need. Rojas is also a driving force behind MOCR's Mama Sana/Vibrant Woman project, which provides free prenatal and postnatal care to MOCR members and other low-income women of color in their community. Women of color are far more likely to delay prenatal care, often for financial reasons, or lack it entirely, and this leads to increased risk of complications, including death; African American women are four times as likely to die as white women from pregnancy or childbirth-related issues.[32]

But almost half these deaths and near-deaths could be avoided if these women had timely access to quality prenatal care. So MOCR members have rolled up their sleeves, and they are providing care with the help of volunteer midwives, nutrition counselors, doulas, and other professionals. Emotional and informational support during labor and childbirth is also important; several members have had obstetricians talk down to them or fail to explain their options, and they felt disrespected and alone. So through their Sankofa Birth Companion Project, MOCR has also raised money to fund doula training for twenty-five women of color. In return, these new doulas now provide birth support to low-income women of color free of charge.[33]

MOCR is a fascinating example because they are creating reproductive justice in their community on their own terms. They have stayed small on purpose. They do not want to be a professional nonprofit; they have only a few fundraising events a year, they are more likely to turn away donations than accept them, and they raise only enough money to support their projects. They work with the state when it suits them, but they try to avoid depending on it. Their model is creative, grassroots, and firmly community-based. So even if you live somewhere more hostile and conservative than Texas (I can't imagine where that might be, but it could happen), you can take inspiration and ideas from this amazing group.

This is what resistance looks like in Texas: varied, interesting, sometimes conventional, sometimes resolutely unique. All these folks give me hope. They work so hard. They work together, they listen to each other, and they take care of each other. Most of us think that government should be a vehicle through which we do all those things, and we will keep advocating for change on that front. It's also wonderful to see people pulling together to do it themselves as best they can. As disheartening as Texas can be for those committed to reproductive justice and sexual freedom, it can also be deeply moving and motivating to see how many folks here retain their fighting spirit, their compassion, and their laughter. As people in other states fight equally hard for their own rights, I hope the beautiful examples set by my friends and colleagues here in Texas will inspire them as much as they inspire me. Even as the legislature approves horror after horror, the people of Texas are fighting back with smarts, humor, creativity, and solidarity. We have to. We are fighting for our bodies, for our right to be sexual, and to choose if and when to parent. We are fighting for our lives.

DISCUSSION QUESTIONS

• What does it mean to say that women's bodies are a battlefield for political fights?

• What new things did you learn about the struggles women of color and the LGBTQ community face when a small group of white, and presumably heterosexual, able-bodied men make decisions of their bodies for them?

- Social movements and political change can happen anywhere at any time. What did you find unique about the resistance work in Texas?
- What role did social media play in enabling social and political change? Did that shift the way you think about social media's role in social movements?
- What were some inspirational moments from this chapter that really spoke to you?
- Often, we find that religious agendas become intertwined with political agendas. This tends to be prevalent in fights surrounding the control of women's bodies. Do you think that it is possible for opposing sides to come together to find some kind of common ground when so many personal feelings are tied into political issues?

NOTES

1. Christy Hoppe, "After Raucous Abortion Fight, Perry Calls Legislature Back for Round 3," *Dallas Morning News*, June 26, 2013, http://www.dallasnews.com/news/politics/headlines/20130626-after-raucous-abortion-fight-perry-calls-legislature-back-for-round-3.ece.

2. Christopher Hooks, "Lone Star," Slate.com, June 27, 2013, http://www.slate.com/articles/news_and_politics/politics/2013/06/texas_abortion_filibuster_and_wendy_davis_the_state_senator_has_revived.html.

3. Elizabeth Nash, Rachel Benson Gold, Andrea Rowan, Gwendolyn Rathbun, and Yana Vierboom, "Laws Affecting Reproductive Health and Rights: 2013 State Policy Review," GuttmacherInstitute.org, 2013, http://www.guttmacher.org/statecenter/updates/2013/statetrends42013.html.

4. Ibid.

5. Ibid.

6. I use gender-neutral language because not only women can get pregnant; transmen, intersex people, and genderqueer or genderfluid people can, too.

7. Nash et al., "Laws Affecting Reproductive Health and Rights," 2013.

8. Ibid.

9. Aaron Blake, "Todd Akin, GOP Senate Candidate: 'Legitimate Rape' Rarely Causes Pregnancy," *Washington Post*, August 19, 2012, http://www.washingtonpost.com/blogs/the-fix/wp/2012/08/19/todd-akin-gop-senate-candidate-legitimate-rape-rarely-causes-pregnancy/.

10. United States Census Bureau, "State and County Quick Facts: Texas," http://quickfacts.census.gov/qfd/states/48000.html.

11. Jaeah Lee, "This Is What Happens When You Defund Planned Parenthood," *Mother Jones*, March 14, 2013, http://www.motherjones.com/politics/2013/03/what-happens-when-you-defund-planned-parenthood.

12. Ibid.

13. Olga Khazan, "The Difficulty of Getting an Abortion in Texas," *Atlantic*, January 14, 2014, http://www.theatlantic.com/health/archive/2014/01/the-difficulty-of-getting-an-abortion-in-texas/283045/.

14. Center for Reproductive Rights and National Latina Institute for Reproductive Health, "Nuestro Voz, Nuestro Salud, Nuestro Texas: The Fight for Women's Reproductive Health in the Rio Grande Valley," New York: Center for Reproductive Rights and National Latina Institute for Reproductive Health, 2013, http://www.nuestro texas.org/pdf/NT-spread.pdf.

15. Christy Hoppe, "Federal Judges Question Whether Texas Abortion Law has Forced Clinics to Close," *Dallas Morning News*, January 7, 2014, http://www.dallasnews.com/news/local-news/20140106-federal-judges-question-whether-texas-abortion-law-has-forced-clinics-to-close.ece.

16. James Rowley, "Federal Judges in Cost-of-Living Suit Collect a 14 Percent Raise After Years of Legal Battles," *Washington Post*, January 16, 2014, http://www.washingtonpost.com/politics/federal-judges-in-cost-of-living-suit-collect-a-14-percent-raise-after-years-of-legal-battles/2014/01/16/c06ee214-7eda-11e3-93c1-0e888170b723_story.html.

17. Jim Vertuno, "Bill Would Add Gays to Texas' 'Romeo and Juliet' Law," *Fort Worth Star-Telegram*, April 8, 2013, http://www.star-telegram.com/2013/04/08/4759215/bills-would-add-gays-to-texas.html.

18. Texas Education Code Section 28.004.

19. Olivia Messer, "At Senate Hearing, Republicans Get Hot and Bothered Over Planned Parenthood," *Texas Observer*, March 5, 2013, http://www.texasobserver.org/at-senate-hearing-republicans-get-hot-and-bothered-over-planned-parenthood/.

20. James Moore, "The Lies of Texas Are Upon You," *Huffington Post*, September 4, 2009, http://www.huffingtonpost.com/jim-moore/the-lies-of-texas-are-upo_b_277749.html.

21. Rev. Beth Ellen Cooper, "Process Matters: Democracy Demands It," Texas Freedom Network, March 6, 2013, http://tfninsider.org/2013/03/06/a-minister-gets-sermon-on-morality-from-legislative-staffers/.

22. Steve Toth, "Who Is Steve Toth?" SteveTothForTexas.com, 2013, http://www.stevetothfortexas.com/about/.

23. Texas Freedom Network, "Religious Right Watch: Republican Party of Texas," Texas Freedom Network 2002–2014, http://www.tfn.org/site/PageServer?pagename=issues_religious_right_watch_txgop.

24. Gerrymandering refers to creating legislative districts that deliberately favor one party over another.

25. Jessica Luther, " 'Use Your Voice': What It Was Like to Be at the Texas Capitol During Wendy Davis' Filibuster Last Week," *Atlantic*, July 2, 2013, http://www.theatlantic.com/sexes/archive/2013/07/use-your-voice/277481/.

26. Eric Dolan, "Watch: Texas State Sen. Leticia Van de Putte Sparks 15 Minutes of Chaos," *Raw Story*, June 26, 2013, http://www.rawstory.com/rs/2013/06/26/watch-texas-state-sen-leticia-van-de-putte-sparks-15-minutes-of-chaos/.

27. Jessica Farrar, "Rep. Farrar's Closing Remarks," Facebook.com, July 9, 2013, https://www.facebook.com/notes/state-representative-jessica-farrar/rep-farrars-closing-remarks-07–09–2013/509826665755465.

28. Molly Ivins, "May 24," Creators Syndicate, 2005, http://www.creators.com/opinion/molly-ivins/molly-ivins-may-24.html.

29. Texas Freedom Network Education Fund, *Sex Education in Texas Public Schools: Progress in the Lone Star State*, TFN.org, 2011, http://www.tfn.org/site/DocServer/Report_final_web.pdf?docID=2941.

30. "Welcome to the Feminist Justice League," http://feministjusticeleague.com/about-fjl/.

31. DONA International, "What Is a Doula?," DONA International, 2005, http://www.dona.org/mothers/.

32. Amnesty International, *Deadly Delivery: The Maternal Health Care Crisis in the USA* (London: Amnesty International 2010), http://www.amnestyusa.org/sites/default/files/pdfs/deadlydelivery.pdf.

33. Darline Turner-Lee, "Mamas of Color Rising," *Austin Woman Magazine*, 2013, http://www.austinwomanmagazine.com/mamas-of-color-rising.

THE ABORTION DEBATE

How Can We Talk With Each Other When We Disagree?

Caroline Heldman

We stood in the rain for hours, huddled together under our spare umbrellas, to rattle our signs at the women walking in and out of our local Planned Parenthood clinic. Now smudged, the sign that I worked on for hours at my church youth group meeting read "Baby Killers."

As a 12-year-old activist on the frontlines of the pro-life movement, it was a straightforward issue: Abortion is murder. I remember the look of panic and pain on the faces of the women I confronted outside abortion clinics, justified in my mind by the heinous act they were intent on committing. One-in-three women in the United States will have an abortion,[1] and fifteen years later, I breathed a sigh of relief that I did not face a crowd of protesters when I entered a clinic to get an abortion.

Regardless of what advocates from the pro-life and pro-choice movements say, abortion is not a one-sided or easy issue. It is a true moral dilemma, a decision where none of the available options resolves the situation in an ethical manner that everyone can agree upon. For many pro-life Americans, abortion will logically and religiously be seen as murder, and legal abortion will never be acceptable. For many pro-choice Americans, the pro-life movement is trying to limit women's reproductive rights, and, in a rights-based society where every person is supposed to share equal value, outlawing abortion is un-American.

I write this piece from the perspective of someone who has been on both sides of the debate, and is now firmly and forever in the pro-choice camp. But I also write this as someone who intimately understands how heartfelt and deeply rooted the pro-life belief is that abortion is murder. I grew up in a Pentecostal Evangelical church where abortion was denounced most Sundays, and

I spent many long hours praying for the souls of the "unborn." Now, as a social justice activist on the political left, the passion I feel for fighting against sexual violence and human trafficking is the same passion I felt as a child, fighting against abortion.

The primary question of this chapter is, how can people who hold pro-life and pro-choice beliefs talk to each other when the disagreement runs so deep? Prior to addressing this question, it is important to understand the basic elements of the abortion debate. I begin with an overview of abortion rates, laws, and public opinion in the United States. I then discuss some strategies for civil dialogue and identify potential common ground.

ABORTION RATES IN THE UNITED STATES

Half of all pregnancies in the United States are unplanned, and four-in-ten of these end in abortion.[2] Each year, approximately 2 percent of women in the United States have an abortion,[3] adding up to 1.1 million abortions annually.[4] Rates of legal abortion increased after *Roe v. Wade* (1973) legalized abortion, stabilized in the 1980s, and have steadily declined in the decades since.[5] This decline is likely due to a combination of more reliable contraceptive methods and the efforts by pro-life activists to stigmatize abortion.[6]

When it comes to who is having abortions, women in their twenties account for half of all abortions performed,[7] while one-in-five abortions are obtained by women under eighteen.[8] White women account for 36 percent of abortions, while African American women account for 30 percent, Latinas account for 25 percent, and women of other ethnicities account for 9 percent of abortions.[9] A majority of abortions (61 percent) are performed for women who have one or more children. In terms of religious identification, 37 percent of women who obtain an abortion identify as Protestant, while 28 percent identify as Catholic.[10] Four-in-ten women who receive abortions are living well below the poverty line.[11] Since abortion became legal in 1973, it has become more concentrated among low-income women of color than white woman (who accounted for three-fourths of all abortions in 1973).[12]

When asked why they had an abortion, 75 percent of women cited concerns about existing responsibilities to other people (e.g., children, elderly parents); 75 percent say they cannot afford a(nother) child; and half report that they do not want to be a single parent or are experiencing problems with their partner or husband.[13] In short, the vast majority of women who have abortions do so out of concern that they will not able to adequately provide for a child. And for many women, the choice to have an abortion will significantly improve their mental health status since unintended pregnancies cause mental distress (but abortion has no short- or long-term negative mental health effects).[14]

ABORTION LAWS

In ancient times, abortion and the killing of infants (infanticide) were decisions made by family patriarchs with little consideration for the rights of women, fetuses, or infants.[15] Questions of when life begins were posed in public discussions, but abortion and infanticide were not legally or socially sanctioned during this time, and patriarchs used them routinely for population control and to ensure that they had male heirs to inherit property. Abortions have been performed for thousands of years in every society humans have studied.

Abortion was legal when the United States was founded, and state restrictions on abortion are a fairly recent development. Connecticut was the first state to criminalize abortion in 1821, and by 1900, every state would have laws limiting abortion.[16] Prior to this wave of laws, abortion was common and acceptable prior to the "quickening" (about four months into a pregnancy), and commercial abortion remedies were widely sold.[17] The American Medical Association (AMA) was instrumental in passing early abortion bans in order to establish their professional credibility compared to midwives.[18] The AMA's anti-abortion campaign played upon the nativist and anti-Catholic sentiments of the time from a decline in white Protestant birthrates coupled with a dramatic increase in non-white and Catholic immigrants.[19] In other words, white, Protestant Americans favored abortion restrictions in order to increase their numbers in the face of immigration "threats."

Making abortion illegal also served as an important tool for controlling women's sexuality. Women who suffered complications from an illegal abortion were routinely denied medical care until they named the "back alley" (illegal) abortion provider and the man who got them pregnant. (It is important to keep in mind that birth control was not widely available in the United States until the 1960s.) Many doctors continued to provide abortions, some estimate at the rate of 2 million a year, twice the number that are performed today.[20] Physicians performed about 90 percent of abortions during the approximately 70 years it was illegal, and "back alley" abortions resulted in an estimated 5,000 to 10,000 deaths per year,[21] disproportionately affecting women of color.[22]

The landmark Supreme Court decision *Roe v. Wade* deemed abortion a fundamental constitutional right in 1973. The justices ruled that a woman's right to privacy is protected under the due process clause of the Fourteenth Amendment that prevents an arbitrary denial of life, liberty, or property by the government. The *Roe* ruling confirmed that the government has two competing interests to consider with abortion: protecting the woman's health and the "potentiality of human life." Given these competing interests, the court held that prior to fetal viability (the ability of the fetus to live outside of the woman),[23] decisions to terminate a pregnancy should be left up to a woman and her physician. The court also ruled that the state's interest in the health of the fetus and the woman increases over the course of her pregnancy, and that states could limit post-viability abortions. Forty-one states now have limits on post-viable abortions.

Over twenty court cases have been decided since *Roe v. Wade*, all of which have upheld a woman's fundamental right to an abortion. However, states have passed many laws limiting access to abortion, including requiring parental permission, banning late-term abortions, mandatory ultrasounds, mandatory waiting periods, and required "counseling sessions" to discourage women from obtaining abortions. From 2011 to 2013, states passed more abortion restrictions than the entire decade before,[24] and since 2010, twelve states have outlawed abortions past twenty-two weeks of pregnancy. The Supreme Court will take up this law in coming years since it appears to violate the viability provision of *Roe v. Wade*.[25]

CRISIS PREGNANCY CENTERS AND YOUR HEALTH

Elizabeth Juarez

When people go to the doctor, they expect to get accurate medical information. We put our trust in the hands of medical professionals to provide clear and factual medical information.

For people who might wonder if they're pregnant, want birth control, or STI testing, medical options might include Planned Parenthood, private doctors, or campus health clinics. The problem is that there are also clinics pretending to be full-service reproductive health providers— when they are not. A Crisis Pregnancy Center (CPC) poses under the guise of providing pregnancy options, ultrasounds, STI testing, or a listening ear. In reality, they offer limited options for people who may be pregnant. Although CPCs promote themselves as a neutral helping hand, the fact is they have an unequivocally anti-choice agenda. The goal of Crisis Pregnancy Centers is to prevent women from getting contraception or abortion.

Even more concerning is that CPCs often provide medically inaccurate information. This misinformation includes false claims about abortion, breast cancer, sex before marriage, condoms, and STI transmission.

In the United States, there are an estimated 2,500 to 4,000 CPCs. With so many clinics and such stealthy tactics, it is difficult for people to discern whether they are entering a credible health-care facility or not.

CPCs target college campuses by strategically placing their fake clinics near schools and by advertising in student newspapers. They've even been seen on campuses using mobile trucks, friendly graphics, pamphlets, and inviting names like Pregnancy Care or Birth Choice.

People receiving services from CPCs have reported that, in addition to getting inaccurate information, they have also been treated in shaming and traumatizing ways. Some report being locked in a room and having the Bible read to them. Others have been subjected to ultrasounds that were unnecessary, and some were told they were not as far along in the pregnancy as they actually were, in an effort to have that person miss the legal time frame for an abortion. In almost all the cases, the messages patients received from CPCs were clear: Sex outside of marriage is bad and abortion should not be an option.

THE PRO-LIFE AND PRO-CHOICE MOVEMENTS

The primary arguments articulated by the pro-life movement are that life begins at conception so abortion constitutes the taking of a life, and that abortion constitutes unjust discrimination against the unborn because it deprives the potential person of a future. The primary arguments of the pro-choice side are that a woman has a right to control her own body, and that denying women the right to abortion promotes inequality between the sexes when it comes to self-determination. Each side has articulated their positions through well-organized public education and lobbying campaigns.

A smattering of organized pro-life efforts were seen in the 1960s and 1970s, virtually all led by Catholic affiliates, but the prominent pro-life movement of today was started by the Evangelical arm of Protestantism in the late 1970s. The pro-life movement has often been characterized as a response to *Roe v. Wade*, but in actuality, it started nearly a decade later when Protestant religious leaders decided they needed to increase their political clout in response to government efforts to desegregate private Christian schools.[26] Prominent reverend Jerry Falwell formed The Moral Majority in 1979 to work with the Republican Party on the school segregation issue and a host of other issues, including abortion.[27] This new alliance of Protestant religious leaders and Republican Party leaders was successful in attracting moral voters away from the Democratic Party, and in giving religious ideas more of a voice in public policy.[28] A pro-life position has become a requirement for serious Republican presidential contenders, and during the presidencies of Ronald Reagan and George W. Bush, the pro-life side enjoyed a vocal advocate in the White House.

Over the years, the pro-life movement developed into a well-funded, sophisticated operation that involves national demonstrations, lobbying of state and national officials, mobilizing voters during elections, picketing clinics that provide abortions, "sidewalk counseling" of women going into clinics that provide abortions, and the creation of Crisis Pregnancy Centers that front as abortion clinics in order to discourage women from having an abortion.[29]

On the pro-choice side, Planned Parenthood is the most prominent pro-choice organization in the United States. In 1955, Planned Parenthood kicked off the national abortion debate when it hosted the conference "Abortion in the United States" that featured experts from across the nation. This conference sparked a national dialogue about the pros and cons of legalizing abortion, and put pro-choice activists on the path to legalizing abortion. As religious groups were organizing to move against the legalization of abortion in the 1960s, more pro-choice organizations formed to fight for legalizing abortions, notably, the National Association for the Repeal of Abortion Laws (NARAL).[30] Abortion activists from the Women's Rights Movement of the 1960s successfully fought to enact *Roe v. Wade*, and since *Roe*, the pro-choice movement has grown in size and membership.[31] Pro-choice organizations continue to engage in legal, legislative, and political battles to keep abortions legal and accessible to women in need. While pro-life advocates "lost" with *Roe* at the federal level, they redirected efforts to the state level, and many of these efforts have come to fruition in the last few years. In short, even though abortion was legalized forty years ago, the abortion debate in America rages on.

PUBLIC OPINION ON ABORTION

Both the pro-life and the pro-choice sides claim that public opinion is on their side, and in different ways, it is. A close examination of public opinion polls shows that a majority of Americans do support abortion rights, but with significant restrictions. Sixty percent of Americans support abortion in the first trimester, but support drops significantly for abortions in the second (28 percent) and third (14 percent) trimesters.[32] Even during the first trimester, support for abortion is only high in cases of rape, incest, and when the mother's health is at risk. Only one in four Americans support abortion with no restrictions.[33] Looking beyond legality to morality, half (49 percent) of Americans think that having an abortion is morally wrong, 15 percent say it's morally acceptable, and 23 percent do not consider it to be a moral issue.[34]

Support for abortion varies by religion, education, race, region, income, political party, and gender. Pro-choice Americans are more likely to be female, Democratic, white; have no religious attachments; have a higher level of education; have higher incomes; and live outside of the South.[35] By contrast, pro-life Americans are more likely to be people of color, male, Republican, Catholic or Protestant; live in the South; and have lower levels of income and education.[36] A majority of women under age 50 identify as pro-choice, while a majority of women 50 and older are pro-life.[37]

When it comes to the *Roe v. Wade* decision, most Americans support *Roe*, but 29 percent want it overturned. Somewhat surprising is the finding that young Americans seem to know little about this landmark abortion rights case. In a 2013 poll, only 44 percent of those under 30 accurately identified that *Roe v. Wade* concerned abortion, while one-third inaccurately linked it to another policy area, and one-quarter stated that they did not know the content of the case.[38] These findings indicate that the pro-life and pro-choice movements have both failed at informing young people about this important policy issue.

Public support for abortion has been fairly stable for decades, but moderate shifts have occurred in the past two decades. The number of Americans identifying as pro-choice dropped from 56 percent in 1996 to 48 percent in 2013, while the number of pro-life identifiers increased from 33 percent to 45 percent during this same time period.[39] In other words, even though more Americans identify as "pro-choice" than "pro-life," the pro-life label is becoming more popular as the pro-choice position is losing popularity. Furthermore, while the percentage of Americans who support abortion with restrictions has remained fairly stable—around 50 percent—the percentage of Americans who support abortion with no restrictions dropped from 34 percent in 1993 to 26 percent in 2013. These shifts indicate that, while the United States is still a majority pro-choice nation, the pro-life movement has successfully persuaded some Americans in recent decades.

HOW CAN WE TALK ABOUT ABORTION?

There is no doubt that the United States is deeply divided when it comes to abortion. This debate ignites moral passions on both sides, inspires Americans to be more politically active than political science models predict,[40] and sometimes instigates violence. Since the 1980s, pro-life activists have killed at least eight people in the name of their political cause, including four doctors who performed abortions, two clinic employees, a clinic security guard, and a clinic escort.[41] Pro-life activists have also perpetrated seventeen attempted murders, 150 physical assaults, and three kidnappings against doctors who perform abortions.[42]

Given the conflict-ridden nature of this issue, how can Americans who disagree about abortion civilly speak to one another? Six pro-life and pro-choice leaders in the Boston area met for over five years to discuss just this question after the 1994 Brookline killings that left two abortion clinic staffers dead and many others injured.[43] The political lines of the abortion debate had already been drawn so tightly that neither side had space to publicly have such a conversation. Indeed, one of the pro-life participants in this group worried that such a dialogue might cause "a scandal if people thought I was treating abortion merely as a matter of opinion on which reasonable people could differ."

This dialogue group came up with several ideas for speaking across the aisle about abortion, and within the first year of meetings, public rhetoric from both sides was noticeably toned down in the press. Additionally, pro-life leaders took a public stance against other pro-life activists who endorsed previous acts of violence, and even alerted pro-choice leaders when the threat of violence was imminent. So what can we learn from this dialogue and an analysis of the contemporary abortion debate? To tone down the rhetoric, move beyond stereotypes, and to find common ground.

Tone Down the Rhetoric

First, in order to have an honest conversation about abortion, both sides need to dial back the divisive rhetoric that defines the debate. An easy olive branch here is to use the preferred terms of each side—"pro-choice" and "pro-life." These labels were obviously selected to inspire divisiveness considering that their opposite terms are "anti-choice" and "pro-death," but those interested in authentic dialogue can sidestep this trap by referring to the opposition with their chosen label.

Another ground rule in civil discourse on abortion is to avoid polarizing phrases that make constructive exchange impossible. For example, pro-choice advocates are offended by pro-life charges that they are "murderers" or likening abortion to the Holocaust or calling it "genocide." These hyperbolic terms are ideal for enflaming pro-choice passions, but they are inaccurate to the point of obscuring the issue. On the other side, many pro-life advocates are infuriated by intentionally dehumanizing terms like "termination of pregnancy" and "products of conception." These sterile terms serve an important pro-choice political function of erasing the potential human life involved, but they also foreclose a more accurate consideration of all of the human elements involved in abortion.

Move Beyond Stereotypes

The second major piece of advice is that we all need to move beyond stereotypes in the abortion debate. "Prolife participants feel maligned when characterized as religious fanatics taking orders from men, or as uneducated, prudish individuals, indifferent to women in crisis and to children after they are born. Prochoice members are offended by labels such as anti-child, anti-men, anti-family, elitist, frivolous, self-centered, and immoral."[44] Painting the "other side" in such broad and inaccurate strokes prematurely closes minds and motivates people to draw conclusions based on these stereotypes rather than the content and quality of opposing arguments. If we were truly able to move beyond stereotypes, we might see that both sides have a deep and abiding sense of social justice and duty in our respective positions.

Finding Common Ground

Another way to achieve civil discourse is to find what little common ground exists in the abortion debate. In my analysis, although both sides vehemently disagree on the issue, we both share the common goal of reducing the number of abortions. Pro-life activists seek to achieve this by restricting and outlawing abortions, while pro-choice activists seek to reduce the number of abortions by reducing unintended pregnancies through better family planning. Research shows that free birth control results in a dramatic 62 percent decrease in abortions,[45] and that family planning through contraceptive use significantly improves the health and economic and social well-being of women and their families.[46] Additionally, teens who use birth control have the same number of sexual partners as those who do not, so contraceptive use does not lead to "promiscuous" sexual behavior.[47] Effective family planning is the best way to reduce the number of abortions that take place in the United States each year.

Opponents of family planning initiatives might point to the Catholic hierarchy's ban on contraceptives; however, contraceptive use is common among women of all religions. Nine out of ten Catholic and Protestant women are currently using a contraceptive method, and virtually all (99 percent) of sexually experienced religious women report that they have used some form of contraception.[48] Another potential barrier is that some Republican leaders are actively working to roll back family planning at the federal, state, and local levels. In 2011, Republican Texas Representative Wayne Christian stated that deep cuts to family planning were "a war on birth control and abortions and everything,"[49] ignoring the inverse relationship between funds for birth control and the number of abortions. Deep cuts in Texas' family planning services in 2011 caused approximately 200,000 women to lose access to contraceptives and cancer screenings, and these cuts increased abortions by 25,000 per year in the state.[50] Congressional Republicans have proposed similar legislation at the national level since 2011, so far without success.

Evidence-based outcomes support the idea that family planning is a common-ground issue for pro-life and pro-choice advocates who share the same goal of reducing abortions, but to date, polarized religious and political leadership have prevented potential collaborative efforts. Family planning is pro-choice because it is provides women with the resources to make real choices before abortion becomes the only alternative, and family planning is pro-life because it reduces the number of unwanted and therefore aborted pregnancies. Perhaps a new generation of pro-life and pro-choice activists will be able to recognize and work from this common ground.

DISCUSSION QUESTIONS

• Which women in the United States have abortions? Does this differ from who you thought had abortions? Does the number of religious women that use some form of contraception surprise you?

• What are the primary reasons why women have abortions?

• How has the social acceptability of abortion shifted over time?

• What reasons did the Supreme Court give in establishing a right to abortion with *Roe v. Wade* (1973)?

• What do Americans think about abortion? Where and how is public opinion divided? How do your beliefs fit with broader public opinion?

• What strategies are offered for how people who hold pro-life and pro-choice beliefs can more constructive talk to each other?

• What are the state laws on abortion where you live? Do you know the process a woman has to go through to obtain an abortion? How many abortion clinics are in your state? How far does the average person have to travel in your state, and is there is a waiting period required by law between an exam and procedure? How much is the cost?

NOTES

1. Guttmacher Institute, "Fact Sheet: Inducted Abortion in the United States," February 2014, http://www.guttmacher.org/pubs/fb_induced_abortion.htm.

2. Lawrence B. Finer and Mia R. Zolna, "Shifts in Intended and Unintended Pregnancies in the United States, 2001–2008," American Journal of Public Health 104, no. S1 (2013): 43–48.

3. Rachel K. Jones and Jenna Jerman, "Abortion Incidence and Service Availability in the United States, 2011," Perspectives on Sexual and Reproductive Health 46, no. 1 (2014): 1–12.

4. Guttmacher Institute, "Fact Sheet."

5. Jones and Jerman, "Abortion Incidence."

6. Erik Eckholm, "Abortions Declining in the U.S., Study Finds," *New York Times*, February 2, 2014, www.nytimes.com/2014/02/03/us/abortions-declining-in-us-study-finds.html.

7. Rachel K. Jones, Lawrence B. Finer, and Susheela Singh, *Characteristics of U.S. Abortion Patients, 2008* (New York: Guttmacher Institute, 2010).

8. Guttmacher Institute, "Fact Sheet."

9. Jones, Finer, and Singh, *Characteristics of U.S. Abortion Patients*.

10. Ibid.

11. Ibid.

12. Sarah Kliff, "CHARTS: How Roe v. Wade Changed Abortion Rights," *Washington Post*, January 22, 2013, http://www.washingtonpost.com/blogs/wonkblog/wp/2013/01/22/charts-how-roe-v-wade-changed-abortion-rights/.

13. Jones, Finer, and Singh, *Characteristics of U.S. Abortion Patients*.

14. Academy of Medical Royal Colleges, "Induced Abortion and Mental Health: A Systematic Review of the Mental Health Outcomes of Induced Abortion, Including Their Prevalence and Associated Factors," National Collaborating Center for Mental Health, December 2011, http://www.nccmh.org.uk/reports/ABORTION_REPORT_WEB%20FINAL.pdf.

15. Carla Spivak, "To 'Bring Down the Flowers': The Cultural Context of Abortion Law in Early Modern England," *William and Mary Journal of Women and the Law* 14, no. 1 (2007): 107–151.

16. George Cole, *Abortion and Protection of the Human Fetus: Legal Problems in a Cross-Cultural Perspective* (New York: Springer, 1987). Also see Katha Pollitt, *Pro: Reclaiming Abortion Rights* (New York: Picador, 2014).

17. Katha Pollitt, "Abortion in American History," *Atlantic*, May 1997, http://www.theatlantic.com/past/docs/issues/97may/abortion.htm.

18. Leslie Reagan, *When Abortion Was a Crime: Women, Medicine, and Law in the United States, 1867–1973* (Berkeley: University of California Press, 1997).

19. Ibid.

20. Ibid.; Guttmacher Institute, "Fact Sheet."

21. Edwin M. Gold, Jacob Jacobziner, and Freida G. Nelson, *Therapeutic Abortions in New York City: A Twenty-Year Review*, in *New York Dept. of Health, Bureau of Records and Statistics* (New York: New York City Department of Health, 1963).

22. Reagan, *When Abortion Was a Crime*.

23. There is not set standard for fetal viability since it varies by organ development and technology. *Roe v. Wade* (1973) placed fetal viability at seven months (twenty-eight weeks), but viability could happen sooner than that. According to Tyson et al. ("Intensive Care for Extreme Prematurity—Moving Beyond Gestational Age," *New England Journal of Medicine* 358, no. 16 (April 2008): 1672–1681), fetuses at twenty-four weeks have a 50 percent chance of surviving on their own.

24. The Guttmacher Institute, "State Policy Trends: Abortion and Contraception in the Crosshairs," April 13, 2012, http://www.guttmacher.org/media/inthenews/2012/04/13/index.html.

25. Julie Rovner, "State Laws Limiting Abortion May Face Challenges on 20-Week Limit," *National Public Radio*, July 22, 2013, http://www.npr.org/blogs/health/2013/07/19/203729609/state-laws-limiting-abortion-may-face-challenges-on-20-week-limit.

26. Jonathan Dudley, "The Not-So-Lofty Origins of the Evangelical Pro-life Movement," *Religion Dispatches*, February 4, 2013, http://www.religiondispatches.org/archive/sexandgender/6801/the_not_so_lofty_origins_of_the_evangelical_pro_life_movement_/.

27. Ibid.

28. Steve Bruce, *Conservative Protestant Politics* (Cambridge: Oxford University Press, 1998).

29. Fred Barnes, "Hidden Persuaders: The Unheralded Gains of the Pro-life Movement," *Weekly Standard*, November 7, 2011, http://www.weeklystandard.com/articles/hidden-persuaders_604174.html?page=1.

30. Susan Staggenborg, *The Pro-choice Movement: Organization and Activism in the Abortion Conflict* (London: Oxford University Press, 1994).

31. Suzanne Staggenborg, "The Survival of the Pro-Choice Movement," *Journal of Policy History* 7, no. 1 (January, 1995): 160–176.

32. David Leonhardt, "In Public Opinion about Abortion, Few Absolutes," *New York Times*, July 17, 2013, http://fivethirtyeight.blogs.nytimes.com/2013/07/17/in-public-opinion-on-abortion-few-absolutes/?_php=true&_type=blogs&_r=0. These statistics are based on Gallup polls that were fielded in 2013.

33. Ibid.

34. Pew Research, "Abortion Viewed in Moral Terms: Fewer See Stem Cell Research and IVF as Moral Issues," August 15, 2013, http://www.pewforum.org/2013/08/15/abortion-viewed-in-moral-terms/.

35. Lydia Saad, "In U.S., Nonreligious, Postgrads are Highly 'Pro-choice,'" *Gallup*, May 29, 2012, http://www.gallup.com/poll/154946/non-christians-postgrads-highly-pro-choice.aspx.

36. Ibid.

37. Ibid.

38. Kliff, "CHARTS."

39. Leonhardt, "In Public Opinion about Abortion."

40. Sidney Verba, Kay Lehman Schlozman, and Henry Brady, *Voice and Equality: Civic Voluntarism in American Politics* (Cambridge, MA: Harvard University Press, 1995).

41. See NARAL, "Anti-Choice Violence and Intimidation," Pro-choice America Foundation, 2006, http://www.prochoiceamerica.org/assets/files/abortion-access-to-abortion-violence.pdf; "Man Arrested in Killing of Mobile Abortion Doctor," *New York Times*, September 5, 1993, http://www.nytimes.com/1993/09/05/us/man-arrested-in-killing-of-mobile-abortion-doctor.html.

42. National Abortion Federation, "NAF Violence and Disruption Statistics," 2009, http://www.prochoice.org/pubs_research/publications/downloads/about_abortion/violence_stats.pdf.

43. Anne Fowler, Nicki Nichols Gamble, Frances X. Hogan, Melissa Kogut, Madeline McComish, and Barbara Thorp, "Talking with the Enemy": The *Boston Globe* Report on Public Conversations, January 28, 2001, http://pubpages.unh.edu/~jds/BostonGlobe.htm. The Brookline killings refer to pro-life activist John Salvi opening fire in two clinics that provide abortions in Massachusetts in 1994. Salvi was convicted of murdering Shannon Lowney and Lee Ann Nichols, both clinic receptionists. Salvi died in 1996 from an apparent suicide.

44. Ibid.

45. Brian Alexander, "Free Birth Control Cuts Abortion Rate Dramatically, Study Says," ABCNews.com, October 4, 2012, http://vitals.nbcnews.com/_news/2012/10/04/14224132-free-birth-control-cuts-abortion-rate-dramatically-study-finds?lite.

46. Rachel K. Jones and Joerg Dreweke, *Countering Conventional Wisdom: New Evidence on Religion and Contraceptive Use*, (New York: Guttmacher Institute, 2011), http://www.guttmacher.org/pubs/Religion-and-Contraceptive-Use.pdf.

47. Kim Painter, "Study: Free Birth Control Does Not Increase Risky Sex," *USA Today*, March 7, 2014, http://www.usatoday.com/story/news/nation/2014/03/06/free-birth-control-sex/6128697/.

48. Jones and Dreweke, *Countering Conventional Wisdom*.

49. Tanya Somanader, "Texas GOP Rep on Family Planning: 'Of Course This Is a War on Birth Control," *ThinkProgress.org*, September 20, 2011, http://thinkprogress.org/health/2011/09/20/323512/texas-gop-rep-on-cuts-to-family-planning-of-course-this-is-a-war-on-birth-control/.

50. Texas Women's Healthcare Coalition, "Texas Women's Healthcare in Crisis," 2013, www.TexasWHC.org http://www.texaswhc.org/wp-content/uploads/2013/01/Texas-Womens-Healthcare-in-Crisis.pdf.

SEX AND THE BODY

A 21st-Century Understanding of Trans People

Noah E. Lewis

How much would someone have to pay you to physically transition and live as the other sex for the rest of your life?[1] Assume that your genitals would be fully functioning. (And that you'd be hot.)

Two hundred thousand dollars? A million? A hundred thousand dollars each year for the rest of your life? You'd never have to work again! Yet most people would be unwilling to make this trade-off. While they might be curious to try it for a day or two, most people find the idea of changing sexes foreign and squicky.

But why is that?

Some problems are practical: You'd have to legally change your name and update all of your documents, buy a new wardrobe, let all of your friends, family, and co-workers know. These things take time, but are not insurmountable.

If you already have a partner, their sexual orientation wouldn't change. So chances are decent that they'd no longer be physically attracted to you. But still, you could find another lover. Your sexual orientation is separate from your sex, so that wouldn't change either. If you are a woman who likes men, you would still like men. But since straight men would no longer be attracted to you, you'd be dating gay men.

These practical concerns aside, the real reason we don't have lots of reality TV shows where we follow someone who changes their sex for cash or have actors who play trans characters actually go on hormones[2]—even temporarily—is because of something far more ineffable. It gets back to the question I posed at the beginning of this chapter: *How much would someone have to pay you to physically transition and live as the other sex for the rest of your life?*

When I give public talks about trans issues and ask audiences this question, no one takes the money. People explain that it just wouldn't *feel* right, that they *like* being the sex that they are now. They often cannot put into words why it would feel wrong to switch, they just know it would.

And that is just what it's like trying to explain being trans. Cis people (that is, non-trans people) can find it fundamentally difficult to understand what's really the deal with trans people. Popular misconceptions lead to everything from rampant employment discrimination, to insurance exclusions for transgender health care, to conflicts over the bathroom. I hope to convey more accurately what I (and countless trans people I've spoken to) experience to bridge that gap in understanding. It is only when trans people are recognized as who we are that we will be able to participate in society as equals.

WHY CIS?

Cis- is the Latin prefix corresponding to trans-. Trans- means "across" or "on the other side" and cis- means "same" or "on this side." As Julia Serano explains in *Whipping Girl: A Transsexual Woman on Sexism and the Scapegoating of Femininity*, cissexual people experience "their subconscious sex and physical sex as being aligned."[3] Cis is far from being an academic term. The word cisgender first appeared on the Internet in 1994 in the alt.transgendered Usenet group.

Being cis doesn't make one normal or natural, it just makes one cis. Just as white people have a race and straight people have a sexual orientation, cis people have a brain sex. But unlike trans people, it just happens to be the same as the sex they were assigned at birth.

There's nothing wrong with being cis! Some people unfamiliar with the term balk at it being applied to them. In reality, developing a positive cis identity helps to show that one is mindful of the issues facing trans people.

It took me a long time before I fully accepted that being cis was a category to which I did not belong. Twenty-seven years to be exact. So if you're struggling to fully accept that trans people exist as a category separate from yourself, I can sympathize.

Like the vast majority of trans people, I knew from a young age that I was male.[4] Tyler, a five-year-old trans boy profiled in the *Washington Post*, told his parents at age two that he was a boy. He persisted, and at three they showed him a toddler version of an anatomy book, explaining that because he had girl parts, he was a girl. He asked, "When did you change me?"[5] One of my legal clients, Coy Mathis, a six-year-old trans girl from Colorado, tearfully asked her mother when she was three, "When am I going to get my girl parts? . . . When are we going to go to the doctor to have me fixed?"[6]

I was not so definitive. When I say that I "knew" I was a boy, it was really a state of simultaneously knowing and not knowing. It was a feeling that I had, but I didn't know how to reconcile it with the seeming objective evidence to the contrary.

While part of me knew that I was a boy, another part knew that my being a boy was not socially acceptable. And even the part of me that "knew" was murky, like trying to see the bottom of a pond, believing that I could see what was down there, but never being entirely sure.

So I would undertake efforts to corroborate these feelings with outside evidence to prove to myself that I was a boy. When I was in kindergarten, I knew that if I was a boy, I had to have a best friend who was a boy. So I was deliberately friends with a neighbor boy my age even though I wasn't particularly wild about hanging out with him. I told myself that this was important so that when I got older, I could look back and remember that I was a boy.

When I was seven, my older brother and I each had guinea pigs who died at the same time. We held a funeral in the backyard and buried them. This seemed like a foolproof way to prove to myself that I was a boy. Since boys don't cry, if I didn't cry, I'd know I really was a boy. I desperately wanted to cry and developed a huge lump in my throat. Of course I knew that boys were allowed to cry. My older brother was standing right across from me, crying. But it was okay for him to cry: Everyone knew that he was a boy. I looked at my mom. She was crying. I looked at my dad. We were not.

Other attempts to prove that I was a boy were less successful. I liked some of my brother's toys: Matchbox cars, Legos, GoBots[7] (though my GoBot collection was actually bigger). There were others that I didn't like but would make myself play with anyway. I would grudgingly get out his Radio Shack circuit board. In my kid logic, if I could just learn to like making circuits, then I would be allowed to be a boy. My brother became an electrical engineer. I never did learn to like circuits.

The efforts to prove to myself that I was a boy only exacerbated another problem common to trans kids:[8] having to hide the fact that I was a boy. My mom wanted a girl, and she'd often remark to people how pleased she was to have "one of each." Since no kid wants to disappoint their mom, I never knew how to get around this. Mom wanted a girl? I guess I'd better pretend to be one.

While I freely played with most of my brother's toys, some I put off-limits. His trucks beckoned to me: the yellow metal road grader that had been my dad's, the orange plastic dump truck. I remember one day giving in and playing with them in full view of the kitchen window. I glanced nervously at the house as I played, fearful that my mom would look out and see that I was a boy.

Sometimes I'd deliberately throw them off the track. My doll collection was mercifully small since adults picked up on the fact that I didn't like them. But I did have this large baby doll with a pink bathtub. I'd sometimes bathe her in front of my mom just so that she would see me playing with it.

My indifference toward baby dolls extended to real babies. When I was seven and met my cousin for the first time, I knew that I'd better act interested. The camera captured my play-acting perfectly, completed by consciously putting my finger to my lip to feign wonder.

Some people think it's hard to tell trans kids from gender nonconforming kids, but there are two distinct features that separate the two. First, trans kids assert that they *are* the other sex whereas gender nonconforming kids simply express a wish that they were the other sex. Second, trans kids also express discomfort with their bodies whereas gender nonconforming children do not. Children such as myself with both of these feelings remain trans once adolescence hits.[9]

In middle school, I began shopping in the boy's department. I didn't shop there out of choice. I was deeply ashamed to do so, just more ashamed not to. I would try to find something in the girls' department, always scouting for the most masculine cuts, something I still catch myself doing while walking past a women's department. The fact that I was buying boys' clothes didn't go unnoticed. My mom, surely having seen some television talk show, asked me if I thought I was a man trapped in a woman's body. I rolled my eyes. "It happens you know," she offered. Despite the glimmer of recognition, I didn't know how one might go about getting untrapped. I admonished her, "No, mom, girls can wear guys' clothes."

There was an invisible line with clothes that I would not cross. I sometimes bought men's clothing that I was too ashamed to wear. I had three rugby shirts that I excitedly bought but rarely wore knowing how unambiguously masculine they were. I had two extra-large plaid button-down shirts, one orange, one lime green, left untouched in the back my closet for years and years. When I finally started wearing them in college, they became my uniform.

In college I had a boyfriend who had a penchant for wearing suit jackets with everything. I coveted them. He liked the look of them on me, but I never felt comfortable wearing them in public. Never mind the long curls that would fall down the back. It seemed to me that I might as well be wearing a sign shouting, "she's really a man!"

I hid behind that hair for many years. I wanted short hair, but with the curls, I could get away with wearing more masculine things. They were my security blanket, my get out of jail free card, my armor to deflect any doubt about my femaleness.

Although I did a good job of pretending to be female, I wasn't happy about it. We went to the shore for the first time when I was four or five. I had a Petunia Pig one-piece bathing suit. I cried and cried at having to wear it. I didn't know why. But part of me knew that boys didn't wear bathing suits like that.

My bedroom was another source of distress. I had a pink canopy bed with Holly Hobby sheets and wallpaper. Whenever my brother wanted to get a rise out of me, all he'd have to do was say that I slept in a "can of peas" while his brown bed, train wallpaper, and Superman sheets silently mocked me.

I was twelve when I came in from playing basketball with my brother and saw bloody underwear for the first time. As the youngest in my class, most of my friends had already started getting their periods. I held out a secret hope that I would never get it. But that was the end of it. I felt like God was punishing me for playing basketball. There was now no denying it: I was a girl.

If I stopped the narrative right there, you might think you know this story: I transitioned because I was masculine and wanted to become a man. But you might wonder, why couldn't I just be a masculine woman? Why didn't I just ask my mom to put the Superman sheets on my bed? Why didn't I just stop caring so much about what other people might think, cut my hair and wear suit jackets all over town? Why did I have to go to the trouble of "becoming a man" at a time when social gender roles are becoming increasingly irrelevant? Had I internalized misogyny? Was I just seeking male privilege? Wasn't I reinforcing the very sex stereotypes that were oppressing me? Why mutilate my body when women can do anything men can do (only better)?

Here's the thing I would want everyone to understand: I transitioned to achieve comfort in my own body. I did not transition because of gender stereotypes, gender roles, or gender expression. I did not transition for the benefit of anyone else. I did not transition in order to be able to express masculinity or femininity, but rather maleness or femaleness.[10] I transitioned not because of my *gender*, but because of my *sex*.

Sex and gender are different. As Supreme Court Justice Antonin Scalia put it: "The word 'gender' has acquired the new and useful connotation of cultural or attitudinal characteristics (as opposed to physical characteristics) distinctive to the sexes. That is to say, gender is to sex as feminine is to female and masculine to male."[11]

We can all agree that no one need abide by sex stereotypes and anyone, male or female, can have any gendered expression they want. Cis people have a hard time understanding why someone would need to change their body in order to express their gender. And rightly so! The masculinity or femininity of trans people, just like cis people, is independent from and not determined by their sex.

Conflating sex and gender paints a confusing picture where a woman can be so masculine that she crosses over a line somewhere and *oops! she becomes a man!* That obviously cannot happen because masculinity and femininity are on a completely separate axis from male and female. You can be a highly feminine man and there's no risk that you'll become a woman.

People mistakenly peg the motivation of transition as having something to do with gender because *most trans people are gender conforming.* This is in contrast with the cultural idea that what defines trans people is that they are gender *nonconforming.* But when viewed from the perspective of the trans individual, a trans man who likes to wear male clothing and has short hair just has typical male gender expression. A trans woman does not wear makeup and dresses in order to access "womanhood." She is doing those things for the same reason that any other feminine woman does those things: because she's female and happens to like those things.[12]

It took me until I was twenty-seven to be able to decouple sex from sex stereotypes. I knew that I wanted to have a male body—there was never any question about that. I wanted a flat chest, bigger upper body muscles. I wanted smaller hips, thighs, and butt. Facial hair I was less psyched about because of my own experience dealing with the rough faces of boyfriends, and I didn't really need more body hair, as my legs had always been hairier than my boyfriends' anyway.

What stopped me from transitioning was this fear that I was going to have to become this stereotype of "a man." I was afraid I was going to become a different person, one who had to behave in totally different ways. I finally realized that men were not monolithic, that there were plenty of other types of masculinities aside from those of my father and brother. I wasn't going to have to start fixing cars, making cabinets, or building those dang circuits. I looked to my past boyfriends. They liked reading and wore cardigans. I, too, would be the nerdy professor type. Once I could see *myself* operating in male form I realized that I wouldn't be transitioning to "become a man." I'd just be *me* with the male body I always wanted.

But back to the story.

Once the fact that I was male had become a distant memory buried deep in my subconscious, I was left with strange compulsions for which I had no explanation. I had to wear bras that would flatten my chest and create a less-breast-like uniboob. All of my T-shirts had to be size extra-large (so that they would cover my hips, butt, and thighs as much as possible). I started doing my own laundry and line-drying my shirts because I would freak out if my mom shrank anything. In sixth grade, I'd pull my pant legs up to just below my knees. I put up with my brother's merciless teasing about "where's the flood?" rather than endure the sight of my huge thighs, which the flood pants somehow minimized.

My subconscious push to mask the female parts of my body even overrode my preferred gender expression. In high school, when I needed to dress up, I really wanted to wear button-down shirts and pants. But that just emphasized my pear-shaped physique and made me dysphoric, so I went with long flowing skirts that covered all of that up.

My concerns about my body were not limited to its overall shape. Something far more dangerous was afoot. When I was in college, I asked my straight boyfriends if they'd like to have strap-on anal sex (oddly, they didn't . . .). But with one I hit upon something that was perhaps even better. I had him lie on top of me on his back. He was slender, and I could reach around and jerk him off. Only it felt like I was jerking off *my* penis. Even though we both liked it, we only did it a couple of times. It felt so good it scared me. Meanwhile, what normally happened after intercourse was that I'd lie there silently sobbing and wondering what was wrong with me.

I figured that I must be a lesbian. Despite coming out as bi at seventeen, I'd always dated men. I finally managed to have my first girlfriend at the age of twenty-six. At one point I said to her, "Remember that time when we went to New York City for Pride and I used a strap-on for the first time?"

I had been on top of her and had this most amazing sensation of having a penis. While in the past I normally shied away from that feeling, that time I allowed myself to fully experience the mind-blowing pleasure of it, only to feel guilty afterward. The only problem? She reminded me that we had not used a strap-on in NYC: The sensation was all in my mind.

MANY FACTORS COMPRISE BIOLOGICAL SEX

While we tend to think of genitals as being the most important physical sex characteristic, the medical community understands that sex is comprised of at least eight factors:[13]

1 Genetic or chromosomal sex—XX, XY, XO, XXY, XYY, etc.;
2 Gonadal sex (reproductive sex glands)—testes or ovaries;
3 Internal reproductive structures—seminal vesicles/prostate or vagina/uterus/fallopian tubes;
4 External sex organs (genitalia)—penis/scrotum or vulva;
5 Hormonal sex—androgens or estrogens;
6 Phenotypic sex (secondary sex characteristics)—facial and chest hair or breasts; face shape; fat/muscle distribution, etc.;
7 Assigned sex at birth (sex of rearing);
8 Brain sex or psychological, self-identified sex.

While some people are drawn to thinking chromosomes are the ultimate arbiter of sex, most people do not even know what chromosomes they have, and many would be surprised if they found out.

Many individuals have characteristics that are both male and female. People born with differences of sex development (DSDs or intersex conditions) are distinct from trans people, who generally have typical male or female anatomy. People with DSDs are often forced to have harmful, nonconsensual surgeries to "normalize" their genitals. Most people with DSDs simply identify as men or women rather than "third sex."

It is well-established that it is no more possible to change someone's internal sense of being male or female than it is to forcibly change someone's sexual orientation.[14]

How must doctors ultimately determine if someone is male or female? It turns out to be remarkably simple: Ask them.

Even today I can feel shame about having a phantom penis instead of a flesh one, or when foolishly reading the comments on a trans news story, revert to questioning my own experiences. So I take comfort that there are some scientists who can explain being trans in a way that actually matches up with my experience.

Neuroscience researcher V.S. Ramachandran has shown that the brain contains its own innate map of the body that is separate from the physical body.[15] This explains phenomena such as phantom limbs where the brain map of the limb is activated, causing the person to feel sensations coming from a missing limb.

When the brain's map and the visual or sensory input from body don't match up, the mismatch disrupts the self's sense of unity.[16] The brain abhors this discomfort and works to eliminate the discrepancy. Certain stroke survivors who have paralysis in their arm suffer from somatoparaphrenia. To the damaged part of the brain's map, the limb is no longer there. If you ask the person to whom the arm belongs, they will respond that it is the doctor's or their mother's as the brain attempts to rationalize the presence of this unrecognizable limb.

People with xenomelia have an overwhelming desire to amputate a limb, to the extent that they lie down on train tracks or stick it in dry ice so that a doctor is forced to amputate it. Ramachandran and his colleagues have performed skin response tests and brain scans to demonstrate that these people's brains literally did not recognize that part of their body. This non-recognition manifests itself in the feeling that the limb is "overpresent" or "redundant" and the person has a desire to get rid of it.

Ramachandran proposed that being trans is similarly caused by an incongruity between the physical body and brain's internal body map, which evidently includes details of sexual anatomy.[17] Many trans women "report feeling that their penis seems to be redundant or . . . over present and intrusive,"[18] while trans men report having phantom penises.[19] When this hypothesis was experimentally tested by Laura Case, one of Ramachandran's PhD students, she found that trans men had heightened autonomic (involuntary) response when their breasts were tapped and that brain imaging demonstrated lesser integration of sensation from a body part that is incongruent with being male.[20] She had found neurological evidence of the dysphoric feelings that trans people try to describe.

Ramachandran has also investigated bigender people who identify as both men and women. Their body map seems to switch back and forth, which he terms alternating gender incongruity.[21]

Brain sex is normally seamless and invisible to cis people, so they may not realize that they too have this internal sense of their sexed body. But if the idea of living as the other sex for the rest of your life is unappealing to you, you're running up against your brain sex.

None of this is news to trans people, who, according to my informal polling, would not transition back to their sex assigned at birth for all of the money in the world. Ramachandran is simply describing in neuroscientific terms the experience of how a mismatch between brain and the body causes the symptoms of bodily incongruity that trans people experience. As trans advocate André Wilson once put it, it "is not about feeling comfortable in our 'gender' or in performing to gender expectations or roles. . . . This is thus not about 'gender dysphoria' or even 'gender identity': it is about facilitating the match between internal sense of our sex, and our external embodiment. This internal sense is not 'in the mind,' it is perhaps more like the internal physical interface of our body. (Like the inside face of a glove, which cannot really be conceived of separately from the exterior surface.)"[22]

Does this describe every trans person's experience? No. There may well be a spectrum of trans feelings. Nevertheless, the vast majority of trans people have accessed hormones and want surgery.[23]

But if brain sex is just about this feeling of embodiment, how does that relate to the discomfort of being misgendered? Why do trans people get so upset about not being seen as their affirmed sex?[24] I don't have an explanation for this other than to say that whatever it is, it applies equally to cis people.

Norah Vincent, a rather masculine lesbian woman, decided to live as a man for purposes of writing *Self-Made Man*. She lived as "Ned" for a year and a half, not even full time. In the end, she ended up checking herself into a mental hospital. She had become depressed from the experience of being seen as male and having to hide the fact that she was female. She unexpectedly realized that sex resides in the head.[25]

David Reimer lost his penis in a botched circumcision, and a misguided doctor convinced his parents to raise him as a girl. David eventually began to live as a boy at age fourteen. But he killed himself at age thirty-eight. He had been through a lot, but the stress of being forced to be a sex he was not and to have a body that did not fully match his sex ultimately proved too much.[26]

Even temporarily having incongruent genitals is stressful. When cis actors Felicity Huffman and Chloë Sevigny played transgender women, they both reported crying at some point because of having to wear a prosthetic penis.[27]

Someone should've told them: It's okay; some women have penises and some men have vaginas—but that doesn't mean they're happy about it.

EPILOGUE

A lot of trans people say that when they were little, they prayed every night, "God please let me wake up and be a girl" or "God please let me wake up and be a boy."

But I was never that naive. After all, God was the one who made me this way. It's not like he was about to admit he made a mistake.

So I didn't pray to God. But I did have this comforting fantasy that I played in my mind, night after night, to help me fall asleep.

I imagined that I was captured by pirates! They took me below deck, tied me to a table, and left me alone. I lay there struggling against the ropes, but could never break free.

Then suddenly a man came to the door! He came in and cut my ropes and I was free. It always ended with me setting off to avenge my capture.

But the little girl? She had vanished. And I was the man who came to my own rescue.

BOOSTING TRANS EQUALITY: 10 TIPS FOR CIS PEOPLE

1 **Develop a healthy cis identity.** Acknowledging that you are cis lets trans people know that you have some understanding of trans issues. Take a cue from Melissa Harris-Perry on her MSNBC episode, "Being Transgender in America" where she explains being cis.[28]

2 **Accept that you may never understand what it's like to be trans.** Being trans and being cis are just different experiences. You don't have to fully understand being trans (not even trans people do!) to accept and respect trans people.

3 **Listen to trans people.** Trans people are the experts on their own experience. They know more about what's happening with them than you do. Resist the urge impose your own theories onto the lived experiences of trans people.

4 **Ensure that trans people can control their own bodies.** This means making sure the insurance plan at your school or workplace doesn't exclude medically necessary, transgender-related health care. Trans people pay the same premiums as everyone else and need equal coverage in return.

5 **See trans people for who they say they are, not who you think they are.** If you're having trouble with someone's preferred pronouns that means you're imposing your ideas onto them rather than seeing them for who they are. This also means ensuring that trans women are welcome in women's spaces.

6 **Don't tell trans people to love our bodies just the way they are.** Dysphoria is real. It is separate from any culturally imposed shame and cannot be willed away. If you think it's important to love trans bodies, start by loving a trans person.

7 **Be aware of your cis privilege.** Society is organized around a cis ideal. You likely have ID that matches who you are, aren't harassed for

using the restroom, and won't face employment discrimination because you're cis. Use your privilege to ensure that trans people have access to the same things.

8 **Boost trans people's voices, don't speak for them.** Trans artists and writers are struggling to get their stories out there. Rather than appropriating trans themes and characters for your project, support a trans person in getting their story out there directly.

9 **View trans people as potential friends and lovers.** Invite us to hang out one-on-one, not just in a group. Don't exoticize us. Don't ask us about our genitals or medical history unless you're talking about yours first.

10 **Educate your cis friends.** If your friends don't understand trans people, help take the burden off of trans people by telling your friends what's what. Speak up when transphobia is happening.

DISCUSSION QUESTIONS

• Author Noah E. Lewis writes, "My transition had nothing to do with *gender*. It had everything to do with *sex*." What does he mean by this?

• What do you make of the author's suggestion that *most trans people are gender conforming*? Is there a difference between someone who is gender nonconforming and someone who is trans?

• Argentina and Denmark allow transgender individuals to change the sex on their birth certificates by submitting a personal affidavit rather than being required to present a doctor's letter or proof of surgery. What might be some barriers to more countries adopting this standard? What would you say to address those concerns?

• How should we as a society classify people for purposes of single-sex facilities (bathrooms, locker rooms)? How do we actually classify people now? What if we got rid of classifications altogether?

• What is cisgender privilege? What does the author suggest can increase awareness about this privilege?

• We've had more stories in the press about schools not embracing their young students who are gender nonconforming. What can you do in your own communities to support the needs of these children and to raise awareness?

NOTES

1. I first heard about this question from Jamison Green in *Becoming a Visible Man* (Nashville, TN: Vanderbilt University Press, 2004).

2. Julia Serano pointed this out in *Whipping Girl: A Transsexual Woman on Sexism and the Scapegoating of Femininity* (Emeryville, CA: Seal Press, 2007).

3. Julia Serano, *Whipping Girl*, 33.

4. Natacha Kennedy and Mark Hellen, "Transgender Children: More than a Theoretical Challenge," *Graduate Journal of Social Science* 7, no. 2 (2010): 25–43. Three out of four children knew they were trans before leaving elementary school, and only 4 percent knew after age 18.

5. Petula Dvorak, "Transgender at Five," *Washington Post*, May 19, 2012, http://www.washingtonpost.com/local/transgender-at-five/2012/05/19/gIQABfFkbU_story.html.

6. Sabrina Rubin Erdely, "About a Girl: Coy Mathis' Fight to Change Gender," *Rolling Stone*, October 28, 2013, http://www.rollingstone.com/culture/news/about-a-girl-coy-mathis-fight-to-change-change-gender-20131028.

7. GoBots are a cooler version of Transformers.

8. Kennedy and Hellen, "Transgender Children," 30–32.

9. Thomas D. Steensma, R. Biemond, F. de Boer, and P.T. Cohen-Kettenis, "Desisting and Persisting Gender Dysphoria after Childhood: A Qualitative Follow-Up Study," *Clinical Child Psychology and Psychiatry* 16, no. 4 (October 2011): 499–516.

10. Anyone who is changing their sex characteristics for the purpose of expressing gender is going to be sorely disappointed. I'm saddened when I hear about young women who have been led by a "gender as performance" subculture into believing that there's no difference between wearing ties and injecting testosterone. There are real consequences to conflating sex and gender. No one should be stuck with unwanted virilization of her body because she didn't understand that being masculine and being male are two different things entirely.

11. *JEB v. Alabama ex rel. TB*, 511 U.S. 127, 157 n.1 (1994) (Scalia, J., dissenting).

12. I will not to try to offer an explanation as to why most women tend toward the feminine and most men tend toward the masculine. But the fact of the matter is that plenty of women *like* being feminine and plenty of men *like* being masculine. These associations of men with masculinity and women with femininity exist in the world, and trans people are no different from cis people in tending to have these preferences.

13. Julie A. Greenberg, "Defining Male and Female: Intersexuality and the Collisions Between Law and Biology," *Arizona Law Review* 41 (1999): 281–282.

14. World Professional Association for Transgender Health, "Standards of Care for the Health of Transsexual, Transgender, and Gender Non-Conforming People, Version 7," *International Journal of Transgenderism* 13 (2011): 165–232.

15. V.S. Ramachandran and William Hirstein, "The Perception of Phantom Limbs," *The D.O. Hebb Lecture. Brain*, 121, no. 9 (1998): 1603–1630; V.S. Ramachandran and David Brang, "Phantom Touch," *Scholarpedia*, 4, no. 10 (2009), http://www.scholarpedia.org/article/Phantom_touch; V.S. Ramachandran, *The Tell-Tale Brain: A Neuroscientist's Quest for What Makes Us Human* (New York: W.W. Norton, 2012).

16. Ramachandran, *The Tell-Tale Brain*.

17. V.S. Ramachandran and Paul McGeoch, "Phantom Penises In Transsexuals: Evidence of an Innate Gender-Specific Body Image in the Brain," *Journal of Consciousness Studies* 15, no. 1 (January 2008): 5–16; V.S. Ramachandran, *The Tell-Tale Brain*, 259.

18. Ramachandran, *The Tell-Tale Brain*, 259.

19. V.S. Ramachandran and Paul D. McGeoch, "Occurrence of Phantom Genitalia after Gender Reassignment Surgery," *Medical Hypotheses* 69, no. 5 (2007): 1001–1003.

20. Laura Case, *How the Body Can Feel Wrong: Sensory Processing and Neural Body Representation in Transsexuality and Anorexia Nervosa*. Dissertation, University of California, San Diego. Ann Arbor: ProQuest/UMI, 2013 (Publication No. 1466303809).

21. L.K. Case and V.S. Ramachandran, "Alternating Gender Incongruity: A New Neuropsychiatric Syndrome Providing Insight Into the Dynamic Plasticity of Brain-Sex," *Medical Hypotheses* 78, no. 5 (May 2012): 626–631.

22. Personal email from André Wilson, February 11, 2010.

23. Three out of four of transgender respondents had accessed hormone therapy. Ninety-three percent of trans men want chest surgery, and 86 percent of trans people want genital surgery. See Jamie Grant, Jamie M. Grant, Lisa A. Mottet, Justin Tanis, Jack Harrison, Jody L. Herman, and Mara Keisling, "Injustice at Every Turn: A Report of the National Transgender Non-Discrimination Survey," *National Center for Transgender Equality* (2011), endtransdiscrimination.org/PDFs/NTDS_Report.pdf.

24. Some of this is certainly related to the effect of bringing to consciousness any body dysphoria that the person may have been able to temporarily suppress while going about their day.

25. "Self Made Man: Norah Vincent Chooses Female Privilege over Male Privilege," *20/20*, 2006, https://www.youtube.com/watch?v=Ip7kP_dd6LU.

26. John Colapinto, "Gender Gap: What Were the Real Reasons Behind David Reimer's Suicide?" *Slate*, June 3, 2004, http://www.slate.com/articles/health_and_science/medical_examiner/2004/06/gender_gap.html.

27. "Larry Discusses Transgender Individuals," *Larry King Live*, February 15, 2006, http://transcripts.cnn.com/TRANSCRIPTS/0602/15/lkl.01.html; Cassie Carpenter, "'I Cried Every Day When They Put It On': Chloe Sevigny Opens Up About Wearing a Prosthetic Penis for New Transgender Role," *Mail Online*, May 18, 2012, http://www.dailymail.co.uk/tvshowbiz/article-2146203/Chloe-Sevigny-opens-wearing-prosthetic-penis-new-transgender-role.html.

28. Melissa Harris-Perry, "Being Transgender in America," MSNBC, 2012, https://www.youtube.com/watch?v=KJOD_SYWKtI.

Part II

Pornography

When it comes to pornography, there are plenty of opinions, billions of page views, lots of questions . . . and no easy answers. Part II of *Gender, Sex, and Politics* includes a series of four chapters with competing feminist perspectives about the role of pornography in regard to pleasure, desire, sexism, and subjugation. This section also includes a Christian cure for addiction and a first-person essay written by a queer porn performer describing his experience on the job (and off).

The section begins with chapter 7 by Lynn Comella, " 'You're Taking a Class on What?!' Studying Pornography in College." Comella is a university professor who teaches a course about the adult entertainment industry. This class includes units on obscenity law, the feminist sex wars, strip club culture, sex toy stores, and yes: pornography. As Comella explains, the goal of the class is twofold: to position public sexual culture as a worthwhile topic of scholarly analysis, and to highlight for students how they can use the same kinds of theoretical tools and modes of critical inquiry that they encounter in more traditional courses to examine an extremely popular and profitable segment of social life. The class is officially titled "Public Sexual Culture," but students on campus commonly shorten the title to "The Sex Class." While misstating the name of the class may seem benign, this pithy revision evokes the serious misunderstandings about what it means to study pornography as an important aspect of university curriculum. In her chapter, Lynn Comella describes students' initial reactions to the course and the transformational experiences students recount as they reflect on how they learned to think in new ways about sex and culture.[1] Talking openly about sex allowed some students to examine their own assumptions about pornography and to share these conversations with others beyond the classroom walls.

In chapter 8, Pastor Craig Gross suggests solutions to porn addiction in "The Porn Pandemic: What Can We Do?" Gross is the founder of XXXchurch.com, which he started as a "response to the hurting he saw both in those addicted to pornography and those who made their living in the porn industry." In Gross's words, "The XXXchurch website mixes the seedy with the sacred in an effort to raise the often taboo subject of pornography as a problem that needed to be dealt with."[2] To that end, Gross writes that pornography has become a pandemic that openly preys on the unwilling. With the easy access of online porn, gone are the days of secretive ventures to the adult bookstore for a brown-paper-wrapped magazine. Today, the porn fix is only a suggestive click away, the tracks easily covered by deleting website history. Given that pornography is more widely available now than ever before, Craig Gross is concerned about the effects this is having on upcoming generations and how the porn pandemic shapes their views on healthy sexuality, on body image, and on gender roles in the touchscreen world. In this chapter, Gross proposes the solution: greater community and accountability among all generations to diminish the adverse effects of pornography on our sexuality and to increase our culture's overall sexual health.

Robert Jensen is also concerned about the impact of pornography in shaping ideas about sex and gender roles. However, Jensen tackles this issue not from a religious Christian viewpoint, but from a feminist political perspective. In chapter 9, "Just a John? Pornography and Men's Choices," Jensen argues that pornography is not really about sexual pleasure. Rather, pornography reinforces gender inequality and women's subjugation.

> Because we live in a culture that buys, sells, and trades women's bodies, Jensen asks men who use porn to take a cold, hard look at why they do. Pornography, he argues, is just another form of buying women's bodies. Instead, there are creative possibilities for new ways of enjoying sex and pleasure that do not require the old tropes of male violence and sexual control of women.[3]

Juxtaposed with Robert Jensen's feminist critique of pornography is a first-person essay written by Ned Henry, a queer porn performer. Like Jensen, Henry identifies as feminist and also applies a gender analysis to pornography but with much different conclusions. In chapter 10, "Male and Queer in the Porn Industry," Henry writes, "I have sex with many different people irrespective of their gender—often people I've just met—and I sell images of these sex acts on the Internet to pay my bills. I am also a Harvard-educated, cisgendered white man who owns his own small business while working on a PhD in experimental quantum nanoelectronics. This will not be a sad story; no downward spiral led me to monetize my sex life. . . . I love my work, I consider it to be ethical, important, challenging, and fun."

As Sut Jhally, Professor of Communication and Executive Director of the Media Education Foundation, comments: All of us present ourselves to be watched and gazed at. We all "watch attractive strangers with sexual desire. To treat another as an object of our desires is part of what it means to be human."[4] The problem arises when women are presented as nothing more than objectified sexual desire and men are presented as only agents of sexual objectification. This wrings out the complexities of human desire and the politics of gender and power. Picking up on this point in his essay, Henry writes, "the experience of being *consensually* sexually objectified can be fun and empowering." The competing views about consuming or producing pornography in this section problematize presumptions about who does porn, who uses porn, who likes to be watched, and who's doing the watching. The arguments that follow encourage us to think carefully about the line between empowerment and exploitation. These chapters hopefully also inspire readers to analyze our assumptions about the politics of heteronormative sexuality and conventional masculinity.[5]

NOTES

1. For more information about pornography research and pedagogical issues, see Lynn Comella and Shira Tarrant, eds., *New Views on Pornography: Sexuality, Politics, and the Law* (Santa Barbara, CA: Praeger, 2015); and Shira Tarrant, "Truth Claims About Porn: When Dogma and Data Collide," in *The Philosophy of Pornography: Contemporary Perspectives*, ed. Lindsay Coleman and Jacob M. Held (Lanham, MD: Rowman & Littlefield, 2014), 35–52.
2. Craig Gross, "Bio," http://www.craiggross.com/bio.
3. Shira Tarrant, "Introduction," in *Men Speak Out: Views on Gender, Sex, and Power* (New York: Routledge, 2013), 69.
4. Sut Jhally, dir., *Dreamworlds 3 (Abridged): Desire, Sex & Power in Music Video.* Northampton, MA: Media Education Foundation, 2007.
5. Shira Tarrant, "Introduction," 70.

"YOU'RE TAKING A CLASS ON WHAT?!"

Studying Pornography in College

Lynn Comella

"**Y**ou teach that sex class, don't you?" the student working behind the counter at the Student Union asked as he handed me a cup of coffee.

I sized him up for a moment before answering. He was a wiry kid with a swath of dark hair, and a thin mustache that barely made it all the way across his upper lip.

"I guess it's *sort* of a sex class," I replied. "But I've never really thought of it quite like that."

"Do you really show pornography in class?" he asked in a conspiratorial half-whisper.

"Sometimes," I told him.

"That's so funny," he said.

"Why is it funny?" I asked, genuinely interested in hearing what he had to say.

"It's just funny to think about pornography in the classroom. It's not a place where you typically expect to find it."

I had to admit that he had a point. Despite the fact that college courses on pornography are increasingly common, the idea of porn making its way into the college curriculum still catches many people—including students—off guard. In this chapter I make a case for why the university classroom should be a place for the study of pornography. In particular, I want to discuss how my students navigate the subject of pornography, and what, according to their own accounts, they have learned from a class that takes what is culturally taboo and repositions it as something worthy of serious academic inquiry.

For the past decade, I have taught a course that surveys various aspects of the adult entertainment industry, from the "Golden Era" of pornography in the 1970s to twenty-first-century labor organizing among sex workers. The syllabus is wide-ranging and includes units on pornography, obscenity law, the feminist "sex wars," strip club culture, sex toy stores, and the cultivation of sexual taste cultures, among other subjects. The goal of the class is twofold: First, I want to position public sexual culture—pornography, prostitution, and strip clubs, for example—as worthwhile topics of scholarly analysis. Second, I want to highlight for students how they can use the same kinds of theoretical tools and modes of critical inquiry that they encounter in more traditional courses to examine an extremely popular and profitable segment of social life. In this sense, the class is both an intellectual endeavor and a recuperative project of writing sexual history and culture into the university curriculum.

The fact that my course calls for students to view pornography in the context of the college classroom has caused some colleagues to shudder, others to raise their eyebrows, and still others to praise what they see as an act of bravery. These responses, however, all fall short of the mark, which is to consider why I teach this class in the first place, and what I hope my students will get out of the experience of taking it.

BRINGING PORNOGRAPHY INTO THE CLASSROOM

More than a decade ago, when I was nearing completion of my PhD in communication and media studies at a large university in the northeast United States, I had the opportunity to design an upper-division undergraduate course based loosely on my dissertation research. I had spent the previous year studying the history and retail culture of women-owned sex toy stores in the United States, a project that had taken me from New York City to Seattle and from San Francisco to Austin, Texas. I conducted in-depth interviews with dozens of retailers, sales staff, and sex toy manufacturers, and spent hours reading dusty memos and profit-and-loss reports. I also spent six months working on the sales floor at feminist retailer Babeland in New York City.[1]

In my capacity as a staff sex educator, I interacted daily with customers. It did not take long for me to realize that adults of all genders, ages, and backgrounds were hungry for accurate information about sexual anatomy, response, and pleasure—basically everything they didn't learn in their school-based sex education. Many people who came into the store were not only interested in hearing about the latest thingamajig that whirled, twirled, and vibrated, but they welcomed the opportunity to talk about sex in an open and nonjudgmental environment. This was especially true of pornography.

On what seemed like an almost daily basis, I found myself standing by the store's porn collection giving the equivalent of a Porn 101 lecture. Customers were fascinated to learn that there were feminist directors making pornography with women in mind, lesbian directors making pornography for lesbians, and a nascent queer porn movement that was challenging normative assumptions about sex and gender. It had never occurred to most of them that pornography—much like Hollywood movies—consisted of different film genres geared toward different audiences with different tastes. People wanted to know about the conditions under which porn was produced, including how performers were treated and what they were paid. Other times, they wanted to discuss how pornography fit with the mission of a feminist-identified sex toy store, which, for some, seemed like an oxymoron. The conversations I had were always compelling and certainly never dull. They also confirmed that pornography was a topic that people from all walks of life were deeply curious about.

It was this kind of on-the-ground and up-close experience with pornography—what I refer to as "porn studies-in-action"—that inspired me to propose a college course that included a focus on pornography.[2] My rationale was simple: If, as a communication department, we were offering courses that analyzed the power and influence of media industries like advertising, television, and music, we should also be discussing the realm of adult entertainment, including the billion dollar pornography industry. The department chair agreed and gave me the green light to develop a course that did just that.

Deciding what to call the class was my first challenge. Although I planned to discuss the history of pornography as both an industry and genre, it wasn't the sole focus of the class. I wanted to encourage students to think about the relationship between sex and public culture in myriad ways, taking into account a variety of spaces where cultural discourses about sexuality circulate, from strip clubs to sex toy stores to the Internet. I wanted students to consider the adult entertainment industry not just as a profit-making enterprise—although it certainly is that—but as a realm of cultural meaning making. In short, I wanted my students to think critically about how sexual consumer culture informs some of their most basic assumptions about gender, race, social class, and sexuality. Given this focus, I decided to call the class "Public Sexual Culture."

The following semester, I was off and running. I was excited to have the chance to teach a course that was so interesting to me. Students seemed to share my enthusiasm. Thus, I was completely surprised when, at the start of the second week of classes, I got an email from the chair of my department telling me that the mother of one of my students had called the chancellor of the university, who had then called the provost, who had then contacted him with the complaint that her daughter was being "forced to watch pornography." In his email the chair assured me that he supported both the course and me but, all the same, could I forward him a copy of my syllabus so he could address the parent's concerns. I did, and later that day, my department chair wrote to tell me that he had spoken to the provost, and made it clear to him that no one was being "forced" to watch pornography. If any student was uncomfortable with the focus of the class—which was an elective and not required—there were other classes they could take that would fulfill the same degree requirements.

As someone who was just beginning her teaching career, it was an instructive moment. It had never occurred to me that a parent might complain about the class. I had assumed—rather naively—that my students would be a self-selective bunch; if they were not interested in the course material, they simply would not enroll. I had not anticipated the likelihood that some students would not bother to read the course description, and that they would therefore be unprepared for a class that included discussions and screenings of pornography. And even though pornography was one topic out of many on the syllabus, it was the one that jumped out and, on a visceral level, provoked the strongest responses from students.

My point of including pornography in this class was not to shock or titillate. Nor was I looking to generate controversy. I see an inherent value in teaching about pornography. For me, porn is an entry point for talking about a number of issues, from the history of obscenity law, to the cultural politics of moral panics, to discourses of disgust and desire. I want my students to develop skills for analyzing public dimensions of sexuality, the politics of sexual representation, and the role of the marketplace in creating conditions—sometimes favorable, other times not—for the production and proliferation of sexual discourse and values. Public sexual culture is part of the world in which we live, and young adults in particular need tools for making sense of it. In what follows, I discuss what the initial cohort of students who took my class had to say about it. The two main questions under consideration are: *What did students learn?* And, moreover, *What did they see as the value of the class?*[3]

STUDENT REFLECTIONS

Initial Reactions

Many students admitted in their final reflection papers that they had absolutely no idea what they were getting into when they enrolled in the course. Some were intrigued by the title, while others were happy just to find a course that fit seamlessly into their class schedule. A few acknowledged that they had failed to read the course description, so they were completely caught off guard to learn that the class included a focus on pornography. Based on nothing but the course title, many had assumed the class would focus on images of women in *Cosmo* magazine, music videos, and sexy Calvin Klein ad campaigns. As one student wrote, "When I saw the syllabus, my heart skipped a beat." She was not alone.

Some students were taken aback by the prospect of publicly watching pornography alongside their professor and fellow classmates. Several said they were intimidated, others embarrassed, and a few never returned after the first day. They used words like "shocked," "stunned," "wary," and "uncomfortable" to describe their initial reactions to the course syllabus. Yet for one reason or another, almost every student who showed up on the first day of class stuck it out and found ways to manage, and eventually conquer, their initial feelings of discomfort. One student had this to say about her experience:

> I had fears about this course, mostly fears that I would not understand some of the material, fears of getting bad marks; but my greatest fear of all was the fear of being uncomfortable. From the start, students were informed that the topics covered were going to shock and challenge you and that pornographic screenings would be frequent; but I committed to the course. The first few weeks of class were uncomfortable, but I was not alone. Others felt the same way and as the course progressed I found it easier to sit back in my chair, let down my guard, and participate in discussions. Besides facing my fears, my misconceptions about pornography were revealed.

Students' initial responses were also highly gendered. Most of the men—who comprised about a third of the class of twenty-five students—said they had been "pleasantly surprised" to have the chance to examine pornography in a critical way. According to one, "A class that already seemed more interesting than most others I've taken started to sound even more interesting." Another noted that he enrolled in the class to "spice up" his "lackluster schedule." "I was pretty optimistic that this course would be interesting and fun," wrote another.

This sense of enthusiasm was far from universal, however. Kara,[4] the student whose mother had called the chancellor to complain about the class, said this about her initial reactions to the syllabus:

> When I received the syllabus my eyes jumped out of my head, and I was utterly shocked. I enrolled in public sexual culture without even thinking that pornography would be discussed. I thought the class was going to be about how sex is so pervasive in our media, such as in music videos, commercials, magazines and television. I expected we would see examples of sexual media, but I never thought the course would be about pornography. The topic was already taboo, let alone having to actually view sex acts as a required part of the class. I immediately knew I wanted out of the class.

Kara did look for another class, but did not manage to find one that interested her, so she opted—quite reluctantly—to stay. She told me later that she thought she would "despise every minute" of it. It was an interesting process, then, to watch Kara's transformation from a resistant, if not downright hostile, student to an involved and engaged member of the class. She later recalled how her perspective shifted, which is worth quoting at length:

> Prior to entering college, I had watched pornography but I had never enjoyed it. The videos I had seen were always geared toward a male

audience, so the videos provided me with little pleasure and enjoyment. Then, upon entering college, I enrolled in a women's studies class. We had a section on pornography and the sex industry, and my professor was vehemently opposed to the idea of pornography and the sex industry because she believed it exploited women. I could not help but agree with her, but it was probably because I was not an independently sexual female. I was moderately sexual because my boyfriends wanted me to be; however, I was sexual for them, not for me, so I could not understand how any female could be truly sexual . . . then I enrolled in this class. This class taught me many things about which I was initially ignorant. I realized that working in pornography (and other aspects of the sex industry) was a choice many women made on their own because they enjoyed the sex, the work, and/or the money. In fact, many of these women were shrewd businesswomen. Additionally, I learned that the pornography that I did not enjoy was not made with my pleasure in mind [and that] there was pornography specifically made for a female audience. That was quite an exciting discovery!

Challenging Stereotypes

Kara was not the only student who began the semester with preconceived ideas about pornography. The dominant narrative that most students bring with them goes something like this: Men make pornography for other (presumably heterosexual) men. Pornography objectifies and degrades women. Thus, all women are hurt by pornography and the sex industry. "Before the beginning of the semester," one female student commented, "I pretty much viewed all pornography as bad . . . there have been times when I have viewed pornography, but I always found it to be degrading to women." According to another: "I had seen pornographic movies, websites and strip clubs before but they all appeared to be made for and only met the needs of men. I always imagined men consuming and enjoying these materials or places and women only participating to please their boyfriends/husbands/lovers." "I thought the only people who watched such videos were men, either young men, such as high school or college kids, or older, dirty men," another woman wrote.

Presented in these near-universal terms, there is little, if any, room in students' preconceived worldviews for diversity, innovation, audience segmentation, or female sexual agency in the world of porn. "I assumed that all pornography was alike," one woman confessed. One of my goals as a professor, then, is to complicate my students' understanding of pornography. This does not mean that I expect (or require) them to become cheerleaders for porn. Rather, my objective is that by the end of the semester students will have learned enough to move beyond a rather simplistic analysis that reduces pornography to either one of two positions: an unequivocal sign of misogyny and social decay, or, conversely, an uncritical celebration of sexual empowerment. Neither position sufficiently captures the complexity of pornography. Indeed, the reality of pornography—much like any other media industry or cultural artifact—is far more layered, nuanced, and multi-faceted than either of these two positions suggest.

My hope is that students are willing to dive into this complexity with an open mind; and this almost always happens. Positioning pornography as a subject of critical inquiry shifts the frame of reference about a topic that many students have never thought about in any serious way—because they've never been asked to. This reframing makes it possible, and indeed gives students permission, to engage with pornography as they would any other subject matter they might encounter in their college classes. "I came to treat [the class] as a film studies class," wrote one student. "That's what we were doing: Viewing clips and discussing the content." Treating pornography as they would a film class or sociology course makes it harder for them to simply dismiss porn as culturally insignificant or lacking in value. And while many students begin the semester with a sense of ambivalence about what the class will entail, it does not take long for most to realize that there is more to the topic of pornography than they had ever imagined.

More Than Meets the Eye

By the time they reach college, most young adults have seen pornography in one form or another, whether it is a *Playboy* centerfold or a hardcore Internet clip. For many, to *see* porn is to *know* porn. To suggest to them, as I do, that pornography is about much more than the visual spectacle of sex, that it might have something to tell us about the politics of gender, race, and class, among other things, is a proposition that knocks many of them sideways. As far as they are concerned, pornography is nothing more than the display of naked bodies and the physical act of sex. In other words, pornography is what it depicts.

Teaching pornography requires upending the way most people think about sex. It involves *denaturalizing* ideas about sexuality, desire, and bodies—a task that is easier said than done. Teaching porn involves taking something that is familiar and making it strange. It also requires giving students the theoretical tools they need to move beyond the default position that what they see on the surface is all there is to the story. For me, this entails introducing students to critical theories of discourse and representation, sprinkled with a little Foucault and a lot of sociology. Most students have never thought about sexuality as a set of discourses or a system of representation; and they certainly have never been encouraged to engage with pornography in any critical way. "My parents were shocked when I told them I was taking a class on pornography," wrote one woman. "My mom asked me what I was going to learn in a class like 'that.'"

Students begin the semester having never considered the business side of pornography, the existence of racial hierarchies, audience niches and market segmentation, or the use of pornography for the purpose of sex education. The idea that women—including those who identify as feminists—might make and view porn, challenges some of their most fundamental beliefs about sex and gender. It often never occurs to them that there might be more to pornography than just sex. As one student observed, the porn industry is about "much more than two people fucking." Others agreed.

> I would have to say that the primary idea I will take away from the class is that the pornography industry is a vast, complicated realm that is much more multi-faceted and complex than I had ever imagined.
>
> Before this class I was ignorant to how large and profitable the pornography industry was. I never regarded it as anything more than entertainment for sleazy, single, middle-aged men who need some visual stimulation to get themselves off once in a while due to the lack of a lady-character in their lives. Now I understand that porn has various uses and genres that can serve other functions, such as 'how to' and erotic videos for couples.
>
> I learned a lot about the different kinds of pornography that exist. I had no idea how many different genres there really were until we started seeing clips and discussing genres in class. I did not have any experience with pornography, so I was not sure as to what existed. After watching clips from the films *Three Sisters*, *How to Fuck in High Heels*, and the Annie Sprinkle video, I have a much better idea. I was interested to watch the clips and analyze them while comparing them to other clips we watched.

That there were occasions when we watched pornography as a class was, at least initially, one of the more challenging parts of the course for many students. However, most came to appreciate just how essential viewing pornography was to learning about it. After all, we would not expect students to discuss the plot of a novel, its character development, and an author's use of metaphors without first reading the book. Yet we consistently expect people to form opinions—and even make policy decisions—about pornography with little knowledge or no direct experience. Instead, the social significance of pornography is treated as so self-evident that the most basic questions, like "What is pornography?" "Who watches it?" "What are people's motivations for viewing pornography?" are treated as largely inconsequential, or the answers are based on opinion, stereotypes, or even prejudice—rather than evidence and data.

Courses on pornography almost always double as sex education classes. This tends to be an unintentional consequence and something that viewing pornography, rather than just talking about it, seems to facilitate. Most students who take my class identify as straight, and most of their ideas about sex and pornography are fairly heterocentric. It is often difficult for many of them to imagine sexual practices and desires that exist outside the bounds of their own, relatively limited, heterosexual experiences. In fact, it rarely occurs to some of them that gay, lesbian, bisexual, and queer porn even exists—let alone what it might look like. Showing examples of lesbian porn, such as SIR Video's *Hard Love & How to Fuck in High Heels*—which includes scenes with dildos and strap-ons—or instructional sex videos, such as *Bend Over Boyfriend*, not only complicates students' understanding of pornography, but it also complicates their understanding of human sexuality. According to one student:

> I have never seen a video about anal sex, especially one done by a 'normal' and somewhat 'nerdy' forty year old couple. Nor had I seen a lesbian video that involved many kinds of lesbians getting off solely by strapping on a dildo and pleasing someone else. My point here is that things that before seemed racy, alternative, or only for sexual daredevils now seem more normalized and acceptable.

In an era when school-based sex education remains inadequate, and opportunities to talk openly about sex are limited, courses on pornography become occasions for people to encounter information about sexual health, pleasure, safety, and diversity.[5] "Until this class I never realized we were not being taught in school the full understanding of sex. We learned about the things that were wrong with sex, but never the benefits. We learned more about risk reduction, but not pleasure," one student noted. For her—and others—the course was transformative.

"My Horizons Have Been Expanded"

Students reported, almost unanimously, that taking the course had not only broadened their understanding of pornography, but it challenged many of their preconceived assumptions. It made them more open-minded, and altered their views about sex. Many also conveyed that the class gave them permission to be curious about a segment of popular culture that they had been taught to dismiss or vilify.

One of the most interesting themes to emerge from student accounts of their experiences was the premium they placed on being able to talk openly and thoughtfully about pornography. "This class and the topic of public sexual culture gave students a chance to talk about a taboo subject in a very educational and informative manner," wrote one woman. "The conversation is what made the class so special," claimed another. "The more you talk openly about sexual ideas, the more open you become to new ideas," noted someone else. Talking openly about sex allowed some students to examine their own assumptions about pornography:

> From this class I will take away the idea that an issue is only taboo if it is hidden away or not talked about freely. There is certainly nothing wrong with sex and sexuality. This class helped me feel comfortable discussing the subject of pornography, and helped me understand individuals' involvement in some of these businesses. Like so many other aspects of life, one shouldn't succumb to stereotypes, and this class has allowed me to leave a lot of stereotypes concerning pornography behind.

The conversations my students were having about pornography spread far beyond the immediate classroom setting. Students shared their response papers with their parents, and talked about the class with friends and roommates. Many of them became "knowledge ambassadors" who took what they were learning back to their dorms and families, using class lectures and discussions as jumping off points to talk about pornography in other contexts. According to Mike:

> I think by reading about porn, watching it in class, and having our open class discussions pornography became something that was easy to talk about. During the first few weeks of the course I would give my housemates updates about what was going on in the 'porn class,' sometimes bragging to them that we got to watch some porn that day . . . after being in the course for over three months now, I feel that talking openly about porn is not really all that different from talking about any other social or political issue.

It was not only students' perceptions of pornography that changed throughout the semester. For some, the class changed the way they thought of themselves as sexual beings. This was especially true for women. "The most important lesson I gained from this course," noted one woman, "is that in order for women to become fully liberated they must also become sexually liberated." According to another:

> I will also take away [from this class] that as a woman, my sexuality should not come second. I have a lot of confidence, but I have never talked about sex much. I think now, after some of the dialogue we have had in class, I am willing to try and change that, because I feel that in being silent, the mainstream taboo around women and sexuality wins and I don't want that to happen.

Of all of the unanticipated consequences of teaching a class on pornography, this was the most significant. That a course on pornography could mimic the effects of a feminist conscious-raising group, and cognitively shift how some young women thought of themselves as sexual agents, was completely unexpected and profoundly meaningful.

CONCLUSION

More than any other course I have taught, I learned the most from this one. I learned to never underestimate my students' ability to negotiate challenging material in the classroom. Limiting students' exposure to certain topics because some people deem them inappropriate or too risqué does young adults a disservice. In an age of the corporate university, where students are positioned as little more than consumers, and essential forms of knowledge are increasingly measured by employability, it is easy to forget that students actually want to learn about things they can apply to the everyday world in which they live. Education is a potentially transformative process, not just the acquisition of a skill set that one ticks off with a series of check marks or measures with a paycheck.

My students did not just like this course, they *loved* it—this, despite the fact that many of them were initially uncomfortable, embarrassed, and unsure about what a class on pornography would entail. They stuck it out, though, which says more about them, and their willingness to take their education seriously, than it says about me as their professor. I was fortunate that I was part of an academic department that recognized the inherent benefit of offering such a course. One student went so far as to say that it made her "intensely proud" to attend a university that allowed a class such as this one into the curriculum. She was not alone in this sentiment. "I think it's important that all campuses have courses like this," another student remarked. "We, as students, and human beings, should expose ourselves to as many things [and] as many subjects as possible. [This is how] we learn and grow." This statement, generated from a student's perspective, is perhaps the strongest rationale I can provide for why pornography should be a topic of study in the twenty-first-century college classroom.

DISCUSSION QUESTIONS

•   The author discusses a number of reasons why taking a class about pornography can be valuable: Do you think there's value to college classes that discuss pornography?
•   Now that you are aware that such classes exist, would you ever take a class that focuses on pornography? Why or why not?
•   Were you surprised by any of the student responses discussed by the author?
•   The author describes how a mother of one student complained to the college because pornography was shown in class. Given that college students are

adults, what role do you think parents and college administrators ought to have in controlling sex-based curriculum?

• The author teaches pornography to encourage her students to develop skills for analyzing public dimensions of sexuality, the politics of sexual representation, and the role of the marketplace in creating conditions that produce and proliferate sexual discourse and values. What does this mean?

• The author writes that one goal as a professor is to complicate students' understanding of pornography. Based on information provided in the chapter, what does this mean? Has it complicated your understanding of pornography?

• After reading student reactions to taking a course on Public Sexual Culture, discuss their responses.

NOTES

1. For a discussion of this research, see Lynn Comella, "From Text to Context: Feminist Porn and the Making of a Market," in *The Feminist Porn Book: The Politics of Producing Pleasure*, eds., Tristan Taormino, Celine Parrenñas Shimuzu, Constance Penley, and Mireille Miller-Young (New York: The Feminist Press, 2013), 79–93; Lynn Comella, "Changing the World One Orgasm at a Time: Sex Positive Retail Activism," in *Commodity Activism: Cultural Resistance in Neoliberal Times*, eds., Roopali Mukherjee and Sarah Banet-Weiser (New York: New York University Press, 2012), 240–253; Lynn Comella, "Repackaging Sex: Class, Crass, and the Good Vibrations Model of Sexual Retail," in *New Sociologies of Sex Work*, eds., Kate Hardy, Sarah Kingston, and Teela Sanders (Surrey: Ashgate, 2010), 213–226.

2. For more on the idea of porn studies-in-action see Lynn Comella, "Studying Porn Cultures," *Porn Studies* 1, no. 1–2 (Spring 2014): 64–70.

3. There is a growing body of literature that addresses the practice of teaching pornography from the perspective of professors. For examples see Shira Tarrant, "Pornography and Pedagogy: Teaching Media Literacy," in *New Views on Pornography: Sexuality, Politics, and the Law*, eds. Lynn Comella and Shira Tarrant (Santa Barbara, CA: Praeger, 2015); Bobby Noble, "Porn's Pedagogies: Teaching Porn Studies in the Academic-Corporate Complex," *Porn Studies* 1, no. 1–2 (Spring 2014): 96–113; Constance Penley, "A Feminist Teaching Pornography? That's Like Scopes Teaching Evolution!" in *The Feminist Porn Book: The Politics of Producing Pleasure*, eds. Tristan Taormino, Celine Parrenñas Shimuzu, Constance Penley, and Mireille Miller-Young (New York: Feminist Press, 2013), 179–199; Mireille Miller-Young, "The Pedagogy of Pornography: Teaching Hardcore Media in a Feminist Studies Classroom," *Signs* 2, no. 2 (Fall 2010), http://www.signs.rutgers.edu/miller-young_essay_1_2–2.htm.

4. All students referred to in this essay have been given pseudonyms to protect their identities.

5. For an example of the limits of school-based sex education in Nevada, see Lynn Comella, "Sex, Lies, and Public Education," *Vegas Seven*, May 31, 2013, http://vegasseven.com/2013/05/31/sex-lies-public-education/.

THE PORN PANDEMIC

What Can We Do?

Craig Gross

When I was a kid, which wasn't all that long ago, it was tough to find pornography. It had to be sought out, searched after, worked at. I was really only exposed to it twice in my childhood: once during middle-school track practice at my private Christian school, when one of my teammates was looking at a magazine and I happened to get a sideways glance at it; and once more, not too long after that, at my friend's house. Let's call him "Sean."

Sean and his family lived just down the street from my house, and since his parents weren't often home during the day, I spent a lot of my after-school time there, just hanging out with my friend, doing what bored seventh-graders do (mostly eating junk food and playing Nintendo). Unfortunately, though, Sean's parents had pretty liberal views on what was appropriate for middle-school boys to look at, and actually considered the type of pornography found in *Playboy* magazine to be a healthy exploration of sexuality for a young adolescent boy.

That's why Sean had no problem showing me his tree house one afternoon (it was really a haphazard collection of plywood boards nailed together in an old maple tree in Sean's backyard), and then, once inside, holding out an issue of *Playboy* to me and asking if I wanted to look at it.

Reflecting back on this moment, I can still recall the intense pounding of my heartbeat, echoing through my chest and making me exceptionally aware of my accelerating pulse rate, as well as the seemingly insatiable curiosity overwhelming my mind with equivocations and reasons why looking would be okay. I can also recall my own innocence and inexperience with such fare, as I gripped the glossy paper and turned to the first page.

Perhaps frustrated that I was doing it wrong, or perhaps with the patience of a mentor, I can't remember which, Sean took the magazine back from my suddenly sweating palms and flipped past all the excess to the heart of the issue: the centerfold. He gave it back to me and the image was branded onto my brain, where it remains to this day.

After a few more minutes looking at the photos in the magazine, Sean put it away and I climbed down the ladder to head home, a different boy than I was when I'd gone up it just a short while before. I had to go through Sean's house in order to retrieve my backpack, and while inside I came upon Sean's mother, who in retrospect was probably older than the women we'd just been gazing at but who, in the mind of a twelve-year-old boy, might just as well have been the same age, or even the same person. The images of those naked women hovered in my mind as I looked at her, and I couldn't bring myself to speak or offer her a farewell. I just grabbed my bag and left as quickly as I could.

I mostly succeeded in putting the images I'd seen out of my mind for the rest of the afternoon and evening, but as I lay in bed that night, they came back with a vengeance, dazzling and entrancing in their audacity. I was both enthralled and ashamed, dual reactions that dueled with one another for supremacy in my heart and soul. Having grown up in church, I had been mostly shielded from any sort of sexuality; I had no framework for dealing with the centerfold I'd seen, and instead of satisfying my curiosity, it only created more.

My innocence had vanished with those simple, single glances and now I felt different. I felt more mature, yet dirtier. That's really the best word to describe the way I felt on the inside: dirty. I didn't even fully comprehend what I'd seen, nor why those women were contorting their bodies into those odd and unnatural poses, nor how those images could be simultaneously so appealing and so repulsive to my mind, nor why they stirred up the kinds of emotions they did, nor how they reached so deeply into my heart. So many questions rose to the surface.

And on top of those philosophical musings, there were the practical questions: How did my friend get such a magazine? Begged? Borrowed? Stole? I wanted to know how to get one because now *I* wanted one. I began to wonder if every boy I knew already had one, and whether it was normal for me both to see what I'd seen and to want to see more.

I didn't know the name for it yet, but that afternoon was my introduction to the shadowy world of pornography, an industry that more often than not leads to an addiction that can quickly spiral out of control. In my own mind, a small spark of curiosity, one that I hadn't even really acknowledged existed, had been fanned into a full flame. Fortunately for my own life, that flame never consumed me in the way it does so many others. Instead, in time—and thanks largely to the inaccessibility of pornography during my childhood and my abiding faith—I was able to control that fire of pornography and effectively put it out.

There's a reason I told that story—because I wanted to point out that, even more today than when I was younger, it's very easy to be exposed to pornography, and usually under innocent pretenses like a misplaced click or mistyped URL into a Web browser. And yet, as innocent as we can be when we stumble into porn, porn does not return the favor. Pornography is a carnivore, and its appetite is insatiable.

Porn doesn't care about its menu or where its prey comes from—it only wants to devour. It sets a lure for the curious and lies in wait. I've known many, many people who were curious about this monster called porn and whose lives, families, and jobs were subsequently swallowed whole by it. I've even known men and women who got addicted to porn simply because they were trying to learn more about avoiding the dangers of the Internet and then their curiosity got the best of them.

Does that make curiosity a bad thing? I would submit that is not the case. In fact, I believe that God created sex and made us with a certain amount of healthy sexual curiosity that is necessary for strong, foundational relationships. But the world of pornography—those who make it and sell it—is cashing in on that curiosity in major ways now.

Sex has obviously always been a central component of the human experience, with ancient civilizations incorporating sexual expression and fertility into their artwork and their primitive forms of worship. And as technology has developed over the centuries, so has the ability to display and distribute the pornographic image, even when it hasn't been defined as such.

Pornography *was* defined in 1969 when President Lyndon Johnson and the U.S. Congress took an in-depth, investigative look called "The President's Commission on Obscenity and Pornography." Their findings became the legal foundation for what we now know as pornography, and revolutionized how the American culture thought about sex and porn.

The commission came to the conclusion that pornography was a mostly benign industry that generated meager revenues (about $10 million annually at the time), that it wasn't a threat to the fabric of society, and that it was perfectly acceptable among adults, as long as impressionable children were kept away from it. This finding dovetailed nicely with the sexual revolution that America was undergoing in the late 1960s and early 1970s as the Baby Boomer generation came of age.[1]

The late film critic Roger Ebert detailed this generational sea change when he wrote, "The modern era of skin flicks began in 1960 with Russ Meyer's *The Immortal Mr. Teas*, which inspired Meyer and others to make a decade of films featuring nudity but no explicit sex."

But then, in 1972, as a result of President Johnson's commission findings, the X-rated pornographic film *Deep Throat* showed up in theaters, and that changed everything. Featuring explicit depictions of hardcore sex, *Deep Throat* reverberated throughout the nation and caused a coast-to-coast scandal, mainly due to, once more, sexual curiosity. Continues Ebert, "[People] lined up for [it] and talked cheerfully to news cameras about wanting to see it because, well, everybody else seemed to be going."[2]

Accounting methods for film profitability were not nearly as accurate in 1972 as they are now, especially for a film as explosively low-budget as *Deep Throat*, so it is practically impossible to divine its legacy in monetary terms. However, when it comes to cultural impact, we can say without hyperbole that *Deep Throat* made porn mainstream, layering a veneer of social acceptability to pornography and laying the groundwork for the future expansion of porn into our world.

From the movie-theater experience of the 1970s, the porn industry added new revenue streams in the 1980s with the growth of home video and again in the 1990s with DVDs (which are easy to duplicate and cheaper to produce). The 2000s and beyond brought the Internet, the advent of widespread streaming video, and the boom in mobile porn on smart phones and tablets.

All of that equals about $57 billion in annual worldwide revenues for the porn industry, a large slice of which (around $12 billion) stays in the United States. For comparison's sake, this number is greater than the revenues from ABC, CBS, and NBC combined (roughly $6.2 billion).[3] Recent polling also estimated that a full 10 percent of websites are pornographic in nature.

Every second of every day, somewhere in the world, $3,075.64 is being spent on pornography. In that same second, 28,258 people are viewing pornography online. Gather up enough of those seconds to make up 39 minutes, and that's how often a new piece of video porn is made, just in America.[4]

The days when twelve-year-old boys were introduced to porn through a friend sneaking them a *Playboy* in their tree house or through being exposed to native nudity in an issue of *National Geographic* are long gone, and they aren't coming back. The Internet is packed with far, far more than just strategically posed centerfolds: If you want to see it, it's out there, and it's usually just a few clicks away. Plus, when it comes to technology, Mom and Dad tend to be nowhere near as proficient as kids—both boys and girls alike—meaning the young ones of the home can usually navigate around the sordid parts of the online world with ease.

Our children are at great risk for exposure to what I call the Pornified World, and once they get a glimpse, something is sparked in them that becomes extremely difficult to extinguish. I've seen it time and again.

As a case study, let's look at a man we'll call Frank. I first met Frank when we arranged to get together at a local coffee house so he could tell me his story over a latte. Frank was punctual, tall, slim, and dressed in business casual attire, as befitting his career in the world of programming. He exuded intelligence and his quick wit became evident after even the briefest conversation.

After we ordered our coffees and sat down, we exchanged pleasantries and Frank began to fill me in on his backstory, namely how he had used his intelligence and computer savvy to work his way to the top of a local tech company. A large portion of his job description was to construct computer systems in such a way that they were secure from the outside world, as well as go through lines of code within programs to ensure they were as safe as possible from potential hackers. Unfortunately, while Frank was able to profit off his computer knowledge, it also gave him the perfect skill set for hiding an addiction that he never intended to develop.

THE PORN ADDICTION DEBATE

Although porn addiction receives a great deal of media attention, the science behind the concept is still being debated. Is there really such a thing as addiction to pornography? Many experts disagree, claiming that scientific evidence is absent or flawed, and that the history of sex addiction, more broadly, is a cultural and moral concept, not a medical condition.

There can clearly be compulsive behavior that is harmful and problematic. Australian scholar Michael Flood notes "that some pornography consumers come to use pornography in ways which are obsessive, compulsive, and have damaging consequences for themselves or others."[5] But that is not necessarily the same thing as an addiction. Jay Clarkson and Shana Kopaczewski go a step further stating that framing pornography use in medicalized language promotes "traditional moralist fears about the effects of pornography while circumventing more complicated analyses of the role of culture" and failing to acknowledge the current limitations in research.[6]

David Ley, Nicole Prause, and Peter Finn argue "the addiction model is based in part upon the assumption that there are negative effects of high frequency use, such as erectile dysfunction, difficulty regulating sexual feelings, and neurobiology changes." The further assumption is treating the addiction will change these negative effects. Yet, there is no scholarly research showing a causative link between high frequency pornography use and health risk behaviors or negative social consequences. Ley, Prause, and Finn explain that pathologizing porn use or assuming an underlying addiction may result in overlooking possible benefits of pornography including improved quality of life, better attitudes about sexuality, some reduced health risk behaviors, and more pleasure with long-term partners.[7]

Frank is, by all accounts, a meek and mild-mannered man. He loves his wife greatly, he is a man of abiding faith and religion, and he not only attends church regularly but is also a very involved member, frequently volunteering and serving where he can. Frank is not the type of person we tend to think of as a pornography addict, the type of person who spends their time in the seedy part of town wearing a trench coat and frequenting the adult bookstore. And yet, as Frank confided in me over coffee, he was indeed an addict, and his addiction had snuck up on him subtly and suddenly, from out of the blue.

Unlike me, Frank was not intrigued by the concept of porn as a young boy or even throughout his adolescence. The allure of the pornographic image held no sway over him as he grew and matured into adulthood, then married and embarked on his career in computers and technology.

Frank's addiction began, innocently enough, through basic cable. One evening his wife, feeling rather tired, went to bed early, so Frank stayed up late with little else to do than surf through the channels on his television to see what the late-night lineup had to offer him. Their cable package included no movie channels and no pay channels, either, so Frank felt there was little chance that he would stumble on anything he deemed inappropriate, the type of programming that can crop up late at night on places like Showtime and Cinemax.

There wasn't much on, but Frank continued to meander his way through the channels as his eyelids grew heavy. Thinking he was about to go to bed, his attention was suddenly grabbed in full when he landed on *Howard Stern*, a video presentation of Stern's daily radio show, notorious for its raunchy and racy content, which was blurred and bleeped out by censors for television but which still left little to the imagination. Frank's finger paused on his remote control as the screen flickered and showed Howard having a conversation with a very shapely and attractive woman who was wearing very little clothing.

It turned out that Howard was interviewing a professional stripper about her career and encouraging her to showcase her skills in front of him, right there on the air. She was apparently all too happy to oblige, going so far as to undress completely, leaving nothing to the imagination of Howard or his raging and cheering studio audience. The network censors pixilated the inappropriate areas so they wouldn't get fined by the FCC for broadcasting nudity over basic cable, but the idea of what was going on, along with the footage and audio, aroused something within Frank's soul that he didn't even know existed.

Frank shared this part of the story with me very deliberately, telling me how crucial that moment was for him. "I wanted to see what the censors had blurred," he told me. "When the stripper plugged her website, it was over." Frank's wife was slumbering deeply and peacefully, and he knew all about how to cover his tracks while on the computer, so he opened up his web browser, took the necessary precautions, and looked up this woman's website.

"My encounter with porn had begun," Frank said.

That was three years prior to the time I had first met with Frank. He has since come to terms with the fact that he has developed an addiction to pornography and is taking practical, valuable steps to controlling that addiction instead of letting it control him. Frank and I now meet regularly to talk about different healthy ways he can go about maintaining his sobriety and avoiding unhealthy visual stimulation, a task that is not easy in our sex-drenched and lust-obsessed media culture.

Still, Frank has done all he can to curb his impulses, because he realizes that pornography offers him nothing of value and instead only brings destruction into his marriage and into his thought life. He now works diligently to develop healthy outlets for his sexual energy and has involved others in his desire for sobriety through accountability, both in person and online through software we developed called X3watch.

The greater reach technology has into our lives, so goes the exponential increase in availability of pornography. PBS's *Frontline* did an entire special called *American Porn* on this issue, and in that episode they estimated that the majority (over 50 percent) of Internet users who are male, have the Internet in their homes partly because it provides quick and easy access to pornography. That same report also indicated that the rapid rise in home Internet subscriptions in the early 2000s, when home Internet was not nearly so ubiquitous as it is now, included the online posting of the infamous "sex tape" made by Tommy Lee, the famous rock-and-roll drummer, and his then-wife Pamela Anderson, a former *Playboy* playmate and actress.[8]

As Frank discovered—along with millions of other men and women—the Internet made porn easy. Now it was simple to satisfy curiosity or explore any possible sexual whim with just a stable Internet connection and a handful of clicks. And best of all, there was no waiting, no worries, and no witnesses. The porn industry saw the opportunity to capitalize on the trend and leapt at it, increasing their profits along with the number of sex addicts worldwide.

Of course, it's easy to paint the entire pornography industry as the villain here, but that isn't always the case and there are solutions to the problem. One answer is XXXchurch.com, an online resource that fights porn addiction by providing recovery help for men, women, parents, and couples. But XXXchurch is not only for people who are addicted to using porn. XXXchurch also reaches out to those who make porn, whether they're in front of the camera or behind it. Many of those who make a living in the industry see their work simply as a product that is demanded by the marketplace, no different than tobacco, alcohol, or even saturated fats and sugars. To them, all of these things are fine in moderation but can easily become addictive; however, it is not up to the manufacturer to prevent addiction but the consumer.

And the consumers are there, especially when it comes to pornography. Porn as a business is highly profitable, and many respectable and reputable mega-corporations benefit from channeling this lucrative product into American hotel rooms and homes, including Time-Warner, AOL, and even General Motors. Of course, these companies rarely trumpet their success in these matters in their financial statements or quarterly earnings reports, instead choosing to bury the porn profits under a mountain of doublespeak, charts, and seemingly incomprehensible numbers. According to a study by the Wharton School of the University of Pennsylvania:

> The common wisdom is that pornographic material is the dirty secret of the Internet, accounting for vast amounts of traffic and enormous revenues. Jupiter Media Metrix, a company which tracks Internet usage,

found that 30 million different users visited adult sites [over the course of one month], accounting for 33.8% of all people who used the world wide web, according to media development coordinator Kumar Rao.[9]

The problem lies in desensitization. The more familiar we become with something, the less sensitive we are to it, and the same holds true with pornography, according to entertainment industry analyst Dennis McAlpine: The porn industry keeps "testing the limits to see how far it can get."[10] The media culture shows "one area that becomes accepted; so you go to the next one. And you go to the next one. And things that ten years ago were not permissible now are accepted by society."[11]

And while porn addiction used to be strictly a "men's" problem, that is no longer the case. The Wharton study I mentioned earlier also unearthed this interesting statistic: Women account for 28 percent of porn use. Our Pornified World is affecting more than we think.

The solution to overturning the porn pandemic and its negative effects on our brains is to foster greater community and accountability among those who find themselves in the throes of this addiction. I don't know anyone who has become addicted to pornography who did it within a group of people—this is a solitary, isolated addiction, and the more you use porn, the more isolated you become.

This is why accountability must become part of the solution that breaks the cycle for the porn addict. Through our efforts at XXXchurch, we have seen this prove true time and again: someone comes to us with a desire to find sobriety, and we counsel them to get accountable. When they do, they find that maintaining that sobriety is much easier; when they don't, they inevitably fall right back into a pattern of addiction.

Accountability can take many forms, and we recommend all of them. For starters, since so much pornography consumption takes place online, we began offering an accountability software that we call X3watch. This software monitors your online consumption; should you happen upon a website that seems like it might contain porn or other questionable material, that site is flagged by the software. X3watch then emails regular reports of any questionable sites directly to someone you designate as an "accountability partner," who will then presumably ask you to account for your activity and why you went to such sites.

The premise then becomes: If you know that someone else—someone you trust and are willing to share your life openly with—is essentially looking over your shoulder while you're online, then you're going to be more likely to make wise decisions about where you go. This is the crux of accountability, the idea that even when you're by yourself, someone is, in a very real sense, right there with you, cheering you on and rooting for you to make healthy and wise decisions with your browser.

In addition to the X3watch software, we also recommend periodic small group accountability gatherings that allow you to foster intentional community. Again, the purpose is to create a strong, tightly knit group of like-minded individuals who can support each other in reaching goals of sobriety. These aren't haphazard groups of random participants; rather, these are intentional, long-term commitments among friends and/or family. Accountability groups provide a safe space where the addict can work through their struggles and find practical help and encouragement.

Beyond accountability, we have also developed a workshop called X3pure that provides information to recovering addicts about the spiritual, psychological, and biological factors that play into a person's sexual dependence. These groups are tailored specifically to each person's needs in order to offer specific knowledge they can use to understand the spiritual, psychological, and biological factors at play in their sexual dependence. Understanding these things helps to disarm any emotional pull they may still possess.

The Pornified World isn't going away any time soon, but the devastating effects of pornography addiction do not have to live on in the individual. By sharing their lives and struggles with others through accountability, countless addicts have found the freedom they crave, which will only make our society stronger and healthier.

DISCUSSION QUESTIONS

• What unexamined assumptions does the author have about the porn industry, the people who create it, and the people who watch it?
• The author says that pornography "more often than not leads to an addiction that can quickly spiral out of control." Do you find his evidence compelling? Why or why not?
• The author finds that his Christian religion helps him with his addiction.
• How can people of various faiths or no faith get help if they think they have a problem with pornography?
• The author argues that porn is isolating, and he presumes that sex is always meant to be with another person. What does this mean about masturbation?

NOTES

1. Lee Rainwater, *Social Problems and Public Policy: Deviance and Liberty* (Hawthorne, NY: Aldine Transaction, 1974), 143, http://en.wikipedia.org/wiki/President%27s_Commission_on_Obscenity_and_Pornography.
2. Roger Ebert, "Inside Deep Throat" (February 11, 2005), http://rogerebert.suntimes.com/apps/pbcs.dll/article?AID=?20050210/REVIEWS/50128001/1023.

3. Editor's note: Although these revenue figures are frequently repeated, they are not entirely agreed upon. Reliable revenue data is particularly difficult to ascertain.

4. Jerry Ropelato, "Internet Pornography Statistics," http://internet-filter-reviews. toptenreviews.com/internet-pornography-statistics.html.

5. Michael Flood, "The Harms of Pornography Exposure Among Children and Young People," *Child Abuse Review* 18 (2009): 384–400.

6. Jay Clarkson and Shana Kopaczewski, "Pornography Addiction and the Medicalization of Free Speech," *Journal of Communication Inquiry* 37, no. 2 (2013): 128–148.

7. For further information see: Steven Bengis, David S. Prescott, and Joan Tabachnick, "What We Know and Don't Know About Addictions and Pornography, *NEARI News* 7, no. 3 (2014), http://www.nearipress.org/newsletter-archive/178-what-we-know-a-dont-know-about-addictions-and-pornography.

8. Michael Kirk and Peter J. Boyer, "American Porn," *Frontline*, WGBH Educational Foundation, aired February 7, 2002. Available online at http://www.pbs. org/wgbh/pages/frontline/shows/porn/view/?utm_campaign=viewpage@utm_medium=viewsearch&utm_source=viewsearch.

9. "Are There Lessons to Be Learned from Porn Sites?" *Knowledge@Wharton* (May 9, 2001), http://knowledge.wharton.upenn.edu/article.cfm?articleid=354.

10. *Frontline* interview with Dennis McAlpine, PBS, August 2001, http://www.pbs. org/wgbh/pages/frontline/shows/porn/interviews/mcalpine.html.

11. *Frontline* interview with Dennis McAlpine, PBS, August 2001, http://www.pbs. org/wgbh/pages/frontline/shows/porn/interviews/mcalpine.html.

JUST A JOHN?

Pornography and Men's Choices[1]

Robert Jensen

There has been much talk about the need for men to love each other and be willing to speak openly about that love. That is important; we need to be able to get beyond the all-too-common male tendency to mute or deform our emotions, a tendency that is destructive not only to ourselves but to those around us. Many have spoken about our need to nurture each other, and that's important, too. But it's also crucial to remember that loving one another means challenging ourselves as well.

I would like to challenge us all—in harsh language—to address men's use of pornography. In an unjust world, those of us with privilege must be willing to do this, especially out of love. The challenge is this: Can we be more than just johns?

Let me start with a story that a female student at the University of Texas told me. She was on a bus traveling from Austin to Dallas for a football game. The bus was chartered by a fraternity and many of the passengers were women. During the trip, someone showed a sexually explicit video. Uncomfortable with the hardcore sexual images of women being used by men, the female student began a discussion with the people around her about it, and one of the men on the bus agreed that it was inappropriate. He stood up and said to the other men, "You all know me and know I like porn as much as the next guy, but it's not right for us to play this tape when there are women on the bus."

No doubt it took some courage for that young man to confront his fraternity brothers on the issue, and we should honor that. But we should recognize that his statement also communicated to his fraternity brothers that he was one of them—"one of the guys"—who, being guys, naturally like pornography. His objection was not to pornography and men's routine purchase and use of women's bodies for sexual pleasure, but to viewing it with women present. He was making it clear that his ultimate loyalty was to men and their right to use women sexually, though that use should conform to some type of code of chivalry about being polite about it in mixed company. In doing that, he was announcing his own position in regard to sex. He was saying *I'm just a john.*

PIMPS AND JOHNS

A john is a man who buys another human being for sex, typically through an intermediary; the pimp. Men sell women to other men for sex: pimps and johns.

There is a lot that could be said about the current cultural practice of using the term "pimp" in a wide variety of other contexts—for example, the MTV show "Pimp My Ride." We live in a world in which men who sell women are glorified. It is also a world in which the dominant white culture implicitly defines a pimp as black and then alternately celebrates and denigrates them. The confluence of racism and sexism in these cultural trends deserves discussion. But I want to concentrate here not on the pimps, but on the johns, on the men who buy women for sex.

I assume that many men reading this masturbate, or have masturbated, to pornography. That makes us johns. I don't mean that most men have necessarily bought a woman from a pimp in prostitution, though no doubt some of us have. I'm talking, instead, about the far more common experience of pornography. In my childhood and young adulthood, I was sometimes a john. Virtually every man I know has been a john. In pornography, the pimp is called a publisher or a video producer, and the john is called a fan or a pornography consumer. But that doesn't change the nature of the relationship: It involves one person (usually a man) selling another person (usually a woman) to a third person (usually a man). What this means is that pornography is a mass-mediated conglomeration of pimps and johns. When you masturbate to pornography, you are buying sexual pleasure. You are buying a woman. The fact that there are technologies of film or video between you and the pimp doesn't change the equation. Legally, it's not prostitution and legally, you're not in trouble. But you are still a john.

THE PORNOGRAPHY THAT JOHNS LIKE

At this point, let me define a few terms. Pornography comes in all forms and all kinds of people consume porn. In this discussion, however, I'm specifically referring to heterosexual pornography. I'm using the term to describe the graphic, sexually explicit material that is consumed by heterosexual men. These DVDs, videos, and Internet sites comprise the bulk of the commercial pornography market. There are three consistent themes in heteronormative pornography:

1. All women want sex from all men at all times.
2. Women naturally desire the kind of sex that men want, including sex that many women find degrading.
3. Any woman who does not at first realize this can be turned with a little force.

The pornography industry produces two major types of films: features and gonzo. Features mimic, however badly, the conventions of a Hollywood movie. There is some minimal plot, a little character development, and a bit of dialogue, all in the service of presenting the sex. Gonzo films have no such pretensions; they are simply recorded sex, usually taking place in a private home or a starkly decorated set. Gonzo porn often starts with an interview with the woman or women about their sexual desires before other men or women enter the scene.

All these films have a standard series of sex acts, including oral, vaginal, and anal penetration, often performed while the men call the women "bitch," "cunt," "whore," and other, similar names. As they are penetrated, the women are expected to say over and over how much they like the sex. As pornography like this has become increasingly normalized—and readily available through-out the country by increasingly sophisticated technology—pornographers have pushed the limits of what is acceptable in the mainstream. As one porno-graphic film director put it, "People want more . . . [so we] make it more hard, make it more nasty, make it more relentless."

The commercial pornography industry grew steadily during the late twentieth-century and seems to have peaked in the mid-2000s. In 2005, 13,588 new hard-core video/DVD titles were released,[2] but in subsequent years the recession, piracy, and DIY (do-it-yourself) pornography ended the wild growth of previous decades. While there are no absolutely reliable statistics on the industry's revenues,[3] annual sales in the United States are commonly estimated at $10 billion or higher,[4] while worldwide revenues have been put at $57 billion.[5] For comparative purposes, the Hollywood box office—the amount of money spent in the United States and Canada to go out to the movies—was $10.2 billion in 2011.[6] Because there is no way to chart the amount of money generated by pornographic web sites, and because there is so much pornography available online for free, it's more difficult than ever to chart the amount of sexually explicit material available.

MEN'S CHOICES AND RESPONSIBILITIES

We know there are women who consume pornography and a few women who make it. In this society, that's called progress. Feminism is advanced, some argue, when women can join the ranks of those who buy and sell other human beings.

This argument is a predictable result of the collaboration of capitalism and patriarchy. Take a system that values profit over everything, and combine it with a system of male supremacy, and you get a situation where pornography is increasingly mainstream and normalized; it is made into everyday experience. Pornography is profitable when men take it as their right to consume women's sexuality. When women join in the patterns of producing and consuming pornography, they join in a practice of exploitation and objectification.

When confronted with this, men often suggest that women choose to participate in pornography, so there's no reason to critique men's use of porn. We should avoid the temptation to take that easy way out. I'm going to say nothing in regard to what women should do, nor am I going to critique their choices. I don't take it as my place to inject myself in the discussions that women have about this.

I do, however, take it as my place to talk to men. I take it as a political and ethical responsibility to engage in critical self-reflection and to be accountable for my behavior, at the individual and the collective level. For men, the question is not about women's choices. The real issue is about men's choices. Do you want to participate in a system in which women are sold for sexual pleasure, whether in prostitution, pornography, strip clubs, or in any other aspect of the sex industry? Do you want to live in a world in which some people are bought and sold for the sexual pleasure of others?

When we ask such questions, one of the first things we will hear is: These are important issues, but we shouldn't make men feel guilty about buying sexual pleasure. Why not? I agree that much of the guilt people feel is rooted in attempts to repress human sexuality. This sort of guilt is unfortunately part of our society's cultural and theological history, and it is destructive. But guilt also can be a healthy emotional and intellectual response to the world and one's actions in it.

Johns should feel guilty when they buy women. Guilt is an appropriate response to an act that is unjust. Guilt can be a sign that we have violated our own ethical norms. It can be part of a process of ending the injustice. Guilt can be healthy if it is understood in political, not merely religious or psychological, terms.

Buying women is wrong not because of a society's repressive moral code or its effects on an individual's psychological process. It is wrong because it hurts people. It creates a world in which people get hurt. And the people who get hurt the most are the people with the least amount of power. When you create a sex-class that can be bought and sold, the people in that group—in this instance, women—will inevitably be treated as lesser, as available to be controlled and abused.

The way out of being a john is political. The way out is feminist analysis. And I'm not referring to a superficial exercise in identifying a few "women's issues" that men can help with. To borrow from Karl Marx, feminist analysis provides ruthless criticism of the existing order. Feminist analysis of pornography will not shrink from its own discoveries. Nor will this analysis shy away from conflict with the powers that be.

We need to engage in this ruthless criticism. Let's start not just with pornography, but with sex more generally. One discovery, I think, is that men are often johns, and that the way in which johns use women sexually is a window into other aspects of our sexual and intimate lives. For many men, sex is a place where we display and reinforce our power over women. By that, I don't mean that all men use sex that way all the time. What I mean is that this pattern of relationships is readily visible in our society. Women deal with it every day, and at some level most men get that.

The issue is not just about pimps and johns and the women who are prostituted. It's about men and women, and sex and power. If you've been thinking, "Well, that's not me. I never pay for it," don't be so sure. It's not just about who pays for it and who doesn't. It's about the fundamental nature of the relationship between men and women, and how that plays out in sex and intimacy.

And if you think this doesn't affect you because you are one of the "good men," then take a closer look. I'm told that I am one of those good men. I work in a feminist movement. I have been part of groups that critique men's violence and the sex industry. And I struggle with these issues all the time. I was trained to be a man in this culture, and that training doesn't evaporate overnight. None of us is off the hook.

WHAT IS SEX FOR?

No matter what our personal history or current practice, we all might want to ask a simple question: What is sex for?

A male friend once told me that sometimes sex is like a warm handshake, nothing more than a greeting between friends. Many people claim that sex can be a purely physical interaction to produce pleasurable sensations in the body. At the same time, sex is said to be the ultimate act of intimacy, the place in which we expose ourselves most fully, where we let another see us stripped down, not just physically but emotionally. Certainly sex can be all those things to different people at different times. But isn't that a lot to ask sex to carry? Can one human practice really carry such a range of meaning and purpose? And in a male-supremacist culture in which men's violence is still tacitly accepted and men's control of women is often unchallenged, should we be surprised that sex becomes a place where that violence and control play out?

This isn't an argument for imposing a particular definition of sex. It's an invitation to confront what I believe is a crucial question for this culture. The conservative framework, often rooted in narrow religious views, for defining appropriate sex in order to control people is a disaster. The libertarian framework that avoids questions of gender and power has also failed.

We live in a time of sexual crisis. That makes life difficult, but it also creates a space for invention and creativity. The possibility of a different way of understanding the world and myself is what drew me to feminism. I was drawn to the possibility of escaping the masculinity trap set for me, and the chance to become something more than a man, more than just a john. I was drawn by the possibilities of becoming a human being.

DISCUSSION QUESTIONS

- To what extent do you think our inability to openly discuss sex contributes to sensationalizing pornography?
- Who defines what is obscene, and what do those legal guidelines look like?
- Do you think there is a gendered double standard in regard to watching porn? Explain your response.
- Robert Jensen questions the extreme value placed upon sex in our culture. Do you agree with his argument?
- The author argues that using pornography is a form of men buying women; that buying other people for sexual pleasure is unjust; that guilt is an appropriate response to an act that is unjust; and therefore, men should feel guilty when they use pornography. Is this argument convincing? Are there ways to be a porn consumer that do not require guilt? If so, what are they?
- When it comes to women who are sex workers, where do we draw the line between exploitation and their agency or free will?
- After reading this chapter, do you view the porn industry and people that watch porn differently?

NOTES

1. This chapter originally appears in *Men Speak Out: Views on Gender, Sex, and Power.* Reprinted with permission from Routledge.
2. "State of the U.S. Adult Industry," *Adult Video News,* January 2006.
3. Jonathan Silverstein, "Is Porn a Growing or Shrinking Business?" ABC News, January 19, 2006, http://abcnews.go.com/Technology/story?id=1522119#.T9Z-fbXvWSo.
4. Frederick S. Lane, *Obscene Profits: The Entrepreneurs of Pornography in the Cyber Age.* New York: Routledge, 2000, p. xiv. For a critique of these estimates, see Dan Akman, "How Big is Porn?" Forbes.com, May 25, 2001.
5. An often-quoted source for this figure is the Internet Filter Review, http://internet-filter-review.toptenreviews.com/internet-pornography-statistics.html.
6. Motion Picture Association of America, "Theatrical Market Statistics, 2011," http://www.mpaa.org/Resources/5bec4ac9-a95e-443b-987b-bff6fb5455a9.pdf.

MALE AND QUEER IN THE PORN INDUSTRY[1]

Ned Henry

I am a queer porn performer. I have sex with many different people irrespective of their gender—often people I've just met—and I sell images of these sex acts on the Internet to pay my bills. I am also a Harvard-educated, cisgendered white man who owns his own small business while working on a PhD in experimental quantum nanoelectronics. This will not be a sad story; no downward spiral led me to monetize my sex life. Despite some important systemic problems in the adult industry, porn has not scarred me physically or emotionally. I love my work, I consider it to be ethical, important, challenging, and fun, and I am in a healthy long-term relationship that I hope will last for the rest of my life. I want to talk about the lessons porn has taught me about gender—lessons that I never would have internalized without stepping in front of the camera.

Participating in the adult industry is, in many ways, what allowed me come out as queer, though mainstream porn has not always been supportive of that part of my identity. When I started in porn I was straight. I do not feel that I was lying to myself or others about my sexual orientation. I enjoyed having sex with women, and the idea of interacting sexually with a male body seemed vaguely icky and uncomfortable to me. In my most private fantasies I was occasionally aroused thinking about fiddling with penises, but only after doing elaborate mental gymnastics to temporarily put aside my discomfort with the idea. Compartmentalizing the ick-factor did not make it go away and I assumed this meant I would not enjoy making my private fantasy into reality. I knew that talking about these fantasies would only make people assume I was a closeted homosexual. I really did enjoy dating women very much, so I kept my occasional male-male fantasies to myself.

Appearing in porn changed my perspective on heterosexuality, although porn started with a heterosexual relationship. When I began dating my partner, she had already been performing in porn under the name Maggie Mayhem. We had been seeing each other (i.e., sleeping together casually) for a few months when she invited me to a filmed live sex party. I was nervous, but I agreed with very little hesitation. Maggie's enthusiasm for screwing with people's preconceptions about porn performers, and for using sexual expression to stand up for the rights of marginalized people, was fascinating and infectious. All of the sexual and intellectual exploration and personal growth and that I intend to describe here come as a direct result of Maggie's loving mentorship and the influence of her nuanced but uncompromising principles. Toward the end of my first filmed sex party, under Maggie's libidinous encouragement, I stepped naked in front of the camera and penetrated her in front of a live Internet audience. I immediately liked it.

For the first time in my life, I proved to myself that I have the confidence to disregard social stigma. It was a very liberating feeling, even more so when the edited footage went up on the Internet with my newly minted stage name. I knew that appearing in porn might close doors for me, but that was part of the appeal. I had always been very cynical about the way people are valued in our society and, as a white guy with a top-tier education, I have always been valued more highly than I deserve. It's easy to talk about how the hierarchy of privilege is bullshit when you're perched at the top of it, and it's easy to talk about destigmatizing marginalized groups while belonging to none of them. I was so privileged I was afraid of losing important opportunities by doing controversial things, but that fear had been holding me back from doing much of anything with my life except following society's expectations for me from college to grad school to research. Performing in porn felt like putting my money where my mouth was for the first time by doing something I believe in, despite the possibility of social stigma or employment discrimination.

Of course, in porn I am also privileged. Being a man in porn means that I am not slut-shamed or threatened with sexual violence on a regular basis, as my partner is. As a man, people do not assume that doing porn means I am stupid, drug addicted, or a traumatized victim of sexual assault. Being Caucasian in porn means I don't have to look for work exclusively on sites that fetishize my ethnic background. Being cisgendered and having a normative body type means that I am offered more work, and I am not publicly mocked or insulted by the same companies that hire me. It took a hell of a lot less courage for me to get in front of that camera than it does for anyone who doesn't look like me.

Yet, for me, porn was a very important first step toward genuinely not caring what people think about my identity. I had been trying for many years to overcome the internalized shame our culture heaps onto any expression of sexuality outside of a rigidly defined patriarchal structure. I suddenly realized that I hadn't fully overcome this shame because I had been trying to be shameless only in my private life and to keep that relatively secret. With porn, I was finally shifting from private shamelessness to public shamelessness, which opened doors in my psyche.

As I internalized this shift, I found that the mild disgust I had felt when I thought about sex with men slowly vanished. I started thinking about sex with men without fear of what my feelings might imply about my identity. It felt like I had already come out, the hard part was over, and I could play with whatever kind of genitals I wanted and take them or leave them. It didn't take long before I added "queer" to my public identity, and started having guilt-free sex with men for fun and profit. Maggie and I have never been sexually monogamous, and she thoroughly encouraged this new development in my sexuality.

Exploring sex with men for the first time was exciting, but I was eager to do gay porn for another reason. I wanted to be the center of attention. Porn is made to sexually arouse, and any given piece of pornography is designed to sexually arouse a certain type of person. We call this "the gaze"—the assumed perspective of the intended audience. Most mainstream porn is made for a heterosexual male gaze. Female bodies are the currency of arousal, and male performers are usually headless stunt cocks—unobtrusive foil characters at most, who should be mostly silent and need not be particularly charismatic or good looking. The assumption is that it would make the (male) audience uncomfortable to sexualize a man's body. As a result, male performers avoid a lot of the intense stigma and shaming that female performers are subjected to, but it is also difficult for male performers to make a name for themselves or to build a fan base.

In contrast, gay porn is made for a homosexual male gaze. Here, the male body is meant to be the visual trigger for arousal. I wanted to be that trigger. I wanted people to look at me and get turned on. Heterosexual men are rarely thought of as visually arousing. Manliness means agency, and men are supposed to be desired for their power, skill, or confidence. For a man to pay attention to his appearance is considered feminine, and is looked down upon by straight men. Before I did porn, even as I conformed to these standards of masculinity, I desperately wanted someone to look at my naked body with the same immediate arousal with which I looked at naked women. I did not think that this would ever be possible. I was sometimes desired for what I could do with my hands or penis or words, but that is different from being desired purely for the aesthetic of my physical appearance. I wanted to be the object of a sexual gaze.

This may sound like I am glorifying the experience of being objectified. In a way, I am. The experience of being *consensually* sexually objectified can be fun and empowering. Many men never have a chance experience this and I believe they should—but consent is key. Women are routinely made the objects of a sexual gaze without their consent, often in nonsexual contexts, and that is used to devalue them. A lot of homophobia among straight guys involves the fear of being objectified nonconsensually by a homosexual male gaze in much the same way that women are by heterosexual male gaze.

I have not yet mentioned a female gaze. Very little porn is made for a female gaze, and none of it is mainstream. I have heard it argued that women are simply not aroused visually the way men are, or that they are for other reasons not capable of enjoying porn the same way. I call bullshit. Women do not make up a large percentage of porn consumers because there is a strong social stigma against women buying porn, and because those who overcome this stigma are disappointed to find that almost all porn is made for a male gaze. I have friends who are shocked that many of the straight female porn consumers enjoy gay male porn. I believe my friends' shock stems from the ingrained idea that male bodies are not visually arousing, or that women are simply not visually aroused. Our culture teaches this idea to people from a young age, and many act as if it were true. Let me say it one more time, from my experience as a male porn performer and producer: This is bullshit. Once my partner and I started making our own porn, which was unafraid to sexualize my body, we found that all of our biggest fans were women.

Gay porn allowed me to be objectified on my own terms, and I enjoyed it. However, I found that doing both gay and straight porn put me under fire from two sides. Some gay performers would see my female partner and turn up their noses at me, calling me "gay for pay." Gay for pay is a term used to describe straight men who perform in gay porn to get more work. The connotation is that these performers take work away from genuine homosexuals, who presumably make better gay porn because they enjoy what they're doing and understand the gaze of their audience. As a queer performer who enjoys sex with men in my personal life as well as on camera, this attitude felt isolating to me.

The response from the straight porn world was even more brutal. Male performers who do both gay and straight films (so-called "crossover" performers) are considered by most of the mainstream straight porn world to be irresponsible HIV risks. This is demonstrably absurd. To perform in straight porn (and most gay porn), performers are required to be tested monthly for Chlamydia, Gonorrhea, and HIV. The HIV tests we use are RNA based, with a "window period" of less than two weeks (rather than six months for a standard antibody-based HIV test). The results of these tests are shared within the industry. If straight porn performers were getting HIV at a high rate, we would know. They are not. Every time a positive HIV result comes up it is a scandal. This happens once every several years, usually due to off-camera activities, and the performer immediately retires. Given the size of the porn industry this makes the HIV rate in porn far lower than that of the general U.S. population. Nonetheless, so-called crossover performers have been publicly condemned and privately banned by some major players in mainstream straight porn due to a perceived HIV risk that has far more to do with homophobia than epidemiology.

Despite the divergent gaze and disinclination to share talent between gay and straight porn, I was discouraged to find that both genres perpetuate the same strict standards of prescriptive masculinity for their male performers. I expected this from the hetero crowd, but as a newly minted queer I was shocked at the extent of stigma against male femininity in gay porn, and in gay culture generally. It is clear that straight culture uses traditional standards of masculinity to perpetuate homophobia by equating male homosexuality with femininity, but I expected to find gay communities more supportive of feminine men. Instead, in porn casting calls and Craigslist personal ads, I found the same stigmatizing words repeated: "straight-acting only," "no femmes," "please be masculine." Any man who even vaguely resembles a feminine homosexual stereotype (lisp, limp wrist, fashionista, for instance) can be mocked and shunned by gay men in the same ways many of them were they were by the jocks in their high schools.

By most of these standards I qualify as "masculine." My experiences in porn, both gay and straight, made me think hard about what made me masculine and why. I had to step back and rethink some of the experiences I had growing up. Like most adolescent boys, every minute aspect of my awkward social presentation was picked apart, and I was rewarded for presenting masculinity and punished for presenting femininity. Everything from my posture, my sports prowess, personal confidence, the violence I showed in dominance battles, my willingness to hurt others, the interest I showed in sexualizing women, and the extent of my participation in misogyny, were all used to evaluate my social merit. The rewards and punishments did not come only from peers; teachers, authority figures, and media representation participated in masculinizing my peers and me. Sometimes this took the form of codified rules rewarding traditional manly behavior. At other times reward or punishment was the difference between a warm smile from a teacher or a disappointed shake of the head. To a large extent I played along, as most do. They were offering me power and privilege in exchange for my performance of masculinity, with the implication that the masculine are the ones who most deserve these perks. Many men's whole lives revolve around this internalized reward system based on their performance of masculinity.

Mainstream gay and straight porn both subject their male performers to this strict standard of prescriptive manliness. I started in the porn business to help me stop caring what people thought of me, so I was unwilling to continue making my appearance live up to a standard I believe is harmful. The more I thought about the depiction of masculinity, especially in sexual performance, the more important it seemed. It is clear that the intense judgment applied to women based on their performance of gender roles is a major symptom of ingrained sexism in our culture. Because men are predominantly the aggressors in sexism and sexual violence, the way we socialize men to perform masculinity is a major cause of these problems. During adolescence, young men are handed privilege on the condition that they participate in abusing it, justifying retroactively the abuses of generations before. Masculinity and male hierarchy are intimately linked to perceived sexual prowess, so the depictions of masculinity in porn are especially important to the way gender dynamics will play out in the next generation. I decided that if I am going to invest a large portion of my time participating in this performance, I want to be much more transgressive about it than I could possibly get away with mainstream porn.

Luckily, there is other porn being made. Just as I was getting fed up with the standards of the adult industry, I found my local indie queer porn scene. The San Francisco Bay Area is home to a growing network of small artisan porn studios turning out really hot content designed to challenge prevailing ideas of what sexuality and gender performance should look like. The label "queer" is liberally self-applied in this group as a general term to signal rejection of prescriptive gender norms in terms of identity, presentation, and orientation. Performers of widely varying ethnic backgrounds, body types, and genders are depicted having the types of sex they actually enjoy, described with marketing language they are comfortable with. By giving sexually marginalized groups a medium to express their sexuality on their own terms, porn is used as a tool for education and empowerment. The results are both inspiring from a political standpoint and, to me, far more arousing than most porn I had seen elsewhere.

By this point Maggie and I had fallen very sweetly in love, and I had taken her stage name. It wasn't long before we started our own DIY porn website titled Meet The Mayhems. We were inspired by some progressive role models in queer porn, and we were skeptical of the ethics, technical standards, and business models of all the big players in the industry (and especially of all the tools available to small adult startups).

We wanted a way to monetize our content on our own terms with little to no startup capital. To make this possible, we had to do everything our-selves, from programming and web development to videography, editing, legal issues, and publicity. This work gave us the freedom to present masculinity and femininity in new ways, to show hot sex acts we always wanted to see in porn and rarely did, and to find our own audience and create our own market. Nine months after the launch, our work was recognized by the Feminist Porn Awards in Toronto, and our small membership continued growing steadily.

The next step for our site is to make the tools we developed, and the information we learned, available to other independent performers who may not have the technical background or the free time to build it all from scratch. By giving performers the tools to take control of their own representation, we hope over time to undermine the mainstream porn industry's exaggeration of cultural gender standards. There are specific expectations for men in porn, but even more harmful are the expectations for people of color, transgendered performers, or performers of different body types. It is generally not for me to decide what is offensive or empowering for marginalized groups to which I do not necessarily belong, especially when it comes to sexual fantasy and media representation. When using independent porn as a tool for sexual expression and social change, it is important to give a diverse range of performers access to that tool.

Working in the porn industry has taught me an immense amount about my own sexuality and gender presentation, and has forced me to face some uncomfortable truths about my culture. Portraying masculinity and queerness in porn in new ways can help change the cultural weight of these identities. I hope the work that we've done building Meet The Mayhems will prove relevant to undoing the layers of stigma I experienced both as a model starting out in porn and as an adolescent starting out in manhood. I do porn because I want to show people that it is okay for them to experience sexual pleasure any way they please with any partners they want, within the bounds of mutual consent. A growing number of pornographers share similar mission statements, and I hope that as a result fewer people will feel personally judged when they look for sexy images on the Internet.

DISCUSSION QUESTIONS

• How does Ned Henry's experience challenge the previous chapters by Robert Jensen and Craig Gross?
• Ned Henry writes that women and marginalized people are often denigrated and objectified in mainstream porn. What does he mean by this? Do you agree with him?
• Do you agree with the author that sexual objectification can be consensual? Is the quality or standards of consenting to objectification the same for women and men?
• Have your ideas about masculinity and queer identity changed after reading this chapter?
• What has the author's story about his career in queer porn taught you about gender presentation and sexuality?

NOTE

1. This chapter originally appears in *Men Speak Out: Views on Gender, Sex, and Power*. Reprinted with permission from Routledge.

Part III

Sex and Social Media

The following six chapters are thematically bound by the intersection of sexual and gender politics and the impact of Internet culture. The authors in this section consider both the benefits and the dangers of online or digital technology by addressing how sexuality is socially—and even legally—policed, how the Internet enables members of allied queer communities to find each other, and how technology is changing the practice and discovery of relationship infidelity.

While rapid changes in technology over the past few decades have yielded a twenty-first-century panic over online safety, some authors reject the presumption that there is always danger lurking on the Internet. There is compelling evidence to acknowledge the real—and sometimes fatal—impact of online gendered and sexual violence. At the same time, authors in this section also explore the constructive possibilities that online communities can yield. This is the challenge and the benefit of navigating digital technology in contemporary society.

Social media involves new technologies, blurring of boundaries, and shifts in how people connect. This can be inspiring, as we see social justice movements gain momentum, increased awareness of sexual violence, or silenced survivors of violence find support in online communities. But there are also new challenges related to the socially entrenched problem of sexual violence: These include abusive partners' use of technology to control, intimidate, or humiliate, additional forms of sexual harassment, and re-victimization of sexual assault survivors. As Rena Bivens and Jordan Fairbairn note, with these new challenges come new efforts to raise awareness about how to protect oneself online.[1] The chapters in Part III present different research perspectives about various issues such as sexting, selfies, and safety. Giving careful attention to these sometimes-challenging perspectives enables us to dispel unfounded alarm, identify bona fide concerns, and to become discerning in how we maximize sexual pleasure, build community, and promote personal and political wellbeing.

In chapter 11, Soraya Chemaly writes about "Slut-Shaming and The Sex Police: Social Media, Sex, and Free Speech." As Chemaly explains, we are immersed in online environments. This creates opportunities for women's free expression of their sexuality, on their own terms. However, the online environment also replicates offline stereotypes about sexual behavior and lends itself to abuse and harassment. The double standard in representations of men and women's bodies and sexuality is undeniable. Nonetheless, the ways in which this double standard is perpetuated online—through corporate policies that govern social media interactions to the habits of snap-chatting teenagers—is rarely acknowledged. "Slut-Shaming and the Sex Police" explores ideas about sexuality, bodily autonomy, and consent. Specifically, this chapter explains how the notion that women's bodies are public property—available for review, comment, rating, and sharing—is reinforced through corporate guidelines and social practices, and enabled by an online environment that is photo-intensive. Internet photography and social media exacerbate harm to girls and women by amplifying common punishments, all too often through slut-shaming and revenge porn.[2]

In chapter 12, Jamie Hagen writes about "The Revolutionary Possibilities of Online Trans and Queer Communities." Hagen was motivated to write because as a femme-identified lesbian, she was irritated and offended by the problematic lesbian representation in pop culture. As she notes in her chapter, "Primetime TV and the few movies with lesbian plotlines available in the LGBT section of movie streaming services more often than not offer storylines where lesbians ultimately decide to be with men, or they end up in bed with a heterosexual couple, sexually satisfying another woman. Mainstream movies and TV about lesbian women that don't have some intervening male-driven plot point remains an anomaly. These story lines are not representative of the queer community I know and love." Facing a dearth of relatable pop culture, Hagan went online in search of sites, stories, and communities that felt exciting and true. "The Revolutionary Possibilities of Online Queer Communities" is an account of what Hagan found.

Ebony Utley moves in a different direction in chapter 13, researching how digital technology has the potential to change what we think of as infidelity and how people find out about unfaithful partners. Infidelity refers to any behavior that breaks the contract that two people have with each other. But what are the rules when the technology changes? Are Facebook "likes" a form of flirting? How many likes does it take to cross the line? "Digital Indiscretions: Infidelity in the Age of Technology" focuses on interviews with women who have been cheated on, women who cheated, and women who were the "other woman." Utley explains that technology shapes infidelity by providing new tools for initiating and maintaining the secrecy of affairs. Infidelity shapes technology by creating tools that more easily facilitate an ancient indiscretion in our twenty-first-century lives. Understanding the feedback loop between infidelity and technology may raise uncomfortable questions and answers—and these are important conversations for us to have.

In chapter 14, Lara Karaian addresses the legal and cultural controversies surrounding consensual sexting among teens. Karaian points out that national and local media across North America commonly warn of the risks of sexting—the practice of sending, posting or possessing sexually suggestive text messages and images by cell phones or the Internet. Responses have included legal sanction, such as Pennsylvania District Attorney Skumanick's threat to bring child pornography charges against teenagers who refused to attend a gender based "re-education" program designed to teach youth about the dangers of sexting. Three girls refused the ultimatum resulting in *Miller v. Mitchell* (2010), the first legal case to challenge the constitutionality of prosecuting teens for their digital sexual expression. This chapter—"Consensual Sexting and Child Pornography: Legal and Cultural Controversies"—critically considers dominant cultural and legal narratives and how these responses create the image of teenage female sexters as both pornographers and dupes of the so-called pornification of a generation.

In chapter 15, Rena Bivens and Jordan Fairbairn explore the relationship between sexual violence and social media among youth. Programs to promote online safety often warn users not to sext or to quit social media. This is the digital equivalent of warning girls to stay safe from rape by staying in well-lit areas at night. In other words, these warnings are well intentioned but misguided.

Based on their survey research of anti-violence prevention organizations, community health and resource centers, educators, and youth-focused agencies based in Ontario, Bivens and Fairbairn conclude there is a crucial need to know more about sexual violence related to social media. Awareness of sexual violence associated with social media is very high but organizations are not keeping track of this specific type of abuse. This means that evidence-based prevention campaigns that tackle sexual violence associated with social media are severely lacking. It is therefore vital, the authors explain, to think critically about how we frame prevention efforts in this context. Based on their findings, Bivens and Fairbairn suggest that individual safety strategies should not be a primary focus of sexual violence prevention related to social media. Instead, identifying the unique ways in which social media technologies contribute to perpetration while recognizing that technologies in and of themselves are not causal factors are both important factors for prevention efforts.

As an avid online dater and fun-lover, Alexandra Tweten enjoyed checking out possible online matches. The offensive comments she received from men on dating sites such as OkCupid and Tinder were routinely predictable in their sexism. As anyone who's dated online knows, Tweten was not alone in this experience. In chapter 16, Tweten describes how she took the problem of online harassment into her own hands, inadvertently launching a popular campaign that quickly went viral and yielded mainstream media coverage by *Good Morning America* and *Cosmopolitan* magazine.

Tweten, who majored in journalism and women's studies in college, explains how she was exposed to feminist theory, intersectionality, and the matrix of oppression. She was inspired to make change, but didn't quite know how to go about doing it. But the right opportunity and an Instagram account gave Tweten the power to share her message with millions of people. In Tweten's encouraging words: "I am continually amazed and overjoyed at the power of everyone to create change and start discussions en masse. You don't have to be a talking head to capture the attention of an entire country anymore." *Bye Felipe* is an inspiring example of how each of us might take action and make a change in the world.

NOTES

1. The previous points are made by Rena Bivens and Jordan Fairbairn, personal correspondence.
2. For more on the subject of slut-shaming, see Leora Tanenbaum, *I Am Not a Slut: Slut-Shaming in the Age of the Internet* (New York: HarperCollins, 2015).

SLUT-SHAMING AND THE SEX POLICE

Social Media, Sex, and Free Speech

Soraya Chemaly

The Internet has revolutionized the way we share information, construct identities, and represent ideas. These realities are, however, not the same for everyone, particularly when it comes to gender and sexuality. Furthermore, just because it's new doesn't mean that Internet technology dismantles stereotypes and repression regarding how bodies are represented and how sexuality is expressed. The use of Internet technology, and of the visual culture at its core, affects men and women, gender conforming and non-conforming people, very differently. These differences reside in our notions about bodies, sexuality, sexual consent, and long-standing ideas about women in public space. When it comes to sex and sexuality, punishment and reward, our laws, corporate policies, and cultural norms ignore harmful, and sometimes deadly, double standards.

Like a public street, platforms on the Internet are contested spaces in which women regularly fight for control over their self-defined image and expression—of ideas, of bodies, of sexuality—most of which have traditionally been out of women's power and instead used against them as weapons of control and shame. Internet technology, coupled with photography and smart phones, provides new ways of carrying out this control and replicating dominant hierarchies of sex, race, and sexuality. When women exhibit control over their own sexuality, online or off, the response is often outrage; when they are harassed or abused, the response is frequently to mock and shame them. When women express agency over their own sexuality, this not only confronts double standards of sex and gender, but it is also a destabilizing threat to other hierarchies including race and class.

Visual imagery is central to both the liberating and oppressive uses of the Internet. When it comes to photography and the Internet, women's consent and self-definition, as in the offline world, are hardly priorities. Women's nudity is exploited but it is also often considered obscene. So, while some Internet users clearly embrace the creativity of easily accessible cameras and technology to express themselves, others exploit these technologies to reinforce conservative cultural norms and negative stereotypes in damaging ways. The result is an online environment that frequently amplifies the effects of gender-based harassment, shaming, and the policing of women's sexual expression. User habits, Internet policies—and the inability of the law to keep up with either—has a chilling effect on girls' and women's free expression, creating material harm in the lives of many.

Sexting, slut-shaming, and revenge porn specifically demonstrate the ways in which technology perpetuates regulation of girls and women's sexuality and curtails our freedom of speech.

SEXTING

Every day millions of people happily share selfies, often sexually explicit ones. Snapchat, "a little sexting app,"[1] enables users to take and share photos that last no longer than ten seconds. In 2013, Snapchat turned down a $4 billion dollar buy-out offer from Google. While the founders of Snapchat insist that their application was not created to enable sexting, the application lends itself perfectly to people sending risqué photographs with reduced risk that they'll be penalized for doing it. The app's popularity with teenagers is a significant driver of success. Given this popularity, competitor apps may soon crowd the market.

So what about teenagers? The "Sex and Tech Survey" conducted by the National Campaign to Prevent Teen and Unwanted Pregnancy reveals that up to 40 percent of teens send racy or explicit messages, and almost 50 percent receive them.[2] A study of more than 1,000 black and Latino Cincinnati tenth graders revealed that teenage boys and girls take sexually explicit photographs of themselves at roughly the same rates.[3] Although the latter study focused on these minority groups, researchers confirmed that their findings reflected similar patterns among non-minority students in the same age range. What is most interesting about this study is that while rates of taking photos and sending them is undifferentiated by sex, the rate at which teens share photos of other people is highly distinguished by sex. Teenage boys were twice as likely to share explicit photographs sent to them by girls, without the girls' intent or consent. As one young man asked me during a lecture on this topic, "What's the difference between sharing a picture of my toaster and sharing a picture of a girl? If she's sent it to me it is mine." His attitude might explain research findings that 52.3 percent of teens exposed to sexting have engaged in "unwanted but consensual sexting with a committed partner."[4] The study found that girls and women (55 percent) were more likely than boys and men

(48 percent) to feel pressured into sexting in response to anxieties about their relationships.[5] The seeming contradiction between "unwanted but consensual" is related to strategic attempts at trying to avoid anger, teasing, bullying, social ostracism, etc. Other surveys and studies confirm and reinforce the findings of this one. Threats and harms from sexting come, generally speaking, from peer groups and negatively affect female technology users who report being subjected online and off to greater sexual pressure more than males.[6]

Girls—who are people, not inert objects—assume a measure of privacy that is routinely denied them by over-sharing male peers. In fact, the right to privacy is considered fundamental to American political ideology. Writing in *Slate*, journalist Amanda Hess describes how school authorities in Cincinnati dealt with this difference in sexting habits after they found that hundreds of teenagers at Madeira High School had been sharing sexually explicit photographs on their phones and computers.[7] The school decided to penalize the students. But the school did not penalize all students. They didn't even penalize those who shared photos of other students without their consent.

Instead, the school administrators punished the girls whose photographs were shared the most. No attempts were made to address the nonconsensual aspects of sharing the photographs, or the violations of privacy and ensuing shaming that the girls experienced. This response is common. In a similar case at Paul VI Catholic High School in Virginia, a 16-year-old girl was asked to leave the school after sending, in response to a dare between friends, a topless photo of herself to two 16-year-old boys. At least one of the boys then sent her photo to others on his sports team, and the photo was then widely circulated.

As Katie J.M. Baker detailed in a *Jezebel* article, the dean of students called the female student into his office and explained that what she had done in sending the photograph was "outrageous," he felt this was particularly true because she wasn't dating either of the boys. The girl was suspended for one day. However, a week later she was called back for another meeting where she was asked if she knew what pornography was and "whether she felt she had 'harassed'" the boys. Among the many questions she was asked was one regarding "what justice" the boys should receive. "Alexis and her parents assumed the administration was referring to Jason and Peter's punishment, but they actually 'wanted to know what I should do to make them feel better if they were distraught.'" The meeting ended with her withdrawing from her school. The boys who dared her and shared the photo (and who already, it was noted, had lacrosse commitments at D-1 universities) remained penalty-free. The breach of trust, privacy, and violation of consent in sharing the photographs was unaddressed by the school administrators, the girl's peers, or, at least publicly, by the parents of the boys.[8]

These actions on the part of parents, teachers, and school administrators do little to communicate to teenagers that girls are different from toasters and that their consent and right to privacy are necessary and legitimate.

Occasionally there is a variation on a theme. When Amber Cole was 14 years old, she engaged in oral sex with a boy. Other people watched, recorded, and shared the event via video on YouTube. All without her permission. The video stayed up on YouTube, despite its illegality (the age of the participants meant that the video was child pornography and disseminating it was a federal offense) long enough to be viewed tens of thousands of times. Cole, who is African American, was publicly reprimanded in a series of "Letters to Amber," which addressed her sexuality, allegedly loose morals, lack of self-respect, failure to represent black girls and women properly, and more. As Latoya Peterson, editor of *Racialicious* asked, "Where were the letters to the boys?"[9] There were no such letters, although another person started a "Leave Amber Cole Alone" video that also had viral success.[10]

The blaming of girls and letting boys off the hook was repeated yet again, but on a global scale, after a photograph of a 17-year-old girl performing public oral sex at an Eminem concert in Ireland went viral. The response to the photo was a relentless outpouring of outrage and misogynistic disgust aimed at the girl, who was later hospitalized. She eventually made a complaint of sexual assault.[11] Messages such as "Slanegirl will suck anything," Tweets calling her a "ho," a "vile slut," and more quickly resulted in the hashtag #Slanegirl trending globally. Media outlets tracked down the girl and ran her photo, name, and age. Only after it became apparent that she was under 18 did social media sites Facebook, Twitter, and Instagram take steps to delete the original images from their sites, now that it was understood as child pornography. At the same time, the boy, who was pictured holding his arms up in victory, was either ignored or lauded as a hero for his sexual prowess.

Simply expressing an interest in sex online often means that women are targeted for harassment, particularly when using popular dating platforms, such as Tinder or OKCupid. Fully 42 percent of women using online dating sites report getting harassing or worrisome messages compared to 17 percent of men.[12]

When artist Anna Gensler decided to try Tinder, a mobile dating app, she did not anticipate the messages that quickly followed. "Bet your [sic] tight," shared one man. "If I was a watermelon, would you spit or swallow my seeds," asked another. "I love anal," was the introductory text of a third. Gensler responded creatively by illustrating her harassers, naked, with the contents of their texts.[13] Her experience is not uncommon. In 2013, a male user decided to pose as a woman on a dating site with the explicit intent of proving how easy it was for women to find dates online; however, his experiment backfired when—just two hours later—he was forced to delete his account because of an onslaught of unwanted attention. He shut down the fake account after just two hours, reporting,

Guys would become hostile when I told them I wasn't interested in NSA [no strings attached] sex, or guys that had started normal and nice quickly turned the conversation into something explicitly sexual in nature. Seemingly nice dudes in quite esteemed careers asking to hook up in 24 hours and sending them naked pics of myself despite multiple times telling them that I didn't want to . . . what I got was an onslaught of people who were, within minutes of saying hello, saying things that made me—as a dude who spends most of his time on 4chan [the popular online imageboard]—uneasy.[14]

Public shaming of the sort described doesn't even require that girls or women engage in actual sexual activity or be sexually assaulted to be targeted for gender-based harassment. In 2012, Facebook was criticized for allowing a page called "12-year-old slut memes" to exist. The page, created by two Australian men, posted photographs of girls and women—taken from their profiles without consent—so that anyone could comment on their "sluttiness." By the time the page was eventually removed, it had more than 200,000 likes.[15] And, although this particular page was taken down, Facebook has dozens of equally egregious links such as upskirt pages, whose sole purpose is publishing photos of women's bodies and underwear without their consent. Platforms such as Ask.FM and Kik are regularly used in this way and implicated in cyberbullying that frequently subjects young girls to intense slut-shaming. It's important to note, however, that most online platforms allow nonconsensual photography, which includes, for example, upskirt photos. While it may seem outrageous, taking upskirt photos in public places is not illegal in most U.S. states. In 2014, the Massachusetts Supreme Court ruled that upskirt photography was legal because women were neither entirely nor partially nude. Legislators acted quickly in the wake of the ruling to ban the practice. The crime is punishable by up to two-and-a-half years in jail or a fine of up to $5,000 in Massachusetts, but is still a common practice online.[16]

Experiences with sexting, appropriation of image and identity, and sharing intimate photographs never intended for public distribution, are often girls' first exposure to sexual double standards for which they pay a high price.

Recently, this scenario was flipped on its head, however, with the release of a new application, Lulu, that allows women to access social media and publicly rate men that they have had relationships with. Use of the app was described by an article in the *Telegraph* as "sexist behavior towards men." In the piece, which described a Brazilian man who was suing Facebook over integration of the app with its service, the writer declared, "It is simply unacceptable that women rate men on Lulu based on their looks and sexual performance."[17]

In several of the instances provided above, girls willingly participated in some capacity with boys before images were shared in nonconsensual, abusive ways. The occurrence of bullying and sexual assault are deeply embedded in social media; persistent sex-based double standards have found new life in this medium. The Internet can make it extraordinarily risky for girls to make mistakes, experiment, express themselves freely, and assume the equality we keep telling them they have.

The use of social media to both reinforce traditional bullying and amplify its effects is epidemic. Cyberbullying combines anonymity, constant accessibility and, quite literally, global audiences who feel free to maliciously target girls and women who are entirely unknown to them. When it comes to bullying, however, the issue is that slut-shaming—a common form of gender-based bullying—was not considered harassment until relatively recently.

Since the 2010 suicide of 15-year-old Phoebe Prince,[18] one of the earliest publicized cases of slut-shaming and cyberbullying resulting in a girl killing herself, similar cases have tragically followed. Prince was a student at a Northampton, Massachusetts, school when she briefly dated a boy in her new school. Her relationship with the boy resulted in disputes with female classmates, at least two groups of whom engaged in relentlessly slut-shaming Prince. Prince hanged herself after a period of intense bullying conducted primarily by nine students who were later indicted for civil rights violations, two for statutory rape. In 2011, Chevonea Kendall-Bryan, 13, threw herself off of a bridge in Southwest London when a boy refused to delete a video from his phone that showed her engaged in a sex act.[19] Felicia Garcia was only 15 years old when she jumped to her death in front of a train in Staten Island after being bullied for having consensual sex with four members of the high school football team.[20]

The trajectory of shame and blame can be even more startling in cases of sexual assault. Similar bullying also resulted in the suicides of teenagers Amanda Todd, Rehtaeh Parsons, and Audrie Pott—all of whom sustained online bullying and slut-shaming after they were raped.

Three 16-year-old boys were arrested for photographing their brutal sexual assault of 15-year-old Pott while she was incapacitated at a party. The boys shared the photos widely. Pott was barraged by gendered obscenities, propositioned, embarrassed, and humiliated. Walking through school one day, grappling with an onslaught of messages reading "u were one horny mofo," and "everyone knows," she was handed a dress code violation by an adult hall monitor. Making connections between the policing of girls' sexuality by adults and the policing of girls by their peers isn't high on anyone's list. Later that day, her mother found Audrie hanging from her bathroom ceiling.[21]

Seventeen-year-old Rehtaeh Parsons's case eerily resembled Pott's. She, too, committed suicide after dealing with an avalanche of malicious social media. Parsons was gang-raped, photographed, and shamed under similar circumstances. "Everybody turned against Rehtaeh and she was a 'slut' and she was the one that they targeted," explained her mother after her death.[22]

Fourteen-year-old Daisy Coleman faced opprobrium after bringing rape charges against two high school seniors who allegedly plied her with alcohol, sexually assaulted her and deposited her, incapacitated, in 23-degree weather outside of her door. Coleman was bullied and harassed by classmates and members of her community. Her family eventually left the town and Daisy has several times attempted suicide since. Eventually one of the attackers plead guilty to charges of "child endangerment." After two high school boys were convicted of raping a 16-year-old Steubenville, Ohio, girl, the victim was deluged with online threats in response to her bringing charges against her assailants. For being raped and pressing charges she was insulted, described as a skank, a liar, a slut, and she received death threats.[23]

After a video of her assault surfaced in social media, a 16-year-old girl in Texas, identified only by her first name, Jada, alleged that she'd been drugged and raped at a party. The video showed her lying on the ground, apparently unconscious. It was not until viewing the video that she realized she'd been assaulted. She lodged a complaint with the Houston police, but even weeks after the incident, no arrests were forthcoming. In the meantime, her peers mocked her by posting photographs of themselves posed as though unconscious on the ground, as she appeared in the video and using a hashtag, #Jadapose, that incorporated her name and publicly identified her.[24]

The Steubenville case pivoted around a now infamous photograph showing two boys carrying the inert girl by her hands and feet. Writing in the *New Statesman*, journalist Laurie Penny called the image, "Rape Culture's Abu Ghraib moment."[25] I'd like to say I agree with Penny, but am concerned we will have many other cases of sexual assault, slut-shaming, and self-harm before reaching a cultural tipping point. The combination of photography and technological ease of sharing it extends the ability to shame girls and amplifies the effects experienced. The majority of these cases involve heterosexual girls, although boys are not immune from viral bullying as the tragic suicide of 14-year-old Matthew Burdette attests. The Southern California teen killed himself two weeks after a video clip of him masturbating in a school bathroom stall was posted to Snapchat and Vine. The video went viral and Burdette was relentlessly taunted at school.[26] And, as is true offline, lesbian, gay, bisexual, or transgender (LGBT) youth—and those thought to be LGBT—are at higher risk of being bullied by their peers. A study led by researchers at Iowa State University found that 54 percent of 444 youth between the ages of 11 and 22 reported cyberbullying related to gender or sexual orientation.[27] Members of the LGBTQ community, like heterosexual women who violate gender rules regarding behavior, particularly sexual norms, are frequent targets of aggression.

When news spread of the first transgender teen, Cassidy Campbell, to be named homecoming queen in Orange County, California, she was inundated with hate. "Oh please die of AIDS you f***ing fag!!!!!" said a typical and typically ignorant commenter on a video showing her winning.[28]

Rutgers University student Tyler Clementi jumped off the Brooklyn Bridge after his roommate used a hidden webcam to livestream a sexual encounter between Clementi and another man in their dorm room.[29] Fifteen-year-old Sinead Taylor explained, in a suicide note written after years of online torment that followed her from school to school, "People used to call me a lesbian or bisexual and they would accuse me of looking at them while they were getting changed, like they wouldn't want to get changed in front of me."[30]

These examples illustrate very traditional distributions of shame and penalty and the degree to which the technology involved is simply a vector for them. Prevailing cultural attitudes reinforce patriarchal norms about gender roles, sex and sexuality and technology does nothing in and of itself to change that. In general, people remain married to the idea that if a girl or woman creates a photograph, allows one to be taken, or engages in sexual behavior without remorse and outside of the bounds of marriage, she deserves whatever happens. The idea that women are a public resource—for representation, comment, abuse, and use—has been well established online.

THE PROBLEM OF REVENGE PORN

In addition to the problems of sexting, slut-shaming, and bullying through social media, there exists a burgeoning revenge porn industry. Revenge porn involves disgruntled ex-sexual partners misappropriating and abusively sharing—with malicious intent—intimate images, sexually explicit photographs, or videos. The photographs are often shared on websites designed for this purpose, along with personal details, such as phone numbers, work and home addresses, and messages such as "really hope ur life get destroyed with this upload. Slut."[31]

Adding to the problem of online revenge porn is the lack of coherent legal recourse for victims and a historic disregard for harms to women. Persistent legal ambiguity about revenge porn raises serious questions about the degree to which we feel culturally comfortable recognizing (or not) women's intentions, autonomy, consent, and privacy. In the United States, thirteen states have created criminal measures to address revenge porn and to provide legal recourse for victims. Plans are underway to introduce similar laws in other states, but throughout the country there are many other states where it is still not illegal to maliciously distribute intimate photographs of another person in these ways. A prevailing undercurrent in the formulation of revenge porn laws is the belief that women who take nude and/or sexually explicit photographs of themselves, particularly if they share them with a presumption of privacy, deserve any ills that might befall them, including loss of privacy, income, reputation, and dignity.

Revenge porn is what led Holly Jacobs to found the Cyber Civil Rights Initiative.[32] Jacobs was forced to legally change her name after an ex-boyfriend shared explicit pictures taken while they were still dating. The police, the FBI, lawyers, service providers, and a host of Internet experts were unable to help Jacobs, whose life was upended by the harassment.

In the case of Kayla Laws, the online exploitation resulted from selfies she took while dressing in her bedroom one night. One photo revealed her unclothed left breast. Three months later, Kayla was mortified when the photograph, which she had saved with hundreds of others on her computer, showed up on the revenge porn site, *Is Anyone Up?*, started by Hunter Moore in 2010. Charlotte Laws, Kayla's mother and a former private detective, became an outspoken anti-revenge-porn activist as the result of her daughter's experience. When Laws contacted Moore to ask that the photo of her daughter be removed, he refused. When she approached a lawyer, his dumb and dumbfounding response was, "The photo will just go away if you ignore it."[33] She discovered that other hacking victims were similarly featured on the site and was able to initiate an FBI investigation. Moore, who removed his site in the midst of the investigation, called himself a "professional life ruiner."[34] Not only do sites like Moore's exist for this purpose of ruining lives, but they benefit doubly by charging women exorbitant fees to remove harassing and nonconsensual content.[35]

Revenge porn, like the teen-focused slut-shaming cyberbullying that precedes it, utilizes current technology to perpetuate power imbalances that discriminate against women, gender non-conforming people, and people of color. A growing movement, focused on establishing a canon of cyber civil rights, is making headway in criminalizing revenge porn in the United States. Countries such as Israel and Australia have already made it illegal to post and distribute intimate photographs without the consent of the subject.

Working with legal scholars and advocates, Jacobs started the End Revenge Porn Campaign to fight for legislation to make this practice illegal. Among these scholars are Danielle Citron, of the University of Maryland, and Mary Anne Franks, of the University of Miami. Citron has written extensively about and created a legal, civil rights-based framework for addressing online abuse. Franks has contributed to developing anti-revenge porn legislation in California and New Jersey. Opponents to these efforts argue that the solution is not in criminalizing speech. However, both Citron and Franks demonstrate the tangible violation of rights and material and dignitary harms that result from this abuse of technology. They make compelling arguments for narrowly defined criminal statutes that recognize the high cost of online harassment and discrimination.[36] Citron and Franks argue that widespread disregard for women's privacy and autonomy, particularly their sexual autonomy, is incorporated into mainstream understandings of "free" speech in such a way that women's civil rights—to privacy and autonomy—are routinely violated.[37] In addition, the criminalization of revenge porn falls squarely in line with legal precedents that are not censoring speech so much as protecting rights of privacy, confidentiality, implied promises. That women have these rights seems to be problematic for advocates of unfettered speech inclined to disregard the fact. It is notable that more than 75 percent of online harassment of this nature is targeted at women.[38]

Citron's and Frank's work challenges current laws (or lack thereof) and ideas about speech, and also creates substantial new challenges to Internet companies who are regulating the content on their sites. Companies such as Yahoo, Facebook, Twitter, Instagram, Snapchat, and other similar platforms have their own unique and deliberately constructed user guidelines and community standards. Dominant cultural ideas about sexuality, bodily autonomy, and consent are manifested not only in user habits, but in the way content is regulated by social media companies.

In the United States, service providers are legally protected by Section 230 of the Communications Decency Act, somewhat ironically called "the Good Samaritan clause," which trusts that companies will act in the best interests of their customers. This law absolves companies of responsibility or liability for content on their sites. As a result, harmful effects are frequently reified by guidelines and policy interpretations that protect free speech for bullies at the expense of the freedom of expression of those they target. However, companies that operate internationally—as most do—run afoul of laws in other countries that do not likewise absolve them of responsibility. For example, the Italian government investigated Facebook in the case of Carolina Picchio, a 14-year-old Italian girl who committed suicide after photos and a video of her appearing inebriated were shared on the platform. As CNN reports, "an ex-boyfriend and his friends posted a steady barrage of abusive, offensive messages aimed at Carolina. And what started out online spilled into her daily life at school, and among her friends."[39] Carolina's sister and several friends reported the ongoing bullying on the site, and Carolina's torment, but Facebook did not remove any content.

One of the primary stated objectives of social media companies is to ensure users that their virtual spaces are safe. These objectives are generally assumed to be gender-neutral propositions, but in execution they are anything but. Normative interpretations of the meanings of words such as "safety," "threat," and "harm" belie these commitments and have a grossly disproportionately negative effect on girls and women. In general, corporations fail to consider the safety gap between men and women, epidemic levels of rape and domestic violence against women, homophobia and transphobia, as well as double standards regarding sexuality and reputational harm. In other words, policies are epistemologically rooted in and normatively interpreted through the reality of straight white men's lives.

Companies persistently demonstrate a lack of understanding of how policies work to make online forums more dangerous for those users who are far more likely to suffer sexualized and racialized harassment. In December 2013, Twitter announced a change in its policy governing how users could block other users on the site. The new policy would have allowed blocked users to continue following those who blocked them. The company was shocked by the immediate outrage expressed by users most vulnerable to cyber-harassment and threats—specifically women, people of color, and members of the LGBTQ community. As a result of protests and an almost instantaneous online petition, the policy was reversed only hours after it was initially announced.[40] Similarly, in May 2013, I worked with the activist-information groups Women, Action and the Media and Everyday Sexism in organizing a successful campaign asking advertisers to boycott Facebook. One catalyst for this campaign was Facebook's decision that threats against administrators of a Facebook page dedicated to fighting Facebook pages promoting rape were not credible. The threats included cannibalistic porn death scenarios, posting pictures of women and young girls being raped or beaten up, and comments such as, "I will skull-fuck your children." Facebook did not consider this content threatening or sufficiently harassing to warrant passing the information on to law enforcement. However, at the behest of the women who were targeted, the FBI considered the barrage of threats worthy of investigation. The boycott campaign asked advertisers to pull their ads from Facebook until that company recognized that misogynistic content, and pages dedicated to shaming, threatening, and harassing girls and women, violated their bullying and hate speech guidelines.[41]

FREE SPEECH ISSUES

Online companies are generally committed to allowing the greatest freedom of expression on their platforms. However, when it comes to women's nudity and female sexuality, definitions of what constitutes speech and freedom of expression often narrow precipitously. First, freedom of speech principles frequently pivot around the definition of "harm" and our society, historically, has failed to consider harms that accrue primarily to women as legitimate, serious, and consequential. This is true, for example, in terms of recognizing domestic violence, sexual assault, workplace sexual discrimination, and, now, online harassment. Second, freedom of speech is subject to cultural norms when its management is privatized through ISP, Internet company or media regulatory agencies. Censorship and ideas about censorship and speech frequently incorporate mainstream ideas about "obscenity." Women's non-objectified use of their own bodies to express themselves presents real problems for companies whose policies conflate all female nudity with obscenity. In a questionable attempt to reduce obscenity on its site, Facebook, for instance, until recently, maintained a "nipple rule" that bans all images of bare female nipples on the site. This means photographs of breast-feeding mothers whose nipples might be revealed, medical representations of women's breasts or genitals, photo images of art featuring women's breasts, or political protest involving female nudity could not be shared among Facebook's one billion users. This recently changed when the company amended policies to allow post-mastectomy and breastfeeding photographs in which women's nipples might be apparent. Instagram's rules continue to require that women's breasts are covered, either actually or with an added digital element, such as a black bar. At the same time, however, these sites are filled with barely camouflaged pornographic content that escapes censure through the use of taped over nipples or creative clothing. These policies thus permit images that objectify and sexualize women while constraining the opportunities to post non-objectifying alternatives. Interestingly, Facebook's changes to policy, allowing survivors of breast cancer and mothers to share their photographs, illustrates a particular aspect of a gender-based double standard. Namely, the new policies seem to reflect a Madonna/whore dichotomy in which "good women" (those who have suffered or are using their bodies to mother) can be seen, but others (those who are expressing artistic, political, or sexual ideas) cannot.

When a young Tunisian woman protesting repressive, religious, and theocratic ideas, posted a picture of herself, topless with the words "Fuck Your Morals" written on her breasts, Facebook insisted that the photo had to be blurred or removed.[42] Her use of her body and nudity were clearly not salacious or pornographic, and the removal of her photography was a suppression of political speech. Women in Facebook, the majority of users, are unable to create and share non-sexualized, self-defined, representations of our own bodies for art, protest, and more. Despite its intent, Facebook's policy is, in effect, retrograde and discriminatory.

In a similar case on Instagram, the company deleted artist Petra Collin's 25,000-follower-strong account, claiming that multiple images violated Instagram's terms of service. Writing in the wake of the deletion, Collin explained, "No nudity, violence, pornography, unlawful, hateful or infringing imagery. What I did have was an image of MY body that didn't meet society's standard of 'femininity'. . . . Up until this moment, I had obviously seen and felt the pressure to regulate my body, but never thought I would literally experience it."[43]

Female nudity is an essential part of the social critique. Women artists—such as Lorna Simpson, Cheri Gaulke, Ana Medieta, Carolee Schneemann, Yoko Ono, Marina Abramovic, and Hanna Wilke—rely on nudity to illuminate social injustices. Additionally, women's deliberate public nakedness as protest is also common. Barbara Sutton has documented naked protests in Brazil over the course of several years. Prior to Tunisia's Amina Sboui's 2013 topless protest (after which she was arrested and subjected to a virginity test), Egyptian activist Aalia Magda posted pictures of herself naked to protest Sharia law and censorship. During multiple protests between 2001 and 2013, hundreds of women in the Niger Delta marched half-naked in protests against Shell Oil Company's exploitative practices in their community. In Argentina, an estimated 7,000 women stormed a cathedral defended by 1,500 rosary-bearing Catholic men. The women fought, spat, yelled, spray-painted people, and were accused, without a shred of irony, of gender-based violence against Catholic men. Many of these women were topless, if not entirely naked. Internet companies who bar these images as "obscene" are working within a well-developed media tradition. Traditional media—including newspapers, broadcast and cable news, and magazines—continue to maintain similar prohibitions in an effort to remain "family friendly." When media networks decline to show women protesting naked, or companies censor their images while allowing grossly objectifying alternatives to proliferate, they silence them doubly.

Social media company policies that equate women's nudity with obscenity are relics of long-standing public ordinances and regulatory norms, such as those of the Motion Picture Association of America and the Federal Communications Commission, both of whose definition of obscenity clearly privileges heterosexuality, conflates women's bodies with indecency, and insist that those bodies (and sex) be private and consumed according to well-understood rules.

These rules have never addressed the issue of consent; and the allowable use, and ubiquitous presence, of nonconsensual photography on these platforms is a primary method used to police women's sexuality and speech and reinforce conservative ideas about them. These policies provide a mechanism whereby new, nominally progressive tech companies enable the replication of objectifying, shaming, and sexist cultural norms while insisting on their own so-called neutrality. All of this takes place in an environment where pornography—most of which constitutes the ultimate representation of women's subjugation and use as sexual objects and marked by racist eroticization of violence against women—is burgeoning.

Nonetheless, our visual online media provide unparalleled and transformative opportunities to those marginalized and silenced in traditional, mainstream media. For women, the Internet allows not only greater freedom of expression and self-representation of our bodies, but of sexual expression on our own terms even as old prejudices, behaviors, and hierarchies are reproduced. Online communities should be attuned to the daily control of representations of girls' and women's bodies that replicate and reinforce double standards in an environment permeated by sexually objectifying imagery and everyday microanalysis of our bodies. In an environment where defining and regulating free speech is increasingly privatized and where companies are operating as quasi-governments across borders, it is vitally important that Internet users and advocates challenge the standards, corporate policies, and legal systems that routinely ignore gendered harms and perpetuate discriminatory norms.

DISCUSSION QUESTIONS

• What does it mean to be a "slut" in our culture? How does the concept of being a "slut" relate to issues of race, class, gender, and sexuality?
• Do you think once someone shares an explicit photo of themselves using their phone, computer, or social media site that they automatically give up the right to be upset if that photo is shared with other people? What about when

hackers illegally access into celebrities' private photos and you view their photos online without consent? Is that abuse? A crime? A scandal? Why or why not?

• How much responsibility do you think social media sites such as Facebook and Instagram have in addressing online sexual harassment or bullying? Could they play a bigger role in preventing such profiles/pages from existing? Should they have a zero-tolerance policy?

NOTES

1. Jeff Make, "Meet the 23-Year-Old Kid Who Turned Down $3 Billion for Snapchat," *Yahoo News*, November 15, 2013, http://finance.yahoo.com/blogs/breakout/meet-the-23-year-old-kid-who-turned-down—3-billion-for-snapchat-010309114.html.
2. "The National Campaign to Prevent Teen and Unwanted Pregnancy," *Sex and Tech Survey*, 2013, http://www.thenationalcampaign.org/sextech/PDF/SexTech_Summary.pdf.
3. Mary Ann Liebert, "Prevalence and Patterns of Sexting among Ethnic Minority Urban High School Students," *Cyberpsychology, Behavior, and Social Networking* 16, no. 6 (2013): 456.
4. Michelle Drouin and Elizabeth Tobin, "Unwanted but Consensual Sexting among Young Adults: Relations with Attachment and Sexual Motivations," *Computers in Human Behavior* 31 (2014): 412–418.
5. Antonia Molloy, "Young People Are Sexting—But That Doesn't Mean They Necessarily Want to Be, Says Research," *Independent*, December 31, 2013, http://www.independent.co.uk/life-style/gadgets-and-tech/news/young-people-are-sexting—but-that-doesn't-mean-they-necessarily-want-to-be-says-research-9031468.html.
6. "Children, Young People and Sexting Study," National Society for the Prevention of Cruelty to Children, May 2012, http://www.nspcc.org.uk/Inform/resourcesfor professionals/sexualabuse/sexting-research-summary_wdf89270.pdf.
7. Amanda Hess, "The Real Difference between Teenage Boys and Girls' Sexting Habits? Boys Forward More," *Slate*, March 4, 2013, http://www.slate.com/blogs/xx_factor/2013/03/04/sexting_statistics_teen_boys_and_girls_sext_in_equal_numbers_but_boys_forward.html.
8. Katie J.M. Baker, "Girl Sends Sext, Gets Kicked Out of School. Lacrosse Players Share Sext, Get Off Scot Free," *Jezebel*, April 10, 2013, http://jezebel.com/girl-sends-sext-gets-kicked-out-of-school-lacrosse-pl-471285308.
9. Latoya Peterson, "Because Amber Cole Is Just a Kid and Boys Will Be Boys," *Racialicious*, October 28, 2011, http://www.racialicious.com/2011/10/28/because-amber-cole-is-just-a-kid-and-boys-learn-to-be-boys/.
10. Laura Matthews, "Amber Cole Video Leads to Two Boys' Arrest, False Rumors of Suicide: Report," October 21, 2011, *International Business Times*, http://www.ibtimes.com/amber-cole-video-leads-two-boys-arrest-false-rumors-suicide-report-325044.

11. Caroline Linton, "Behind #SlaneGirl: Young Girl Hospitalized after Photographed Having Oral Sex," August 8, 2013, *Daily Beast*, http://thebea.st/1d6YLHu.

12. Aaron Smith and Maeve Duggan, "Online Dating & Relationships," Pew Research Center, October 21, 2013, http://www.pewinternet.org/2013/10/21/online-dating-relationships/. (Editor's note: For more discussion, see Alexandra Tweten's chapter, "Bye Felipe," in this volume.)

13. Audra Schroeder, "This Tinder User Got Back at Creepy Dudes by Drawing Them Naked," *Daily Dot*, April 22, 2014, http://www.dailydot.com/technology/tinder-harassment-art/.

14. "Comments," *TwoXChromosomes*, January 8, 2014, http://bit.ly/1ewpoCI.

15. Soraya Chemaly, "The 12-Year-Old Slut Meme and Facebook's Misogyny Problem," *Huffington Post*, September 26, 2012, http://huff.to/S8hLWV.

16. Haimy Assefa, "Massachusetts Court Says 'Upskirt' Photos Are Legal," *CNN*, March 6, 2014, http://www.cnn.com/2014/03/05/us/massachusetts-upskirt-photography/. Upskirt photos are also illegal in states including New York, Florida, and Washington. In general, however, the law has not kept up with the photo practice or with gender justice principles.

17. Brooke Magnanti, "Lulu App: Why Women's Sexist Behaviour towards Men Needs to End," *Telegraph*, December 10, 2013, http://www.telegraph.co.uk/women/sex/online-dating/10508593/Lulu-app-Why-womens-sexist-behaviour-towards-men-needs-to-end.html.

18. Russell Goldman, "Teens Indicted after Allegedly Taunting Girl Who Hanged Herself," *ABC News*, March 29, 2010, http://abcnews.go.com/Technology/TheLaw/teens-charged-bullying-mass-girl-kill/story?id=10231357.

19. Mark Duell, "Chevonea Kendall-Bryan: Schoolgirl, 13, 'Plunged 60ft to Her Death after Rumours of Sex Video,' " January 8, 2013, *Mail Online*, http://bit.ly/11d1xEV.

20. Vivien Yee, "On Staten Island, Relentless Bullying Is Blamed for a Teenage Girl's Suicide," *New York Times*, October 25, 2013, http://nyti.ms/QJ9QkM.

21. Nina Burleigh, "Sexting, Shame and Suicide," *Rolling Stone*, September 17, 2013, http://rol.st/1f1Lf7q.

22. Selena Ross, "Who Failed Rehtaeh Parsons?" *Herald News*, April 9, 2013, http://thechronicleherald.ca/metro/1122345-who-failed-rehtaeh-parsons#.UWQfNmLG6Jg.twitter.

23. Andrew Welsh-Huggins, "Girls Threaten Steubenville Rape Accuser on Facebook, Twitter; 2 Face Charges in Ohio," *Huffington Post*, March 19, 2013, http://www.huffingtonpost.com/2013/03/19/girls-threaten-steubenville-rape-accuser-twitter_n_2906270.html.

24. Inea Oh, "16-Year-Old's Alleged Rape Goes Viral and Now She's Speaking Out," June 10, 2014, http://www.huffingtonpost.com/2014/07/10/jada-teen-rape-_n_5574831.html.

25. Laurie Penny, "Steubenville: This Is Rape Culture's Abu Ghraib Moment," *New Statesman*, March 19, 2013, http://www.newstatesman.com/laurie-penny/2013/03/steubenville-rape-cultures-abu-ghraib-moment.

26. Tony Perry, "Bathroom Video, Bullying Led to Teen's Suicide, Parents Say," *Los Angeles Times*, July 14, 2014, http://www.latimes.com/local/lanow/la-me-ln-bathroom-video-bullying-suicide-20140714-story.html.

27. "Cyberbullying Hits LGBT Youth Especially Hard," *CNET*, March 10, 2010, http://www.cnet.com/news/cyberbullying-hits-lgbt-youth-especially-hard/.

28. Devin Cordero, "Trans Teen Wins Homecoming Queen, Faces Onslaught of Hate and Cyberbullying," *SAVE*, September 23, 2013, www.savedade.org/trans_teen_homecoming.

29. "Tyler Clementi," *New York Times*, March 16, 2012, http://topics.nytimes.com/top/reference/timestopics/people/c/tyler_clementi/index.html.

30. "Teenage Girl Sinead Taylor Kills Herself Over Bullies' 'Lesbian' Taunts," *International Business Times*, August 29, 3013, http://www.ibtimes.co.uk/london-teenager-commits-suicide-bullying-tomboy-online-502253.

31. Charlotte Lyntton, "When Sexting Gets Ugly," *Daily Beast*, January 7, 2014, http://www.thedailybeast.com/articles/2014/01/07/when-sexting-gets-ugly-flirting-can-become-fodder-for-revenge-porn.html.

32. See cybercivilrights.org.

33. Charlotte Laws, "I've Been Called the 'Erin Brockovich' of Revenge Porn," *XOJane*, November 21, 2013, http://www.xojane.com/it-happened-to-me/charlotte-laws-hunter-moore-erin-brockovich-revenge-porn.

34. Rheana Murray, "IsAnyoneUp? Shuts Down," *New York Daily News*, April 20, 2012, http://www.nydailynews.com/news/money/isanyoneup-shuts-revenge-porn-forum-bought-anti-bullying-website-article-1.1064608.

35. Meghan Kenaeally, "Revenge Porn Website Operator Arrested," *Mail Online*, December 12, 2013, http://dailym.ai/J4vrot.

36. Danielle Keats Citron and Mary Anne Franks, "Criminalizing Revenge Porn," *Wake Forest Law Review* 49 (2014): 345–392, http://digitalcommons.law.umaryland.edu/cgi/viewcontent.cgi?article=2424&context=fac_pubs.

37. Ibid.

38. Saul Levmore and Martha C. Nussbaum, eds., *The Offensive Internet: Speech, Privacy, and Reputation Paperback* (Boston: Harvard University Press, 2012).

39. Ben Wedemen, "Facebook May Face Prosecution Over Bullied Teenager's Suicide in Italy," *CNN*, July 31, 2013, http://www.cnn.com/2013/07/31/world/europe/italy-facebook-suicide/.

40. Lauren C. Williams and Aviva Shen, "Why Doesn't Twitter Take Gender-Based Harassment More Seriously?" *Think Progress*, December 13, 2013, http://thinkprogress.org/health/2013/12/13/3061151/twitter-block-policy-backlash/.

41. Zoe Klineman, "Facebook Sexism Campaign Attracts Thousands Online," *BBC*, May 28, 2013, http://www.bbc.co.uk/news/technology-22689522.

42. Emily Greenhouse, "How to Provoke National Unrest With a Facebook Photo," *New Yorker*, April 8, 2013, http://www.newyorker.com/online/blogs/elements/2013/04/amina-tyler-topless-photos-tunisia-activism.html.

43. Petra Collins, "Why Instagram Censored My Body," *Huffington Post*, October 17, 2013, http://huff.to/1cznDoN.

THE REVOLUTIONARY POSSIBILITIES OF ONLINE TRANS AND QUEER COMMUNITIES

Jamie J. Hagen

When I initially proposed a chapter on queer sexuality for this anthology, I suggested the title: "Straight Lesbians and Bisexual Sluts: Mainstream Media's Confused Representation of LGBT Women in Bed."

This chapter title was motivated by my experience as a femme-identified lesbian irritated and offended by the problematic lesbian representation in pop culture. Primetime TV and the few movies with lesbian plotlines available in the LGBT section of movie streaming services more often than not offer storylines where lesbians ultimately decide to be with men, or they end up in bed with a heterosexual couple, sexually satisfying another woman. Mainstream movies and TV about lesbian women that don't have some intervening male-driven plot point remains an anomaly. These story lines are not representative of the queer community I know and love.[1]

WHERE THE QUEERS ARE: THE ONLINE QUEER LANDSCAPE

Met with this dearth of relatable representation in mainstream media, I went elsewhere with my questions and curiosities about queer sex and the type of community I wanted to be a part of as an out, political, feminist, sexually active lesbian. What does feminist queer porn look, sound, and feel like, anyway? Can kinks between a butch and femme couple be feminist instead of simply a new twist to old patriarchal relations? How can a lesbian who presents in a masculine way be read socially as handsome? What is tribbing and how does it work? These were some of the questions I Googled excitedly at home when I was too nervous to check out a book about lesbian sexuality at the library. I had so many questions about the ethics of BDSM power play in the bedroom. Exploring queer sexuality is a political act, deeply tied to acknowledging first and foremost who we are as a queer community and whom we desire. Because of this, online communities provide more than just an opportunity to find a date or a friend, but also a possibility to find something as essential as the vocabulary and stories we use to understand and share our world. For example, Eli R. Green and Eric N. Peterson compiled definitions for common trans and sexuality terms, shared online at Trans-Academics.org.[2] Another helpful resource, *The Gender Book*, was created by a group of individuals in Texas to "educate everyone (for example: doctors, friends, school teachers, family, and individuals who are exploring their gender) about gender." This ebook covers an extensive array of topics including gender identity, masculine women, gender through history, and the transgender umbrella.[3]

Like-minded queers seeking to communicate with one another around the world have been doing a spectacular job of creating our own valuable online spaces. Using our own technology, photography, writers—and often our own funds—we have created online spaces for each other.[4] We built them from the ground up. Sometimes we shared this with our community away from the computer, and sometimes we remained closeted. Perhaps we didn't feel safe being open about our queer selves. Not all of us have the privilege and opportunity to be open about our gender and sexuality depending on how class, race, age, or gender dynamics impact our own life. But we have been able to find others in similar circumstances and share and learn in meaningful and revolutionary ways.

So, why is this poor representation of the queer community still occurring when America has gay parents on TV sitcoms and award-winning music about same-sex marriage? One example of this poor representation is conflating sex with gender—and conflating gender with genitals. This occurs in frustrating ways: A January 2014 episode of the Katie Couric show received extensive backlash when her interview with model Carmen Carerra was sidetracked by questions about Carrera's physical transition and genitalia.[5] During the interview Couric was met with a refusal to respond to such questions by both Carrera and Couric's other guest actress and trans advocate Laverne Cox. Couric explained she aired the segment with the inappropriate questions as a "teachable moment." But many trans rights advocates pushed back, arguing America has had enough teachable moments and it's time for more responsible representation of trans awareness and education. This interaction represents the type of careless and harmful environment many queers find in popular culture representation and conversation about queer identity.

KEY TERMS AND DEFINITIONS

The definitions used here are part of a project by the LGBT Resource Center at the University of California, Riverside. For the complete definitions of those terms listed here, as well as a more comprehensive list of LGBTTSQI terminology, please visit Trans-Academics.org.

BDSM—Bondage, Discipline/Domination, Submission/Sadism, and Masochism. The terms "submission/sadism" and "masochism" refer to deriving pleasure from inflicting or receiving pain, often in a sexual context. The terms "bondage" and "domination" refer to playing with various power roles, in both sexual and social context. These practices are often misunderstood as abusive, but when practiced in a safe, sane, and consensual manner can be a part of healthy sex life.

Bisexual—A person emotionally, physically, and/or sexually attracted to males/men and females/women. This attraction does not have to be equally split among genders and there may be a preference for one gender over others.

Butch—A person who identifies as masculine, whether physically, mentally, or emotionally. Butch is sometimes used as a derogatory term for lesbians, but it can also be claimed as an affirmative identity label.

Femme—Feminine identified person of any gender/sex.

Gay—1. Term used in some cultural settings to represent males who are attracted to males in a romantic, erotic, and/or emotional sense. Not all men who engage in homosexual behavior identify as gay, and as such this label should be used with caution. 2. Term used to refer to the LGBTQI community as a whole, or as an individual identity label for anyone who does not identify as heterosexual.

Gender—One's expressions of masculinity, femininity, or androgyny in words, persons, organisms, or characteristics.

Genderqueer—A gender variant person whose gender identity is neither male nor female, is between or beyond genders, or is some combination of genders.

Gender Binary—The idea that there are only two genders—male/female or man/woman—and that a person must be strictly gendered as either one or the other.

Heteronormativity—The assumption, by individuals or institutional practices, that everyone is heterosexual, and that heterosexuality is superior to homosexuality and bisexuality.

Homophobia—The irrational fear or hatred of homosexuals, homosexuality, or any behavior or belief that does not conform to rigid sex role stereotypes. It is this fear that enforces sexism as well as heterosexism.

Lesbian—Term used to describe female-identified people attracted romantically, erotically, and/or emotionally to other female-identified people.

Queer—1. An umbrella term for a matrix of sexual preferences, orientations, and habits of those who are not members of the exclusively heterosexual and monogamous majority. Queer includes lesbians, gay men, bisexuals, transpeople, intersex persons, and radical sex communities. 2. Sometimes used as a sexual-orientation label instead of bisexual as a way of acknowledging that there are more than two genders to be attracted to, or as a way of stating a non-heterosexual orientation without having to specify to whom they are attracted.

Sex—A medical term designating a certain combination of gonads, chromosomes, external gender organs, secondary sex characteristics, and hormonal balances. Because "sex" is usually subdivided into the binary categories of male and female, this term does not generally account for intersex bodies.

Trans—An abbreviation that is sometimes used to refer to a gender nonconforming person. This use allows a person to state a gender-diverse identity without having to disclose hormonal or surgical status and intentions. This term is sometimes used to refer to the gender-diverse community as a whole. The term trans may include (but is not limited to) those who identify as transgender, transsexual, genderqueer, androgynous, agender, bigender, two spirit, and gender nonconforming.

Transphobia—The irrational fear of those who are gender diverse and/or the inability to deal with gender ambiguity.

FINDING OURSELVES BY FINDING EACH OTHER

For the queer community, as with any other, cultural knowledge is created through sharing our experiences. These stories may be shared through personal blogs, Tumblrs, Twitter accounts, Facebook groups, or other social media outlets with a broad reach and diverse audience. Through reading and writing our shared stories some of us learned how to come out. Some of us learned how to have sex! Some of us learned how to love. And some of us learned how to experience the pain of loss that comes along with this love, especially as part of an ostracized community.

In this chapter, I consider three ways that online communities provide radical new opportunities for social and sexual connection. The most popular independently owned lesbian website, *Autostraddle* is an exciting example of content made by and for queers and the type of community this can create.

Lesbians, and those who love them, have an accessible place to connect with relatable stories of how they live and love. Queer sex–focused websites such as *Sugarbutch Chronicles* and Queerie Bradshaw's blog *The Frisky Feminist* have also changed the way we talk, read, and write about sexuality (and gender), as do the queer fashion website *DapperQ*, *The Handsome Butch Tumblr*, and *Test Shot Tumblr*. Online spaces created by trans individuals for other trans individuals on YouTube, Facebook, and websites such as Ftmguide.org and TQ Nation provide helpful resources for those unable to find supportive communities or reliable information elsewhere.

The *Autostraddle* Community

The founders of *Autostraddle* very clearly state the purpose of the online intentional community when they write, "Autostraddle's girl-on-girl culture is rooted in basic social values and ideals—we want women to feel good about themselves, we want equality and visibility for all marginalized groups and ultimately, we'd like to change the world." As this stated mission of the site exemplifies, the website is a feminist, queer space for writers and readers to create a revolutionary community. After I came out to my family, I wanted to write about LGBTQ politics. I was particularly drawn to the possibility of writing for a site with an accessible, intersectional audience. When I discovered *Autostraddle* in the 2011 Pride issue of *GO Magazine* detailing the year's top 100 "Women We Love" with a feature on the website's CEO/editor-in-chief Riese Bernard, I knew I wanted to be a part of the team.[6]

Unraveling my sexual identity was both exhilarating and unnerving, and my time as a contributing editor at Autostraddle was a big part of that process. Writing for *Autostraddle* opened doors to find confidence in my sexuality I never found anywhere else. I don't think I am alone in this experience: Having a community to firmly point to and say, "See, this is who I am. Let me help you understand us!" is powerful. While working as a contributing editor, our team was awarded the Bloggies Weblog of the Year Award and was a nominee for "Outstanding Blog" in the Annual GLAAD (Gay and Lesbian Alliance Against Defamation) Awards.[7] These are clear signs that beyond all the positive feedback from our readers, our website is having a meaningful and noticed impact on the community. All of this for a website that defines itself as, "an intelligent, hilarious & provocative voice and a progressively feminist online community for a new generation of kickass lesbian, bisexual & otherwise inclined ladies (and their friends)" is no small accomplishment![8]

Bernard argues the Internet has radically changed what it is like to be LGBTQ and explains that having an online presence is "one of the most transformative things to ever happen to our community. We've always been a hungry group of far-flung aspirants desperately hunting down means of connection to other people like us, whether that came in the form of Daughters of Bilitus newsletters, hidden copies of lesbian pulp fiction or queer punk 'zines."[9] *Autostraddle* offers a space for the discussion of lesbian and queer sexuality where queer folks self-define what they want—and how they want it. Bernard continues, "One of the best things we've been able to do on *Autostraddle* recently is to publish a lot of personal essays about more specific intersectional experiences and those really connect with people who didn't know anybody else in their situation, like, 'To Be Queer, Black, and Sick,' 'Sex, Kink, & Cerebral Palsy,' and 'Sober in the City.' "[10] The articles address diverse social and political issues in addition to media criticism, fashion, cooking, and dating advice.

Coming Out in California: A-Camp

Autostraddle's first international queer meet-up beyond the computer screen launched in 2012 with Camp Autostraddle. "We get asked *a lot* about how to meet other queer people and when we finally wrote a post about it . . . the comments exploded with people wanting to host meet-ups in their towns to meet other 'straddlers. It's still our most commented upon post of all time."[11] The launch of A-Camp offered an opportunity for *Autostraddle*'s online readers to gather offline with hundreds of other readers and dozens of the site's staff (including myself), for a summer camp experience full of queer love, poetry, panels, campfires, and dancing in the woods of California at Alpine Meadows. Bernard notes, "After the first A-Camp it was fascinating to see how many campers moved. Like, they moved from where they lived to another city. This happens after every camp: A-campers moving to L.A., Chicago, New York, San Francisco, usually moving in with other A-Campers or moving in nearby. They host parties and camping trips and go to each other's homes for major holidays—it's wild!"[12] The group photos of hundreds of the campers, with their camp counselors, celebrating their community is a tangible piece of the weight and meaning of this experience.

   Autostraddle team member, writer, and activist Carmen Rios explains, "I came of age with the Internet, so it makes sense to me when I call it 'my home.' *Autostraddle*—its staff, its commenters—had always felt like a community to me as a writer, but going to the first A-Camp (and each since its genesis) really drove home what we were doing."[13] This sense of affirmation is incredibly important for those who may, for the first time, be openly identifying as the person they truly are. This is revolutionary when so many people still seem to have trouble understanding our community and continue to make us feel invisible or "abnormal" rather than something whole and all our own. Many readers have said that *Autostraddle* and A-Camp provided their first experience of living their true identity in a caring and loving space.

365-Days-a-Year Queer: The Calendar Projects

To many feminists, what is sexy is ultimately politically aware and one way that *Autostraddle* has accomplished this intersection is through an annual calendar project. For this project, models are styled and posed for a photo shoot for women who love women, by women who love women. Robin Roemer, the photographer for the *Autostraddle* calendar, writes in a post about the selection of models, "We wanted people who really had a sense of what the project was all about, were readers of *Autostraddle*, and were involved in their communities at home. We wanted women bursting with energy and love. Second, we wanted to represent our incredibly diverse community: beauties of all different shapes and styles and backgrounds and gender expressions."[14] Importantly, all posts on Autostraddle about the calendar have a statement asking that only positive and on-topic comments be posted to the story to celebrate the women featured in the calendar.

Other calendar projects intended to meet similar needs for representation in the queer community include a project of the queer collective, bklyn boihood, founded by Genesis Tramaine and Ryann Makenzi Holmes. As their website explains, "Funded entirely through our community, created with artists and designers who are growing with us, this calendar is as much about our self-love as our power of honest expression."[15] The calendar photos of models from all over the continent are available online for the past three years of the project. Another like-minded calendar project out of Ontario, Canada, The Trans Calendar Project raised over $11,000 through a Kickstarter campaign and is a "non for profit collective of trans* identified individuals working for positive social change through art." As their mission statement explains, the goal "is to create an annual calendar as a way to represent ourselves through our own eyes, in all our diversity of identities and narratives. This not only empowers our own trans communities, but serves as a way to raise awareness and combat transphobia."[16] Half of the proceeds from the project go to fund gender transitions of project members.

Sex Blogs, Fashion Tumblrs, and Queer Sex

How we express and pursue sexual and gender identity involves many factors beyond desire. These include socialization, spirituality, and family to name a few. The question, "How do you have sex?" is one many lesbians can't help but respond to with an eye roll. Yet, it is still a legitimate question, just as any sexually active individual would have. This is particularly the case for those who are just becoming sexually active. Queer sex blogs and fashion Tumblrs provide intimate, direct, and detailed answers for curious queers in an approachable, non-judgmental way. A number of websites provide fashion advice for those who are female bodied but desire to dress in more masculine, butch, or transmasculine attire. Some of the most popular of these websites providing an alternative to heteronormative sex and fashion imagery and advice include the website *DapperQ*, *The Handsome Butch Tumblr*, and *The Test Shot Tumblr*.

One project that has provided one of the most radical spaces for discussions about queer sexuality is The Peculiar Kind, a web series that, "candidly explores the lives and experiences of queer women of color with eye-opening and unscripted conversations."[17] Episode four of season one, entitled "Pillow Talk," is an earnest discussion of the women's experiences with lesbian sex and how this relates to stereotypical assumptions about lesbian sex. The episode includes a visit to the NYC sex shop Babeland and also addresses stereotypes about the way people who may present as masculine or feminine enjoy sex and debunks these assumptions with personal accounts from some of the women. One participant explains, "I think it takes a lot of courage to one admit to yourself what you like, and then to admit to others what you like."

Lauren Marie Fleming (aka Queerie Bradshaw), a self-described feminist queer sex blogger, began her website FriskyFeminist.org as an offshoot of the lesbian magazine *Curve*. Her most recent educational guide "Choosing a Harness for Strap-On Sex" is available for free online along with other educational guides offered by the Frisky Feminist Press that is "dedicated to providing accessible, judgment-free, comprehensive sex education."[18] Fleming describes the change in resources online since she came out. She writes, "I like to think of twelve-year-olds Googling what it means to be queer and finding so much more positive, quality, shame-free, information now than I did those years ago back in AOL chatrooms." Fleming continues, "I'm in a serious relationship with a woman I met through online dating and most of my friends come from connections made on social media, including online dating sites, most notably OKCupid. This is a phenomenon I don't see nearly as often in the straight community, who—as the majority—have more chances to meet and identify people of similar lifestyles and interests."[19]

The award-winning *Sugarbutch Chronicles* is a website that offers "dirty stories, essays, advice and journal entries about queer sex, kink, gender and relationships." In describing the project, author Sinclair Sexsmith explains, "Through this project, I used writing as a way to uncover the kind of gender I wanted to present, get into the relationships I was seeking, and have the sex life I craved."[20] In a piece for *Bitch* magazine, researcher Megan Lieff explains, "Widespread access to the Internet has changed our lives, but this is especially true for sexually marginalized communities. Historically, BDSM has existed underground, and often anonymously, which meant it was difficult for folks with these interests to find one another safely."[21] Websites such as *Sugarbutch Chronicles* provide a space to express and understand sex kinks. The "Ask Mr. Sexsmith" feature, where readers can write in with questions for thoughtful feedback and additional comments, provides a platform that allows readers to engage in an open dialogue about power play, masculinity, and feminism. The website offers advice about how to have a healthy and fulfilling sex life as a member of the queer BDSM community. Two of those most popular essays have included "Reconciling Feminism & Sadism" and "How to Come Out as Genderqueer." In a non-stigmatizing or shaming way, essays like this allow individuals in the queer community to be complicated and kinky but also responsible to one another. This is especially important for people who may not know anyone offline to talk to about these topics as they learn how to experiment and grow into their own identity.

MĀHŪ: IN THE MIDDLE

Many cultures have language to describe third gender persons. "Two-spirit" is a modern term used by Native North Americans to describe gender variant individuals. In Tonga, the term *fakaleiti* refers to third gender, or men and boys who identify as female. And the *burrnesha*, a dwindling community in the Albanian Alps, are biological women who live as men. These terms, and many others around the world, are similar to, but not analogous with, Western concepts of transgender.

Mahu is a native Hawaiian term referring to people "in the middle" or those who straddle the male–female binary. Some people use the term "mahu" as disparaging slang. But before white Christian contact in Hawai'i, the word was not pejorative. In pre-contact Hawai'i, mahu were highly respected as teachers, particularly of hula dance and chant. Today, many identify as mahu, rather than as transgender, in part to reclaim the honor of the mahu tradition. Hinaleimoana Wong-Kalu is a well-regarded Native Hawaiian teacher, community leader, and cultural practitioner. She is also the subject of the documentary film *Kumu Hina*, which challenges viewers to rethink assumptions and even the language used to identify and describe those beyond a gender binary. A mahu is a person who straddles the middle of the male and female binary, Hina explains. Mahu "does not define their sexual preference or gender expression, because gender roles, gender expressions and sexual relationships have all been severely influenced by changing times. It is dynamic. It is like life." Asked her opinion about "the trans umbrella," Hina explains this is not a concept she prefers. "LGBT," and other identity terms under the trans umbrella, are constricting labels with cultural and spiritual limitations. These labels are the product of Western linguistic colonialism. While trans people from the continental United States may describe themselves as "born into the wrong body," as Hina says: "I was born into the *right* body."

To find out more about Hinaleimoana Wong-Kalu and the documentary about her life, go to http://kumuhina.com/.

YOU HAVE THE RIGHT TO BE HANDSOME

Learning how to be comfortable with one's own gender presentation is a very public act. Rae Tutera, a founder of *The Handsome Butch* Tumblr and clothier at Bindle & Keep explains, "As I approached menswear with my body, I had to learn to practice dressing braver than I felt, and I also had to remind myself that I had the right to be handsome. I wanted my blog to be a resource to folks learning to do that themselves. Most of my clients have found me through *The Handsome Butch*."[22] The headline on Tutera's Tumblr reads, "In case you ever forget I'm here to remind you that you have the right to be handsome."[23] Speaking to the value of online community, Tutera continues, "Meeting the audience I had imagined might exist for my blog has been an emotionally-charged and uniquely powerful way to participate in and build community. I never imagined that *The Handsome Butch* community would exist offline and face-to-face, and being able to tell each other our stories has been affirming and inspiring for all of us."[24] Another Tumblr project, *The Test Shot*, was launched by Jamie Pallas and LGW with a specific focus on transmasculine style. Pallas explains, "*The Test Shot* aimed to do two things, principally: to create a space to celebrate transmasculine aesthetics and lives through style; and to approach trans-ness and identity in a way that wasn't biographical in the conventional sense. We were a bit tired of chronological trans narratives; style re-arranges the temporal thread of personal trans histories."[25] Also important to Pallas and LGW is representing the multiplicity and complexity of transmasculine identity.

Similarly, the website *DapperQ*'s mission is to be "a visibility project that celebrates the inner and outer beauty of masculine-presenting lesbians, gender-nonconformists and genderqueers, and transmasculine individuals of all colors, shapes, and sizes."[26] The website works to move beyond the fashion focus to provide a safe space, "to document and discuss how gender role expectations, particularly with respect to gender identity and expression, shape who we are as individuals and as a community."[27] *DapperQ* Founder Anita Dolce Vita explains, "Many of our readers experience stress, depression, anxiety, and low self-esteem when they cannot find clothing that affirms their gender identities. Since our desire for sex and our psychological and emotional well-being are interdependent, dressing in a manner that makes us feel attractive and affirms our gender identities plays an integral role in developing a healthy 'sex-esteem' and sex life."[28] For femme-identified lesbians such as myself the experience of femme invisibility is also a daily frustration in a heteronormative society. It wasn't until I found a community of queers who could explain and understand this phenomenon that I was better able to find confidence in the clothing I wear and identity I embrace as a femme.

For many people who begin to question their gender identity or sexual orientation, it can be difficult to know who to talk to, especially considering the lack of knowledge by many professionals about healthcare and well-being for trans and queer individuals. "I can say with certainly that most of what I learned about transitioning physically (surgeries, hormones, etc.) was learned online," explains Andrew Spiers, co-coordinator of the Trans-Health Information Project at GALAEI, who primarily used Facebook groups for trans individuals, TQ Nation (transqueernation.com), Susan's Place (susans.org), and Instagram as resources. The website Ftmguide.org is another commonly accessed website and is "intended to provide information on topics of interest to female-to-male (FTM, F2M) transmen, and their friends and loved ones."[29] Some of the topics covered on the website fall under the categories testosterone, presenting as male, grooming and surgery, and common concerns for those making female-to-male transitions. Spiers adds, "The primary care physician I was seeing in 2010 and 2011 didn't know anything about trans folks or differently gendered individuals and I ended up having to educate her about a lot of things I had learned online."

Author Margaret Talbot writes about transgender youth who use You-Tube as a place to find community and express identity during, before, and after transition explaining, "Often shot in poster-covered bedrooms or in the family basement, on wavering Webcams, they range from diary-like accounts to pop-ballad accompanied montages and practical tutorials on subjects like makeup for MTFs (male-to-females) or binding (compressing breasts) for FTMs."[30] For Spiers and others, online trans resources prove fundamental to navigating their transition and meeting their health care needs.

Yet for all its advantages, there are limits to what online resources can provide. First, there are issues of online safety. Internet bullying has real and detrimental consequences. Second, online spaces should be a supplement to, not a solution for, offline community. Living online runs the risk of unintentionally closeting, isolating, or segmenting queer people. All the same, these online spaces offer a new capacity among queer communities for connection in deep, meaningful, and radical ways.

Online communities are more accessible, intersectional spaces than those available to queer and trans people in the past. With online communities there is a greater ability to be inclusive regarding age, race, and class—though this requires a constant commitment and attention to criticism from both inside and outside the community. By moving our communities out of closets and bars, and online and into the open where a myriad of voices can be heard, we create a broader more authentic spectrum of the experiences our queer community shares.

Photo 12.1 Transgender Umbrella page from *The Gender Book* © thegenderbook.com 2014. Reprinted with permission.

DISCUSSION QUESTIONS

•   Has your understanding of sex or gender changed since reading this chapter? Do you see yourself represented in the media, in textbooks, and in information available at your local health clinic?

•   After reading this chapter which aspects of sex and gender addressed do you know the least about and where would you look for more resources?

•   How do you think communities you are a part of (school, sports, civil society organizations, local health care services like doctors and dentists) work to incorporate the topics addressed by these revolutionary online communities?

•   Did you know there were so many helpful resources online for the queer community? How can these resources become more widespread and accessible to more people?

•   Where do you see the online queer community going from here?

NOTES

1. As a cisgender lesbian, I prefer the pronouns "she" and "her" for myself and strive in all of my quotes to honor the pronoun usage preferred by the people I'm quoting. I use "we" and "us" to express my experience as part of a queer community, and hope I speak to the experience of many, but understand I am limited by my own perspective

and point of view. Another important term in this chapter is the word "queer," which both liberates and complicates the gender binary of male and female. How LGBTQ (lesbian, gay, bisexual, transgender, queer) signifiers are used to define sex and gender is very personal. A helpful way of distinguishing between sex and gender is to understand the biological and psychological aspects of being male or female as sex, and the socially constructed roles that express this sex as gender. With this in mind, it's easier to understand that, for a transgender person, transitioning is not just about genitals. Queer is the complicated space between, around, and throughout the two categories of male/female, masculine/feminine, and how we live this experience.

2. "Trans and Sexuality Terminologies," *Trans-Academics.org*, http://trans-academics.org/trans_and_sexuality_termi.

3. *The Gender Book*, http://www.thegenderbook.com/.

4. For instance, an *Autostraddle* Indiegogo fundraising campaign in 2012 to fund an upgrade and redesign for the site led to over $116,000 in donations. http://www.indiegogo.com/projects/autostraddle-the-actual-website.

5. Carmen Carrera, interviewed by Katie Couric, "Carmen Carrera's Quest to Become a Victoria's Secret Angel," http://katiecouric.com/videos/carmen-carreras-quest-to-become-a-victorias-secret-angel.

6. Kat Long (ed.), "100 Women We Love: Class of 2011," *GO Magazine*, June 17, 2011, http://www.gomag.com/article/100_women_we_love2/16.

7. *Autostraddle* won the 2012 Bloggies Weblog of the Year Award and was also nominated for "Outstanding Blog" in the Annual GLAAD Awards in both 2013, when I was a contributing editor, and again in 2014.

8. "About," *Autostraddle*, http://www.autostraddle.com/about/.

9. Riese Bernard, interview by Jamie J. Hagen, email, July 15, 2014.

10. Ibid.

11. Ibid.

12. Ibid.

13. Carmen Rios, interview by Jamie J. Hagen, email, January 31, 2014.

14. Robin Roemer, "Autostraddle Calendar Girls 2014: Cynthia is Miss January," *Autostraddle*, January 4, 2013, http://www.autostraddle.com/autostraddle-calendar-girls-2014-cynthia-is-miss-january-152867.

15. "The Calendar / 2014," *Brooklyn Boihood*, http://bklynboihood.com/bbh-calendar/.

16. "The Trans Calendar Project," *Indiegogo*, last modified October 10, 2013, http://www.indiegogo.com/projects/the-trans-calendar-project-2014.

17. "The Peculiar Kind: A Web Series & Doc," http://www.thepeculiarkind.com/episodes.

18. "Educational Guides," *Frisky Feminist*, http://www.friskyfeminist.com/guides/.

19. Lauren Marie Fleming, interview by Jamie J. Hagen, email, January 10, 2014.

20. "About," *Sugarbutch Chronicles*, http://www.sugarbutch.net/about/.

21. Megan Lieff, "Safe Words: The History of Anti-Abuse Activism in BDSM," *Bitch Magazine*, Fall 2013, http://bitchmagazine.org/article/safe-words.

22. Rae Tutera, interview by Jamie J. Hagen, email, January 29, 2014.

23. "The Handsome Butch," http://thehandsomebutch.tumblr.com.

24. Ibid.

25. Jamie Pallas, interview by Jamie J. Hagen, email, January 25, 2014.

26. "About," *DapperQ*, http://www.dapperq.com/about/.

27. Ibid.

28. Anita Dolce Vita, interview by Jamie J. Hagen, email, January 31, 2014.

29. "Hudson's FTM Resource Guide," http://ftmguide.org.

30. Margaret Talbot, "Being Seen: Video Diaries of Transgender Youth," *New Yorker*, March 12, 2013, http://www.newyorker.com/news/news-desk/being-seen-video-diaries-of-transgender-youth.

DIGITAL INDISCRETIONS

Infidelity in the Age of Technology

Ebony A. Utley

Digital indiscretions are infidelities aided by technology. As people reach out to each other through new technology, new types of relationships and new types of relationship conflicts occur. Researchers Katherine Hertline, Joseph Wetchler, and Fred Piercy define infidelity thusly: "At its very core, infidelity refers to any behavior that breaks the contract that two people have with each other. What is especially complex about the broad definition of infidelity is that two different people in the same relationship might have different ideas about what represents infidelity or constitutes an affair."[1] In addition to the normal differences of opinion about what constitutes infidelity, couples may find it even more difficult to agree about what constitutes infidelity given the possibilities created by technology. For example, there are apps that play fake background sounds to help corroborate a lie, apps with disappearing or self-destructing messages like Snapchat and Wickr, dating sites for married people such as Ashley Madison and Victoria Milan, revenge sites like Don't Date Him Girl and Cheaterville, as well as a plethora of GPS and spying sites to keep tabs on a partner.

It is difficult to be clear about unacceptable relationship behaviors when the opportunities for connection and betrayal escalate so quickly. Is it acceptable to reconnect with exes via Facebook when you are in a relationship? How much liking on someone else's page is too much? Under what circumstances should you share passwords with a partner? Is there a difference between a private infidelity that only the parties involved know about and a public infidelity that plays out via social media? What happens when a betrayed partner can stalk an affair partner on social media? How much spying is too much spying? The age of technology raises serious questions about the boundaries between public and private as well as commitment and infidelity. This chapter suggests answers to some of these questions through the stories of women who experienced digital indiscretions.

METHOD

As the research shows, men are socialized to be sexual and women are socialized to keep silent about their sexual experiences and desires; men's infidelities are normalized as "men being men" while women's infidelities are policed by strong social shaming consequences.[2] My research focuses on the lesser-publicized aspects of infidelity by interviewing women who had been cheated on, women who cheated, and women who were the "other woman." I conducted 110 interviews with women across the United States using snowball sampling. Just as a snowball gathers more snow as it rolls down a hill, interview participants increasingly came to me through word of mouth, social media, and two Los Angeles talk radio programs that gave my number on air when I spoke on their shows about infidelity. As per the agreement that I made with my university's Institutional Review Board, an approval organization that ensures no researcher harms a human subject, interested interviewees contacted me and we either met at a location of their choice or spoke on the phone. Each woman chose her own pseudonym and, to further protect her privacy, I omitted all geographical references. I used an open-ended interview protocol that asked each woman to define infidelity and then tell me about her experiences with infidelity. Many women told multiple stories during interviews that lasted an average of approximately sixty minutes.

The data for this study includes fifty-five interviews where women who were cheated on, were cheaters, and/or were the other woman mentioned technology. Because I did not ask about technology, the scope of these references is wide and ranges from technology used to cheat to the technology used to catch a cheater. There were eighty-two incidents of being caught in a digital indiscretion, which totals approximately 1.5 incidents per interview. Discoveries aided by technology included, in order of frequency: phones (texts, pictures, calls, call history, etc.), websites, email, Facebook, and other social media. The most popular sites that revealed digital indiscretion were dating websites. The most frequently mentioned email providers were Gmail, Yahoo, and Hotmail. In addition to Facebook, the mentioned social media sites were MySpace, YouTube, Twitter, and Instagram. Other technologies used to cheat or to discover cheating included MapQuest, PayPal, Skype, the iPhone, iPad, and Xbox. The interviewees' ages ranged from 21 to 60; the average age was 35. The women self-described their sexual orientation and race: Forty-six (84 percent) identified as heterosexual, four identified as heteroflexible, three identified as lesbian, and two identified as bisexual.[3] Thirty-one (56 percent) women identified as African American, fourteen identified as white, five identified as Latina, two identified as Asian, and three identified as biracial (one, black and white; two, white and Latina).

Although qualitative research is cemented as a legitimate social science method, the veracity of interview data is often questioned. What if an interviewee is lying? What if lying is not intentional but the memories are inaccurate? Many people who agree to share their stories with a stranger are people who have given their narratives careful consideration and may have even crafted the story in their favor prior to agreeing to participate. Others may be reticent to tell the entire story about their biggest betrayal or their deepest regret. Finally, these stories only consider one perspective; and infidelity, by definition, includes at least three.[4] While these are each reasonable concerns, this research focuses on validating these women's stories and not verifying whether their stories are true.[5]

Using methods associated with grounded theory,[6] I read each interview transcript and coded it for emergent themes. I noted the number of times certain incidents regarding technology recurred. The numerical data reporting how many times someone was caught via text message, however, was less interesting than the behavioral data that provided insight into the relationship between technology and infidelity. Thus, this chapter is less about the technology used to cheat—or to get caught cheating—and more about how behaviors are shaped by the role that technology now plays in infidelity.[7] The five emergent themes of connection, obsession, hateration, humiliation, and vindication focus on women's stories that explain how infidelity in the age of technology shifted or shaped their own behavior.[8]

ANALYSIS

Connection

It is easier to connect with people in the age of technology. Technology relationship maintenance is managed using phone, text, video chats, social haptic networks, and social media.[9] Geographic distance is no longer a reason to reject a potential relationship. Long-distance relationships are not as convenient as the partner who lives a fifteen-minute drive away, but these relationships are no longer as inconvenient as when letters were the primary means of communication.

Vanessa's unfaithful boyfriend was in the military. She described their constant communication by explaining, "We talked on the phone two to three times a day. We were communicating on Facebook. We traded emails, so we were constantly in touch and in each other's lives, and for someone still to be leading that type of life outside of the life you think they're leading . . ."

As Vanessa discovered, and as another interviewee, Evelyn, counted on, maintaining a secret relationship is also made easier by technology. Evelyn's lover lived in another state. Since they were both married they relied on phone, email, and text to sustain a connection that was only consummated once a year. When XeenaSummer ended a sexual relationship with her married best friend, she avoided seeing him even though they lived in the same town. But through Google chat and texting every morning five days a week, her affair partner sustained a connection beyond just friendship. XeenaSummer explained, "He'll throw a flirt dagger here and there, to kind of like make me aware that 'I'm still attracted to you some kind of way' or that 'I'll still do you,' but he hasn't asked, like, 'so can I go to your place?' "

Technology obviously plays an impactful role in relationship maintenance with or without infidelity. The ubiquity of technology, however, makes its role in relationship initiation even more pertinent to infidelity. The interviewees recounted several stories of partners' digital indiscretions via online relationship initiation. Dawn's husband initiated "an inappropriate Facebook phone affair" with a woman he knew thirty years ago in high school but was always afraid to approach. Other husbands had profiles on PlentyOfFish.com and AshleyMadison.com. Lassie's husband and Fifi's boyfriend both hid their Facebook activity from their partners. India's husband met his second wife on MySpace while he was still married to India.

Women also initiated online relationships. The possibility that Charlotte would leave her husband became even more certain after she reconnected with a friend on Facebook who is now her fiancé. Ebony decided her husband's affair was no reason to break up their family, but she admitted to being unhappy until she discovered the computer.

> So my niece turns me on to the computer. Mind you I don't know nothing about a computer. She tells me, 'Auntie you outta see on this computer. You can go on these sites and you can do this and you can do that.' So one day I go over to her house and I'm looking at her computer and they have this site called Unhappily Married. I'm like, oh, ok. So she shows me how the thing goes and we're doing it. And I'm like, 'Aahh, this is fun.' I'm just enjoying it. So, next thing you know, I want a computer.

Even after being caught by her husband, Ebony changed her screen name and was back in the online dating and cybersex game.

Technology not only helps people meet to cheat, but it can also expedite interactions and disassociate those same interactions from in-person constraints. Sasha noted how texting accelerated her relationship with an older married mentee. She explained how their casual interactions about common interests became flirtatious, "I really attribute [texting] to both of our boldness, and how it progressed. Things that I never would have said. Things that he never would have said except it could be said in a text message." Sadie's long-term relationship with a married man also began with texting. She admitted, "I didn't even think about the wife. It didn't even cross my mind." Since texting was their primary means of communication, Sadie's partner's wife was not part of her life.

Ishtar had the exact opposite experience. Ishtar was in an open relationship and her husband would help her take sexy photos for her lover. Yet Ishtar watched her lover's very different life unfold on Facebook. She said, "By being on Facebook I got to see his wife, I got to see his kids, and I started to feel really guilty because my marriage was solid. I was being honest with my husband. He knew everything and encouraged everything and this man that I was basically in an affair with was lying to his family." Ishtar confessed that his wife "wasn't real until I made that connection with him on Facebook." Because of this insight that was only made possible through social media, Ishtar decided to end the relationship.

Obsession

The use of technology is not only about whether one can and will be unfaithful. A betrayed partner is also in the position to decide how much she wants to know, and technology plays a prominent role in this. Some women do not want to know any details about their partner's infidelity; some women want to know everything. The discovery options aided by technology are vast—cell phones, caller ID, voicemail, email, PayPal, bank records, digital cameras, instant messages, texts, MapQuest, and social media profiles including (but not limited to) Facebook, Twitter, and Instagram.

Some discoveries among the women I interviewed were accidental, but most were the result of a focused and intentional obsession with discovering information about a partner's affair. Irene acknowledged, "For a number of years I lost my mind and started going through every email, every file, every underneath." Pauline noticed that her boyfriend of two years was leaving his phone face down and liking smiley faces that women posted on his Facebook pictures. One night while he was sleeping, she went through his phone, because as she said, "I turn into an FBI agent when all this stuff happens."

Several women admitted that were not proud of their actions. Janet confessed to stalking her boyfriend's other girlfriend on social media—mostly Instagram. "I was literally stalking. I'm not even going to lie. I'm checking and I was like, 'What are you doing?' It's consuming some hours of my day because every hour I'm checking. Is she saying something? Are they together? Are they around each other? I have to stop." Ironically, Janet did not have a Twitter or an Instagram account; she would log onto friends' accounts to gather information. Alesia conceded to going too far while confirming her boyfriend's infidelity when she said, "And then another time, there was this girl who left a message on his cell phone. I called that girl, which is so out of character for me. I hated that! I'm calling these girls asking what the dude is doing and stuff like that. I hated that. Because that's the girl I always tried to avoid being. Looking through cell phone bills and bank accounts; he took me out of my element and I didn't like that."[10]

Linda's husband was a serial cheater. She perused cell phone records and financial statements, called hotels, searched his computer and iPad, and read messages. She even emailed one of his mistresses.

> So I did something that's not very nice. I created a fake Gmail account that sounded just like it would be his Gmail account and I emailed her and I said, 'Hey, what's going on? This is the best way to contact me right now. How're you doing?' She writes back, 'Oh I feel like somebody that's lost her best friend. I've missed you so much and not being able to talk to you is just awful. You can't live like this. Your wife is crazy. Just go get a disposable cell phone. Go to the pay phone if they still have them. Do anything. I have to talk to you.' And so then I started asking questions. I made up questions that I supposed he would ask, like 'What do you want from us?' And she said, 'I want to be walking down the beach hand in hand, growing old together but I know that's not what you're telling me is going to happen.' That made me feel sad. I probably hurt her.

Linda admitted, "I have a PhD in each of his affairs." Later in the interview she mused, "I think I got addicted to the hunt, the hunt for information." A hunt that was made possible by the same technology her husband used to be unfaithful.

Hateration

Technology often reveals information about the affair partner that may have otherwise remained unknown. Hateration—an intense disdain for someone— is what can happen when the primary partner receives digital information about the secondary partner.

India expressed hateration towards her husband's affair partner who he met on MySpace and eventually married.

> I don't want to label somebody, but a lot can be said about somebody that goes to the Internet to get their spouse. I can understand being too busy. I can understand dedicated dating systems that you actually have to have somebody helping you try to find somebody. That's fine, but when you're just openly putting stuff out there on MySpace and Black People Meet. It wasn't Black People Meet—what was that other website called—some black—I don't know. Anyways, she had like three or four of them where she openly was, 'I'm looking for a husband. I'm taking applications for a husband.'

For some of the women interviewed, hateration developed from looking at social media profiles and was based on the affair partner's appearance. Janet described her boyfriend's other girlfriend.

> She is real vain as far as her looks. Everything is a picture. You would think she's a superstar the way she'd post stuff on Twitter, Facebook, and now Instagram. Everything is me, me, me, me, me, me. I know this because I'm kind of like a low-key stalker. I've gotten better because I can go like days, even weeks without wondering what she is doing or if she's around here or if they're together or something like that. But that's what it came out of. So it had gotten to the point where I knew exactly all her flaws. She's knock-kneed, something wrong with her eye, [she's] a mixed chick, [and her] hair doesn't grow; usually mixed girls have nice hair. It got really bad. I knew when she would be talking subliminal.[11] She was talking about him. Just little stuff she was real, real, real, real put it in your face-type chick not knowing that I would see it or know about it.

The visual nature of social media lends itself to judgment. People put themselves out there to be seen, but everything about an affair partner is more harshly judged by a betrayed primary partner.

When FiFi saw the "slut girls" her boyfriend was interacting with on Facebook, she immediately worried about her sexual health. She said, "I was like 'hell no I don't want to have anything wrong with me' so I went and got checked out so everything was clear thankfully." When pressed to define a "slut girl," FiFi explained, "Just the way that they were dressed. They had their little club outfit on or they take their picture of themselves in the mirror. They don't even have people take pictures of them; they are the ones that take them. Stuff like that. Heavy makeup, their hair done, and their heels, and their nice little club-going-out outfit. I don't know. I guess I can't call them a slut because they didn't know he had a girlfriend so it's not their fault." As she explained, FiFi realized that she was harshly judging other women because of her boyfriend's behavior and not theirs. Social media leaves us with impressions and not necessarily accurate representations, but even when what we see is not true, knowing that other people think it is true, can be a profound form of humiliation.

Humiliation

Discovering a partner's affair can be embarrassing. Women are apt to blame themselves. The shame, silence, and insecurity that develops from being cheated on is commonplace.[12] What may be even more humiliating, however, is having your privacy broadcast without your permission. Several of the women interviewed told stories of feeling devastated from having to involuntarily share their intimate moments with another woman.

Melanie was upset that even though the father of her daughter was there for her birth, he celebrated their first baby's arrival with his other woman by cell phone. Melanie said, "When my daughter was born in May, he stayed with me for the four days that I was in the hospital, but he used to take pictures of her and like text and text and text. And later I found out that he was texting the girl pictures of my daughter, and that when he used to go smoke outside of the hospital he would call her." Melanie was unaware at the time that their private celebration as new parents was being shared.

In hindsight, Anne's happy memories of her thirtieth wedding anniversary and a romantic vacation became tainted when she realized her husband shared them with his affair partner. She recalled telling him, "You promised that you would call me. You forgot, but yet during this romantic weekend you did not forget to call your mistress."

Sharing intimate moments with strangers can be humiliating and so can sharing those intimate moments with your entire social circle. Janet was ready to fight her boyfriend's girlfriend. She justified her anger by telling the other woman, "These are the consequences of sneaking around with someone else's man and putting it all over the social network for everybody to see." The infraction was not just cheating but its publicity. Sarah lamented about her boyfriend's infidelity: "I think it would've been less painful had I known about her, had he been straightforward with his feelings. Instead he tried to hide it. I had to find out through Facebook and my cousin, and it was very humiliating for me."

Hope was humiliated by her husband in multiple ways:

> The week that we got married I saw on some social networking site some girl mentioning him in a status. I don't know if it was Facebook or MySpace, but she mentioned him in a status saying that she was in love with him and I was thinking 'What in the world?' So I sent her a message. I go, 'You talking about this same person?' And she said 'Yes. That's my boyfriend.' And I said 'That's crazy. We just married last week.' And she said, 'Well I don't believe you.' So I emailed her some of the photos and she said, 'Well he was just over here,' and I was just horrified. I had a big wedding and I felt like how stupid would I be to go back and tell my parents and everybody else that a week in and he has somebody else.

Hope went on to describe her husband's disregard for her privacy.

> I think the worst part was I saw where he had been reaching out to some of my Facebook friends. They were people that I had gone to college with. He didn't know them and he was reaching out to people on my Facebook friend list. That's how he had been talking to a girl that had

lived in my freshman dorm. They had been talking about me and he had been lying. This girl wasn't really a friend of mine but she knew me and she wasn't somebody I wanted in my business but she is somebody that's okay enough to be a Facebook friend. I saw where he had just told her all kinds of stuff. He told her the reason we weren't having sex was because I was getting a gut and he told her that I had a drinking problem, which wasn't true. I guess he was just setting that up to be his reason things didn't work out. I don't know why he did it.

A public affair is devastating for private people. For many women, there is nothing more private than their sexual lives. Once this private information is made public through technology in general, and social media in particular, the genie cannot be returned to the bottle. There are, however, subtle ways that a woman scorned on social media can be vindicated.

STI TESTING: THERE'S AN APP FOR THAT

Jessica Ross

Healthvana is a downloadable phone app that allows users to locate the closest STI test centers, privately and securely hold their sexual health records, and then share this info with whomever they choose. Excited to hear about this new technology promoting sexual safety and pleasure in the twenty-first century, we arranged an interview with the CEO and founder of Healthvana, Ramin Bastani, to learn more.

Jessica Ross: What motivated you to create Healthvana?
Ramin Bastani: After being slapped in the face for asking a woman about her sexual health status, the app was created to allow people to verify someone else's STD status in a way that was hopefully a little less awkward and unreliable. [The app was originally called Hula; the name was changed to Healthvana in 2014.]

Even if people say that they have been tested, it doesn't really matter because they may be lying or they may not even know what their real status is. Whenever you get tested, the doctor generally says, "Hey if you don't hear from us within two weeks, no news is good news" and then you never actually get your results. Sadly, we know of a lot of people who test positive but fall through the cracks and never actually find out. We think Healthvana makes for a more meaningful and reliable conversation in a fun and appealing way. It's funny though, it didn't take long for us to realize that the biggest problem we are actually solving has nothing to do with STDs or HIV, it actually just has to do with empowering patients to get their medical records because that is honestly the hardest thing to do. The rest we can take care of once their records come in, but ensuring patients receive their records is the biggest challenge that Healthvana is solving.

JR: How does Healthvana change up the conversation regarding STIs between current/potential sexual partners?

RB: There are two ways Healthvana changes the conversations, and the first one is online. About 50 million people are dating online in the United States. People can initiate this conversation about STD and HIV status online with potential partners and people can also share their personal medical information online with a partner if they want. At some point, a lot of these same people will actually get tested and put on their dating profile that they have been tested, but there is no way of knowing if that is really true. Healthvana only displays the records from verified test centers and doctors. So, in this online context, we really help because people can have this conversation before they even meet up. We are also useful for the people who use the apps like Tinder and Grindr that are geolocated because on Healthvana you can see when people were last tested and decide who you would like to hook up with. If you had a choice, would you rather hook up with the person who was tested a month ago, or nine months ago?

The second way Healthvana helps change up the conversation is in person. We hear stories all the time about people saying things IRL like, "Unzip me," which refers to a feature on the Healthvana app that appears when someone shares their profile with you. "Unzip me" has become an easy and fun icebreaker into the conversation of STI and HIV status. Users have shared stories with us that it becomes this sexy conversation-starter of "I'll show you mine, if you show me yours." At the same time, this promotes more testing especially if one person hasn't been tested recently. This feature also means that partners are able to show each other medically accurate records.

JR: Do you think Healthvana helps combat the stigma associated with positive test results?

RB: That's a good question. . . . We do know that a lot more people talk about it, especially if they are dating online. That's our hope and intent. We are trying to create more discussion even if that includes positive test results, which is great because [it's important that people] know their status. You've got to keep in mind that a lot of STDs are curable or manageable. If you are HIV positive, you can actually share information about your viral load, which indicates whether or not you're taking your medication. If you take your medication every day, your viral load can become undetectable and the odds of transmitting the virus can be greatly reduced. This still sounds terrifying to some people, but others think this sharing this information is a huge move towards de-stigmatizing positive HIV. HIV is not at all a death sentence anymore; it is a chronic condition that is totally manageable.

Visit www.healthvana.com to learn more about Healthvana and to create your free profile today. You can download Healthvana onto iPhones from the app store, or use Healthvana's mobile optimized website from any other smartphone.

Vindication

In the past, infidelity was more difficult to prove—until it met technology. In these interviews, women found creative ways to prove their suspicions of infidelity, specifically when their partners refused to confess. When Hope, mentioned in the previous section, found evidence of her husband's inappropriate behavior on Facebook, she told herself, "I have to print it out so if I ever change my mind or he makes up a really good lie I can go back and look at it and remember why this won't work out." When her husband continued to lie, she showed the printed messages to his parents. She recalled, "It wasn't until probably my fourth instalment of emails, pictures, and video that I sent [to] his parents and they were over there crying, that he said 'Okay, I did it. Just stop sending stuff to my parents.' " Hope admitted that she did not want to send so much proof to his parents, but she desperately needed them to know the truth.

Hope's decision to print her evidence was an opportunity to create physical proof of his digital indiscretions. Lassie also printed all of the sexual communications between her husband and the other women that she found in his email. She said, "I printed them out and I just left them—I wanted to really screw with him, so I left them on the floor with my engagement ring on top of them and then left the apartment and waited for him to come home."

Whereas Hope and Lassie printed the virtual evidence so they would have physical proof, Pauline engaged in what she called "a whole different game of technology" when she found virtual evidence of her boyfriend's emotional affair.

> I screen shot all the messages to myself and I had thought about posting them to Facebook. I thought, 'No, I'm not going to be public like that, then I'd be one of those messy girls. At my age, that's not okay.' So I screen shot them to myself . . .

I had seen the girls' numbers [and] I had all their numbers in my phone. I had the screen shot text messages and when I woke him up I'm like 'Why were you saying–?' And then I said the woman's name. I'm like, 'Why were you telling her this when you–?' I just said everything that I had found and I was like, 'Before you say anything, don't try to deny it because I've screen shot everything to my phone and I have their numbers.'

Pauline didn't need physical evidence. She used technology for her record keeping.

Like Grace and Pauline, Teah considered going public with videotape proof that her husband was having sex with strippers and prostitutes. She said, "I had dreams of sending those sex tapes to his mama and his family and friends. I was going to call it our special day and it was going to be him fucking a whore or somebody like that in his car or something like that." She never did because thinking about it made her feel worse.

Irene confessed, "If I have any regrets in my life it would have been the amount of energy that I put in, just cause I always just felt like I wanted him to admit it. I wanted to know the truth. I was partially insane during those years cause that's all I would do sometimes, just go through stuff, tear up, and call numbers."

In contrast to Teah and Irene, Maria found a way to feel vindicated once she tricked her husband into confessing. She used a calling card that would display an untraceable number on the caller ID and then she called their house. She told her husband that a woman with a high-pitched voiced called claiming, "He's mine. You need to let him go so I can have him." With the assistance of the phone card, she convinced her husband that she received this call over and over until he confessed that there was another woman. In the absence of a willing confession, vindication made possible by technology is one step women may choose in beginning the healing process after infidelity.

CONCLUSION

Infidelity in the age of technology means the possibilities for connection, obsession, hateration, humiliation, and vindication are greater than they were before technology became such an integral aspect of infidelity. A private indiscretion gone digital has a permanence and a viral capability that was previously unmatched. Al Cooper, author of *Sex and the Internet*, identified "accessibility, affordability, and anonymity" as three factors that can distinguish Internet infidelity from traditional infidelity.[13] The ability to get online any time for free, and to interact with people without them knowing more than you share with them, makes infidelity irresistibly sexy to some.

The issue, however, is not just how people cheat but how people respond to cheating. What if a woman connects with an affair partner online who seems perfect on phone, text, and email, but is actually a dangerous, abusive, and violent man? What happens when an obsession or hateration turns into stalking and threatening? There is only a thin line separating hateration and humiliation from cyberbullying and slut-shaming. What if someone goes public with vindicating evidence that turns out to be false? What happens when vindication is violence? What happens when the offending partner turns violent against the person seeking vindication?

The social implications of infidelity in the age of technology are greater than interpreting the actions of a partner who turns the phone face down or refuses to share social media passwords.

Technology shapes infidelity by providing new tools for initiating and maintaining the secrecy of affairs. Infidelity shapes technology by creating tools that more easily facilitate an ancient indiscretion in our twenty-first-century lives. Understanding the feedback loop between infidelity and technology means understanding our new sexual selves.

DISCUSSION QUESTIONS

• How do you think technology has changed or impacted relationships? Has it opened up new possibilities that never existed before?
• What has been your experience using technology to engage in intimate relationships?
• Do you think technology has made it easier for people to cheat on their significant partners?
• Do you think it was ethical for some of the women to access their partners phones, profiles, and personal records?
• What are your reactions to hearing so many women tell similar stories about how they caught their cheating partner and how they reacted to the indiscretion?

NOTES

1. Katherine M. Hertline, Joseph L. Wetchler, and Fred P. Piercy, "Infidelity: An Overview," *Journal of Couple & Relationship Therapy* 4, no. 2–3 (2005): 6.
2. Jack De Stefano and Monica Oala, "Extramarital Affairs: Basic Considerations and Essential Tasks in Clinical Work," *Family Journal* 16, no. 1 (2008): 14.
3. Heteroflexible is defined as a person who primarily identifies as heterosexual but occasionally participates in homosexual activity.
4. An exception would be in cases where people consider porn to be infidelity. In this instance, a third person is not necessarily directly involved.

5. Raquel K. Bergen, "Interviewing Survivors of Marital Rape: Doing Feminist Research on Sensitive Topics," in *Researching Sensitive Topics*, eds. Claire M. Renzetti and Raymond M. Lee (Newbury Park, CA: Sage, 1993), 197–211.

6. Kathy Charmaz, *Constructing Grounded Theory: A Practical Guide through Qualitative Analysis* (Thousand Oaks, CA: Sage, 2006).

7. For this reason, the diversity of the sample is not entirely reflected in the analysis. Women who simply mentioned the use of infidelity are not quoted in the subsequent section.

8. Although the research data includes queer women, there are no queer stories in the analysis because they do not address changes in behavior.

9. Social haptic networks allow individuals to send "touch messages." Signals are sent through technology to elicit physical sensations. Frixion.me is one example that allows individuals to touch and have sex at any distance.

10. Interestingly, Alesia accomplished her sleuthing using public and work computers because she did not own one.

11. A "subliminal" is a slang term for a social media message clearly received by the intended recipient and her/his social circle even though that recipient was not tagged or mentioned in the original message.

12. Ebony Utley, "Infidelity as a Form of Intimate Partner Abuse," unpublished article.

13. Al Cooper, ed., *Sex and the Internet: A Guidebook for Clinicians* (New York: Brunner-Routledge, 2002).

CONSENSUAL SEXTING AND CHILD PORNOGRAPHY

Legal and Cultural Controversies[1]

Lara Karaian

News media, mainstream books, and popular culture across North America have pronounced girls the disempowered and duped victims of the "pornification" of a generation and the rise of sexualized cyberculture.[2] The teenager's world, we are told, is "steeped in highly sexualized messages" as well as "extreme pornography . . . hit songs and music videos [which] promote stripping and sexting"[3]—the practice of sending or posting sexually suggestive text messages and images, including nude or semi-nude photographs, via cell phones or over the Internet. A growing body of research on sexting highlights the distinctions between consensual and nonconsensual sexting, and considers its potential influences and effects within our contemporary context.[4] Consensual sexting is predominantly framed, however, as a risky consequence of childhood sexualization. Tween and teenage girls are purportedly being mal-socialized to deny their natural "innocence," to prematurely embrace and express the characteristics of porn culture, and to engage in "self-sexualization" in the form of sexting.[5] For instance, the Canadian documentary *Sext Up Kids: How Children Are Becoming Hypersexualized*[6] warns of Western mainstream media's sexualization of young people and its negative effects on girls' self-esteem and their sexual health. The film also advances the claim that hypersexualization works in conjunction with easy access to Internet pornography to allegedly force teenage girls to expose their semi/naked bodies using digital technology, "often with grave consequences." M. Gigi Durham describes this cultural landscape as one tainted by what she calls the "Lolita Effect"—the apparently "distorted and delusional set of myths about girls' sexuality that circulates widely in our culture and throughout the world, that works to limit, undermine, and restrict girls' sexual progress."[7] Durham draws on the tragic and infamous 12-year-old love interest of Humbert Humbert, the pedophile narrator of Vladimir Nabokov's 1955 classic novel, *Lolita*, to symbolize mainstream culture's production of "prostitots"—hypersexualized girls who, Durham alleges, are being harmed in large numbers for having become "involved in a sphere of fashion, images, and activities that encourage them to flirt with a decidedly grown-up up eroticism and sexuality."[8]

Given this cultural context, the mobilization of laws in the name of girls' safety comes as little surprise. The most recent form of this protectionism criminalizes teens who consensually sext by using child pornography laws to prosecute offenses. However, this legal strategy raises serious concern.[9] In this chapter, I argue that hegemonic legal discourse regarding sexting—including laws that frame sexting as child pornography—employ a "mechanism of censorship" that circumscribes what Judith Butler describes as "the social parameters of speakable discourse, of what will and will not be admissible in public discourse."[10] In other words, legal strategies to address sexting that use child pornography legislation as a solution, paradoxically reify teenage girls as sexual objects, to be seen and not heard.

Part of the solution I propose requires centering girls' narratives in this debate. Doing so makes visible the extent to which pleasure and power may inform and be derived from girls' decisions to sext. Using girls' own perspectives on digital sexual expression, this chapter explores first-hand perspectives on sexting as well as the potential harms of the hyperbolic cultural and legal responses in the United States. At issue is the broadening of criminal law's punitive powers, the over-breadth of American child pornography laws, as well as their over-zealous application by American prosecutors.

CULTURAL CONSTRUCTIONS OF THE SEXTING SCARE

My analysis of international, national, and local media coverage of sexting within the United States reveals that sexting is constructed as an overwhelmingly harmful practice for youth and for teenage girls in particular. Sexting is commonly described as "shockingly common,"[11] an "epidemic,"[12] and a "scare."[13] This "disturbing"[14] and "dangerous teen trend"[15] is also described as "risky and alarming" behavior[16] resulting in "tragic consequences"[17] such as sexual exploitation,[18] imprisonment,[19] sex offender registration,[20] and emotional and psychological damage resulting in suicide.[21] Teens are warned that there is no such thing as "safe sexting,"[22] and parents are implored to "Fight Back"[23] and to help their children avoid negative consequences such as shame, humiliation, social isolation, depression, cyberbullying, cyber stalking, criminal charges, sex-offender registration, imprisonment, suicide, and assault. Only a small portion of the overall media coverage of sexting that I examined refers to the practice in less alarmist terms such as "modern-day spin the bottle"[24] or "high tech flirting."[25]

In their article on teenage girls, sexual double standards, and sexting, Jessica Ringrose and her coauthors describe sexting as framed by risk discourses that often construct "girls' sexuality as a particular problem to be surveilled and regulated."[26] The nature and the extent of this surveillance and regulation is informed by girls' race, sexual orientation, and economic privilege.[27] Fueling the moral panic over sexting is an apparent desire to protect white, heterosexual, middle- and upper-class, "respectable" girls from both sexual predators and themselves.[28] The figure most often depicted as needing protection in both media coverage and crime prevention responses to the practice is that of a white, thin, well-dressed, usually fair and long-haired, feminine teenage girl.[29] This demographic of teenage girls is featured in daytime talk shows such as *Dr. Phil* or the *Tyra Banks Show*, where sexting is labeled both a "Crazy Teen Trend"[30] and a "Scary Trend"[31] and the female sexters are derided for their behavior. For instance, the *Tyra Banks* episode on "Teen Sexting" ends with Tyra shaming the girls for their decisions to sext. Tyra then proceeds to explain to the girls that they are "beautiful on the inside," information that might help them refrain from participating in this presumably self-objectifying practice. Such examples further promote the long history of defining white, heterosexual femininity[32] as pure, respectable, and good, while also idealizing and fetishizing white heterosexuality as the most passive and dependent of femininities worthy of addressing and protecting.[33]

A similarly situated girl also dominates the fictional representation of sexting in an episode of *Law and Order: Special Victims Unit* entitled "Crush." In this episode, a high school student named Kim sends nude images to her boyfriend.[34] These are quickly passed around her school. Kim is subsequently taunted, sent death threats, and eventually pushed down a flight of stairs. While in a coma, it comes to light that Kim's boyfriend, the intended recipient of the original sext, has been physically abusing her. When Kim comes out of the coma and refuses to reveal her abuser's name, the prosecutor attempts to protect her from further victimization by forcing Kim to reveal her abuser or face prosecution for possessing and distributing child pornography.

The episode's title, "Crush," has multiple tacit and explicit negative connotations: It implies that girls who develop a crush on someone, and who then express their desire digitally, could face bullying, physical abuse, the destruction of their "good girl image," and even the crushing weight of legal sanction.

LEGAL CONSTRUCTIONS OF THE SEXTING SCARE

The leap from cultural representation to legal reality is a short and interconnected one. Much of the moral panic around sexting is fueled by media coverage of the punitive legal response to this practice. A great deal of media coverage, for example, focuses on the decision by the U.S. Court of

Appeals for the Third Circuit in *Miller v. Mitchell* (2010), the first case to challenge the constitutionality of prosecuting teens for sexting.

Miller v. Mitchell is the result of a sexting scandal that came to light in a high school in Tunkhannock, Pennsylvania, in October 2008, when school officials discovered photographs of nude and semi-nude white, heterosexual, middle-class teenage girls on several students' cell phones. Two of the three girls, Marissa Miller and Grace Kelly, were 12 to 13 years old at the time and are shown from the waist up wearing white opaque bras. One was talking on the phone, the other was making a peace sign.[35] The third girl, Nancy Doe, was wrapped in a white opaque towel, just below her breasts, appearing as if she'd just emerged from the shower.[36] After learning that male students had been trading these images over their cell phones, officials turned the phones over to the Wyoming County District Attorney's Office, where District Attorney George Skumanick stated publicly that "students who possess inappropriate images of minors may be prosecuted for 'sexual abuse of children.' "[37] A few months later, Skumanick sent a letter to the parents of about twenty students. These included students who appeared in the photographs, and those on whose cell phones the pictures were stored, not those who had distributed the images. The parents were informed that felony child pornography charges would be filed unless the teens submitted to probation, paid a $100 program fee, and completed a six- to nine-month education program developed by Skumanick in consultation with the Victims Resource Center and the Juvenile Probation Department.[38] If convicted of these felony offenses, the minors would face a seven-year prison sentence and a permanent record. They would also have their names and pictures displayed on the state's sex-offender registry and its website for at least ten years, as required under Megan's Law.[39]

Three families, in conjunction with the American Civil Liberties Union of Pennsylvania, refused these conditions and brought suit for a temporary restraining order to prevent the District Attorney from bringing criminal charges against their daughters. The plaintiffs alleged that Skumanick's directive was retaliation for their refusal to attend the education program. This retaliation, they claimed, violated: (1) the minors' First Amendment right to free expression, the expression being their appearing in two photographs; (2) the minors' First Amendment right to be free from compelled speech, the speech being the education program's required essay explaining how their actions were wrong; and (3) the parents' Fourteenth Amendment substantive due process right to direct their children's upbringing, the interference being certain items in the education program that fall within the domain of the parents, not the District Attorney.[40]

The plaintiffs argued that while Skumanick may personally disapprove of the fact that the girls allowed themselves to be provocatively photographed, the two photographs in question "were not made by abusing or coercing the girls, were not made for commercial purposes, and do not depict sexual activity or lascivious display of the genitals or pubic area."[41] As such, the pictures were legal expression protected by the First Amendment of the U.S. Constitution.

When deciding on this matter, the District Court focused its constitutional review of the issue on the second and third claims noted above. (The plaintiffs did not appeal the first claim.) The District Court granted the plaintiff's motion for preliminary injunctive relief. Upon appeal the newly elected district attorney, Jeff Mitchell, acknowledged that Pennsylvania's child pornography law is specific enough that photos of girls in bras would likely not qualify as "nudity" and therefore decided not to file criminal charges against two of the three plaintiff minors.[42] The remaining minor, Nancy Doe, had exposed her breasts and therefore she and her mother, Jane Doe, proceeded to defend their constitutional retaliation claims.

Ultimately, the Court of Appeals agreed with Jane Doe's opposition to the value lessons entrenched in the education program of a District Attorney who had "stated publicly that a teenage girl who voluntarily poses for a photo wearing a swimsuit violated Pennsylvania's child pornography statute."[43] The court upheld Doe's Fourteenth Amendment claim and found that "an individual District Attorney may not coerce parents into permitting him to impose on their children his ideas of morality and gender roles."[44] The court went on to write, "While it may have been constitutionally permissible for the District Attorney to offer this education voluntarily (that is, free of consequences for not attending), he was not free to coerce attendance by threatening prosecution."[45] With respect to the minor's rights, the court found that the government violates the First Amendment right to refrain from speaking when it requires that a person's speech assert a specific message favored by the government.[46] The court also condemned the requirement that the minor explain why her actions were wrong in the context of a program that "purports to teach . . . '[w]hat it means to be a girl; sexual self-respect, [and] sexual identity.' " The court acknowledged that asking girls to reflect on "what it means to be a girl in today's society" may constitute an important sociological endeavor, but this line of questioning is disconnected from the goals of the criminal and juvenile justice systems.[47]

Although the Court of Appeals found in favor of the plaintiffs, the fervor of criminal prosecution captures the punitive and objectifying disciplinary relations between parents, school administrators, prosecutors, and teens. Alarmist, reductionist, and moralistic media portrayals of sexting underscore and perpetuate these problems. At the same time, those at the center of media representations, child protectionist efforts, and lawsuits are mainly white, middle-class, heterosexual teenage girls. These girls are presumed to be disempowered and duped victims of childhood sexualization, as self-sexually exploiting, or as asexual subjects.[48] The dominance of this discourse ignores teenage girls' own diverse narratives about the complex social, psychological, and sexual/erotic dimensions of their experiences. In effect this reifies (white) teen girls as Lolitas—the vulnerable object of sexual desire.

SPEECH, CENSORSHIP, AND THE DENIAL OF
TEEN GIRLS' SEXUAL SUBJECTIVITY

According to constitutional law professor Amy Adler, American statutory provisions and case law on child pornography have expanded the definition of child pornography greatly since its supposed discovery by the public in the 1970s.[49] Statutory provisions include passing the Protection of Children Against Sexual Exploitation Act of 1978, the Child Protection Act of 1984, and the Child Pornography Prevention Act of 1996. In the *New York v. Ferber* (1982) decision, a unanimous U.S. Supreme Court created an exception to the First Amendment by proclaiming that child pornography constituted a category of speech without constitutional protection. Subsequent legal decisions have further broadened the definition of child pornography. In the case of *United States v. Knox*, the Third Circuit Court upheld convictions of Knox for possessing videotapes that zoomed in on the genital region of clothed girls. The Court found that the definition of child pornography did not require the child to be nude. In response, Adler notes, "If we pushed the definition in the evolving case law to the extreme, it seems to threaten all pictures of unclothed children, whether lewd or not, and even pictures of clothed children, if they meet the hazy definition of 'lascivious' or 'lewd.' Thus, the capacious law has proved an excellent vehicle for prosecutorial vigilance."[50] As a result of these decisions, young people who sext can be prosecuted as child pornographers even when their sexting is entirely consensual.

Given the high-stakes concerns, it is notable that there are few scholarly sources and media reports soliciting commentary by young women and teenage girls about their sexting behaviors and their understanding of its risks and opportunities. Even less has been said about sexting that involves queer teens and teens of color. Emerging qualitative studies with teens have, however, opened up a space for alternative perspectives. For instance, in her study on teenage sexting with Australian teens, Kath Albury finds that the sample media campaigns and public education materials viewed by focus group participants were rejected by some participants for failing to acknowledge young women's capacity for consensual production and exchange of images.[51] In addition she notes,

> The majority of participants did not seem to view naked or semi-naked pictures as inherently shameful or shaming for their subject (though they were considered embarrassing, particularly if viewed by parents or teachers). Only one participant (a 16-year-old female) used moral frameworks to discuss "sexters." For some others the choice to participate (or not participate) in taking or distributing naked or semi-naked self-portraits was primarily seen as an outcome of bodily autonomy and 'self-confidence' rather than sexual shamelessness.

One participant claimed,

> I think it also raises issues about . . . are you allowed to do what you want with your body? I mean, if you are that confident that you want to post a naked picture on Facebook, should you be allowed to do that? I mean, if it's yours, if you're autonomous.[52]

With respect to media discourses on sexting, one of the earliest online forums dedicated to this topic emerged following the Tyra Banks episode on sexting. Given Banks's expressed disapproval of girls who sext it comes as little surprise that the discussion-board responses largely reflect her interpretation of the practice. Nevertheless, dissenters took advantage of this opportunity to make their voices heard. For instance, Elizabeth wrote,

> i think a ton of girls my age (15) are sexting ALL THE TIME and they think its no big deal because everyone does it and it might not necessarily be a picture but it would be discussing what they're going to do . . . *and why aren't guys being held at fault for any of this*?? . . . i myself have never sexted and don't ever plan to but all of my friends do and they don't see anything wrong with it.[53]

Elsewhere on the site, Molly, Emily, and Katherine offer the strongest condemnation of Banks's response to her guests. They write:

> We are teenage girls, and we are watching the sexting episode. Tyra and the audience are overreacting [sic]. Texting a boy sexual things is just another way of expressing yourself. People say these things outloud [sic] all the time what is the difference putting them into a text message? Expressing yourself is not an issue that should be discussed with such disgust. . . . Using your phone to express yourself really should be the least of parents concerns. This is ridiculous. Tyra's tone is condescending and she doesn't let the girls say what they want to say. She makes the girls seem embarrassed. There is no shame in being a sexual person.[54]

When narratives such as these, generated by young people themselves, are dismissed by parents, scholars, and legal actors, gendered double-standards and norms of so-called respectable girlhood are reified through denying one's ability to "consummate [their] status as a subject of speech."[55] Here, the dual meaning of consummation, that is, the completion of status as a subject, and the sexual completion of a relationship, are revealed as linguistically and ontologically intertwined and made concrete by the expressed fear that sexting behavior will lead to girls engaging in actual (read: heterosexual, penetrative) sex. This then fuels an "abstinence from sexting" discourse that parallels the "abstinence from sex" discourse that prevails in American culture. This abstinence discourse is a form of censorship by linking the "respect yourself" and "protect yourself" messages.[56] Only now, in order to adequately protect against the harms of sex, one must refrain from expressing themselves in the form of sexting.

This conflation informs the sex-segregated curriculum that made up the education program designed for the sexters—and rejected by the court—in *Miller v. Mitchell*. For both the female group and the male group the first two sessions focused on sexual violence, and the third on sexual harassment. One of the stated goals of the first session of the girls' program was to teach them about "behaviors which foster or encourage violence."[57] The fourth session, for girls, was titled "Gender Identity-Gender Strengths," and the fifth was titled "Self Concept." The former listed among its objectives that the participants "gain an understanding of what it means to be a girl in today's society, both advantages and disadvantages. Identify women in history who have had an influence in the advancement of women's rights. Identify non-traditional societal and job roles. Learn how girls/women can overcome social barriers and achieve all their goals."[58] One of the stated goals of the first session of the boys' program was to teach them about "violence against women."[59] The fourth and fifth sessions of the boys' group were titled "The Relationship Between Ideas About Masculinity and Violence" and "What Can Boys and Men Do to Stop Violence Against Women?" The boys were to "examine the messages that boys and men receive from society about the concept of masculinity" and "become more cognizant of thoughts, ideas and reactions to media images."[60] Underlying this gender division, and the way in which the danger of sexuality is constructed differently for the boys' and girls' groups, is an implicit censorship of girls' sexual desire and their digital expression. While both boys and girls are encouraged to resist mainstream media representations of femininity and masculinity only the girls are implicitly cast as inviting sexual violence via their behaviors; that is to say, their disrespectful sexual expression. The girls were required to watch Jean Kilbourne's documentary video *Killing Us Softly*, described as "messages from advertisers" while the boys were to watch Jackson Katz's *Tough Guise*, described as "an examination of the relationship between images of popular culture and its influence on the concept of masculinity in the United States."[61]

Both films speak to the social construction of gender but *Killing Us Softly* deals largely with the sexualization and objectification of girls and women while *Tough Guise* deconstructs a cultural construction of masculinity that is linked to violence and domination. These videos are of great significance in educating teens about gender identity and the need to be critical media consumers. Yet there remains the tacit message, that girls' consensual sexual self-expression is sexual self-*exploitation* and an invitation for others to sexually exploit them, as well. It is therefore up to the girls to abstain from sexual behaviors that "foster or encourage" violence: Teenage girls remain the gatekeepers of sexual propriety. They must choose between digitally expressing desire and the right to be free from violence. In this way then, while participating in sexting is deemed bad for both groups it is only morally unacceptable for girls. Much like rape myths that suggest a woman asked to get raped when she wore such a short skirt, linking self-respect to a girl's ability to censor her sexual expression makes her the problem when it comes to sexting. What's more, this line of argument forecloses the domain of her speakability and thus her sexual subjectivity. The problems of such a foreclosure are aptly explained in the anthology *Yes Means Yes! Visions of Female Sexual Power and a World Without Rape* where the prevailing no-means-no strategy for combating sexual assault is critiqued for "stop[ping] short of envisioning how suppressing female sexual agency is a key element of rape culture, and therefore how fostering genuine female sexual autonomy is necessary in fighting back against it."[62]

SEXTING!: WHAT DO YOU THINK ABOUT IT?

"If I ever received one . . . I don't know, I think it would be interesting. I mean I'm not opposed to it . . ."—*A.G., 20, Student*

"It doesn't really do anything for me. Always kind of wondered like what if we break up, what's going to happen to these pictures?"—*Ryan, 18, Student*

"It's normal. Depends on the relationship though. It's interesting too, when guys do it it's considered 'ok,' but if a girl does it she's considered slutty."—*J.H., 25, Student*

"I think it's weird . . . if you're going to send something like that it's most likely going to get shared with someone you didn't intend to see it."—*A.R., 18, Student*

"I've gotten a few, sent a few. Initially, I wasn't sure what to do with it when I got it, but then I found that I liked sending them a lot more than receiving them. If it's consensual, then go for it, if it makes you feel good, awesome, just be careful who you send them to."—*Annie, 18, Student*

"It's okay . . . Kind of a shady activity, I guess. If I were to get one I'd be ok with it though."—*Steve, 19, Student*

"I have received multiple sexts and guys seem to like it, but it just doesn't turn me on . . . I look at the sext and all I see is a naked body. Penises are ugly!"—*Tovah, 20, Juice Barista*

"I have received sext messages. The sext pictures make me laugh. It shows really how little respect some people have for their own body. I don't initiate, but I definitely respond back with words."—*Eric, 21, Artist*

"I'm not totally sure I understand the definition of a sext but if I've got the right idea, I have received a few . . . all from the same person. It was someone I was involved in a little affair with so it was quite welcome and appropriately inappropriate. I thought it was sexy and it led to one of the more exciting and racy sexual encounters I've had."—*Anonymous, 32, Farmer*

"I masturbated to that content. I think sexting is a liberating and exhilarating experience that enhances sexual relationships, making them more intimate and physically concrete."—*Anonymous, 18, Student*

"I am not into sexting at all. When I was a sophomore in high school this picture of a butt naked girl who was posing in a mirror was sent to everyone by her ex-boyfriend after they broke up. I didn't know her or her name, but somehow even I got the picture sent to me by a guy friend as a 'joke' and I just thought to myself 'I will never do this.' "—*Anonymous, 19, Student*

"I have received a sext. I read it, got turned on and deleted it. I feel it can be safe if you don't include faces in images."—*Alexandria, 20, Disney Employee*

"I think photos might be risky because you feel that you trust the person you're sending it to, but they can later use it against you. Once you've sent something, you now have no control over it."—*Anonymous, 20, Student*

"It depends who the message is from. If I received the message from an acquaintance or from someone I have only known a short time, it is usually unwanted. After I receive a message, I usually respond with a one-word response, such as 'nice' or 'damn' (with no emojis). Then I usually follow with 'someone hasn't been laid in awhile' and usually the subject changes quickly. If the message came from an intimate partner, it is much more pleasant and enjoyable the relationship is more complex and deeper than sex."—*"Rochelle," 27, Retail Fashion Trend Analyst*

"I enjoyed it when it was from someone I was dating, and when it was something I requested. Sometimes people would send me explicit content without any warning and it's not like we were dating, either. It made me feel uncomfortable because it felt like I didn't have any power in the situation."—*Jessica, 19, Microbiology student*

CONCLUSION

In *The BUST Guide to the New Girl Order*, a popular feminist compilation, Debbie Stoller writes, "American porn culture is here to stay."[63] To paraphrase Stoller, it appears that American sexting is here to stay, as well. And, indeed, a new generation of young women and teenage girls (along with their tech-savvy elders) appears to have acknowledged and accepted the role that digital technology may play in their sexual lives. Rarely, however, does this re-envisioning of the relationship of sexuality to technology, and shifting notions of risk, respectability, and privacy, factor into cultural and legal assessments of youths' right to digital sexual expression or into prevailing cultural and legal assessments of teenage girls' sexual agency. This may be, as some feminists have argued, due to failures to theorize pleasure alongside danger,[64] particularly for heterosexual women. More recently this has been framed in terms of the need to theorize young women's ability to say "yes," and for law to hear this yes to sex or to sexual expression. Legal theorist Katherine Franke asks whether the time "might have arrived when we would want to de-sacrilize the sex-danger alchemy within feminist legal theory."[65] In doing so, the point is not to discount the significance of sexual violence for women, but rather to "de-essentialize sex's *a priori* status as a site of danger for women and one best cleansed of such danger." To illustrate her point, Franke writes,

> I now ask my students which practice they would find most humiliating, objectifying, or objectionable: having a male boss ask you, out of nowhere, to (i) kiss him, (ii) babysit for his kids, or (iii) be responsible for serving coffee at staff meetings. Few of my female students select the kiss as the most objectionable encounter. When we discuss their reasons for their selections, I cannot easily write off their failure to get the 'right feminist answer' to an impoverished feminist education or false consciousness. Rather, sex seems to have become a less 'dense transfer point for relations of [gender-based] power' for some women a generation younger than my feminist peers and I.[66]

Whether or not she is entirely correct in her supposition, Franke arrives at this reassessment through actively canvassing, and refusing to disavow, her students' perspectives. It serves as a counter-point to the assumption that the corrective to girls' purported false consciousness is " 'right consciousness' . . . imposed from the outside by 'right thinking' feminists [and other adult actors] who know what [girls] want."[67] As legal scholar Drucilla Cornell acknowledges, such an approach of imposing our views on others reinforces—rather than resists—the degraded status of those on whose behalf those with right-consciousness' speak.[68] To put it simply, this means when one group thinks they have the right answer and they impose this view on others, it paradoxically takes agency and self-definition away from the very same people who are presumed to lack it in the first place. Thus, by rendering girls' ability to say yes to sexting unspeakable, dominant anti-sexting cultural and legal discourses have not only subjected girls to further regulation they have produced teenage girls ontologically as unknowable sexual subjects. Instead, I suggest that a framework that acknowledges teenage girls' ability to desire, to play with sex, be thrilled by her sexual power—and yet simultaneously recognizes the extent to which she is influenced and even subjugated by hegemonic forces—is necessary for any legal assessment of, and response to, sexting. Prosecuting teens who engage in consensual sexting demonstrates the negative consequences of ignoring agency, autonomy, and desire. In light of this, the relationship between the Lolita Effect and digital sexual expression, adolescent sexuality, and the law merits further consideration. Doing so may help deter youth endangerment that is exacerbated by constructing them as the ultimate objects of sexual desire.[69] Rethinking the Lolita Effect and the law may also work to curb the expanding definition of child pornography that subjects teens to the harms of criminal sanction for youthful and consensual actions.

DISCUSSION QUESTIONS

• Before reading this essay, did you know that sexting between minors, in some cases, violates child pornography laws? Do you think using child pornography law to address sexting is excessive? Or is this type of legal response necessary to protect youth?
• Author Lara Karaian states that white, middle-class, heterosexual teenage girls are at the heart of media representations, child protectionist efforts, and lawsuits because they are presumed to be disempowered and duped victims of childhood sexualization. If these laws and media representations are geared toward protecting these particular groups of children, then what does that mean for teens who don't fit into those categories?
• Do you think there is moral panic over youth sexuality? If so, how can the conversation shift from shame, panic, and morality to pleasure, agency, and empowerment?
• The author states, ". . . young women and teenage girls (along with their tech-savvy elders) appear to have acknowledged and accepted the role that digital technology may play in their sexual lives." Can you ever opt out from inviting technology into your sexual life? How?
• Should schools be required to teach their students the laws pertaining to sex exploitation in sex education courses? Why or why not?

NOTES

1. A previous version of this chapter appeared in *Crime, Media, Culture*. See Lara Karaian, "Lolita Speaks: 'Sexting,' Teenage Girls and the Law," *Crime, Media, Culture* 8, no.1 (2012): 57–73.
2. See, for example, Gigi M. Durham, *The Lolita Effect: The Media Sexualization of Young Girls and What We Can Do about It* (New York: Penguin, 2009); Carmine Sarracino and Kevin M. Scott, *The Porning of America: The Rise of Porn Culture, What It Means, and Where We Go From Here* (Boston: Beacon Press, 2008); Diane E. Levin and Jean Kilbourne, *So Sexy So Soon: The New Sexualized Childhood and What Parents Can*

Do to Protect Their Kids (New York: Random House, 2009.) For the purposes of this chapter, teens refers to girls between the ages of 14 and 17 years old. Alternately, I refer to teenage girls as girls, youth, and minors.

3. Jan Hoffman, "A Girl's Nude Photo, and Altered Lives," *New York Times*, March 27, 2011, http://www.nytimes.com/2011/03/27/us/27sexting.html?pagewanted=all&_r=0.

4. See, for example, Amy Hasinoff, *Sexting Panic: Rethinking Criminalization, Privacy, and Consent* (Champaign: University of Illinois Press, 2015); Kath Albury and Kate Crawford, "Sexting, Consent and Young People's Ethics: Beyond Megan's Story," *Continuum* 26, no. 3 (2012): 463–473; Kath Albury et al., "Young People and Sexting in Australia: Ethics, Representation and the Law," *ARC Centre for Creative Industries and Innovation/Journalism and Media Research Centre* [Report], 2013, http://jmrc.arts. unsw.edu.au/media/File/Young_People_And_Sexting_Final.pdf; Jessica Ringrose, Rosalind Gill, Sonia Livingstone, and Laura Harvey, *A Qualitative Study of Children, Young People and "Sexting:" A Report Prepared for the NSPCC* (London: National Society for the Prevention of Cruelty to Children, 2012), http://www.nspcc.org.uk/inform/ resourcesforprofessionals/sexualabuse/sexting-research_wda89260.html; Michael Salter, Thomas Crofts, and Murray Lee, "Beyond Criminalisation and Responsibilisation: Sexting, Gender and Young People," *Current Issues in Criminal Justice* 24, no. 3 (2013): 301–316.

5. Linda Papadopolous, *Sexualization of Young People Review* (London: Home Office, 2010); American Psychological Association, *Report of the APA Task Force on the Sexualization of Girls*, 2007, http://www.apa.org/pi/women/programs/girls/report.aspx.

6. Maureen Palmer, dir., *Sext Up Kids: How Children Are Becoming Hypersexualized*. Media Education Foundation, 2012.

7. Durham, *The Lolita Effect*, 12.

8. Ibid., 21.

9. There are a growing number of scholars concerned about sexting and child pornography laws. See for example, Clay Calvert, "Sex, Cell Phones, Privacy, and the First Amendment: When Children Become Child Pornographers and the Lolita Effect Undermines the Law," *CommLaw Conspectus* 18 (2009): 1; Mary Graw Leary, "Self-Produced Child Pornography: The Appropriate Societal Response to Juvenile Self-Sexual Exploitation," *Virginia Journal of Social Policy and the Law* 15 (2008): 1; Leigh Goldstein, "Documentation and Denial: Discourses of Sexual Self-Exploitation," *Jump Cut: A Review of Contemporary Media* 51 (Spring 2009): 1–25; http://www.ejumpcut.org/currentissue/ goldstein/text.html#n (February 2010); Karaian, "Lolita Speaks"; John A. Humbach, "Sexting and the First Amendment," *Hastings Constitutional Law Quarterly* 37 (2009): 433; Catherine Arcabascio, "Sexting and Teenagers: omg ru going 2 jail???" *Richmond Journal of Law and Technology* 16 (2010): 10–11; and Amy F. Kimpel, "Using Laws Designed to Protect as a Weapon: Prosecuting Minors Under Child Pornography Laws," *New York University Review of Law and Social Change* 34 (2010): 299.

10. Judith Butler, *Excitable Speech: A Politics of the Performative* (New York: Routledge, 1997), 132.

11. "'Sexting' Shockingly Common among Teens," *CBC News*, February 2009, http:// www.cbsnews.com/stories/2009/01/15/national/main4723161.shtml.

12. Rosemina Nazarali, "MTV Tackles 'Sexting' Epidemic," *Kiwi Commons*, February 5, 2010, http://kiwicommons.com/2010/02/mtv-tackles-%E2%80%98sexting%E2%80%99-epidemic/.

13. "The Sexting Scare," Macleans.ca, March 12, 2009, http://www2.macleans.ca/2009/03/12/the-sexting-scare/.

14. Gigi Stone, "'Sexting' Teens Can Go Too Far: Sending Provocative Images Over Cell Phones Is All the Rage, But It Can Go All Wrong," *ABC News*, March 13, 2009.

15. "Sexting: New, Dangerous Teen Trend—A New, Dangerous Trend Is Growing among Teenagers," *ABC 7 News*, May 15, 2008, http://www.wjla.com/news/stories/0508/520195.html.

16. "Sexting: Pornography or High Tech Flirting," Lawyers.com, http://criminal.lawyers.com/juvenile-law/Sexting-Pornography-or-High-Tech-Flirting.html.

17. Annalisa Barbieri, "You Don't Know What Sexting Is? Texting Explicit Photographs Has Become a Common Part of Courtship among Teenagers. But the Consequences Can Be Tragic," *Guardian*, August 7, 2009, http://www.guardian.co.uk/lifeandstyle/2009/aug/07/sexting-teenagers-mobile-phones.

18. "Teenagers Risk Sexual Exploitation on Web, Group Warns," *CBC News*, February 10, 2009, http://www.cbc.ca/technology/story/2009/02/10/tech-safer-internet.html.

19. Wendy Koch, "Teens Caught 'Sexting' Face Porn Charges," *USA Today*, November 3, 2009, http://www.usatoday.com/tech/wireless/2009–03–11-sexting_N.htm.

20. Deborah Feyerick and Sheila Steffen, " 'Sexting' Lands Teen on Sex Offender List," *CNN's American Morning*, April 18, 2009, http://www.cnn.com/2009/CRIME/04/07/sexting.busts/index.html.

21. Cindy Kranz, "Nude Photo Led to Suicide: Family Wants to Educate Teens about Dangers of Sexting," Cincinnati.com, March 22, 2009, http://news.cincinnati.com/article/20090322/NEWS01/903220312/Nude-photo-led-to-suicide.

22. Belinda Goldsmith, "Safe 'Sexting'? No Such Thing, Teens Warned," *Reuters*, May 4, 2009, http://www.reuters.com/article/internetNews/idUSTRE5430V420090504.

23. "Fight Back Against Sexting," Readers Digest.ca, May 2009, http://www.readersdigest.ca/money/cms/xcms/fight-back-against-sexting_2861_a.html.

24. Kathryn Blaze Carlson, "Sexting Like 'Spin the Bottle Online,' Prof Argues," *National Post*, May 27, 2009, http://amyhasinoff.wordpress.com/press/sexting-like-prof-argues/.

25. Olivia Baniuszewicz and Debra Goldstein, *Flirtexting: How to Text Your Way to His Heart* (New York: Skyhorse, 2009).

26. Jessica Ringrose, Laura Harvey, Rosalind Gill, and Sonia Livingstone, "Teen Girls, Sexual Double Standards and 'Sexting': Gendered Value in Digital Image Exchange," *Feminist Theory* 14, no. 3 (2013): 305–323.

27. Lara Karaian, "Policing 'Sexting': Responsibilization, Respectability and Sexual Subjectivity in Child Protection/Crime Prevention Responses to Teenagers' Digital Sexual Expression," *Theoretical Criminology* 18, no. 3 (2014): 282–299.

28. Ibid.

29. Ibid.; Hasinoff, *Sexting Panic*.

30. "Crazy Teen Trends: Sexting," *Dr. Phil Show*, CBS Television Distribution, January 27, 2009.

31. "Teen Sexting," *Tyra Banks Show*, the WC, April 20, 2009.

32. Richard Dyer, *White: Essays on Race and Culture* (New York: Routledge, 1997), 131.

33. Beverly Skeggs, *Formations of Class and Gender: Becoming Respectable* (Thousand Oaks, CA: Sage, 1997), 99. See also Robin Bernstein, *Racial Innocence: Performing American Childhood from Slavery to Civil Rights* (New York: New York University Press, 2011).

34. "Crush," *Law and Order: Special Victims Unit*, NBC, May 5, 2009.

35. *Miller v. Mitchell*, No. 09–2144, 2010 WL 935766, at *1 (3d Cir. Mar. 17, 2010): 8.

36. Ibid., 9.

37. *Miller v. Skumanick*, 605 F. Supp. 2d 635 (M.D. Pa. 2009): 15.

38. *Miller v. Mitchell*, No. 09–2144, 2010 WL 935766, at *1 (3d Cir. Mar. 17, 2010): 7–8.

39. *Miller v. Skumanick*, 605 F. Supp. 2d 635 (M.D. Pa. 2009): 16–17.

40. Witold J. Walczak, Valerie Burch, and Seth Kreimer, *United States District Court for the Middle District of Pennsylvania: Verified complaint. Miller et al. v. Skumanick: Legal Documents*. March 25, 2009: 18–20. Skumanick eventually decided not to bring charges against Marissa Miller and Grace Kelly. While this was stated orally, Skumanick did not withdraw his appeal with respect to these two minors and their mothers and therefore their names, along with the newly appointed District Attorney, Jeff Mitchell, who took office in January 2010, are those cited in the case name (*Miller v. Mitchell*, 9 & 14).

41. Marsha L. Levick, and Riya S. Shah, "Brief of Juvenile Law Center as Amici Curiae in Support of Appellees," *Miller et al. v. Skumanick: Legal Documents*, 25 September 2009. http://www.aclupa.org/downloads/Amicusmiller.pdf (April 2010): 23.

42. *Miller v. Mitchell*, No. 09–2144, 2010 WL 935766, at *1 (3d Cir. Mar. 17, 2010): 4.

43. *Id.* at 23–34.

44. *Id.*

45. *Id.*

46. *Id.* at 25–26.

47. *Id.* at 27.

48. Karaian, "Policing 'Sexting'"; Hasinoff, *Sexting Panic*.

49. Amy Adler, "The Perverse Law of Child Pornography," *Columbia Law Review* 101, no. 2 (2001): 230.

50. Ibid., 240.

51. Albury et al., "Young People and Sexting in Australia," 1.

52. Ibid., 9.

53. http://tyrashow.warnerbros.com/2009/07/sexting.php?page=5#comments

54. http://tyrashow.warnerbros.com/2009/07/sexting.php?page=8#comments

55. Butler, *Excitable Speech*, 133.

56. Karaian, "Policing 'Sexting.'"

57. *Miller v. Skumanick*, 605 F. Supp. 2d 635 (M.D. Pa. 2009): Exhibit 2, "Course Outlines" 2, 5.

58. *Id.*

59. *Id.*

60. *Id.* at 7.

61. *Id.* at 7; Jean Kilbourne, *Killing Us Softly: Advertising's Images of Women* (1979) Cambridge Documentary Films; Jackson Katz, *Tough Guise: Violence, Media and the Crisis in Masculinity* (1999), Media Education Foundation. The most recent version of the Kilbourne film title required by the court is Jean Kilbourne, *Killing Us Softly 4: Advertising's Image of Women* (2010), Cambridge Documentary Films.

62. Jaclyn Friedman and Jessica Valenti, eds., *Yes Means Yes: Visions of Female Sexual Power and a World without Rape* (Berkeley, CA: Seal Press, 2008), 6.

63. Marcelle Karp and Debbie Stoller, *The Bust Guide to the New Girl Order* (New York: Penguin, 1999), 82.

64. Carole. S. Vance, "Pleasure and Danger: Towards a Politics of Sexuality," in Carole S. Vance, ed., *Pleasure and Danger: Exploring Female Sexuality* (New York: Routledge & Kegan Paul Books, 1984); Gayle Rubin, "Thinking Sex: Notes for a Radical Theory of the Politics of Sexuality," in Vance, ed. *Pleasure and Danger*; and Friedman and Valenti, *Yes Means Yes*.

65. Katherine M. Franke, "Theorizing Yes: An Essay on Feminism, Law, and Desire," *Columbia Law Review* (2001): 201.

66. Ibid., 202–203.

67. Drucilla Cornell, *At the Heart of Freedom: Feminism, Sex and Equality* (Princeton, NJ: Princeton University Press, 1998), 169.

68. Ibid.

69. James R. Kincaid, *Erotic Innocence: The Culture of Child Molesting* (Durham, NC: Duke University Press, 1998); Adler, "The Perverse Law of Child Pornography."

SOCIAL MEDIA AND SEXUAL SAFETY

Quit Facebook, Don't Sext, and Other Futile Attempts to Protect Youth

Rena Bivens and Jordan Fairbairn

As for the girls, they are forward, immodest and unladylike in speech, behavior and dress.
—Attributed to Peter the Hermit (1274 AD)

Women and children: Stay safe! Stay vigilant! New technologies are lurking around every corner, inviting you to use them, and then ruthlessly putting you in dangerous situations. We are here to protect you. We've always tried to protect you. Remember our unease when electricity was coming to your homes? "If you electrify homes you will make women and children vulnerable. Predators will be able to tell if they are home because the light will be on, and you will be able to see them."[1] You've told us that electricity increased your quality of life and gave you more opportunities to be social, but it is in your interests to have us evaluate every new technology carefully. It's the twenty-first century and so many of you are connected to our dangerous world through multiple electronic devices—your phone, your computer, your tablet. We keep trying to tell you about the risks and dangers and that, as women and children, you have to behave differently, but are you even listening?

This admittedly tongue-in-cheek narrative reveals a number of social anxieties that are caught up in the trajectory of technological development. Consider the invention of the telephone, a technology intended for businessmen. Women quickly appropriated it for what was, at the time, seen to be a radical and unexpected use: to socialize with others.[2] Genevieve Bell[3] argues that it is women and children, especially girls, who are targeted first when moral panics ensue following the introduction of a new technology that may alter relationships with time, space, and other people. Staying safe in the new society, which supposedly materializes following widespread adoption of a new technology, becomes conflated with changing the behaviors of would-be victims instead of the behaviors of dangerous perpetrators.

AN INCONVENIENT FOCUS: SEXUAL VIOLENCE PREVENTION STRATEGIES

Focusing on victims is a common tendency within societal conversations about sexual violence, which can include actions ranging from unwanted sexual comments to rape.[4] Also known as victim-blaming, this perspective places the responsibility on victims to prevent the violence they endure. Sexual violence prevention advice frequently follows this logic by focusing on individual risk-reduction strategies: Young women and girls are told not to walk alone at night, to protect their drinks, and to think carefully about how they dress and act, particularly when drinking. However well intentioned, what is omitted from these and similar prevention strategies is advice for would-be perpetrators, along with societal-wide strategies that target root causes of sexual violence. With this in mind, organizers behind a march against victim-blaming in Tempe, Arizona, posted a list of sexual assault prevention tips online that puts the onus instead on would-be perpetrators. Consider the first three: "1. Don't put drugs in people's drinks in order to control their behavior. 2. When you see someone walking by themselves, leave them alone! 3. If you pull over to help someone with car problems, remember not to assault them!"[5]

One reason why risk-reduction strategies that focus on victims rather than perpetrators remains prominent is that they are rooted in myths and stereotypes related to sexual violence. Here are a few examples: Sexual violence is always or primarily physical; potential victims can identify and react to sexual violence before or while it is happening; and sexual violence primarily consists of attacks by strangers, rather than force or coercion administered by partners, friends, family members, colleagues, and acquaintances.[6] Perhaps the most deeply entrenched falsehood of all is the notion that preventing sexual violence is the responsibility of individuals, not broader communities.

By examining current sexual violence prevention strategies and advice, we can reveal a great deal about societal attitudes and beliefs concerning gender and sexual violence. When Emily Yoffe of *Slate* told college women to stop getting drunk to prevent sexual assault,[7] and Constable Michael Sanguinetti, a Toronto police officer, asked women to "avoid dressing like sluts"[8] to protect themselves, no would-be perpetrators were asked to change their behaviors and beliefs to avoid assaulting. These attitudes are connected to widespread beliefs about sexual violence: Alcohol is a cause (rather than a correlate, or a tool) of sexual assault, and clothing is a cause because perpetrators cannot control their sexual urges upon viewing skin (rather than understanding sexual violence to be about power and entitlement).

IS QUITTING FACEBOOK THE SOLUTION?

Google's search engine has made us stupid.[9]
Twitter's 140-character restriction has rewired our brains.[10]

When we place all of the blame on a technology that is supposedly causing a social problem, we are adopting a technologically deterministic perspective. Following this logic, technologies appear and then begin to change society either for the better, by solving social problems, or for the worse, by wreaking havoc with social norms. What is missing from these arguments is the wider sociocultural contexts that surround technological development and consumption. As political scientist Langdon Winner explains, a technology is seen to develop "as the sole result of an internal dynamic, and then, unmediated by any other influence, molds society to fit its patterns."[11] If Facebook alone caused cyberbullying, asking a victim to quit would solve the problem. However, cyberbullying takes place with the help of many technologies and is connected historically to bullying behaviors that existed prior to social media. People use Facebook to bully; therefore responsibility lies with these people and the specific aspects of the technology that make bullying possible, not the technology on its own. The bully and the victim exist within a sociocultural context that both perpetuates and condemns cyberbullying while also positioning social media sites as important spaces for socializing. Asking a victim of cyberbullying to terminate his or her presence on a social media site can be akin to asking a young person to commit social suicide.[12] Safety-focused prevention campaigns must be evaluated to consider whether their advice will produce serious social costs for youth.

To avoid technological determinism, many scholars have adopted a mutual shaping perspective to demonstrate how technologies and societies shape one another. Designers and innovators of technologies are influenced by their wider sociocultural context and the product they develop is in part a consequence of this context. At the same time, the technology can reproduce problematic myths and stereotypes that are rooted in the designer's sociocultural context. For example, rape whistles, electric bras, pink pepper spray, and anti-rape underwear have been developed and marketed to women and girls as a response to the widespread problem of sexual violence. While these technologies may be of use in particular settings or for particular people, they also contribute to the societal problem of victim-blaming that perpetuates myths and stereotypes about sexual violence. Consider the anti-rape underwear that was designed to "prevent a significant number of rapes":[13] The onus is on the would-be victim (portrayed in the product's fundraising campaign as a slim, able-bodied white woman) to purchase and wear the underwear, sexual violence is seen to be primarily about forced penetration, and strangers are positioned as likely perpetrators.[14]

Along with a mutual shaping perspective, we argue that it is vital to pinpoint what precisely is new in the social media-youth-sexuality nexus. Social phenomena like cyberbullying and sexting cannot be divorced from their historical lineage. Neither came into being in a social vacuum and neither would cease to exist once the technologies they have become associated with disappear. For instance, cyberbullying without social media is bullying that takes place in person or through notes shoved inside school lockers. Sexting is also not completely new—people have drawn sexy photos of themselves to give to their would-be lovers and a wide variety of professional and amateur cameras have been used to take sexy photos.

So, what is new? Digital data has at least four unique qualities: persistence (recording and archival properties); replicability (easy duplication); scalability (can reach large audiences); and searchability (easy to locate).[15] Using this framework, let's consider what makes cyberbullying distinct from non-technologically mediated bullying. The text or images used to bully are recorded and archived by the social media site, no longer under the control of the perpetrator or the victim. Others can easily copy and paste the offending material or take screenshots, lifting and reposting it within a different location. The text or images are often shared, reaching many people in the victim and perpetrator's social circles, as well as outside of those circles. The material is often easy to locate through a search engine and due to archival properties it is likely to remain available for a long time or reappear without the victim's consent.

DEFINING YOUTH

Societal debates around sexuality, sexual expression, and sexual violence online tend to invoke a category of youth that is rarely well defined. Conversations that consider social media, in particular, often explicitly or implicitly focus on youth.[16] Of course, many youth are frequent users of social media sites and certainly a focus on minors in the context of sexual exploitation and child pornography crimes is highly relevant and reasonable. Yet there is more to it: The "state of youth today" has historically been a key area of social focus, and a way to either express hope or despair about where we are headed as a society. In many different historical contexts, sexual expression and use of technologies by youth have been framed as excessive in relation to the activities and expectations of older generations.[17] This broader social context is important to keep in mind when analyzing social responses to sexual expression and sexual violence related to youth and social media, as is the recognition that the moral panic pendulum can swing in a variety of directions. For example, there is a common tendency to trivialize or patronize youth and youth activities, and to accept a certain degree of abuse and harassment as somewhere on the spectrum of an unfortunate byproduct of youth to an accepted rite of passage. Similarly, by focusing on cyberbullying, the broader context is often made invisible. For instance, a gendered, racist, or ableist context (or an intersection of multiple contexts) may be particularly important for victims who are bullied on the basis of social categories they hold or appear to hold. A black youth may be bullied because his peers deem his behaviors too feminine and this bullying may be expressed with racist undertones, whereas a white youth may experience strong, problematic reactions to his feminine behavior in ways that are not racialized.

While we define youth between the ages of 12 and 24 for this chapter, the importance of thinking about youth as a category extends beyond age. One way to unpack this is to consider what else we are referring to: beyond age, what qualities or characteristics do youth share? Are we simply referring to people who use social media a lot? Many people assume that both technical competence and enthusiasm for new technologies are inversely related to age.[18] Following this logic, a high level of social media use may be seen as a defining feature of youth, who are also understood as one generalized group with no major differences between individuals.

We may speak about youth as one homogenous group, but are we equally concerned about all youth? Or, are there particular groups or communities that we mistakenly assume to represent the whole? A recent *Vanity Fair* article exploring the role of social media in youth hookup culture noted that the young women interviewed "were pretty girls with long straight hair—two blonde, two brunette, all aged 16. They wore sleeveless summer dresses and looked fresh and sweet. They went to a magnet high school in L.A."[19] This description does not mention that they are white, heterosexual, able-bodied young women who are from middle- or upper-class families—and, indeed, perhaps they are not. However, given the strong tendency by the mainstream media to focus on "ideal" victims—most often equating to white, middle- or upper-class, and chaste or virginal female victims[20]—we should be critical of any representation that speaks about youth as a homogenous group. Focusing on gender and sexism is not enough, and "youth" are no more a homogenous group than "parents" (and, of course, youth can also be parents simultaneously).

To summarize, beyond being 12 to 24 years old, we approach youth as a group that is (1) the object of much social analysis and scrutiny and (2) a heterogeneous demographic of diverse identities and experiences. A third and final point is that youth are sexual beings (though asexuality should not be discounted as a valid identity) and their sexuality and sexual expression is constructed and regulated by society in specific ways. As such, youth receive regulatory responses that are dependent upon how others categorize them into social groupings. A young woman with a visible physical disability may be perceived as having no sexual desires simply on the basis of her disability and as a result, parents, teachers, police and her peers may respond to her in ways that do not correspond to her own experience.

DON'T SEXT

Now we will explore these issues by examining two information and safety campaigns about sexting. MTV's *A Thin Line* campaign shows a young woman front and center, with young men, blurred in the background, mocking her.

Figure 15.1 A Thin Line

Sexting is defined in the campaign as: "Sending or forwarding nude, sexually suggestive, or explicit pics on your cell or online. For some people, it's no big deal. But real problems can emerge when the parties involved are under 18, when people get pressured into sexting, and when sexts go viral."[21] It is great to see that sexting is not positioned as the problem; instead, coercion and nonconsensual sharing of images is the problem. Along with statistics, questions to ask before making or sharing sexts, and advice on how to decide when to draw your own line, readers are invited to consider sexting consequences:

> 'You get a reputation—because that 'private' sext somehow escaped the phone it was sent to. You get rejected—because the girl/guy you *really* want to go out with thinks you send naked pictures of yourself to everyone, since everyone's seen them, and s/he's not psyched. . . . You get arrested. Taking, sending, and possessing naked images of a minor is a federal crime. Sex offenders' registry? Not the honor roll you were hoping for.'[22]

This fear-based messaging does not differentiate between sexting, and coercion or consent. As a result, the cautionary message emphasizes the potential victim's behaviors: Don't sext. You will be seen as a slut, no one will want to date you, and you might even get a criminal record. The overall message is that this behavior is too risky and, essentially, you are stupid and at fault if you take these risks.

The second campaign, from Youthlaw and the South Eastern Centre Against Sexual Assault,[23] begins to shift the conversation towards the perpetrator.

In the poster (Figure 15.2), we see a man pressuring a woman for photos in the first frame and nonconsensual sharing in the final two frames. However, the message appears to conflate consensual and nonconsensual sexting. "Don't sext me" could be read as "Don't share my image without my permission,"

Figure 15.2 Respect Me. Don't Sext Me

Reprinted with permission from South Eastern Centre Against Sexual Assault, Melbourne, Victoria, Australia.

but by focusing on the woman's decision to take the photo ("CLICK") as the pivotal aspect of the story, she is more directly seen as bearing responsibility for the consequences while his decision to share the photo is understood as inevitable. By positioning sexting and respecting someone as opposites, there is no room for the possibility of being enthusiastic about sending a picture and respectfully receiving one, nor any thoughts on how to sext more safely by, for instance, not revealing your face in the photo.

As a final, minor point, the man's phone can be viewed as a non-human actor in this scenario. The software he was using to receive the photo was designed in a sociocultural context where sharing is the norm. The software reflects this by making the suggestion to share the sext with his friends. While this may not be a particularly amenable example, it is noteworthy that designers can and should also bear some responsibility in terms of how their designs can thwart or facilitate sexual violence.

HOW TO SHIFT THE PREVENTION FOCUS

Concerned about these issues of technology and sexual safety, we undertook a study funded by Crime Prevention Ottawa and conducted in partnership with the Ottawa Coalition to End Violence Against Women.[24] We gathered information from community organizers, educators, violence prevention advocates, and frontline workers about sexual violence that occurs in and through social media sites, with a focus on youth. Our framework, which was reinforced by the community responses through surveys, interviews, and a community forum, was that it is important to understand what is unique about social media while recognizing that it does not cause sexual violence and cyberbullying. Prominent issues identified by the community included: the challenge of anonymity and rapidly changing technologies; intersections with other factors (e.g., racism, substance use, mental health); the ambiguity and apolitical nature of the terms bullying/cyberbullying; awareness of slut-shaming as sexual harassment; and the importance of youth-driven initiatives.[25] There are many types of sexual violence that can be considered in relation to sexual media (e.g., recording and distributing images of sexual assault through social media, cyberstalking and digital dating abuse, luring/online exploitation of minors, and human trafficking). This chapter has focused on social responses relating to the nonconsensual sharing of digital images and cyberbullying because we see these as particularly salient areas of social and political attention and debate where beliefs and policies around gender, sexuality, and technology are co-constructed.[26]

Drawing from this research and the above discussion of technology, sexual violence, and online prevention campaigns, we have three recommendations to help shift the prevention focus. First, avoid victim-blaming and victim-shaming in all contexts. Decades of sexual violence research has detailed the additional harm that blaming and shaming cause survivors of violence, and it clearly does not prevent sexual violence.[27] Second, challenge social norms that promote violence and abuse online and offline—including slut-shaming, homophobia and transphobia, ableism, and racist bullying—and encourage others to do the same when they see sexual violence taking place. Bystander intervention—when a person tries to stop a situation between others that could become violent or takes an action that promotes non-violent social norms[28]—is recognized as an increasingly important and promising area in sexual violence prevention,[29] and should therefore be a core element in any campaign. Finally, youth should be accepted and embraced as sexual beings. At a societal level, healthy relationships and sex education that includes conversations about power, consent, and coercion should be promoted.

That's Not Cool[30] and *Draw the Line*[31] are two examples of online campaigns that spotlight coercion and nonconsensual sharing as problems, avoiding the traditional focus on victims and the victim-blaming that accompanies it. These campaigns also do not position sexual expression as the cause of abuse, allowing youth the freedom to be sexual.

That's Not Cool focuses on redefining sexting pressure as uncool, challenging social norms dictating that a relationship is only serious if sexting is occurring (see Figure 15.3). In Figure 15.4, part of the *Draw the Line* campaign, is followed by the caption: "Is it a big deal to share it with others?"[32] Individuals are depicted as having the capacity to decide which images to share, and they are responsible for how they treat intimate photos of others. This campaign includes both online and offline behaviors, which allows us to

Figure 15.3 When You Pressure Me
©That's Not Cool programs by Futures Without Violence. Reprinted with permission.

Figure 15.4 A Friend Sends You a Naked Picture
Reprinted with permission from Draw the Line.

connect a broader range of problematic behaviors and actions to sexual violence and avoids the tendency to divorce issues like cyberbullying from wider sociocultural contexts. Here are two examples: "The coach spends extra time with a player—on and off the field. Do you tell someone?"; and "After the chemistry final, your friend says that he 'raped the exam.' Do you say something?"[33] These examples also use the bystander approach, encouraging us to consider intervening even if we are not directly involved.

CONCLUSION

As social and legal responses to sexual expression, technology, and sexual violence continue to evolve, it is important to maintain a critical lens. What do community responses to sexual violence look like? Do they challenge myths and stereotypes that surround sexual violence? Who (or which technology) are we holding responsible for violence, abuse, and harassment? What are the effects of current advice and policies developed in the name of safety? What are our underlying assumptions and fears about youth, and how are these influenced by factors such as sexism, racism, and ableism?

Discourse around sexual exploitation online tends to focus on regulating the behavior of potential victims. Girls and young women are told not to sext. They are cautioned to respect themselves enough not to take and send sexual photos. Underlying the advice is the assumption that youth sexuality is bad and that sexting is inherently exploitative. We believe a more nuanced approach is vital. Scholars have drawn attention to the lack of girls' voices and refusal to acknowledge their sexual agency in current conversations about consensual, pleasurable sexting.[34] Similarly, new research is beginning to problematize the age- and gender-related double standards experienced by teen girls who sext.[35] Our previous research findings and discussion in this chapter further highlight the need to build additional narratives and a new social reality. Online sexual chastity does not have to be the approved default option. Emerging conversations that focus on eliminating rape culture, promoting bystander intervention, and developing healthy sexual relationships can be mobilized and integrated into all spaces where we socialize, consume, and produce.

DISCUSSION QUESTIONS

• What have been your experiences dealing with cyberbullying or being coerced into sexting?
• According to the authors, all of the blame cannot be placed onto technology because social problems have existed before technological advances. Do you think we would still see high rates of bullying and sexual coercion without technology?
• How has technology made social issues such as bullying and sexual coercion seem more commonplace? Do you think this has to do with the ability of people to remain anonymous online?
• Do you think social problems would be erased if there were stronger repercussion/restrictions for people that engaged in cyberbullying or other abusive behaviors online?
• Do you agree with the authors that sexting can be consensual as long as both parties involved "don't cross the line" and share private photos or texts publically? What have been your experiences with consensual sexting? Do you think sexting is inherently exploitative?
• Have you dealt with issues related to cyberbullying? Do you feel as if your school or community has dealt with these issues efficiently? Do you have any advice for people that are dealing with cyberbullying?
• How do you think society can start to have a conversation about youth sexuality without the conversation turning into victim-blaming or victim-shaming?

NOTES

1. In this quote Genevieve Bell is speaking about reactions to electricity in Ben Rooney's article "Women and Children First: Technology and Moral Panic," *TechEurope*, July 11, 2011, http://blogs.wsj.com/tech-europe/2011/07/11/women-and-children-first-technology-and-moral-panic.
2. Claude S. Fischer, "Gender and the Residential Telephone, 1890–1940: Technologies of Sociability," *Sociological Forum* 3, no. 2 (Spring 1988): 211–233.

3. As cited in Rooney, "Women and Children First."

4. Rachel Jewkes, Purna Sen, and Claudia Garcia-Moreno, "Sexual Violence," in Etienne G. Krug, Linda L. Dahlberg, James A. Mercy, Anthony B. Zwi, and Rafael Lozano, eds., *World Report on Violence and Health* (Geneva: World Health Organization, 2002), 149. http://whqlibdoc.who.int/hq/2002/9241545615.pdf.

5. "How to Prevent Rape," Slutwalk Phoenix/Tempe, http://slutwalkphoenix.wordpress.com/how-to-prevent-rape. For the original and complete list of tips see Colleen Jameson, "Sexual Assault Prevention Tips Guaranteed to Work," *Alas! A Blog*, September 15, 2009, http://amptoons.com/blog/2009/09/15/sexual-assault-prevention-tips-guaranteed-to-work/.

6. Patricia Weiser Easteal, "Rape Prevention: Combating the Myths," in Patricia Weiser Easteal, ed., *Without Consent: Confronting Adult Sexual Violence: Proceedings of a Conference* (Canberra: Australian Institute of Criminology, 1992), 314–318.

7. Emily Yoffe, "College Women: Stop Getting Drunk," *Slate*, October 15, 2013, http://www.slate.com/articles/double_x/doublex/2013/10/sexual_assault_and_drinking_teach_women_the_connection.html.

8. Raymond Kwan, "Don't Dress Like a Slut: Toronto Cop," *Excalibur*, 2011, http://www.excal.on.ca/news/dont-dress-like-a-slut-toronto-cop.

9. Nicholas Carr, "Is Google Making Us Stupid?" *Atlantic*, July 1, 2008, http://www.theatlantic.com/magazine/archive/2008/07/is-google-making-us-stupid/306868.

10. Elisa Rice, "John Mayer 2011 Clinic—'Manage the Temptation to Publish Yourself,'" *Berklee College of Music: Berklee Blogs*, July 11, 2011, http://www.berklee-blogs.com/2011/07/john-mayer-2011-clinic-manage-the-temptation-to-publish-yourself.

11. Langdon Winner, "Do Artifacts Have Politics?" *Daedalus* 109, no. 1 (1980): 121–136.

12. Nicole S. Cohen and Leslie Regan Shade, "Gendering Facebook: Privacy and Commodification," *Feminist Media Studies* 8, no. 2 (2008): 208–212.

13. "AR Wear—A Clothing Line Offering Wearable Protection for When Things Go Wrong," *Indiegogo*, http://www.indiegogo.com/projects/ar-wear-confidence-protection-that-can-be-worn.

14. For commentary and critique on this campaign, see Von Diaz, " 'Anti-Rape Wear' Reinforces Every Rape Myth You Can Think Of," *Colorlines*, November 5, 2013, http://colorlines.com/archives/2013/11/anti-rape_wear_reinforces_every_rape_myth_you_can_think_of.html; and Tara Culp-Ressler, "What the Company Marketing 'Anti-Rape Underwear' Gets Wrong about Rape," *ThinkProgress*, November 5, 2013, http://thinkprogress.org/health/2013/11/05/2889411/anti-rape-underwear-sexual-assault.

15. danah boyd, "Social Network Sites as Networked Publics: Affordances, Dynamics, and Implications," in *Networked Self: Identity, Community, and Culture on Social Network Sites*, ed. Zizi Papacharissi (New York: Routledge, 2011), 39–58.

16. This focus is likely related to high-profile cases of victimization and suicides of young women following the distribution of photos or video footage of their sexual assaults (e.g., Steve Almasy, "Two Teens Found Guilty in Steubenville Rape Case," *CNN*, March 17, 2013, http://www.cnn.com/2013/03/17/justice/ohio-steubenville-case/

index.html); nonconsensual sharing of intimate photos (e.g., Meaghan Keneally, "Tragedy as Girl, 15, Kills Herself Just One Month after Posting Desperate YouTube Plea Begging Bullies to Stop Tormenting Her," *Daily Mail*, October 12, 2012, http://www.dailymail.co.uk/news/article-2216543/Amanda-Todd-Canadian-teen-kills-desperatevideo-plea-begging-bullies-stop.html), and/or sexual bullying in the form of slut-shaming (e.g., Paula Newton, "Canadian Teen Commits Suicide after Alleged Rape, Bullying," *CNN*, April 10, 2013, http://edition.cnn.com/2013/04/10/justice/canada-teen-suicide/index.html?iref=allsearch).

17. For example, see Margaret Beetham, "Periodicals and the New Media: Women and Imagined Communities," *Women's Studies International Forum* 29, no. 3 (2006): 231–240, where Beetham explains on page 231: "for us at this historical moment it is not so much the fact of changing technologies as the pace of change which threatens to dissolve the solidarities of the past." Also, David Finkelhor talks about "juvenoia" as "the exaggerated fear about the influence of social change on children and youth." See David Finkelhor, "The Internet, Youth Safety and the Problem of 'Juvenoia,'" Crimes Against Children Research Center, January, 2011, http://www.unh.edu/ccrc/pdf/Juvenoia%20paper.pdf, p. 13. Alice Marwick, "To Catch a Predator? The MySpace Moral Panic," *First Monday* 13, no. 6 (2008) has highlighted technopanic as "an attempt to contextualize the moral panic as a response to fear of modernity as represented by new technologies."

18. Similar questions have been raised about the use of the terms "digital natives" and "digital immigrants" to describe Internet users. For a description of these constructs see Mark Prensky, "Digital Natives, Digital Immigrants," *On the Horizon* 9, no. 5 (2001): 1–6, doi:10.1108/10748120110424816. For an analysis of surrounding critiques see Sue Bennett, Karl Maton, and Lisa Kervin, "The 'Digital Natives' Debate: A Critical Review of the Evidence," *British Journal of Educational Technology* 39, no. 5 (2008): 775–786.

19. Nancy Jo Sales, "Friends without Benefits," *Vanity Fair*, September 26, 2013, http://www.vanityfair.com/culture/2013/09/social-media-internet-porn-teenage-girls.

20. For newspaper coverage see Yasmin Jiwani and Mary Lynn Young, "Missing and Murdered Women: Reproducing Marginality in News Discourse," *Canadian Journal of Communication* 31 (2006): 895–917; and Kristen Gilchrist, " 'Newsworthy' Victims? Exploring Differences in Canadian Local Press Coverage of Missing/Murdered Aboriginal and White Women," *Feminist Media Studies* 10 (2010): 373–390. For female sexual activity and type of death in horror movies see Andrew Welsh, "On the Perils of Living Dangerously in the Slasher Horror Film: Gender Differences in the Association Between Sexual Activity and Survival," *Sex Roles*, 62, no. 11–12 (2010): 762–773.

21. "Sexting: What Is It?" *MTV: A Thin Line*, January 26, 2012, http://www.athinline.org/facts/sexting.

22. Ibid.

23. This Australian campaign is a partnership of the Youthlaw and the South Eastern Centre Against Sexual Assault (SECASA), http://youthlaw.asn.au/wp-content/uploads/2012/05/Sexting.pdf.

24. Jordan Fairbairn, Rena Bivens, and Myrna Dawson, "Sexual Violence and Social Media: Building a Framework for Prevention," Ottawa: Crime Prevention Ottawa/Ottawa Coalition to End Violence Against Women, http://www.crimeprevention ottawa.ca/. The views expressed in this paper are the authors' and do not necessarily represent those of Crime Prevention Ottawa or the Ottawa Coalition to End Violence Against Women.

25. The full report is available at http://www.crimepreventionottawa.ca/en/publications/violence-against-women-publications.

26. For example, in November 2013, the Canadian Government announced a bill to make it illegal to distribute intimate images without consent. See "Cyberbullying Legislation to Target Spread of Intimate Images," *CBC News*, November 20, 2013, http://www.cbc.ca/news/canada/nova-scotia/cyberbullying-legislation-to-target-spread-of-intimate-images-1.2433914.

27. See, for example, Courtney E. Ahrens, "Being Silenced: The Impact of Negative Social Reactions on the Disclosure of Rape," *American Journal of Community Psychology* 38, no. 3–4 (2006): 263–274; Avigail Moor, "When Recounting the Traumatic Memories Is Not Enough," *Women & Therapy* 30, no. 1–2 (2007): 19–33; Rebecca Campbell, Emily Dworkin, and Giannina Cabral, "An Ecological Model of the Impact of Sexual Assault on Women's Mental Health," *Trauma, Violence & Abuse* 10, no. 3 (2009): 225–246.

28. Patricia Cook-Craig, "Youth Sexual Violence Prevention," *National Online Resource Center on Violence Against Women: Applied Research* (Harrisburg, PA: VAWnet, 2012).

29. Victoria L. Banyard, Mary M. Moynihan, and Elizabeth G. Plante, "Sexual Violence Prevention through Bystander Education: An Experimental Evaluation," *Journal of Community Psychology* 35, no. 4 (2007): 63–81.

30. "Where Do You Draw Your Digital Line?" *That's Not Cool*, http://thatsnotcool.com.

31. Draw the Line, http://www.draw-the-line.ca/scenario/online.

32. Ibid.

33. Ibid.

34. Lara Karaian, "Lolita Speaks: 'Sexting,' Teenage Girls and the Law," *Crime, Media, Culture* 8, no.1 (2012): 57–73.

35. Jessica Ringrose, Laura Harvey, Rosalind Gill, and Sonia Livingstone, "Teen Girls, Sexual Double Standards and 'Sexting': Gendered Value in Digital Image Exchange," *Feminist Theory* 14, no. 3 (2013): 305–323.

BYE FELIPE

Online Harassment and Straight Dating

Alexandra Tweten

One night in October, a woman from a secret Facebook group posted a screenshot of a message she received on the free dating website OkCupid. The message read "4:20am: I really want to message you and say how pretty you are but than [sic] again I'm scared to message you because attractive women seem to repel me all the time :\" Then fifteen minutes later, at 4:35 a.m. another message came in: "Asshole." The photo above the message had the man's smiling, clean-cut mug as his profile picture.

I laughed. The guy's desperation was high, his attempt at wooing her clearly failed, and in his frustration he probably thought insulting her would make her feel bad or at least get a reaction. I, too, had recently received a message that was clearly dripping with desperation:

> Hi there. You're really pretty and seem like a lot of fun. I'm looking for a cute, easy-going woman who I can date and with whom I can explore the town during my free time at night. You seem to be very much my type. People have described me as tall, dark and handsome, but I don't expect you to take my word for it. So if you'd like to see more pictures of me, I can send you a few immediately. I just don't feel comfortable posting too many online because of my profession as a lawyer. Would you like to chat? :)

The problem was that this guy had sent me this same exact message three times in the last month, and I ignored them because in his profile he seemed like a sleaze who was just looking to hook up.

"No," I finally responded.

"WHY THE FUCK NOT?!? If you weren't interested then you shouldn't have fucking replied at all! WTF!"

I found the juxtaposition of the two messages to be rudely paradoxical, and I did my best to laugh it off. In the first instance, the woman from Facebook didn't respond to a guy's attempt to connect and she was insulted as a result. In the second instance, I did respond after a guy repeatedly tried to meet me . . . only to be insulted. Damned if you do reply, damned if you don't reply. It's easy to see that women can't win with these types of men.

Other women in the secret Facebook group responded to the post about OkCupid with similar stories of online harassment. Anytime one of us posted an ugly message from a man, we'd respond in the Facebook thread with "Bye, Felipe," a spin on the meme "Bye, Felicia," signifying that the person who received the message should dismiss the man or not respond.[1] Realizing that men's hostility was a common experience of online dating shared by the women in the Facebook conversation, someone suggested starting an Instagram account to chronicle all of the "Bye Felipe" moments. In a split-second decision, I decided to do it.

I wanted the collection of Instagram posts to expose an all-too-common theme in online dating where men become hostile after being rejected or ignored. Any woman who has tried online dating has probably experienced this reaction: Man hits on woman, woman rejects or ignores him, man lashes out with insults or even threats. Are we supposed to entertain any man who is interested in conversation or a date just because we exist online? This ridiculous notion was both hilarious and extremely sad at the same time. And, by the same token, there have to be men out there who feel entitled to insult, harass, and even threaten women who aren't interested in dating or hooking up with them. Or who simply don't respond quickly enough to please them.

After I launched the Instagram account, I received about twenty-five submissions and posted them. My objectives for the project were (a) to commiserate with other women and make fun of these idiots (we all get creepy messages from men online); (b) to let men know what it's like to be a woman online; and (c) to expose the problematic entitlement some men feel they need to exert over women.

Only a few days later, the account had already picked up 600 followers. On Wednesday, I received an email from a journalist at the *Atlantic* saying she had come across my Instagram account, and she would like to interview me for a story about the creeps women interact with while online dating.

After the story in the *Atlantic* came out, "Rise of the Feminist Tinder-Creep-Busting Web Vigilante," *Bye Felipe* followers rose to 6,000.[2] Other news outlets immediately jumped at the chance to interview me, and by the following Monday, *BuzzFeed* had picked up the story, catapulting followers to 137,000 by the end of the day. There was a flurry of activity: I was contacted by *ABC News* and my hometown newspaper. I was featured on both *Good Morning America* and *Nightline*, *Cosmopolitan* magazine, and *Huffington Post*. By the end of the week, "Bye Felipe" was officially a viral news story and I was spreading my message.

The Instagram account speaks for itself. It simply chronicles the ongoing pattern of hostile things that men say to women. After seeing these text exchanges grouped together, it's easy to conclude that our society has a misogyny problem. Being a woman and simply existing in the world, we come to anticipate and expect to deal with being treated as items for men to possess and use. Examples of men's entitlement are rampant, there's only a difference in severity. The cultural atmosphere that says it's okay for hundreds of men to catcall any woman in a public space[3] is part of the same continuum of misogyny that drives men to brutally injure women, as exemplified by the man in New York City who slashed a woman's neck because she ignored him.[4] These same forces of toxic entitlement taught Elliot Roger that he was justified in murdering six people and injuring thirteen others near the campus of the University of California, Santa Barbara, because women had sexually rejected him.[5] This is why *Bye Felipe* matters: There are clear messages in society telling men that they deserve to go on dates with women simply because the men want to and simply because they are male. Some men believe these messages.

It didn't take long after launching *Bye Felipe* before the site was inundated with thousands of submissions from women who saw the Instagram account and identified with the behavior exhibited by these men. There was immediately a constant photo stream of terrible messages. Women sent screenshots of frightening messages from stalkers, violent ex-boyfriends, and legitimately scary threats. Because *Bye Felipe* exposes absurd attempts at insulting women and uses humor to take away some of the power men's insults may carry, I don't post the most violent messages that women send me. Serious threats should not be taken lightly, and I refuse to make fun of the most extreme examples of violence.[6] So what kinds of posts do I include in *Bye Felipe*? Most fall into the following categories:

1. Men attacking women's appearance.

The pattern usually follows a predictable routine. As soon as she declines his advances, he puts her down and calls her fat or ugly.[7] In a society that chronically tells women that her number-one asset, and the most important aspect of her worth, is her looks, these men try to harness the power they think they have over women's self-esteem. Ads, television, movie stars, and everything in popular culture that features impossibly thin and perfect women aren't the only things leading to women's bodily hatred. When it is an everyday battle to keep liking yourself and your body, comments from entitled men giving their critiques on what exactly is wrong with us becomes hard to swallow. I hope to help these women find a smidgen of relief in calling out these absurd comments.

2. Petty insults.

While some of the *Bye Felipe* men dig to the women's deepest insecurities, others are grasping at straws to try to insult her.[8]

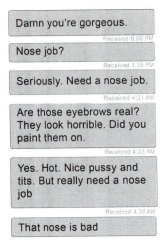

Damn you're gorgeous.	we cuddle then when u come same day
Received 8:50 PM	
Nose job?	Haha nah, I'm not looking for just cuddles or whatever cuddles will lead into.
Received 1:35 PM	
Seriously. Need a nose job.	hahahahahahahahahahahahahahahah u are ugly as fuck anyways
Received 4:21 AM	
Are those eyebrows real? They look horrible. Did you paint them on.	So why the fuck did you want cuddles?
Received 4:23 AM	
Yes. Hot. Nice pussy and tits. But really need a nose job	*Figure 16.2*
Received 4:39 AM	
That nose is bad	

Figure 16.1

Here's what I'm thinking.
We get to know each other and inevitably hit it off. Then, we go on this epic amazing date and then you'll have the story you want.

Oct 15, 2014, 5:48 PM

Guess not lol

Oct 15, 2014, 10:00 PM

Ur not even anything special

Y ignore me

U look like a fuckin tranny

Figure 16.3

3.   Premature frustration.

Some men get extremely frustrated when women don't respond to them. Immediately.[9] In one particular post (Figure 16.6), the man gets outraged after a five-minute gap, the woman had fallen asleep in the middle of a text conversation. Here is her explanation about what happened on *Thoughtcatalog.com*:

> Background: we've been texting since last Friday and have gotten along really well. We've been planning to get coffee or something this week and see how that goes. Late last night (11pm) we talked more about it and he invited me over. I declined because I had already taken a melatonin and

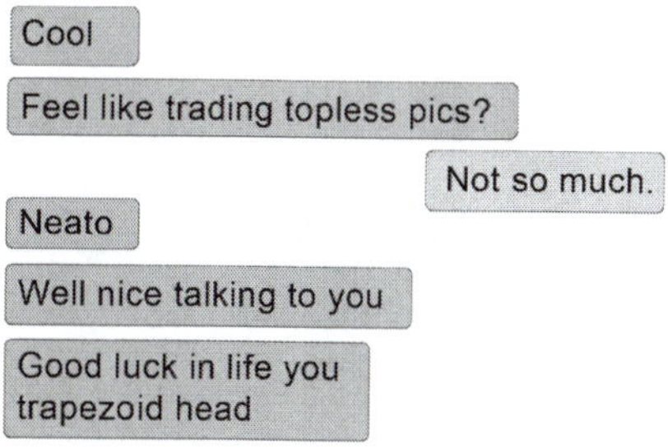

Cool

Feel like trading topless pics?

Not so much.

Neato

Well nice talking to you

Good luck in life you trapezoid head

Figure 16.4

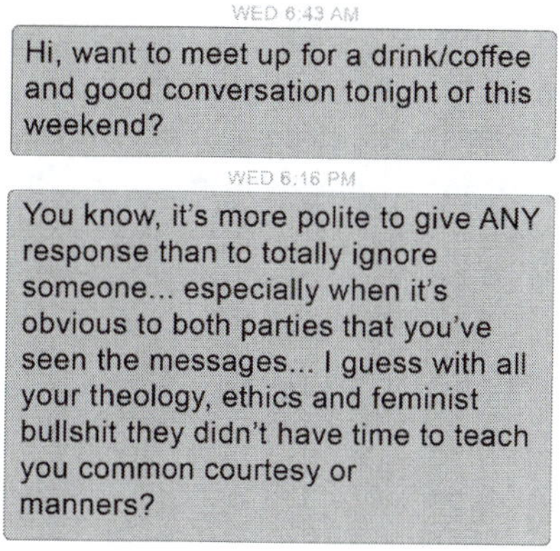

WED 6:43 AM

Hi, want to meet up for a drink/coffee and good conversation tonight or this weekend?

WED 6:16 PM

You know, it's more polite to give ANY response than to totally ignore someone... especially when it's obvious to both parties that you've seen the messages... I guess with all your theology, ethics and feminist bullshit they didn't have time to teach you common courtesy or manners?

I'll give you 5 minutes to write something back, if you don't, I'll never talk to you again.....you might be able to play other dudes but not this one!!!

5 minutes is up....don't ever text me again, don't, have fun being a cunt to other people.....besides you're too fat for me anyways!! Delete my number and leave me alone bitch!!!!!

Figure 16.5 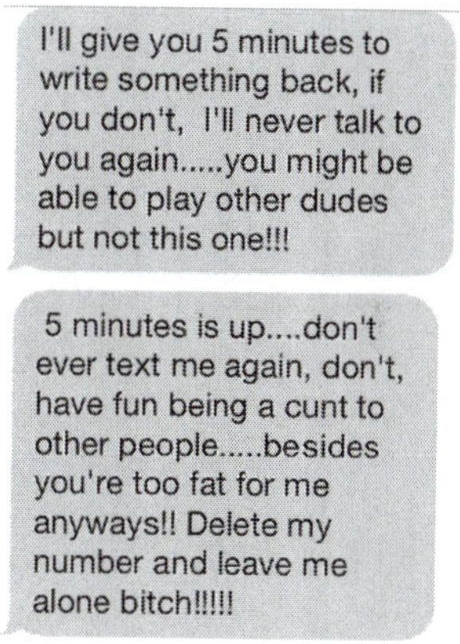   *Figure 16.6*

wouldn't let myself go straight to the home of someone I didn't know anyway, even if it sounded fun.

If I was reading this I would think, there's got to be more to the story, but there really isn't. We'd only had pleasant exchanges. I said it was too late to come over and didn't think much of it, assuming he'd understand that it was late and we'd figure out a time that worked better. Then I woke up to a few messages about how I was inconsiderate, ending with these two (I isolated them because, identifying information).[10]

4. Sheer stupid blame.

If you somehow haven't been convinced yet that some men feel entitled to access women's bodies, the following post takes the cake in this category.[11]

The blatant objectification of women is obvious when these messages are grouped together. And yet, sometimes a theme of internalized responsibility

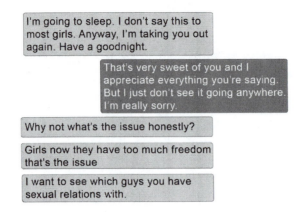

Figure 16.7

shows up on *Bye Felipe*. Even when we know it's not our fault, some women still feel bad about making a guy upset, as with this woman who wrote: "He seemed *so* nice. He *called* himself nice. He called himself a hopeless romantic. So why do I feel like if he had my address I'd be hearing him pound on the door right about now?"

CRITICS AND TROLLS

As soon as *Bye Felipe* hit 100,000 followers, the trolls came out to play in full force. While I was pretty glad that the comments about my posts were generally positive before *BuzzFeed* published an article about the site, the sudden and widespread exposure meant the site became a bit like the old West. Sometimes, a men's rights activist will come along and point out why he thinks the account is stupid or hypocritical and other followers will call him out, which then leads to a full-on comment war. Among the ideas that usually start heated debates on *Bye Felipe*, the most common include the following:

Why Is *Bye Felipe* Only for Women? Men Get Crazy Messages, Too

The site is for women because they are disproportionately targeted and harassed online, and in real life, because of their gender. I have not received any submissions from men as examples of similar behavior from women. It's not really a problem that needs to be addressed. In addition, taking into account the networks of power and institutionalized oppression women are under, it would be comparing apples to oranges to post threatening messages from women. Men possess more power. In our society, men don't have to face the same hostile messages every day that women have come to accept and deem as normal. Men don't have to be wary of strangers walking down the street, or be afraid for their safety because of the outfits they wear. This is a struggle women deal with all the time.

These Posts Are Photoshopped. The Woman's Responses Are Edited Out

These are all real. I wouldn't post them if I thought they had been doctored. There's no way to know that they haven't been photoshopped, unless investigated by an expert, but judging by the sheer volume of similar submissions I get, it would be very improbable that women are making these up. The messages I'm posting are very common, and that's why so many women identify with the project.

What Do You Expect? You Shouldn't Go on Hookup Sites If You Don't Want These Guys to Talk to You

This is victim blaming. Just because a woman is on a dating website doesn't mean men have the right to demean them. No one deserves to receive this type of bullying. Ever. Many women feel guilty, as we are taught to make men happy. We are told that we can avoid this harassment if we are more careful. If a man reacts in a violent way, we must have done something to make him do it. This assumption unjustly absolves him from responsibility. Also, it's not contained to dating sites. I post text conversations and Facebook messages as well. This problem definitely goes far beyond the scope of dating sites.

Why Do You Hate Men?

I most definitely do not hate men. I have met many great guys from online dating. I realize that it is a minority of men who send these hostile messages, but the purpose of the account is to draw attention to the issue as a whole. If you look at the *Bye Felipe* posts it's easy to see this mindset is prevalent in our culture.

All Men Aren't Like This. Why Do You Group Us All Together?

It's true that not every guy sends hostile messages, but all women have received a hostile message like this from a man online or in real life. That's what *Bye Felipe* is about: the subset of men who believe they are entitled.

I Don't Think What He Said Was That Bad. She Deserved It

I can't reason with someone who thinks a woman deserves to be insulted because she refused.

The comments are mostly self-policing, meaning that Instagram followers call out the trolls. Occasionally, though, I have to say goodbye to the most egregious ones and block their accounts. I don't hesitate for a second in doing so.

ONLINE DATING

Here's a piece of information no one tells you before you graduate college: It becomes progressively harder to meet strangers in public. After graduation, it may take a while to wrap your head around how to make friends in a new city. When I graduated from college in Minnesota and moved to Los Angeles to intern at *Ms.* magazine, I had no friends, and I certainly didn't know how to meet men in the city. There were no more campus mixers, classes in which to meet people, or dorms in which to hang out. In the years since graduation, it's become even more difficult to meet people in public as everyone is increasingly addicted to their phone. Enter OkCupid (and Tinder). They take the guesswork out of going into a bar and eyeing who you think is attractive and who also thinks you are attractive. By cutting out (most of) the ambiguous guesswork, they have made modern dating much more efficient. It seems that most people would rather flip through potential mates from their couches using their phone rather than actually go to a bookstore and bump into an attractive stranger on the off chance that they are single and want to go on a date.

While this process cuts down on actually having to interact with people you don't want to meet, and creates an extra screen before you meet for a drink, it is a pretty close approximation to the people you would meet if you were to walk down the street.

In the weeks before *Bye Felipe* was created, the group Hollaback! created a video that filmed Shoshana B. Roberts dressed in a black crewneck T-shirt and jeans walking silently in Manhattan for ten hours. She was catcalled more than 100 times in that period. The video went viral, and people seemed shocked at the volume and content of the comments she received by simply existing in public.

"Hey beautiful."
"Smile."
"God bless you, mami."
"Someone's acknowledging you for being beautiful. You should say thank you more."[12]

These are all comments Roberts received as she walked down the street.

"I'm harassed when I smile and I'm harassed when I don't," Roberts said in a press release accompanying the video. "I'm harassed by white men, black men, Latino men. Not a day goes by when I don't experience this."[13]

This isn't surprising or groundbreaking news for women. If you live in a metropolitan area, simply going out your front door, you become accustomed to this type of behavior from men. "The thing about that @iHollaback video is that it depicts something so familiar to me, I didn't realize it needed to be depicted at all," tweeted Lori Adelman.[14] In contrast, the reaction from men was mostly that they had no idea harassment was a problem. "When I first reported on #streetharassment in NYC, I had no idea men could be so disrespectful to women. I was blown away. #YouOKSis," Terrell J. Starr posted on Twitter.[15]

Publicly exposing the harassment that so many women experience every day has become an important framework for pushing back against the problem. *Bye Felipe* is just another facet of this emerging discussion about exposing and ending harassment. Using Instagram lets us speak up. It exposes harassments that infiltrate our daily lives, but that we often only talk about with other women. I have received hundreds, if not thousands of thank you's from women in my inbox and in the comments saying that they, too, have received similar insulting or threatening messages. One woman wrote, "Here I sat feeling bad for being called names and apologizing for turning guys down politely. Until I just saw that it's a norm for a lot of men to be complete sickos. Thank you!"

Bye Felipe has acted like an immortalized record of catcalling, which links the harassment women see on the street to the same types of harassment they see in their own living rooms, when they are simply online. The fact that these accounts of daily life were picked up by major news outlets, and viewed and shared by millions of people, speaks to the fact that so many women can relate (and so many men are learning something new). The idea was so simple, yet revelatory. Widespread online harassment is obvious to most women who have ever swiped right on Tinder, and to most anyone who has taken a women's studies course. Online straight dating generally tends to be very different for men than it is for women. As the typical senders of first communication, men must sometimes send hundreds of messages before a woman responds. Women often don't send the first message because of social norms that tell us men must be the courter. Many men clearly don't know what it's like being on the receiving end of these messages since women are disproportionately the target of aggressive and hostile language online.

I have been asked multiple times, "What's the answer to this? What can these dating sites do to curb this problem?" And I struggle to answer because this is just a symptom of a larger problem. Censoring these messages may help in the short term, but the messages featured on *Bye Felipe* are a public record of the catcalls and threats women receive on the street every day, just walking around and existing. Until we change the cultural atmosphere, women will continue to receive these hurtful messages online and in real life.

Is it working? I would argue *yes*. *Bye Felipe* is still growing its audience and starting conversations about what is acceptable behavior for men and women. I received an anonymous email from a man who said in the past he messaged women in offensive ways: Once "I browsed through your posts . . . seeing it as an outsider, seeing someone else doing it, I know now how low I was. It feels awful to know that I was doing this to a woman just because she wouldn't reply or when I didn't like their replies. I know there are women with issues, and maybe ignoring guys make them feel better about themselves or something, but I should have learned that this is THEIR issue, THEIR problem, and it doesn't give me any right to abuse or be mean to them." If this is an example of the fact that change is possible, then it gives me hope.

When I went to college, I majored in journalism and women's studies. I was exposed to feminist theory, intersectionality, and the matrix of oppression. I was inspired to make change, but I didn't quite know how I wanted to go about doing it. I knew that I had a voice, and that I could use it to make waves. I was just waiting for the right opportunity to do it. Instagram and social media gave me the power to share my message with millions of people. I am continually amazed and overjoyed at the power of everyone to create change and start discussions en masse. You don't have to be a talking head to capture the attention of an entire country anymore. I hope to continue the movement of *Bye Felipe* and change the attitudes of at least a few people.

DISCUSSION QUESTIONS

• Some people may find that these online exchanges aren't "that serious," and may argue that Alexandra Tweten is overreacting or causing an issue. Is *Bye Felipe* potentially a form of retaliation harassment? Or is it productive to bring attention to such unacceptable behavior?
• Do you see a correlation between the messages on *Bye Felipe* and street harassment? Does digital communication provide a screen of relative anonymity to hide behind, which allows some men to lash out?
• Have you ever experienced online sexual harassment? What did you do?
• Have you ever messaged someone in a way that could be construed as sexual harassment? Why did you do it? After reading this chapter, do you feel differently about these texts or other messages you sent?

NOTES

1. http://www.urbandictionary.com/define.php?term=bye%20felicia.

2. Olga Khazan, "Rise of the Feminist Tinder-Creep-Busting Web Vigilante," *Atlantic*, October 27, 2014, http://www.theatlantic.com/national/archive/2014/10/rise-of-the-feminist-creep-busting-web-vigilante/381809/.

3. Inae Oh, "Watch a New York Woman Get Catcalled 108 Times in Less Than One Day," *Mother Jones*, October 28, 2014, http://www.motherjones.com/mixed-media/2014/10/watch-new-york-woman-get-catcalled-108-times-less-one-day.

4. Ben Yakas, "Video: Queens Woman Slashed after Ignoring Man's Advances," *Gothamist*, October 8, 2014, http://gothamist.com/2014/10/08/video_queens_woman_slashed_after_ig.php.

5. Ralph Ellis and Sara Sidner, "Deadly California Rampage: Chilling Video, But No Match for Reality," *CNN*, Tuesday, May 27, 2014, http://www.cnn.com/2014/05/24/justice/california-shooting-deaths.

6. The Tumblr site, *When Women Refuse*, chronicles the serious problem of actual violence women receive at the hands of men who have been rejected, sharing the stories of women who have been brutally beaten or even killed by men who had been rejected. For more information see http://whenwomenrefuse.tumblr.com/.

7. To find the original screengrabs for the following comments that are posted online go to http://instagram.com/p/vW778oJK4p/; http://instagram.com/p/vOlBn9pK1P/; and http://instagram.com/p/uOEqfWpK20/.

8. http://instagram.com/p/u83wgBpK17/.

9. http://instagram.com/p/uqiFpzpK9U/; http://instagram.com/p/uN5nvgpK2t/.

10. Anonymous, "Accidentally Fell Asleep in the Middle of Texting a 'Nice Guy' from Tinder, This Is What I Woke Up To," *Thought Catalog*, October 8, 2014, http://thoughtcatalog.com/anonymous/2014/10/i-accidentally-fell-asleep-in-the-middle-of-texting-a-nice-guy-from-tindr-this-is-what-i-woke-up-to/.

11. See http://instagram.com/p/uvRdi9JK4p/.

12. Inae Oh, "Watch a New York Woman Get Catcalled 108 Times in Less Than One Day."

13. Jillian Sederholm, "Woman Catcalled More Than 100 Times in Single Day in NYC," *NBC News*, October 28, 2014, http://www.nbcnews.com/pop-culture/viral/woman-catcalled-more-100-times-single-day-nyc-n235936.

14. @ladelman

15. @Russian_Star

Part IV

Dating, Desire, and the Politics of Hooking Up

Part IV, "Dating, Desire, and the Politics of Hooking Up," includes first-person perspectives on sex and disability, dating while fat, debates about orgasms, why some people hook up, and why other people don't.

Chapter 17 is titled "Can Disabled People Have Sex? and Other Questions You Probably Shouldn't Ask Me If We Just Met." Sexual violence prevention educator Jennifer Scott calls out copious examples of ignorance, rudeness, and misinformation when it comes to sexuality and people with disabilities. For starters, Scott writes, there is a powerful and wrong assumption that people with disabilities are asexual. Blending personal experience and academic scholarship, Scott covers a range of issues such as SlutWalk, misguided sexual health care, inappropriate comments and touching from strangers, and the disproportionately high rates of sexual violence and abuse perpetrated against people with disabilities.[1]

In chapter 18, "Big Girls Need Love, Too: Dating While Fat (and Feminist)," author and scholar Brittney Cooper poses a compelling demand to readers and daters alike: "I'm a short, dark-skinned, fat Black girl with a natural. I'm all those things in a culture that . . . hates fat and finds it repulsive," Cooper writes. Concerned about good health and not opposed to weight loss, Cooper remains acutely aware of the politics of size. As Deborah Lupton points out in her book titled *Fat*, fat-phobia is infused with racist ideology. There is a long history of ethnic, race, and class oppression shaping views on health and illness, beauty and self-worth. Dating back to the 1800s in the United States, for instance, hegemonic policies attempted to contain the "contamination" of Jewish immigrants and newly emancipated black Americans by framing any sign of fatness as the inherited trait of "inferior" and "primitive" groups. In contrast the slim, upper-middle-class white (and Christian) American body "was positioned as the most civilized type," Lupton writes, "as it represented the privileged cultural values of self-restraint and self control which members of 'primitive' social groups were seen to lack."[2]

"The idea that we're only attractive within a range of sizes is absurd. And narrow. And it is absolutely a function of patriarchy," Cooper writes. And, because men deal with fat phobia (or fetish) at some level, too, they are not off the hook of this conundrum, either. While there is no easy or quick fix to the inextricably linked issues of gender, race, and size, Cooper's quick-paced personal and political account ends with a solid pronouncement: "I'm prioritizing self-care and that includes being loved on and getting my groove on. Regularly. And I know for sure that those things are feminist."

Sociologist Lisa Wade takes a different tack, focusing on quantitative data to investigate the frequency of women's orgasm during hookup sex. While it is doubtful that both kissing and anal intercourse rank the same, both tend to be lumped together in publications about hook-up activities. Books and articles by academic experts and ace reporters writing on the subject lump a wide range of sexual activity under the hook-up umbrella. Young adults are often sketchy in defining what's going on, too. Journalist Sharon Jayson writes, "The cryptic nature of what a hookup involves appeals to many young people: They deliberately want to be vague so they can exaggerate or hide their actions from their friends, analysts say."[3] Along with vaguely defined descriptions about what activities, exactly, constitute hooking up, other questions remain, as well. In chapter 19, "Are Women Bad at Orgasms? Understanding the Gender Gap," Wade explains that, much like the gendered wage gap, there is also a gendered orgasm gap. This chapter suggests the reasons why and what is at stake.

Despite the impressed given by attention-grabbing headlines about teens and hooking up, this isn't only the purview of teens and young adults; nor is it true that hooking up is a twenty-first-century invention. Heather Corinna, executive director of the sex info site Scarleteen.com, is also interested in multigenerational experiences with casual sex. Corinna comments, "if anyone thinks that all of a sudden way more college students are having sex than they used to, they're probably mistaking the incidence of reporting [sexual activity] with the incidence of it happening." It helps to keep in mind, Corinna notes, that in the past, "especially before 1950 or so, casual sex was much more commonly framed as pre-marital. It was still happening, and likely just as much, but it was viewed differently since it was more common for marriages to result soon after."[4]

In chapter 20, "Why We Hook Up: Searching for Sex or Looking for Love?," Justin Garcia and Helen Fisher continue the theme of casual sex, specifically exploring the motivations for why people choose to hook up. Garcia and Fisher—both sexuality scholars affiliated with The Kinsey Institute—note that most hook-up research has focused on white heterosexual college students, rather than the general population. It is an understatement to say this is a problem. As a corrective, Garcia and Fisher collected data from a far broader nationally representative sample of U.S. singles. This data about sexual hookups included 3,905 unmarried Americans between the ages of 18 and 75+ years, of all sexual orientations, from every major ethnic group, and from every region of the country. This data collection is important for its scope and inclusivity, and broadens the attention about hookups from the presumption that it's something only young adults do.

In their astute and potentially controversial conclusion, the authors explain that along with the historical, cultural, and psychological reasons that undoubtedly play a role in hooking up, there appear to be some evolutionary biological factors that also contribute to the practice.

Part IV closes with Mark Carrigan's interview of David Jay, founder of the Asexuality Visibility and Education Network (AVEN).[5] Although popular media might give the impression that college students are practically majoring in hooking up, as the chapter title makes clear: "Everybody's *Not* Hooking Up." Research suggests that hooking up may be more talk than action. According to research findings, 90 percent of one study's participants assumed that a so-called typical student hooked up at least two times during the school year. Yet, in contrast, only 37 percent of students reported they'd actually had two or more hookups during that time frame. Similarly, while approximately 45 percent of students said they had never hooked up with anyone, a scant 3.7 percent believed that a "typical student" had never hooked up.[6]

These rhetoric and reality gaps notwithstanding, chapter 21 is not about whether people talk a big talk about what they did last weekend. Rather, this chapter hones in on asexual individuals who enjoy the social company of others and sincerely have no desire to engage sexually. This conversation between Carrigan and Jay about *not* hooking up raises important questions and controversial issues about how we define and understand asexuality, and is definitely poised to encourage further discussions about the topic.

NOTES

1. Readers may also be interested in the compilation of first-person reflections collected in Katherine Duke, ed., *Kissability: People With Disabilities Talk About Sex, Love, and Relationships* (Amherst, MA: Levellers Press, 2014).

2. Deborah Lupton, *Fat* (New York: Routledge, 2013), 47. Also see Ragen Chastain, ed., *The Politics of Size: Perspectives From the Fat Acceptance Movement* (Santa Barbara, CA: Praeger, 2015).

3. Sharon Jayson, "More College 'Hookups,' But More Virgins, Too," *USA Today*, March 30, 2011. http://usatoday30.usatoday.com/news/health/wellness/dating/story/2011/03/More-hookups-on-campuses-but-more-virgins-too/45556388/1.

4. Shira Tarrant, "Why Are Conservatives Obsessed with the Sex Lives of College Kids?" *AlterNet*, April 17, 2011, http://www.alternet.org/story/150639/why_are_conservatives_obsessed_with_the_sex_lives_of_college_kids.

5. For an additional interview listen to Shira Tarrant and David Jay on "Asexuality Comes Out of the Closet," *Patt Morrison Show*, KPCC 89.3 FM, Los Angeles, April 6, 2012, http://www.scpr.org/programs/patt-morrison/2012/04/06/25911/asexuality-comes-out-of-the-closet.

6. Amanda Holman and Alan Sillars, "Talk about 'Hooking Up': The Influence of College Student Social Networks on Nonrelationship Sex." *Health Communication* 27, no. 2 (2012): 205–216.

CAN DISABLED PEOPLE HAVE SEX?

And Other Questions You Probably Shouldn't Ask Me If We Just Met

Jennifer Scott

My favorite cousin made me go speed dating with her once. Spending an evening making small talk with strangers—and paying money to do it—seemed to me like a special version of hell. But I was single, new to the city, and whatever alter ego my cousin decided to invent for the evening was bound to be hilarious, so I agreed to go.

We arrived at the bar and discovered that the event was taking place upstairs and there was no elevator. I took this as a sign that we should turn right around and go home, but the speed-dating host offered to carry me up the stairs. I generally only let friends do this in a pinch, but the alternative would have been to hobble up them and become a spectacle in front of a bunch of potential dates. No, thank you, so I let him pick me up. About halfway up the stairs, the host blatantly grabbed my butt. It was the first time that had ever happened to me. (Leave it to me to find the only way for someone who uses a wheelchair to get their ass grabbed in a bar.) Startled, I couldn't think of anything to say. What, exactly, is the appropriate response to a guy who grabs your ass while he is also that the person keeping you from tumbling down an entire flight of stairs? He put me down without a word and proceeded to get on with his hosting duties.

Later that night, after the merry-go-round of awkward conversations ended, it was time to go. I was trying to avoid giving the host another opportunity to cop a feel, so some conversation ensued about how I was going to get back down the stairs. One of the daters commented that I seemed light enough for him to carry, to which the speed-dating host replied, "Yeah, her body really doesn't fit with someone in a wheelchair." It made me wonder about what kind of body would have matched his expectations. A lumpy one? One with long legs? Short legs? A super-skinny one? One with really awesome arm muscles? A grotesque one? He certainly didn't expect me to have a butt he found worth grabbing. He didn't expect to find me attractive because folks with disabilities are often left out of discussions of sexuality and sexual desire.

The assumption that we are asexual is one of the most powerful myths that folks with disabilities have to confront. People with disabilities[1] and chronic illnesses don't fit into the narrow confines of what's considered attractive, so others assume it must be impossible for us to find partners, or that we don't want them at all. Another myth is that if we do manage to find partners, those partners must also have disabilities. There are plenty of people in relationships where both people are disabled. There are also many fantastic couples where one partner has a disability and one does not. Each of the relationships is built on love, trust, companionship, adoring the same punk bands or cheesy comedies, complementary career passions, or any of the other myriad things that bring people together. It wouldn't surprise me, though, if each of those couples, at one time or another, had to respond to comments about their relationships. The non-disabled partners are often viewed as noble, self-sacrificing, or overly compassionate. While we were out for my birthday, a complete stranger once told my ex-boyfriend it was nice of him to date me. My ex replied that he was only in it for the karmic brownie points, but the stranger missed his sarcastic tone and just smiled and patted my hand before walking away. It hadn't occurred to her that my ex might be dating me *because he wanted to be.*

Perhaps this unintentional ignorance is one of the reasons that sex-positive and anti-violence movements have largely left out folks with disabilities. Take the recent popularity of SlutWalk. As a sexual violence prevention educator, I find hope in the grassroots activism and passion that radiates from SlutWalk. Anything that gets people talking, that breaks down the myths about sexual assault, and that reduces victim-shaming, is a necessary step in the right direction. This activism is so badly needed in a society that still justifies violent victimization according to what women are wearing or how they choose to spend their Friday nights. But, there are serious problems with who gets to reclaim their sluthood. Many women of color, in particular, have made it clear that they don't want to reclaim the word because of the way their sexuality has been constructed throughout America's racist history. Folks with disabilities have never been granted sluthood in the first place. While women all over the world are waiting for people to stop seeing them as sex objects, women with disabilities are still waiting to be seen as sexual—or to be seen at all. We are less than a woman, somehow—certainly less than "slut." Too often we are viewed as pitiable, pathetic, and devoid of desire. We could never be sluts.

Assuming that people with disabilities are not sexual leads to more serious problems and clueless comments. It also means there is a dearth of accurate information about sexuality and disability; for example, the Department of Health and Human Services' Office on Disability notes that they have no information on the prevalence of sexually transmitted infections (STIs) for disabled people.[2] None. Sex education programs in this country are woefully inadequate, but many folks with disabilities aren't allowed to participate in them at all. It's assumed that the information just won't be necessary. In college, I worked nights at a group home for adults with intellectual disabilities. During training we were explicitly told never to discuss sex, sexuality, or intimacy with the residents even though they were all adults. Many individuals with intellectual disabilities are not taught the words for the parts of their own bodies, let alone provided with information like what sex is or what consent is, or that they're entitled to experience pleasure just like everyone else.

Additionally, sex ed information is often not available in formats that are accessible to folks with disabilities. How many public schools have videos with closed captioning, or materials in Braille? The disability-specific information that is out there, at best, only addresses form and function. Most doctors rarely talk with disabled patients about sexuality or sexual health. It was a running joke at my college health center that you had to answer "Are you pregnant or is there any chance you could be pregnant?" at least five times over the course of an appointment, regardless of whether you were there for a cold, a broken toe, or just to get out of class. But the doctors rarely asked me that question. I remember the day they finally did. I ran home to my roommates and announced proudly, "Yay, the doctors finally realized I can get pregnant!" We all had a good laugh, but it felt like an accomplishment.

I also had a difficult time finding a physician who would write me a prescription for birth control. One physician refused, saying my risk of blood clots would be too high. (Folks who use wheelchairs sometimes have poor circulation in their legs, increasing the chance of a blood clot.) I explained to the doctor that my circulation was normal and I had already done some research about the best option for me. She said that she still didn't think it was worth the risk. She asked, "Really, how sexually active are you going to be?" I wanted to shout at her "ALL THE TIME. EVERY DAY. WITH LOTS AND LOTS OF BOYS," but I doubt it would have helped matters. A friend of mine who is a paraplegic had to go to three different doctors before one agreed to provide care throughout her pregnancy.

Often, individuals who acquire a disability during or after puberty are provided a video about sex and disability while they are in rehab. The video is narrated by physicians and makes sex feel about as enticing as watching paint dry. Nowhere in these videos is there a disclaimer that there's no "right way" to have sex or that sex can still be a blast even though your body may have changed in some way. There are no tips about finding positions that are comfortable, or communicating new challenges or preferences to your partners.[3] People just figure all those things out on their own later. If you acquire your disability at birth or at a young age, and thus don't have to suffer the awkward video, you figure things out by talking to your peers. Parents often cannot answer questions about what sex and intimacy might be like with a disability because they don't have the answers either. Not to mention that most young people would rather do just about anything than have a candid conversation with their parents about sex.

A lack of information and knowledge makes people vulnerable. Research shows that individuals with disabilities face extremely high rates of sexual violence and abuse. More than half of women with physical disabilities are sexually assaulted and studies estimate that the figure is closer to 70 percent or 80 percent for women with developmental disabilities. They are also more likely than women without disabilities to face multiple perpetrators.[4] Every single one of my residents at the group home had a trauma history. Despite these astronomical numbers, people with disabilities have almost no credibility in the criminal justice system. Testifying is incredibly difficult for any assault survivor, and for those with intellectual disabilities, difficulties with communication or vocabulary can make it even harder. People with intellectual disabilities are also seen as manipulative and prone to lying, and since rape culture already teaches us to assume victims are fabricating their stories, they have essentially no chance of being believed. Perpetrators are most likely parents, caregivers, and partners. They are often viewed as good people who hit their limits, whose altruism should excuse their abuse. Rape culture allows the putative burden of caring for the victim to be used as an excuse for the violence.

On the other hand, the sexuality of folks with disabilities is sometimes viewed as dangerous. There are many who believe that folks with disabilities, especially intellectual disabilities, should not be allowed to have children. The United States has a long history of forced sterilization as part of its leadership in the eugenics movement. People who were Deaf, blind, and those with physical and intellectual disabilities (along with Native women and African American women) were targets of the eugenics movement because they were seen as genetically weak and inferior. It was believed that if they were allowed to pass on their substandard genetic material, the entire society would suffer as a result. Often sterilizations were performed without the patient's knowledge.[5] It remains a widespread practice of legal guardians to make life-altering decisions for persons with disabilities, including the decision to sterilize. This lack of agency over their own bodies makes people with disabilities even more vulnerable to sexual abuse. Abusers are often the ones serving as medical guardians. If they authorize sterilization, they can continue their abuse with impunity. They don't have to worry about a pregnancy serving as evidence.

Bodily agency is a core element of humanity, not just sexuality, and it is something that folks with disabilities contend with on a daily basis. They are often seen as not owning their bodies. It's assumed that caregivers, doctors, or even strangers can act on them under the guise of helping or because they supposedly know more about what is best for the person than they do.

People start pushing me without asking, without saying anything at all, while ignoring my objection if I do say no. I once dumped an entire vanilla latte down my shirt when a stranger grabbed my chair while I was crossing the street and pulled me over backwards. It was an accident, of course. He was only "helping." But here's the thing: He didn't ask me. He didn't speak to me. He just assumed and acted. If Latte Guy had asked me if I needed help, I'd probably have said "No, I got it" because I get coffee and go to the office every day. Doubtless, his next question would have been "Are you sure?" That's always, always the next question, and it gets exhausting. Many people ignore me and "help" anyway. I move through the world independently every single day, so yes, I am sure that I can determine whether I need your help or not. If everyone had to answer this question as often as I do on any given day, they might understand. Folks without disabilities don't go out of their way to offer help to one another as much as they should, but people will stop what they are doing and literally run down the street to open a door for me. Let's be clear: Offering to help someone—anyone—is never offensive. We should all do it more often. But it is exhausting to deal with the assumption that help is always needed or wanted and then to contend with complete disregard for the choice to reject it. I can't help but wonder at the connection between the ways that "no" is fully ignored here, and in the epidemic of violence against people with disabilities.

Most of the time, the ways that folks ignore my boundaries end up being funny and awkward, but not dangerous. My life is full of awkward interactions like the latte guy. It's a long-standing joke among my family and friends that I should document these encounters in a book. People seem to think that they can say or do whatever they want, and they expect me to be polite and compliant no matter how far outside the lines of appropriate their behavior has strayed.

Here's another example. I was at dinner and drinks one night with a group of friends for a girls' night out. We were tucked away in a tiny back room behind the bar, with room only for our group. It was great, given that the band was setting up on the other side of the bar and things were bound to get loud. So it seemed strange when a woman and her child walked through the doorway staring at me. The little girl was probably about six years old, and she was hiding her head shyly in her mother's back. The mother just kept staring at me, and everyone was becoming uncomfortable, including me. I expected the mother to say something, but she didn't. So, I said to the little girl, "Hello, did you want to talk to me?"

This made her bury her head in her mother's back. My friend chimed in, "Don't worry she doesn't bite."

This finally got the mother talking and she said, "Oh, don't say that to my daughter." She dragged the little girl to within about six inches of me. Even though she was now well inside any reasonable personal space bubble, she still had not spoken to me. The little girl finally looked at me and said, "I hope you feel better."

I explained to her that I was not sick, and that I use a wheelchair to get around because I cannot walk. She went back to hiding behind her mother. At this point, the mother repeatedly told the youngster to hold my hand. The woman still hadn't said so much as "hello" to me. The little girl clearly had no desire to hold my hand, and I told her it was okay not to.

"Oh don't tell her that," the mother said again, finally actually speaking to me. She was still trying to coax her daughter into holding my hand.

"Well, you have to think about whether I may not want to do that. We are strangers after all."

Again, all the mother said was, "Don't tell her that." I seriously began to wonder if she was capable of saying anything else. This cringe-worthy interaction had already gone on far longer than most, and my patience was thinning at this point. It was a Friday night, and I just wanted to have dinner, a cocktail, and some laughs with the girls. So I said to the mother, "Look, I am not an educational tool. You need to talk with your daughter if you want her to learn something." She was utterly shocked. The woman stammered a couple times that she was sorry if she bothered me and then she left. I tried to return to our very uncomfortably interrupted dinner. Luckily the server returned almost immediately and asked us if we wanted drinks. She was a little surprised at the enthusiasm in the "yes!" coming from all of us.

This was one of the most awkward encounters with strangers I have ever had, because the adult was the one whose behavior was so inappropriate. I don't mind when kids ask questions. They're simply trying to make sense of a world so much bigger than they are. I cringe when kids ask things like "What happened to her?" as I walk by and their parents shush them or give them some ridiculous answer. It teaches them to be wary, to not engage with people with disabilities like ordinary people. However, I was flabbergasted that this woman tried to force her child to hold my hand. She didn't come in and say, "I'm sorry for interrupting your dinner, but Suzy Q has a question she'd like to ask you." She didn't ask me if I would be okay holding a strange child's hand. She didn't really acknowledge me at all. I was simply a prop in whatever experience she was trying to provide her daughter. She had no respect for her daughter's boundaries or mine. She fully expected me to be fine with this invasion of time and privacy. I had no social space to be irritated, to point out how absolutely ludicrous she was. She would not have understood me if I had. It would have reinforced some of the stereotypes of folks with disabilities—that we are all bitter and pissed off at everything and everyone. She would never have read my reaction as being irritated or taken aback at her behavior in particular.

The same thing applies for the random fellas who ask me about sex before they ask me my name. More than one guy has started a conversation by asking me which body parts I could feel and which ones I couldn't or whether I was able to have sex. (The answer to that last question is *Yes, but not with you, buddy. You should have led with hello.*) Unless you're someone I am seriously considering having sex with, you don't need to know, but these guys fully expect an answer. They're not asking to ensure that sex we might have later would be enjoyable for me. It would be revolutionary if they were. Up-front conversations about sexual pleasure? No way! That doesn't happen nearly as often and as easily as it should. But wouldn't it be amazing if pleasure and boundaries were typical topics when negotiating a sexual encounter or relationship—regardless of ability.

DISCUSSION QUESTIONS

• This author speaks from a very personal place, but connects issues related to the body, sexuality, and agency that she feels everyone should incorporate into their lives. How does her story resonate with your own understandings of sexuality, agency, and the body? What part of her story resonates with you the most?
• Why do you think some people are uncomfortable with people who have disabilities? How can people become more aware of their interactions and recognize their behaviors can be offensive to people with disabilities?
• What do you think it will take for people with disabilities to be more consistently seen as sexual beings?

NOTES

1. Some people prefer the term "people with disabilities" instead of "disabled" or "disabled person" because it puts the person rather than the disability first. It is used here to emphasize that, while someone may have an impairment, their own bodies are not what causes disability, but that outside forces like discrimination, ignorance, and inaccessible spaces cause one with an impairment to become disabled.
2. Department of Health and Human Services Office on Disability, "Sexually Transmitted Diseases and Disability," 2010, http://www.hhs.gov/od/about/fact_sheets/stdchapter25.html.
3. For further discussion about the attitudes of educators, nurses, physiotherapists, and social workers toward people with physical and intellectual disabilities having sex, see M. Parchomiuk, "Specialists and Sexuality of Individuals with Disability," *Sexuality and Disability* 30 (2012): 407–419.
4. M.E.Young, M.A. Nosek, C.A. Howland, G. Chanpong, and D.H. Rintala, "Prevalence of Abuse of Women with Physical Disabilities," *Archives of Physical Medicine and Rehabilitation* 78 (1997): S34–S38.
5. Open Society Foundations, "Against Her Will: Forced and Coerced Sterilization of Women Worldwide, September 2011, http://www.soros.org/initiatives/health/focus/law/articles_publications/publications/against-her-will-20111004/against-her-will-20111003.pdf.

BIG GIRLS NEED LOVE, TOO

Dating While Fat (and Feminist)

Brittney Cooper

I have recently come to the conclusion that I'm going to have to lose a significant amount of weight in order to have a viable chance at a love life.

Let me be clear: This is not a fat-hating announcement. When I look in the mirror, for the most part, I like what I see. I like my curves, I like my ass, I like my legs, I like my boobs (which I only have in abundance, when I'm tipping the scales), and I like my face.

But the fact remains that I'm a short, dark-skinned, fat Black girl with a natural. I'm all those things in a culture that not only hates fat and finds it repulsive, but also in a culture where fat dark-skinned women typically can only find roles in movies as maids. Even so, one could argue that these mainstream films reflect the desires of white America, or more to the point, white men, and not Black men, which up to this point is the only group of men I've dated.

But with brothers I find, that they, too, have internalized a particular relationship to the body-type most associated with the mammy figure. They see girls like me as sisters, as homegirls, but not as love options. They don't find big girls sexy. They usually find us *comforting. Strong. Stable.* Huge difference.

I know there is this myth in Black America that brothers like their sisters thick, thick like a luscious milkshake, that "brings all the boys to the yard," as it were. But what I call thick, and what the average brother calls thick is not the same thing. I'm (pre-weight-loss) Mo'Nique thick. (Sister looks fabulous, by the way.) Not quite Gabourey Sidibe thick. But thick nonetheless. And when I was doing the online dating thing (I've tried it twice, and I'm taking a break), I saw one brother that specifically said, "I'm not into the Mo'Nique thing, ladies." Translation: "No fat girls need apply."

Even Demetria Lucas, author of a fabulous memoir on Black love and dating called *A Belle in Brooklyn*, has (reluctantly) said as much, in her online dating advice column.

> It's not popular to say (and I'm sure I'll be e-stoned for saying it anyway), but if you're overweight and serious about expanding your dating options, it may be worthwhile to shrink your waistline. I've interviewed thousands of men in my career as a dating expert and journalist, and I've noticed that on every rundown of what it is that men are looking for in a woman, weight inevitably sneaks high on the list, usually in the form of 'She works out' or 'She stays fit' or 'She is concerned about her weight and personal appearance'—i.e., she's not fat.[1]

No stones to throw over here. The girl speaks the truth. My experience with straight Black men indicates that many of them do have these proclivities. That holds true even when the brother I'm dating is large himself. Britni Danielle, writing for *Clutch Magazine*, echoes a similar experience of dating as a sister of size.[2]

Acknowledging these larger structural issues around the commodification of straight male desire and the way it affects our dating options *and choices* as cis, hetero women is difficult, because it can make us feel powerless and/or less-than-feminist. So pieces like this make folks uncomfortable, often leading to three kinds of reactionary (and unhelpful) comments. The first will be from those folks who insist that I must really have low self-esteem about my weight and that it must be coming through to the dudes I'm meeting. Um, that would be a Negative. That ain't it. Even though we all have insecurities, self-confidence is not my major struggle. The only way to live in my body, doing the work I do, is to be confident.

Others will come over and lecture about weight loss and health.

Before you do it, don't.

I know that we have huge problems with obesity in Black communities. I have thought long and hard about my relationship to food (and exercise), and I have started to make some changes in order to remain healthy. I also have both short- and long-term goals for doing so. I made those choices for myself, not for a man. So please save the condescending lectures (and armchair therapy) for someone else. This big girl (and I suspect every other big girl with access to a TV) doesn't need it.

And a third, fundamentally more well-meaning group, will come over and give anecdotes about all the thick chicks they know who have male partners. The number will usually total up to no more than two or three, mind you. Those stories ring hollow to me, because they ultimately amount to a futile attempt to amass enough exceptions to disprove the rule. Moreover, perhaps folks aren't considering that the partnerless fat girls simply remain invisible to you, and the thick girls with guys are visible, precisely because they are an anomaly.

What I'm getting at is something much more fundamental. Because desire is socially constructed (no matter how much folks justify their limited dating choices based on "natural preference"), the fact that we live in a fat-hating culture greatly affects who we're attracted to and what we find attractive. Now, I personally have dated men who are skinny, fat, short, tall, light-skinned, dark-skinned, and a range of combinations of all of these. The idea that we're only attractive within a range of sizes is absurd. And narrow. And it is absolutely a function of patriarchy. And I do not deny that men deal with fat phobia at some level, too.[3] Beyond a certain weight range, dating is difficult for many people of size. Still I wonder how race inflects the conversation for men of size, because I think that while, as Virgie Tovar argues, fat often feminizes men, narratives about aggressive and scary large Black men, suggest that fat might make them seem masculine and stronger. And in my experience, I've seen far more brothers on the heavy side happily partnered, married or dating, than not. Sometimes those brothers are the very ones who insist on being with a thin woman. So even though I'm aware of how these structures of patriarchy and desire function more broadly, I live daily and personally with the impacts of those realities.

Some (admittedly anecdotal) examples:

(One)

Several months ago, I was in a bar/lounge type spot, with a group of seven or eight homegirls. We ranged in size and skin tone, from short and petite, to tall and lanky, from light-skinned to dark-skinned, from skinny to fat (me being the fat one), and everything in between. The homeboy of one of my homegirls happened to be in the club. Now in many ways, he was my type. Mid-height, stocky, dark-skinned, bald-headed. My girl gave us his vital statistics and it turns out the brother is highly intelligent and very accomplished. He was also a natural flirt. This I discovered, as I watched him at different points during the evening, strike up a conversation and flirt with every single girl in the crew—except me. My homegirl indicated to me at some point that I should make sure to meet him, because she thought we'd have similar interests. Not one to be shy, I did at some point attempt to strike up a conversation. He barely acknowledged me! I mean he literally did not look me in the eye, made no real attempt at conversation, and pretty much gave me the brush off. *And then starting talking to another one of my homegirls!*

It was clear to me that he wasn't really that interested in a serious thing with any of the girls at the bar that night. He was just doing the bar/lounge thing, as was I. But why the cold shoulder, from a brother I'd never met? Why the unique snub reserved for the one fat girl in the crew? I wish I could say that this experience was isolated, but it's been more the rule rather than the exception for me.

(Two)

I think of all that CRUNK club-hopping I did in ATL back in the early days of the CFC.[4] Nothing makes me dance with joy-filled abandon more than a smoke-filled club strung out on CRUNK. And when me and my girls would go and shut the club down, routinely, I'd be the only chick that hadn't been approached, danced with, hit on. Now I never thought I'd find my prince charming in a club. But everyone likes to be desired. So no matter how much Big Boi proclaimed back in 2003 that "Big Girls need love, too," I don't think the other ATLiens got the message.

(Three)

There is also the story of that time that Crunkadelic and I went to one of those Big Beautiful Women parties. But, um, I'm not trying to date a dude with a fat fetish. No hate on fetishes, but being the object of that particular one feels . . . *objectifying*. I want to date a man that has a range of desires wide enough to see a big girl as attractive. Just like I find a range of men attractive.

Getting back to Big Boi, the reality is that Big Girls do need love. This big girl, anyway. So as much as I resent the limited range of desire that it seems (Black) men have, and the ever-present male privilege that allows them to never have to interrogate their sexual and romantic investments, I hate my limited partnering prospects much more. As un-feminist as I'm sure it is, and as much my Sagittarian self wants to say f**k the world and embrace my life of singleness in a blaze of principled feminist big girl glory, the #truestory is that I'm seriously trying to figure out how I can get my J.Hud on. (Well, maybe not to that extreme!) In my thirties, I'm prioritizing self-care and that includes being loved on and getting my groove on. Regularly. And I know for sure that those things are feminist. I also know being thinner won't guarantee me a date, but I'm willing to bet it'll improve my chances.

DISCUSSION QUESTIONS

• Do you agree with the author that desire is socially constructed? What's your definition of desire? Is it the same after reading this essay?
• The author states that women are subject to a very limited, absurd beauty and body standard that operates as a function of patriarchy. Do you think men have to deal with a similar beauty and body size standard? How is it different/similar for them? What about gay men or men of color?
• Do you think that it is "un-feminist" of the author to admit she still wants to lose weight instead of just accepting who she is because losing weight will increase her chances of a date? How does one decide what is feminist and not feminist?

NOTES

1. Demetria Lucas, "Do I Have to Lose Weight to Land a Date?" *Root*, December 7, 2011. http://www.theroot.com/articles/culture/2011/12/losing_weight_for_love_ask_demetria.html.

2. Britni Danielle, "Big Love: Is Your Weight Holding You Back?" *Clutch Magazine*, November 30, 2011, http://www.clutchmagonline.com/2011/11/big-love-is-your-weight-holding-you-back/.

3. Virgie Tovar, "Fat Men Are a Feminist Issue," *Everyday Feminism*, October 30, 2013, http://everydayfeminism.com/2013/10/fat-men-feminist-issue/.

4. Crunk Feminist Collective. To read more go to http://www.crunkfeministcollective.com/.

ARE WOMEN BAD AT ORGASMS?

Understanding the Gender Gap

Lisa Wade

Women who have sex with men have about one orgasm for every three her partner enjoys.[1] We call this the "orgasm gap," a persistent average difference in the frequency of orgasm for men and women who have heterosexual sex. I want to discredit one common explanation for this gap—the idea that women are somehow bad at orgasms—and offer alternative explanations for the gendered asymmetry in this one type of sexual pleasure.

The common cultural narrative about men's orgasms is that, if anything, they arrive too easily and too quickly. Sex advice for men tends to focus on the need to prolong sexual activity by delaying orgasm. Premature ejaculation, we are frequently reminded, is among the few sexual dysfunctions that plague men. The idea that men have orgasms at will, even against their will, is part of what we collectively understand to be true.

In contrast, the female orgasm is portrayed as elusive.[2] If women don't have orgasms, the narrative about women's bodies suggests that it's because the clitoris is hard to find and complicated to operate; it's shy and persnickety. It requires special attention on his part and the right mindset on hers and, even so, it often fails to show. And perhaps it doesn't matter anyway, the myth continues, because we're not sure that women are as interested in orgasm as men. They're physiologically different, we tell ourselves. Nah, women just don't *need* orgasm as much; they're really in it for the eye contact and the cuddling.

These types of justifications—that women's bodies are less primed for physical pleasure and that women likely care less about it anyway—are part of how we naturalize the orgasm gap. They make the prioritization of men's sexual release seem normal and unproblematic. There is nothing, however, inevitable about this.

VARIATION IN THE FREQUENCY OF FEMALE ORGASM

We know that the orgasm gap isn't natural because rates of orgasm for women vary. Women who sleep with women, for example, have many more orgasms than women who sleep with men.[3] Lesbians and bisexual women have orgasms about 83 percent of the time. That's three times as often as women who have sex with men, or about the same frequency that *men* who sleep with women enjoy.

Women also have no problem experiencing orgasm through masturbation.[4] Fewer than 5 percent of women who masturbate fail to reach orgasm routinely as a part of doing so.[5] In masturbation, orgasms come easily and quickly to women. On average, they need just four minutes, the same amount of time it takes men who are masturbating.[6] Even women who don't frequently have orgasms with other people, often easily find ways to climax when they're by themselves.[7]

New data offers another window into women's varying orgasm rates. Sociologist Elizabeth Armstrong and colleagues analyzed quantitative data on the likelihood of orgasm among about 15,000 heterosexual college students.[8] Table 19.1 shows the likelihood that men and women will orgasm in a first-time hookup (a casual sexual encounter), higher order hookups (more hookups with the same person), and relationships.

The orgasm gap between men and women in first-time hookups reflects the national average: Women have one orgasm for every three orgasms that men have. But the chance that she will have an orgasm increases when they hook up a second or third time, and relationships offer women the most orgasms. Men experience more orgasms over repeated encounters as well, but women's likelihood increases faster, such that the orgasm gap shrinks too: he has 3.1 orgasms for every one of hers in first time hookups, 2.5 in second and third hookups, 2.1 in fourth and further hookups, and 1.25 in relationships. Women in relationships, then, are having almost seven times as many orgasms as women hooking up for the first time. In other words, the gendered orgasm gap shrinks by more than half.

Table 19.1 Percent of Men and Women Having an Orgasm in Four Sexual Contexts

# of hookups	men	women
1st hookup	31%	10%
2nd or 3rd hookup	43%	17%
4+ hookups	64%	31%
In a relationship	85%	68%

Table 19.2 Percent of Women Having an Orgasm in Four Sexual Contexts, by Occurrence of Selected Sexual Behaviors

# of hookups	oral sex	intercourse	intercourse + oral	intercourse + self-stimulation	all three
1st hookup	15%	26%	37%	32%	63%
2nd or 3rd hookup	31%	32%	29%	50%	62%
3rd+ hookups	22%	40%	55%	63%	71%
In a relationship	66%	55%	80%	74%	92%

If we add another variable—whether each sexual encounter included oral sex performed on the female partner, intercourse, or self-clitoral stimulation—the data gets even more interesting. In Table 19.2, looking now only at rates of orgasm for women, we see a dramatically wide range of frequency: from a 15 percent chance of orgasm on the far upper corner (a first time hookup including oral sex only) to a 92 percent chance on the far right bottom corner (a relationship event including all three activities). Both additional hookups and a wider range of activities tend to increase women's rate of orgasm. When couples in relationships engage in all three activities, women's orgasms become nearly universal and her rate of orgasm almost converges with men's. Men in that situation have an orgasm 96 percent of the time, so the orgasm gap has shrunk to 1.04.

A woman's likelihood of experiencing an orgasm with sexual activity, then, varies according to whether she is alone or with someone else, the sex of the person she's with, the nature of her relationship with that person, and the types of sexual activities they include. Under the right circumstances, her chance of orgasm is almost exactly that of his.

This suggests that the orgasm gap cannot be driven purely by biology, but instead is related, at least in part, to decisions that individuals and couples make about whether and how to involve clitoral stimulation in sexual activity. In the remainder of this chapter, I will discuss four sociocultural forces that contribute to the orgasm gap: a lack of knowledge about sexual pleasure; the prioritization of male sexual pleasure; the expectation that women be sexy, but not sexual; and the coital imperative in the sexual script.

A LACK OF KNOWLEDGE ABOUT FEMALE ORGASM

When I teach college classes on sexuality, I am on the frontlines of American sex education failures. I've been asked to confirm if it's true that women are physically incapable of orgasm before the age of thirty. I've explained to a truly confused listener why women are unlikely to orgasm from anal sex,

WHAT'S YOUR CLITORAL LITERACY?

Jessica Ross

Here is a quiz to test your knowledge on the clitoris. Give yourself one point for each correct answer.

1. The clitoris has _____ nerve endings.

    a. 700
    b. 0
    c. 8,000
    d. 5,500
    e. None of the above

2. The clitoris is the only human organ that exists solely for pleasure.

    a. True
    b. False

3. About _____ of the clitoris is externally exposed.

    a. ½
    b. All
    c. ¾
    d. No part
    e. ¼

4. Vaginal orgasms are not related to clitoral orgasms.

    a. True
    b. False

Answers

1. c. The clitoris also interacts with 15,000 additional nerve endings within the vulva!
2. a. Other body parts associated with sexual pleasure have at least one additional bodily function.
3. e. This means three-quarters of this pleasure-inducing organ isn't even visible. This also explains why other areas of the vulva can feel so pleasurable!
4. b. All female orgasms are related to the clitoris, thus a vaginal orgasm is really a clitoral orgasm.

For more information see *Scarleteen: Sex Ed For The Real World* at www.scarleteen.com.

anatomically speaking. Students ask eagerly about how to find the g-spot—a scientifically-debated structure that might be found inside some women's vaginas and, if properly stimulated, may produce orgasm-like experiences for some women. Yet these same students seem nervous to ask about the clitoris, an external organ that appears to have no purpose except to easily provide sexual pleasure to women.[9] "Do we all have one of those?" asked one female student when I talked about the clitoris in a basic anatomy lesson.

If knowing the clitoris exists and finding it is a challenge, operating one seems even more so. I've seen the incredulous faces of my students when I tell them that they can't "make" a woman have an orgasm but should, instead, talk to her about what she likes; I may as well have told them to go to the moon to find out.

There's a good reason that young people (and many older people, as well!) are ignorant and unsure about female orgasm. Compared to the volume of conversation about other parts of our sexual anatomy—the homologous male organ, the penis, breast size, or female body parts more directly involved in reproduction—there is a cultural silence about the clitoris. It often gets short entries in dictionaries, anatomy textbooks, and sex education materials, if it's included at all.[10] Only 15 percent of young adults report that they've learned anything of importance about the clitoris from their parents.[11] Sex education classes, which typically focus more on reproduction than sex per se, discuss male orgasm in the context of ejaculation but usually don't address female orgasm at all.[12]

Young people, then, often have limited knowledge of the clitoris and sometimes carry some major misconceptions. In one study, I tested college students' knowledge about the clitoris.[13] Almost two-thirds of the students agreed with the false statement: "The clitoris is on the front wall of the vaginal canal." Nearly half of women and almost a third of men agreed with the statement, also false, that "the g-spot is another name for the clitoris." Ten percent of students believed that women urinate through their clitorises, as men do through their penises.[14] More than a quarter—29 percent of women and 25 percent of men—failed to find the clitoris on a diagram. On average, they scored a 63 percent on the "cliteracy test." Interestingly, men and women performed equally badly.

A general lack of knowledge about the clitoris, then, may explain part of the orgasm gap. But there's another problem: Neither men nor women may prioritize female orgasm.

DE-PRIORITIZING THE FEMALE ORGASM

As Tables 19.1 and 19.2 reveal, the orgasm gap in first-time hookups is three-to-one, but the gap in relationships is half that. What changes as couples move from hooking up to a relationship?

There is good evidence that the importance of female orgasm changes. Both men and women often deprioritize the female orgasm in hookups. "I'm all about making her orgasm," said a man interviewed for a study about orgasm among college students.[15] "The general her or like the specific her?" he was asked. "Girlfriend her," he responded, "In a hookup her, I don't give a shit." Some other men agree:

> If it's just a random hookup . . . Say they meet a girl at a party and it's a one night thing, I don't think it's gonna matter to them . . . But if you're with somebody for more than just that one night . . . I know I feel personally responsible. I think it's essential that she has an orgasm . . .[16]

Women know the difference. Said one: "When I . . . meet somebody and I'm gonna have a random hookup . . . from what I have seen, they're not even trying to, you know, make it a mutual thing."[17] My own research confirms that college women often accept that hookups don't include orgasms for women. One woman had hooked up with thirteen men, but not one had given her an orgasm. "The guy kind of expects to get off," she explained, "while the girl doesn't expect anything."[18]

Some women are disappointed by this state of affairs, but others feel that expecting an orgasm from a male hookup partner would be demanding or rude. One woman explained how she felt like she didn't have the right to ask for an orgasm: "I didn't feel comfortable I guess . . . I think I felt kind of guilty almost, like I felt like I was kind of subjecting [guys] to something they didn't want to do and I felt bad about it."[19]

While women's interest in having an orgasm varies, there is some evidence that women may be coping with men's disinterest in their orgasm by deemphasizing its value to themselves. They then put their energies into giving their partners pleasure.[20] Speaking of hookups, one woman insists: "I will do everything in my power to, like whoever I'm with, to get [him] off."[21] Another confessed, "Even if I was in charge, I did not make sure I was being pleased."[22]

Reflecting the quantitative data, women in relationships often feel very differently. They may feel entitled to orgasm and certain that their partners are concerned with their pleasure: "I know that he wants to make me happy," said one college student about her boyfriend, "I know that he wants me to orgasm . . . we are connected and like we're going for the same thing and that like he cares."[23]

The different rates of orgasm for men and women, then, may be partly caused by a consistent interest in giving men orgasms, but a varying interest in the same for women. This isn't the sexual double standard that women of the 1970s objected to—in which one group of women were "good girls" that men treated well and another group were "bad girls" they felt comfortable disrespecting. After all, on today's college campuses women often transition from being hookup partners to girlfriends. Nevertheless, men are still the arbiters of when women are "worthy" of their care and attention—not when she's "just" a hookup partner, but more so when she's a girlfriend—whereas men's orgasms are considered important by both men and women regardless of the context.

THE IMPERATIVE FOR WOMEN TO BE SEXY, BUT NOT SEXUAL

In a telling statement, Paris Hilton once told *Rolling Stone* magazine: ". . . my boyfriends always tell me I'm not sexual. Sexy, but not sexual."[24] There's a big difference. Sexual people *experience* desire. They feel lust, desire, and passion. In contrast, sexy people *inspire* desire. They stir sexual people to have those feelings.

Most people want to be both sexy *and* sexual, to be desired and to have desire. In the American cultural imagination, however, we tend to bifurcate those roles by gender. Men are sexual, women sexy. Men want, women want to be wanted. This is a problem; a sexy body is not necessarily a sexual body. The sexiness we're talking about is sexy like a sports car is sexy. It's a thing to be looked at, consumed, used, or owned. Admired, but only as we admire an object.

Women's disinterest in their own orgasm may be caused by a sense that their role in sex is solely to deliver a sexy body. What's important isn't how she feels, what she thinks, or who she is; . . . it's how she looks. By this logic, women's sexual desire and satisfaction is not really what sex is all about.

When a woman internalizes this message, we see self-sexual objectification, the process of identifying as an object of desire for others. This can lead to spectating, which means being worried about how one looks from a partner's perspective. A woman who self-objectifies might try to stay in sexual positions that she thinks are flattering, arrange her body and limbs to make herself look thinner or curvier, try to make sure her face doesn't do anything unattractive, and avoid making any embarrassing noises. She may even try to prevent her own orgasm because climaxing means losing control of these things.

Some women have "out of body sexual experiences" in which they are constantly thinking about how she *looks* to the other person instead of focusing on how she *feels*. And, sure enough, irrespective of actual attractiveness, the degree to which women self-objectify correlates with lots of different measures of sexual dissatisfaction and dysfunction. In other words, the more a woman worries about how she looks, the less likely she'll experience sexual desire, pleasure, and orgasm.

THE COITAL IMPERATIVE IN THE SEXUAL SCRIPT

While we like to think that our sexual encounters are spontaneous, they actually follow a rather rigid sexual script. This script is a set of rules that guide sexual interaction.[25] It tends to be quite closely followed much of the time, especially when two people are first becoming sexual together.

The sexual script involves a "coital imperative," a rule that, if heterosexual people are going to have sex, it must (eventually) include penile-vaginal intercourse.[26] In fact, penile-vaginal intercourse, or coitus, is the only act that almost everyone agrees counts as "real sex."[27] It also quite consistently produces orgasm for men.

In contrast, only about 20 percent of women regularly have orgasms from the thrusting of coitus alone, while the activities that are more likely to produce orgasm in women—cunnilingus and manual stimulation of the clitoris—are often not considered sex at all.[28] Likewise, most people call themselves virgins until the first time they have intercourse, no matter how many other sexual activities they've engaged in. And, if two people have never engaged in coitus, it's often an open question whether they've ever had sex, even if they've done other sexual things. A sexual encounter that doesn't include intercourse may even be seen as a failed encounter, because the couple didn't "go all the way."

So, by virtue of the coital imperative, the sexual script includes a concerted effort to give him an orgasm, but not her. Moreover, partly because coitus is so often treated as the end goal of sexual activity, his orgasm signals the end whether she's had an orgasm or not.[29] Her orgasm rarely signals the end of sexual activity, nor is it a measure of whether sex was had. Her orgasm is, instead, incidental: a nice addition, a sign that the sex was good perhaps, but wholly unnecessary to the endeavor.

To close, it is high time we stop pretending that women are bad at orgasms. The gap between men's and women's frequency of orgasm is not an inevitable fact of life. It is, instead, strongly impacted by social forces that privilege men's pleasure over women's. These social forces include ignorance about the clitoris, a prioritization of men's pleasure, the gendered sexy/sexual binary, and a coital imperative. Both men and women tend to internalize this logic, naturalizing and justifying the orgasm gap. In fact, the orgasm gap is a social artifact and it can be changed at will.

DISCUSSION QUESTIONS

•   Lisa Wade argues that the orgasm gap between men and women can't possibly be a purely biological phenomenon. What evidence does she provide to back up this claim? What sociocultural explanations does she offer? Do you agree or disagree?
•   What is the difference between feeling sexy and feeling sexual? How is this difference gendered? Can you imagine how it might contribute to an orgasm gap between men and women?
•   What is the order of activities in the sexual script common among the people you know? You probably can repeat it whether you are sexually active

or not. How might it contribute to a difference in the rates or orgasm for men and women?
• What does it mean to say that his orgasm is essential and hers incidental?

NOTES

1. John Gagnon, Robert Michael, and Stuart Michaels, *The Social Organization of Sexuality: Sexual Practices in the United States* (Chicago: University of Chicago Press, 2000).
2. Stevi Jackson and Sue Scott, "Faking Like a Woman? Towards an Interpretive Theorization of Sexual Pleasure," *Body & Society* 13, no. 2 (2007): 95–116; Maya Lavie-Ajayi and Hélène Joffe, "Social Representations of Female Orgasm," *Journal of Health Psychology* 14, no. 1 (2009): 98–107.
3. Heather Armstrong and Elke Reissing, "Women Who Have Sex with Women: A Comprehensive Review of the Literature and Conceptual Model of Sexual Function," *Sexual and Relationship Therapy* 28, no. 4 (2013): 364–399; Marcia Douglass and Lisa Douglass, *Are We Having Fun Yet?* (New York: Hyperion, 1997); John Harvey, Amy Wenzel, and Susan Sprecher, *The Handbook of Sexuality in Close Relationships* (Mahwah, NJ: Lawrence Erlbaum Associates, 2004); Alfred Kinsey, Wardell Pomeroy, Clyde Martin, and Paul Gebhard, *Sexual Behavior in the Human Female* (Philadelphia: Saunders, 1953); Elisabeth Lloyd, *The Case of the Female Orgasm: Bias in the Science of Evolution* (Cambridge, MA: Harvard University Press, 2005); Sharon Thompson, "Search for Tomorrow: On Feminism and the Reconstruction of Teen Romance," in Carole Vance, ed., *Pleasure and Danger: Exploring Female Sexuality* (London: Pandora, 1989).
4. John Harvey, Amy Wenzel, and Susan Sprecher, *The Handbook of Sexuality in Close Relationships* (Mahwah, NJ: Lawrence Erlbaum Associates, 2004).
5. Shere Hite, *The Hite Report: A Nationwide Study of Female Sexuality* (New York: Seven Stories Press, 1976); Kinsey et al., *Sexual Behavior in the Human Female.*
6. Kinsey et al., *Sexual Behavior in the Human Female.*
7. Lisa Wade, Emily Kremer, and Jessica Brown, "The Incidental Orgasm: The Presence of Clitoral Knowledge and the Absence of Orgasm for Women," Women & Health 42, no. 1 (2005): 117–138.
8. Elizabeth Armstrong, Paula England, and Alison Fogarty, "Accounting for Women's Orgasm and Sexual Enjoyment in College Hookups and Relationships," *American Sociological Review* 77, no. 3 (2012): 435–462.
9. Lloyd, *The Case of the Female Orgasm.*
10. Virginia Braun and Celia Kitzinger, "Telling it Straight? Dictionary Definitions of Women's Genitals," *Journal of Sociolinguistics* 5, no. 2 (2001): 214–232; Janet Holland, Caroline Ramazanoglu, Sue Sharpe, and Rachel Thomson, *The Male in the Head: Young People, Heterosexuality and Power* (London: Tufnell Press, 1998); Judith Levine, *Harmful to Minors: The Perils of Protecting Children from Sex* (Minneapolis: University of Minnesota Press, 2002); Lisa Jean Moore and Adele Clarke, "Clitoral Conventions and Transgressions: Graphic Representations in Anatomy Texts, c1900–91," *Feminist*

Studies 21, no. 2 (1995): 255–301; Shirley Ogletree and Harvey Ginsburg, "Kept under the Hood: Neglect of the Clitoris in Common Vernacular," *Sex Roles* 43, no. 11/12 (2000): 917–927.

11. Sinikka Elliott, *Not My Kid: What Parents Believe about the Sex Lives of Their Teenagers* (New York: New York University Press, 2012); Wade, Kremer, and Brown, "The Incidental Orgasm."

12. Christine Beyer, Roberta Ogletree, Dale Ritzel, Judy Drolet, Sharon Gilbert, and Dale Brown, "Gender Representation in Illustrations, Text, and Topic Areas in Sexuality Education Curricula," *Journal of School Health* 66, no. 10 (1996): 361–364; Linda Brock and Glen Jennings, "What Daughters in Their 30s Wish Their Mothers Had Told Them," *Family Relations* 42, no. 1 (1993): 61–65; Holland et al., *The Male in the Head*; Levine, *Harmful to Minors: The Perils of Protecting Children from Sex* (Minneapolis: University of Minnesota Press, 2002); Ogletree and Ginsburg, "Kept Under the Hood"; Deborah Tolman, "Doing Desire: Adolescent Girls' Struggles for/with Sexuality," *Gender & Society* 8, no. 3 (1994): 324–342.

13. Wade, Kremer, and Brown, "The Incidental Orgasm."

14. Author's unpublished data.

15. Armstrong, England, and Fogarty, "Accounting for Women's Orgasm and Sexual Enjoyment in College Hookups and Relationships," 456.

16. Elizabeth Armstrong, Paula England, and Alison Fogarty, "Orgasm in College Hookups and Relationships," in Barbara Risman, ed., *Families as They Really Are* (New York: W.W. Norton, 2009): 456.

17. Armstrong, England, and Fogarty, "Accounting for Women's Orgasm and Sexual Enjoyment in College Hookups and Relationships," 455.

18. Lisa Wade and Caroline Heldman, "Hooking Up and Opting Out: What Students Learn about Sex in Their First Year of College," in John DeLamater and Laura Carpenter, eds., Sex for Life: From Virginity to Viagra, How Sexuality Changes throughout Our Lives (New York: New York University Press, 2012): 142.

19. Armstrong, England, and Fogarty, "Orgasm in College Hookups and Relationships," 457.

20. Ellen Laan and Alessandra Rellini, "Can We Treat Anorgasmia in Women? The Challenge to Experiencing Pleasure," *Sexual and Relationship Therapy* 26, no. 4 (2011): 329–341.

21. Armstrong, England, and Fogarty, "Accounting for Women's Orgasm and Sexual Enjoyment in College Hookups and Relationships," 455.

22. Wade and Heldman, "Hooking Up and Opting Out," 141–142.

23. Armstrong, England, and Fogarty, "Orgasm in College Hookups and Relationships," 454.

24. Ariel Levy, *Female Chauvinist Pigs: Women and the Rise of Raunch Culture* (New York: Simon and Schuster, 2006).

25. John Gagnon and William Simon, *Sexual Conduct: The Social Sources of Human Sexuality* (Chicago: Aldine, 1973).

26. Kathryn McPhillips, Virginia Braun, and Nicola Gavey, "Defining Heterosex: How Imperative is the 'Coital Imperative'?" *Women's Studies International Forum* 24, no. 2 (2001): 229–240.

27. Marian Pitts and Qazi Rahman, "Which Behaviors Constitute 'Having Sex' among University Students in the U.K.?" *Archives of Sexual Behavior* 30, no. 2 (2001): 169–176; Stephanie Sanders and June Machover Reinisch, "Would You Say You 'Had Sex' If . . .?" *Journal of the American Medical Association* 281, no. 3 (1999): 275–277.

28. Lloyd, *The Case of the Female Orgasm*.

29. Virginia Braun and Celia Kitzinger, "Telling It Straight? Dictionary Definitions of Women's Genitals," *Journal of Sociolinguistics* 5, no. 2 (2001): 214–232.

WHY WE HOOK UP

Searching for Sex or Looking for Love?

Justin R. Garcia and Helen E. Fisher

About 65 percent to 85 percent of U.S. college students have had a sexual "hookup"—a no-strings-attached uncommitted sexual encounter between two people not currently in a romantic relationship with each other. But if one were to also count other varieties of uncommitted sex, such as "booty calls" (late night visits for sex) and "friends-with-benefits" (ongoing sexual but supposedly not romantic relationships),[1] the rates of allegedly casual sexual encounters would be considerably greater. Of course, casual sex is not a new American phenomenon;[2] however, twenty-first-century social discourse about casual sex, contemporary cultural representation of hooking up, and the shifting relationship between uncommitted sex and committed romance today is unprecedented, particularly among the young.

Hooking up has caught the attention of the American public. Books on casual sex now range from self-guided diaries, such as *Hook-ups & Hangovers*, to self-help handbooks such as *The Happy Hook-up* and *The Hook-up Handbook*; most of these aim to guide young women to get the most out of their uncommitted sexual encounters. Popular movies on the topic, including *No Strings Attached* and *Friends with Benefits*, feature A-list actors as they fumble through the ups and downs of practicing uncommitted sex; most notably, these films follow the characters as they attempt to manage their developing romantic feelings. Countless songs contain allusions to uncommitted sex, either advising to avoid or pursue it. Advertisements for websites and mobile phone apps encourage men and women—across sexual orientations and relationship statuses—to realize their sexual urges and find a nearby hook-up partner.[3] Magazine editorials ask why people hook up, or give tips on how to be more successful at it. The February 2012 cover story in the American Psychological Association's flagship magazine urged practitioners to know the data on the health consequences of hooking up.[4] Even the *New York Times* has tackled this phenomenon several times, questioning whether we should be concerned for America's youth, and asking what has and hasn't changed since the sexual revolution of the 1960s.

Academic research on the motivations for, and the consequences of, sexual hook-up behavior has also proliferated among scholars in a wide range of disciplines. Most of the research to date has focused on the occurrence of sexual hookups among *emerging adults*, individuals between the ages of 18 and 25 years, who are in the developmental transition stage between adolescence and young adulthood.[5] Researchers vary in their theoretical approaches, methodologies, definitions, sample sizes, and campus locations. Some have studied small regional college populations while others have collected data in large urban universities.

WHAT IS EMERGING ADULTHOOD?
THE EXPERTS DISAGREE

When it comes to explaining young-adult brain development, there is disagreement among the experts. Some researchers believe that 18- to 25-year-olds are still in a developmental transition stage between adolescence and young adulthood; others cite evidence that 18-year-olds are, neurologically speaking, adults.

Robert Needlman, MD, professor of Pediatrics at Case Western Reserve University and editor of *Dr. Spock's Baby and Child Care*, explains "the brain of an eighteen-year-old is neurologically quite similar to that of a twenty-eight-year old. Most of the sensitive periods for learning are essentially over by eighteen. Developmental psychologist Jean Piaget believes—as do other psychologists—that most eighteen year olds have the ability to think abstractly (even if they don't always use that ability—much like the rest of us!)."[6]

A great deal of media attention about hook-up culture focuses on college students. If we consider college students to be adults, then peering into the bedrooms of grown-ups and judging their private activities is infantilizing.[7] What do you think?

Despite many unanswered questions about sexual hookups, the collective data has produced some consistent patterns: A majority of men and women on North American college campuses today have hooked up at least once; undergraduate students regard hooking up as distinct from romantic dating; and both sexes experience myriad negative *and* positive reactions after having hooked up.

Several historical trends have contributed to this hook-up phenomenon.[8] Along with rapidly changing social conventions and patterns of leisure activity, the rise of the automobile, and the growth of college parties and entertainment venues such as cinemas and drive-in movie theaters in the early to mid-twentieth century, parental supervision of dating and traditional patterns of courtship began to diminish.[9] For centuries, a young man visited the natal home of a young woman to woo her in the presence of her family. But by the mid-1900s, a courting couple could speed off in a car—where they could get to know each other more fully, even sexually, in private. Then, along with the rise of the feminist movement, mixed-sexed parties, the use of alcohol and drugs, increasing access to birth control (condoms and oral contraceptives), and changing attitudes about virginity, marriage, and reproduction in the 1960s, American emerging (and older) adults became even more sexually liberated, increasing one's opportunities to hook up.

A few psychological factors may also be key in contributing to the current hook-up phenomenon: Today emerging adults tend to push away from parental figures to test their social and personal boundaries, define their identity, and experiment with sex, romance, alcohol, and other drugs. Many emerging adults also have a deep desire to belong to a peer group, and thus follow social—and sexual—norms. Most emerging adults in the United States and other postindustrial societies are not yet constrained by marital and parenting responsibilities; many attend college where they are surrounded by other singles of the same general age. So, many emerging adults, especially on college campuses, have the time and opportunity to engage in casual sex. In fact, in one study the average U.S. college student had more recent sexual hookups than first dates.[10]

For demographic reasons, the frequency of contemporary casual sex is likely to continue.[11] The average age at first sexual intercourse in the United States is 17 years. But adolescents are entering puberty at historically younger ages. The average age that boys in the United States experience their first major pubertal landmark (first ejaculation) is age 13 years; for girls, menarche or first menstruation occurs between ages 12 and 13 years.[12] The ages of physiological sexual maturity have been consistently dropping. Interestingly, in one national study, close to 16 percent of female teenagers and 28 percent of male teenagers reported that their first sexual experience was with someone they had just met or who was just a friend,[13] although the degree to which these first sexual encounters may have been hookups is unclear. However, in a study of middle school and high school students, 32 percent had experienced sexual intercourse and 61 percent of those who were sexually experienced had sexual encounters with someone who was not a dating or relationship partner.[14] American youth are engaging in sexual activity, including non-relationship sex.

While age of sexual maturation is becoming younger, Americans are also delaying first marriage and first childbirth, further increasing the opportunities to hook up. In the United States, the current median age of marriage for women is age 27 years and for men it is age 29 years, providing millions of people with even more time to have sex outside of a committed, long-term, romantic relationship. The amount of time between sexual maturation and marital pairing is greater than it has ever been. Moreover, the U.S. divorce rate is about 45 percent, providing many previously married men and women more time for casual sex in middle age and their later years. In fact, according to the 2013 U.S. Census, there are now 111 million unmarried people age 18 years and older in the United States, approximately one-third of the adult population. We know of no society in the historical or anthropological literature that has had so many single adults with the time and opportunity for casual sex for such extended periods of adulthood.[15]

WHO IS HOOKING UP?

Because most of the hook-up research has focused on white heterosexual college students, rather than the general population,[16] we collected data on hookups in a far broader sample of U.S. singles. This investigation was part of *Singles in America* (SIA), an annual study conducted in collaboration with the Internet dating site Match.com.[17] Participants were not members of this dating site; instead, data were collected on a large nationally representative sample of single Americans based on demographic distributions reported in the U.S. Census. The 2013 sample from which we collected data about sexual hookups was a sub-sample of 3,905 unmarried Americans between the ages of 18 and 75+ years, of all sexual orientations, from every major ethnic group, and from every region of the country.

Results showed that 58 percent of these men and women had experienced a one-night stand; and 53 percent had been in a friends-with-benefits relationship. Moreover, casual sex had been experienced by individuals in every age cohort, not just among the young. For example, among individuals in the age cohort 50 to 59 years, 65 percent of men and women had experienced a one-night stand and 47 percent had had a friends-with-benefits relationship. Among those aged 60 to 69, 61 percent had had a one-night stand and 41 percent had had a friends-with-benefits relationship. Among those aged 70 and older, 44 percent had had a one-night stand and 35 percent had had a friends-with-benefits relationship. It is not known whether these men and women aged 50+ experienced these one-night stands and friends-with-benefits relationships when they were younger or more recently, as the question did not specify a time frame. But the frequency of uncommitted sex was relatively high across all age cohorts, including older men and older women. In other words, casual sex cannot be regarded as a phenomenon unique to emerging adults, or specifically to college students. (See Figure 20.1.)

Equally interesting, among those between the ages 18 to 20 years, 33 percent had had a one-night stand and 42 percent had had a friends-with-benefits

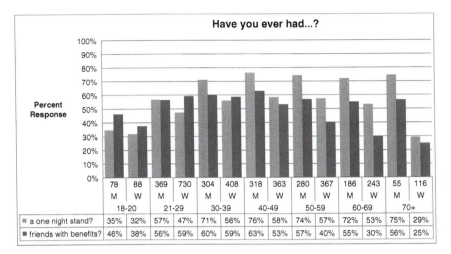

Have you ever had...?													
	78 M	88 W	369 M	730 W	304 M	408 W	318 M	363 W	280 M	367 W	186 M	243 W	55 M	116 W
	18-20		21-29		30-39		40-49		50-59		60-69		70+	
▨ a one night stand?	35%	32%	57%	47%	71%	56%	76%	58%	74%	57%	72%	53%	75%	29%
■ friends with benefits?	46%	38%	56%	59%	60%	59%	63%	53%	57%	40%	55%	30%	56%	25%

Figure 20.1 Hooking Up and Friends With Benefits: The Data

relationship. Among those between the ages 21 and 29, 51 percent had experienced a one-night stand and 58 percent had experienced a friends-with-benefits relationship. As we noted earlier, some 65 to 85 percent of U.S. college students have had a hookup. So individuals on college campuses do appear to engage in more uncommitted sex than those of the general population, even compared with those of their own age cohorts. This is consistent with a recent interview study that reported that college students who live on campus engage in hookups more regularly than commuter students. However, all students noted that hooking up is part of what they perceive as the typical college experience.[18] The authors of this study also established that hooking up was most prevalent among white, middle-class students who did not hold a job.

The available data suggest that college campuses create a special environment for casual sexual encounters, despite the fact that a considerable number of men and women of every age cohort and region in America have experienced casual sex. This may be due to opportunity. When asked where hookups take place, college students report a variety of locations, including parties (67 percent), dormitories or fraternity houses (57 percent), bars and/or clubs (10 percent), cars (4 percent), and unspecified available places (35 percent).[19] In another study, approximately 30 percent of undergraduates had engaged in sex with someone they met over spring break.[20] Alcohol and other drug use most likely further fuel the hook-up phenomenon. In one study, only 27 percent of college-age respondents reported being sober during a sexual hookup.[21]

Curiously, results from a qualitative study indicate that nearly half of college students are also unconcerned about contracting a sexually transmitted infection from a hookup, possibly because they believe their partners (largely other college students) do not match their preconceived image of a person carrying a sexually transmitted infection.[22] Nevertheless, in one study, nearly 71 percent of college students reported using a condom during their most recent sexual hookup.[23]

CASUAL SEX FOR PLEASURE?

Casual sex poses considerable potential risks, including the possibility of emotional trauma, sexually transmitted infections, unwanted pregnancy, relationship violence, and intoxication-related harm.[24] Yet both men and women do it. Why?

It is commonly believed that men and women hook up for sexual pleasure. Yet hooking up is not always as sexually gratifying as tabloids, TV shows, movies, or blogs would lead us to believe. Data show that both men and women are less likely to achieve orgasm during a hookup than during sex with a committed partner. Sociologists Elizabeth Armstrong, Paula England, and Alison Fogarty found that 85 percent of men and 68 percent of women reached orgasm during sex with a committed partner, whereas only 31 percent of men and 10 percent of women reached orgasm during hook-up sex.[25] Justin Garcia, Sean Massey, Ann Merriwether, Susan Seibold-Simpson replicated and extended these findings showing that both sexes had fewer orgasms when hooking up, and also found that on average, men and women *desired orgasm less* in a sexual hookup than in a romantic relationship.[26] Although orgasm should not be equated with sexual satisfaction, most would agree that orgasm is a deeply pleasurable aspect of a sexual encounter. Those partaking in hookups have fewer of them.

A variety of factors are likely to contribute to reduced sexual pleasure, or at least reduced orgasm, during a hookup. Some people enjoy sex only in the context of a partnership; others enjoy sex in both committed and uncommitted relationships. Thus, a negative attitude toward uncommitted sex could limit one's ability to orgasm during an uncommitted sexual encounter, reducing the pleasure of the experience. Levels of comfort with various sexual behaviors in an uncommitted encounter can also impact feelings of pleasure and satisfaction. Several scholars have also noted that college students tend to over-perceive the comfort level of their hookup partners while engaging in a variety of sexual behaviors (what psychologists call *pluralistic ignorance*); men, in particular, tend to overestimate a woman's comfort with sexual intercourse.[27]

Sexual double standards may also limit the potential for pleasure in casual sex. Some women who engage in casual sex worry about being negatively perceived, harshly judged, and stigmatized.[28] Other women feel they have been denied a partner's sexual attentiveness. Still others feel that casual sex jeopardizes their ability to negotiate safer sex via condom use.[29] College women report greater thoughts of worry and vulnerability during sexual hookups than do college men, indicating a gender difference in attitudes about casual sex.[30]

These worries are perhaps well founded. Research has shown that women who engage in uncommitted sex are judged more negatively and stigmatized by both men and other women.[31] Even Sigmund Freud noted that women, and the men who engage in sexual activity with them, struggle with a "Madonna-Whore dichotomy" wherein women experience difficulty being viewed as either a potential virginal spouse or a potentially promiscuous sexual object, rather than occupying the more realistic space between these polar opposite stereotypes.

The data on the pleasure of hooking up is varied. Some people report feeling sexually aroused, satisfied, happy, and/or proud, while others report feeling disappointed, confused, embarrassed, and/or scared.[32] Some report that a majority of men and women are glad that they have had their hookup experiences.[33] Still other researchers find that a majority of both men and women have felt regret for engaging in sexual hookups.[34] In an innovative longitudinal study evaluating the putative effect of casual sex on well-being, developmental psychologist Zhana Vrangalova followed a group of undergraduate students across an academic year; after controlling for a variety of variables, on average those students who identified engaging in sexual hookups for "autonomous" reasons reported no negative outcomes, while those who engaged in sexual hookups for "non-autonomous" reasons (self-imposed pressures, external forces, lack of intentionality) were more likely to report lower self-esteem, higher depression and anxiety, and more negative health outcomes.[35] Taken together, the data suggest that when hooking up, people experience a wide variety of concomitant positive, negative, and ambiguous feelings.

Since hookups tend to result in lower rates of orgasm, and are often associated with high rates of regret and other negative emotional outcomes, how do people describe their own reasons for engaging in hookups? Justin Garcia and Chris Reiber[36] asked college students who had experienced a sexual hookup about their motivations. Men and women gave remarkably similar reasons for hooking up: 89 percent reported that their motivation was physical pleasure and gratification; 54 percent reported emotional gratification; 33 percent said their hookups were unintentional, likely due to alcohol or drug use; 8 percent said they felt others were doing it; and 4 percent said they felt peer pressure.

But here's the catch: In that same study, *51 percent reported that they hooked up hoping to initiate a romantic relationship*. Further, over one-third of participants reported that the *ideal* outcome of a hookup would be the beginning of a romantic relationship. Studies of U.S. undergraduate students corroborate this evidence. Cindy Meston and David Buss asked participants why they had engaged in sexual intercourse.[37] Respondents provided 237 varied reasons. But among the top five responses were: "I was attracted to the person"; and "I wanted to show my affection to the person." These results indicate that many men and women link sex with some form of romantic attraction and/or attachment to a partner.

One's hopes of turning casual sex into love may be realized more regularly than people think. In the 2013 *Singles in America* study noted earlier, we asked a sub-sample of 1,042 U.S. singles whether they had ever had a one-night stand or casual hookup that turned into a long-term, committed, romantic relationship. In the survey, 40 percent of men and 24 percent of women said "yes." And when we queried American singles about whether they had ever had a friends-with-benefits relationship that turned into a long-term committed partnership, 36 percent of men and 23 percent of women in the 2013 survey said "yes."

Casual sex can trigger love, perhaps for several reasons. Foremost, during sex one gets to know some basic things about one's partner. Five of the twelve cranial nerves are triggered when kissing, sending powerful signals to the brain to record extensive data on a partner's smell, taste, touch, and sounds, as well as bodily details perceived through vision. During sexual activity one collects even more data through the senses, as well as valuable information about a partner's degree of kindness, empathy, patience, ability to listen, their mental and physical health and flexibility, and perhaps even their sense of humor. Thus, when the casual sex meets one's expectations, he or she may become more receptive to romance.

Casual sex may also prime the brain for love. This is possible due to complex biological interactions between three primary brain systems that evolved for mating and reproduction: the sex drive; feelings of intense romantic love; and feelings of deep attachment.[38] The sex drive is characterized by the craving for sexual gratification (or "libido"). It is associated primarily with the androgens, particularly testosterone, in both men and women. Romantic love is characterized by intense energy, focused courtship attention, ecstasy, mood swings, anxiety, sexual possessiveness, emotional dependency, obsessive thinking about the beloved, craving for emotional union with the beloved, and extreme motivation to win this preferred mating partner. Romantic love is primarily associated with elevated activity in dopamine pathways of the brain's reward system. Attachment is associated, instead, with feelings of calm, security, social comfort, and emotional union with a long-term mating partner, as well as mutual territory defense, home building, maintenance of close proximity, separation anxiety, shared parental chores, and affiliative gestures. Several lines of evidence link feelings of attachment primarily with the neuropeptides oxytocin and vasopressin.[39]

The sex drive most likely evolved principally to motivate individuals to seek sexual union with a *range* of potential mates. Romantic love developed to motivate individuals to prefer a *specific* mating partner, thereby conserving courtship time and energy. And the brain circuitry for partner attachment most likely evolved primarily to motivate individuals to sustain an affiliative connection at least long enough to raise a child through infancy as a team.[40] It is important to note that a growing body of data demonstrates that the biological substrate of romantic love is consistent across sexual orientations and does not appear contingent upon one's gender preferences.

These three brain systems interact in myriad different ways. Most important to this chapter, however, is their role in casual sex. Genital stimulation and arousal can produce elevated activity in the dopamine system,[41] potentially triggering feelings of romantic love. Moreover, rising dopamine activity can stimulate the release of testosterone, and increasing testosterone can promote even more dopamine release[42]—potentially intensifying one's feelings of romance. Casual sex can also trigger feelings of deep attachment, because any form of pleasing massage or touch can elevate the oxytocin system, associated with feelings of attachment.[43] Moreover, if one reaches orgasm during casual sex, this release can also elevate the activity of oxytocin and vasopressin, neurochemicals associated with feelings of bonding[44] (although the relationship between orgasm and promotion of sociosexual pair-bonds is somewhat controversial among evolutionary behavioral scientists).[45]

"Casual sex," it appears, is not always casual. Sex—even uncommitted sex—provides individuals with an abundance of information about a potential longer-term partner, information that may stimulate romance and/or feelings of attachment. Interestingly, the frequency of orgasm and sexual pleasure increase as men and women repeat their hook-up encounters together,[46] most likely in part because pleasurable sex can trigger the neuropsychological mechanisms associated with romance and attachment and stimulate pair-bonding.

Along with the many historical, cultural, and psychological reasons that undoubtedly play a role in the frequency of casual sex, there appear to be some foundational evolutionary biological factors that also contribute to the practice and frequency of hooking up. Foremost, it can turn short-term sexual activity into a long-term, committed relationship—with the crucial opportunity to send one's DNA on to future generations. Long-term romantic relationships typify humanity. Thus, for many twenty-first-century lovers, the (most likely unconscious) potential payoffs of casual may far exceed the potential costs.

DISCUSSION QUESTIONS

• If people have always engaged in casual sex, why do you think contemporary hookups have interested researchers across multiple fields?
• Can you think of any major societal shifts (e.g., technology) that have influenced hook-up culture? Do you think any of these shifts are the reasons why casual sex seems to be popular amongst college-aged people?
• What role has the media played in popularizing hook-up culture? Would you consider it a positive or negative influence?
• If casual sex cannot be regarded as a phenomenon unique to emerging adults, or specifically to college students, then why does so much of the media

attention, conversation, moral panic, and research typically focus on college students? What is it about college students that make them different from the rest of the population?

NOTES

1. S.E. Claxton and M.H.M. van Dulmen, "Casual Sexual Relationships and Experiences in Emerging Adulthood," *Emerging Adulthood* 1 (2013): 138–150.

2. B. Reay, "Promiscuous Intimacies: Rethinking the History of American Casual Sex," *Journal of Historical Sociology* 27 (2014): 1–24.

3. Several mobile phone apps use geospatial location to find those nearby (e.g., Grindr is such an app designed specifically for men looking for casual sex with other men). In addition to the "casual encounters" section of Craigslist, several websites exist for the purported purposes of finding a casual sex partner.

4. J.R. Garcia, C. Reiber, S.G. Massey, and A.M. Merriwether, "Sexual Hookup Culture," *APA Monitor on Psychology* 44 (February 2013): 60–67.

5. J.J. Arnett, "Emerging Adulthood: A Theory of Development From the Late Teens through the Twenties," *American Psychologist* 55 (2000): 469–480; J.J. Arnett, *Emerging Adulthood: The Winding Road from the Late Teens through the Twenties* (New York: Oxford University Press, 2004).

6. Personal correspondence with the author, April 28, 2011.

7. Shira Tarrant, "Why Are Conservatives Obsessed with The Sex Lives of College Kids?" *AlterNet*, April 17, 2011, http://www.alternet.org/story/150639/why_are_conservatives_obsessed_with_the_sex_lives_of_college_kids.

8. Much of the hook-up research to date has primarily focused on white, heterosexual youth, with most samples stemming from North America.

9. B.L. Bailey, *From Front Porch to Back Seat: Courtship in Twentieth Century America* (Baltimore, MD: Johns Hopkins University Press, 1988); E. Laumann, J.H. Gagnon, R.T. Michael, and S. Michaels, *The Social Organization of Sexuality: Sexual Practices in the United States* (Chicago, IL: University of Chicago Press, 1994); R.D. Stinson, "Hooking Up in Young Adulthood: A Review of Factors Influencing the Sexual Behavior of College Students," *Journal of College Student Psychotherapy* 24 (2010): 98–115; J.R. Garcia, C. Reiber, S.G. Massey, and A.M. Merriwether, "Sexual Hookup Culture: A Review," *Review of General Psychology* 16 (2011): 161–176.

10. C. Bradshaw, A.S. Kahn, and B.K. Saville, "To Hook Up or Date: Which Gender Benefits?" *Sex Roles* 62 (2010): 661–669.

11. J.R. Garcia and C. Reiber, "Hook-Up Behavior: A Biopsychosocial Perspective," *Journal of Social, Evolutionary, and Cultural Psychology* 2 (2008): 192–208; K.A. Bogle, "The Shift From Dating to Hooking Up in College: What Scholars Have Missed," *Sociology* Compass 1–2 (2007): 775–788.

12. Marcia E. Herman-Giddens, "Recent Data on Pubertal Milestones in United States Children: The Secular Trend toward Earlier Development," *International Journal of Andrology* 29, no. 1 (2006): 241–246.

13. G. Martinez, C.E. Copen, and J.C. Abma, "Teenagers in the United States: Sexual Activity, Contraceptive Use, and Childbearing, 2006–2010 National Survey of Family Growth," National Center for Health Statistics. *Vital and Health Statistics* 23 (2011): 1–35.

14. W.S. Manning, P.C. Giordano, and M.A. Longmore, "Hooking Up: The Relationship Contexts of 'Nonrelationship' Sex," *Journal of Adolescent Research* 21 (2006): 459–483.

15. Garcia and Reiber, "Hook-Up Behavior."

16. Garcia et al., "Sexual Hookup Culture"; C. Heldman and L. Wade, "Hook-Up Culture: Setting a New Research Agenda," *Sexuality Research and Social Policy* 7 (2010): 323–333; L.J. Rupp, V. Taylor, S. Regev-Messalam, A. Fogarty, and P. England, "Queer Women in the Hookup Scene: Beyond the Closet?" *Gender & Society* 28 (2014): 212–235.

17. Singles in America (SIA) is sponsored by the online dating company Match.com; however, participants were not drawn from the Match.com population or subsidiary sites. Data access and analysis procedures were approved by a university institutional review board. Data for the current study were drawn from the 2013 wave of the ongoing Singles in America (SIA) study. Data were collected by Research Now (Plano, TX) using Internet research panels for population-based cross-sectional survey. Nationally representative research panels are compiled based on demographic distributions reflected in the most recent Current Population Survey, released by the United States Bureau of the Census. However, the current study also includes augmented oversampling of certain demographic categories. All data were collected over the Internet.

18. A. Rachel and B.J. Risman, "It Goes Hand in Hand with the Parties: Race, Class, and Residence in College Student Negotiations of Hooking Up," *Sociological Perspective* 57 (2014): 102–123.

19. E.L. Paul and K.A. Hayes, "The Casualties of 'Casual' Sex: A Qualitative Exploration of the Phenomenology of College Students' Hookups," *Journal of Social and Personal Relationships* 19 (2002): 639–661.

20. S. Sönmez, Y. Apostolopoulos, C.H. Yu, S. Yang, A.S. Mattila, and L.C. Yu, "Binge Drinking and Casual Sex on Spring-Break," *Annals of Tourism Research* 33 (2006): 895–917.

21. M.L. Fisher, K. Worth, J.R. Garcia, and T. Meredith, "Feelings of Regret Following Uncommitted Sexual Encounters in Canadian University Students," *Culture, Health & Sexuality* 14 (2012): 45–57.

22. T.M. Downing-Matibag and B. Geisinger, "Hooking Up and Sexual Risk Taking among College Students: A Health Belief Model Perspective," *Qualitative Health Research* 19 (2009): 1196–1209.

23. S.M. Seibold-Simpson, J.R. Garcia, S.G. Massey, A.M. Merriwether, and A.N. Gesselman, "Hook-Up Behavior, Condom Use, and Perceptions of Sexual Risk among U.S. College Students." In preparation.

24. S.E. Sandberg-Thoma and C.M.K. Dush. "Casual Sexual Relationships and Mental Health in Adolescence and Emerging Adulthood," *Journal of Sex Research* 51 (2014): 121–130; J.J. Owen, G.K. Rhoades, S.M. Stanley, and F.D. Fincham, " 'Hooking Up'

among College Students: Demographic and Psychosocial Correlates," *Archives of Sexual Behavior* 39 (2010): 653–663.

25. E.A. Armstrong, P. England, and A.C.K. Fogarty, "Orgasm in College Hook-ups and Relationships," in B.J. Risman, ed., *Families As They Really Are* (New York: W.W. Norton, 2009): 362–377; E.A. Armstrong, P. England, and A.C.K. Fogarty, "Accounting for Women's Orgasm and Sexual Enjoyment in College Hookups and Relationships," *American Sociological Review* 77 (2012): 435–462.

26. J.R. Garcia, S.G. Massey, A.M. Merriwether, and S.M. Seibold-Simpson, "Orgasm Experiences Among Emerging Adult Men and Women: Gender, Relationship Context, and Attitudes Toward Casual Sex." In review.

27. M. Hill, J.R. Garcia, and G. Geher, "Casual But Not Always Wanted: Exploring the Occurrence of Unwanted Sexual Experiences in the Context of Hookups." In review; T.A. Lambert, A.S. Kahn, and K.J. Apple, "Pluralistic Ignorance and Hooking Up," *Journal of Sex Research* 40 (2003): 129–133; C. Reiber and J.R. Garcia, "Hooking Up: Gender Differences, Evolution, and Pluralistic Ignorance," *Evolutionary Psychology* 8 (2010): 390–404.

28. T.D. Conley, A. Ziegler, and A.C. Moors, "Backlash from the Bedroom: Stigma Mediates Gender Differences in Acceptance of Casual Sex Offers," *Psychology of Women Quarterly* 37 (2012): 392–407.

29. J. Kelly and D.G. Bazzini, "Gender, Sexual Experience, and the Sexual Double Standard: Evaluations of Female Contraceptive Behavior," *Sex Roles* 45 (2001): 785–799; V.R. Schick, A.N. Zucker, and L.Y. Bay-Cheng, "Safer, Better Sex through Feminism: The Role of Feminist Ideology in Women's Sexual Well-Being," *Psychology of Women Quarterly* 32 (2008): 225–232.

30. J.M. Townsend and T.H. Wasserman, "Sexual Hookups among College Students: Sex Differences in Emotional Reactions," *Archives of Sexual Behavior* 40 (2011): 1173–1181.

31. Conley, Ziegler, and Moors, "Backlash from the Bedroom."

32. Paul and Hayes, "The Casualties of 'Casual' Sex."

33. Garcia and Reiber, "Hook-Up Behavior."

34. Fisher et al., "Feelings of Regret Following Uncommitted Sexual Encounters in Canadian University Students."

35. Zhana Vrangalova, "Does Casual Sex Harm College Students' Well-Being? A Longitudinal Investigation of the Role of Motivation," *Archives of Sexual Behavior* (February 2014). http://link.springer.com.mcc1.library.csulb.edu/article/10.1007/s10508-013-0255-1/fulltext.html.

36. Garcia and Reiber, "Hook-Up Behavior."

37. C.M. Meston and D.M. Buss, "Why Humans Have Sex," *Archives of Sexual Behavior* 36 (2007): 477–507.

38. H.E. Fisher, "Lust, Attraction, and Attachment in Mammalian Reproduction," *Human Nature* 9 (1998): 23–52; H.E. Fisher, A. Aron, and L.L. Brown, "Romantic Love: A Mammalian Brain System for Mate Choice," *Philosophical Transactions of the Royal Society: Biological Sciences* 361 (2006): 2173–2186; H.E. Fisher and J.A. Thomson, "Lust, Romance, Attachment: Do the Side-Effects of Serotonin-Enhancing

Antidepressants Jeopardize Romantic Love, Marriage and Fertility?" in S.M. Platek, J.P. Keenan, and T.K. Shackelford, eds., *Evolutionary Cognitive Neuroscience* (Cambridge, MA: MIT Press, 2007), 245–283; H.E. Fisher, *Why We Love: The Nature and Chemistry of Romantic Love* (New York: Henry Holt, 2004).

39. C.S. Carter, "Oxytocin and Sexual Behavior," *Neuroscience and Biobehavioral Reviews* 1 (1992): 131–144; C.S. Carter, "Neuroendocrine Perspectives on Social Attachment and Love," *Psychoneuroendocrinology* 23 (1998): 779–818; H. Walum, L. Westberg, S. Henningsson, J.M. Neiderhiser, D. Reiss, W. Igl, J.M. Ganiban, E.L. Spotts, N.L. Pederson, E. Eriksson, and P. Lichtenstein, "Genetic Variation in the Vasopressin Receptor 1a Gene (AVPR1A) Associates With Pair-Bonding Behavior in Humans," *Proceedings of the National Academy of Sciences* 105 (2008): 14153–14156; P.J. Zak, R. Kurzban, and W.T. Matzner, "The Neurobiology of Trust," *Annals of the New York Academy of Sciences*, 1032 (2005): 224–227.

40. H.E. Fisher, *Anatomy of Love: The Natural History of Monogamy, Adultery, and Divorce* (New York: Norton, 1992).

41. C.M. Meston and P.F. Frohlic, "The Neurobiology of Sexual Function," *Archives of General Psychiatry* 57 (2000): 1012–1030.

42. E. Adkins-Regan, *Hormones and Animal Social Behavior* (Princeton, NJ: Princeton University Press, 2005); Fisher and Thomson, "Lust, Romance, Attachment."

43. P.J. Zak, *The Moral Molecule: The Source of Love and Prosperity* (New York: Dutton, 2012).

44. M.S. Carmichael, R. Humbert, J. Dixen, G. Palmisano, W. Greenleaf, and J.M. Davidson, "Plasma Oxytocin Increases in the Human Sexual Response," *Journal of Clinical Endocrinology and Metabolism* 64 (1987): 27–31.

45. P.B. Gray and J.R. Garcia, *Evolution and Human Sexual Behavior* (Cambridge, MA: Harvard University Press, 2013).

46. Armstrong, England, and Fogarty, "Accounting for Women's Orgasm and Sexual Enjoyment in College Hookups and Relationships."

EVERYBODY'S *NOT* HOOKING UP

Asexuality on Campus and Beyond[1]

Mark Carrigan interviews David Jay

Asexuality is a sexual orientation defined as the lack of sexual attraction. It is different from intentional celibacy or voluntary abstinence, which are choices not to have sex. The leading group in asexual rights and visibility is AVEN, the Asexuality Visibility and Education Network. In this chapter, Mark Carrigan interviews David Jay, the founder of AVEN and an outspoken supporter of asexual understanding.

Mark Carrigan: How visible do you think asexuality is in contemporary society? It seems much more broadly recognized now than has previously been the case, but is there still a long way to go?

David Jay: Yeah, I think that we've made huge strides and we still have a long way to go. Asexuality is getting recognized among key stakeholder groups like the LGBTQ community and sex educators, the kinds of people who need to be aware that our community exists in order for us to become more widely recognized. So for example at the biggest national LGBTQ organizing conference in the United States this year, asexuality was mentioned on the main stage. There were multiple workshops about asexuality; it was something that all of the NGOs were working on with LGBTQ youth, and adults and seniors around the country [are becoming] aware of asexuality, or aware they need to learn more about it. The same is beginning to become true among people who do sex education at a high school and a college level, at least here in the States. So we're becoming a part of the dialogue about sexuality and we're becoming part of the dialogue that the experts are having. That's a huge important first step.

I think that we still have a long way to go because knowledge of us in popular culture is still pretty spotty. Things like Angela Tucker's documentary film, *(A)sexual*, have helped a lot. It's not uncommon when I run into someone randomly, for them to be aware that asexuality exists. But I think there still is not a deep understanding, and we're coming up on a few critical opportunities that can promote better understanding about asexuality. The first is when we start seeing "Ace" characters portrayed in popular TV shows. We already have characters like Sherlock and Dr. Who, who kind of seem like they're based on Ace experience, but they don't identify as Ace. When [pop culture] identification starts happening it's going to give a lot of people their first in-depth understanding of what the community is about. For better or worse, that is going to shape a lot of people's thoughts about asexuality. Having some influence in the way those first pop-culture characters are portrayed is an important goal for our movement.

The other big thing that is on the radar for me, is how Ace folks are discussed [and often pathologized] by mental health professionals. We're just in the early stages of really engaging with counselors and therapists and talking with them about best practices for helping Ace people who need their services. That's not to say that many of them are bad, a lot of them intuitively get that this is a thing, that they should allow people to explore, that you don't need sex to be happy. I'd say that if an Ace were to need to walk into a therapist's office right now, if the therapist is good, they are probably are going to have a good experience. But there needs to be a much better dialogue among the mental health community. I think that will inform the broader cultural dialogue because that is a group of experts that everyone else turns to, to ask whether or not asexuality is okay.

MC: So one might say that there is a massive increase in visibility and recognition, but perhaps understanding asexuality still trails behind. And these are the different fronts where the fight for more understanding can be fought.

DJ: Exactly.

MC: Do you think there have always been asexual people? It seems obvious to me that people who now identify as asexual didn't just magically pop into existence overnight in the early 2000s, when asexuality gained public visibility.

DJ: There has always been a spectrum of human sexual diversity. Across non-human species, there are plenty of documented examples of animals experiencing a wide range of sexual behavior, including asexual behavior. I think in many ways it took a modern cultural articulation of sexuality for the concept of sexual identity to come into being. So asexual experience has been around forever. I'm pretty certain that there have been people not experiencing sexual attraction for as long as there have been people experiencing sexual attraction. What's new is talking about asexuality as an identity. Talking about asexuality as an identity dates back to the early 2000s. There might have been people for whom that identity would have made sense maybe twenty or forty years before that, but not much more. I mean sexual identity itself, as a concept, is only really 100 years old and far younger than that as a widespread cultural concept. And so the idea that I identify as asexual and that means something to me, that entire experience is new. We are exploring what sexual identity or sexual orientation means during one of the first cultural moments where we are historically capable of doing that.

MC: Do you think there is more cultural pressure or expectation on people to experience sexual attraction? Do you think it might have been easier a century ago for someone to be asexual without it being a "thing" with a label?

DJ: I don't know about easier, but it would have been really different a century ago. I would say that we've moved to a culture where sexuality is more explicitly celebrated and more overtly fetishized. So I think that sexuality has become a thing that everyone is expected to articulate, to experience, and to express publicly. Sexuality is discussed much more actively as a core component of relationship formation—and much earlier in a relationship—than it was in the past. In some ways that's made being Ace harder because I think that forty or fifty years ago, there used to be a cultural concept of getting to know someone, and becoming really emotionally into them without sexuality, compared with how things are today.

That being said, I also think we live in a time where it is much safer to say, *You know what? I'm not experiencing the sexual feelings that everyone else is experiencing and that's awesome and I'm going to explore what I'm experiencing on my own terms.* I think it's much easier and safer to say that now than it was forty or fifty years ago—and that is a huge benefit to our community.

In the past, in most parts of the world, we would have been seen as just insufficiently sexual and maybe it would have been less of a crime to be insufficiently sexual back then but that's still the most that we could have hoped to. Whereas now, I think we can really become fantastic at being something new and interesting that we define on our own terms, and that's way more powerful.

KEY TERMS AND DEFINITIONS

Ace is a popular or slang term for someone who is asexual.

Sometimes a person's sexual and romantic orientations are not the same. The term for describing this is **allosexual**.

An **aromantic** person feels little or no romantic attraction toward others. Because sexuality and romance are not the same thing, people anywhere on the sexual spectrum (sexual, gray-A, etc.) may also be aromantic.

Asexual allies include family, friends, and partners who identify as sexual and also support members of the asexual community.

A person who is **demisexual** feels sexual attraction to others only after a strong emotional bond has been formed.

> **Gray-A** refers to those who fall along the continuum between asexual and sexual identity. People who identify as gray-A can include those who do not usually experience sexual attraction, but do experience it sometimes; those who sometimes experience sexual attraction but with a low sex drive; and people who can enjoy and desire sex but only under very specific circumstances.
>
> For more information, see "Gray-A," *AVENwiki*, http://bit.ly/1iZxHfa; "Demisexual," *AVENwiki*, http://bit.ly/1irtu4w; "Gray Space," http://bit.ly/1yjRASx; and Katherine Richard, "Column: 'A' Stands for Asexuals and Not Allies," http://bit.ly/1plmPvu, and "Asexuality 101," http://acesandallies.org/asexuality-101/.

MC: There still seems to be a quite a lack of understanding about asexuality. On the one hand, people might tolerate the idea, but intellectually they just don't get it. Is this a problem? How could it be addressed?

DJ: Yes, I think that this is definitely a problem. I think this has a lot to do with the way that people think about intimacy and human connection. In my experience, when people have a hard time understanding or accepting asexuality, it is often because when they hear the word "asexual" they think this means someone who does not connect with other people, does not have the desire to connect with other people, or does not have the desire to deeply connect with themselves. The misunderstanding is that an asexual person is someone who is isolated.

If someone has these misconceptions about asexuality, I think that it is very hard for them to accept us and it is very hard for them to take us seriously. There will be times when they may give lip service to acceptance because they consider that politically correct, but they won't really get it. It behooves us as a community to tell stories about how we are forming deep connections with other people and with ourselves, and how we're living extremely fulfilled, connective lives because of that.

When I have been able to pepper my descriptions of asexuality with those kinds of stories, I think it clears up that kind of mental webbing really effectively. So to answer your question: Yes, I think there is still widespread misunderstanding. Addressing that misunderstanding is going to mean rewiring how people think about connection, and how people think about intimacy, in a broader cultural context.

This is part of why I'm excited about potential for visibility of Ace characters on TV and things like that. Honest and open stories about asexuality are really important.

The biggest reason I'm excited about asexual visibility is that there are a lot of isolated Aces out there and letting everyone know that a community exists is really powerful. But I'm also excited about asexual visibility because I think that just hearing about us and hearing about the way that we form connections with one another, also opens up a lot of possibilities for sexual people and for sexual culture.[2]

I see this happening again and again when I talk about asexuality with people. It is often a very profound experience for non-asexual people that I talk to. I think this is because asexuality helps us rethink and articulate our cultural assumptions about how human connection works.

At World Pride,[3] I described this "click" moment that happens when I give talks to sexual people about asexuality. Something switches in the way they perceive sexuality and other things that are important to them in their life. This switch is really cool and gets them really excited, it makes them want to engage.

I think this effect of talking about asexuality is something the Ace community should really lean into. The fact that we can get sexual people that engaged in the conversation is a huge benefit to us. We can use this engagement to build cultural dialogues about sexuality.

MC: Do you think this might lead to a new kind of identity called "sexual"? This is something that's come to fascinate me. . . . Until people who aren't asexual encounter asexuality, they don't think of their sexual nature as being one option amongst others.

DJ: The clearest place I've seen this is the adoption of romantic identities among sexual people. At the fringes of many Ace communities that I hang out in there are people who actively identify as sexual, and who have a romantic orientation that is not the same as their sexual orientation. They don't have another place to talk about that. They really like that there is a community of people who understand that they can have romantic experience that is not sexual—and they can have romantic attraction that is not sexual—and that doesn't mean that they're doing sexuality wrong.

MC: So in a way, the conceptual vocabulary that the asexual community provides has opened up more options for describing our sexual and romantic identities?

DJ: Exactly. The most powerful example of this is a woman I was talking to in New York who identifies as heterosexual and aromantic and she says, "I form incredibly close relationships with my friends that I'm not sleeping with and I occasionally very much enjoy sleeping with people that I do not want to be romantic or intimate with. There are words for that in the sexual world that are pretty scarring for someone who wants to be sexual with people but does not want to be intimate with them. At the same time, there are no terms that describe the non-sexual intimacy that is happening in my life. So how do I explore intimacy without being sexual? The sexual world wants me to glom these things together when I don't want to glom them together."

This woman hangs out in the asexual community in part so she can talk about her intimate relationships and have everyone celebrate them without being distracted by the sexual relationships she's not being intimate in.

MC: So Ace discourse gives sexual people awareness and conceptual tools to express things they might not have otherwise been able to. In this sense, do you think there are affinities to other groups within society? I'm thinking about the way in which the trans movement for instance might sensitize people to gender who would not themselves identify as trans. Or even the poly community—do you think there are affinities here?

DJ: The Ace community includes people who identify along a spectrum as asexual, gray-A, demisexual, allosexual, and as asexual allies. There are people who are getting a lot of benefit from the identity explanation that's going on in the Ace community, the same way that hanging out with trans people since I was in early college has informed the way that I shaped my identity as a cis-male. I think that we're helping people rethink their identities by turning a lot of unstated assumptions into questions.

When a sexual person hears about asexuality prior to hearing about the Ace community, they often think of themselves as enjoying sexuality, which they assume is a healthy thing that everyone does to some degree. They think of themselves as being in relationships that they define as intimate connections involving sexuality and they often assume everyone is like them in struggling to make sexuality work as well as they would like it to work in those relationships. They think of sexuality as this thing that is really awesome and exciting and fun and sexy and gets them to touch their bodies and lets them connect with other people, and yet also this thing that sort of fails to do that on a regular basis.

Every time sexuality fails to create the connection that is promised by every billboard around them, people feel like they fall short or their relationship is lacking in some way. For some people this is a minor annoyance, but for many people this is a significant preoccupation. The idea that they are deeply flawed and that things need to be fixed, with them or with their partner, is associated with a lot of shame. Part of what's powerful about discussing asexuality is it gives people permission to not be ashamed. Instead, people can see [sexuality] like *there are times when I'm being more sexual and there are times when I'm being less sexual*. The times when I'm being less sexual don't necessarily mean that there is a deep crack in the foundation of all that matters about me and my life, it just means that I'm not feeling it as much. This lets me think about all the other things I can do to be happy in those times rather than feeling like there's something that needs to be fixed.

MC: That natural ebb and flow that many people experience with their sexual desire is something that seems to be captured by the term gray-A. Do you think gray-A is an identity that would attract more attention if it were more widely known?

DJ: Even though I think identity words matter a lot, I think it is more powerful to talk about our experiences—especially our experiences of connection—than it is to talk about our identities. There are powerful, common threads that connect us with people that get lost when we talk about identity. [But] we still need identity, especially for people who want to figure themselves out, and need a container for that process of exploration, and for those who need a flag they can wave to find other people like them. Identity words are extremely important for that. But . . . I guess part of the risk of identity categories, as necessary as they are, is that it atomizes these experiences and obscures the continuities that exist [among people].

MC: It seems to be the gray-A category that provokes the most natural affinity with people.

DJ: I think that does a disservice to people who identify as gray-A who have a unique experience that they feel is not what everyone in the world is experiencing. They want to be able to articulate that. At the same time, I think that there's a need to tease out the gray-A discussion [to find words for describing the sexual ebb and flow that] everyone is experiencing. We should have a way to talk about [this topic] more explicitly.

MC: Just to bring this conversation to a close, do you think there's a risk in talking about the pressure of sexual norms as oppressive? Is there a tension between recognizing the extent to which people feel subjugated to sexual norms but at the same time resisting a conservative agenda and wanting to maintain some sense of sex positivity?

DJ: I think that there is risk in people only hearing part of what we're saying. What we want is for people to be able to explore sexuality on their own terms. That means celebrating *not* being sexual as much as it means celebrating sexual connection. If we can frame the conversation about asexuality in such a way that it is about self-discovery and finding what works for you, not about enforcing some cultural norm of what should and should not be sexual, then we can maintain a sense of sex positivity.

To anyone who says our society is talking about sex too much, I would argue that our society is not talking about sex honestly enough. Because talking about sex honestly means talking about the fact that it is not fun all the time and that's okay. And if we make our push for more honest discussion of sexuality then we can avoid accidentally associating with people who just don't want sexuality talked about, because not talking about sex is not going to help the Ace community or anyone else.

DISCUSSION QUESTIONS

• In this interview, David Jay states: "I'm pretty certain that there have been people not experiencing sexual attraction for as long as there have been people

experiencing sexual attraction." What is the evidence for his claim? Do you find it compelling?
• David Jay suggests that asexual visibility opens up a lot of possibilities for sexual people and for sexual culture. What does he mean by this? Do you agree?
• How does asexuality challenge us to rethink our prevailing understandings of sexuality and sexual identity?
• Why do many non-asexual people initially find asexuality difficult to understand?
• How and why might non-asexual people inadvertently act in marginalizing or stigmatizing ways toward those who are asexual?

NOTES

1. A previous version of this interview appears as a podcast titled "Why Asexuality Matters for the Future of Sexual Culture," June 9, 2013, http://markcarrigan.net/2013/06/09/an-interview-with-david-jay-why-asexuality-matters-for-the-future-of-sexual-culture/. This interview is transcribed here with permission of the interviewer.
2. For further discussion about dating and asexuality, see Wiley Reading, "Dating While Asexual," *Everyday Feminism*, June 9, 2014, http://everydayfeminism.com/2014/06/dating-while-asexual.
3. World Pride is an annual, international event that promotes lesbian, gay, bisexual, and transgender pride with parades, festivals, and other cultural programs. The first Asexual Conference took place at the 2012 World Pride in London; the second International Asexual Conference was held in 2014 at World Pride in Toronto. Historically there has been debate as to whether asexuality should be included under the LGBTQ umbrella. Speaking to the *Huffington Post*, asexuality rights advocate Sarah Beth Brooks says, "Asexuality is very much a part of the broader conversation in our society about gender and sexual diversity. [It's] certainly queer, and it's certainly part of the LGBT community." See "Second Ever Asexual Conference at World Pride Toronto 2014," *Pink News*, June 23, 2014, http://www.pinknews.co.uk/2014/06/17/second-ever-asexual-conference-at-world-pride-toronto-2014/.

Part V

Issues in Sexual Pleasure and Safety

The final section of *Gender, Sex, and Politics* explores subjects that may be challenging or difficult to think about. Some topics might seem taboo. In chapter 22, philosopher Marjorie Jolles explores the ethics and debates surrounding BDSM. Sexual pleasure that centers on consensual pain or degradation, Jolles writes, "seems to be at once both (a) protected by our rights to pursue happiness however we please, and (b) a violation of our rights to be protected from physical and verbal injury." Jolles walks readers through ways we might we make sense of these seemingly paradoxical conditions.

Chapter 23 begins with Janet Rosenbaum's observation that "sex can be such a taboo topic that sometimes people don't tell the truth about their sexual behavior, not even to themselves." This chapter examines when people tell the truth about sex and when they don't. Rosenbaum also investigates whether people seem most interested in lying to themselves or to others. This issue of sexual honesty is presented in four contexts: the author's research on virginity pledgers in the United States; a study of premarital sex among Southern Baptists in Texas; laboratory tests for showing when people have been exposed to semen in the recent past (as compared to their self-disclosure about condom use during recent sexual activity); and whether parents deceive themselves about how much they teach their adolescents about sex. As readers might guess, people sometimes fail to be honest about their sexual activity—not because they are hypocrites who are trying to deceive others but because they have deceived themselves. In some cases misreporting about sex has severe consequences. Rosenbaum explains that virginity pledgers who have sex are less likely to use condoms, adolescents who report using condoms 100 percent of the time but test positive for semen exposure have a greater risk for pregnancy than even adolescents who admit to unprotected sex, and parents who believe that they provide comprehensive sex education to their adolescents—but don't—miss an important opportunity to influence their teen's behavior at a formative time.

Chapter 24 concerns the serious matter of sexual violence on college campuses. After generations of activism and outreach, this issue has finally come the forefront of attention. And with good reason: In 2014, *Mother Jones* magazine reported that 40 percent of colleges had not investigated a single campus sexual assault case in five years.[1] In "Campus Sexual Assault: Myths, Facts, and Controversies," Nina Flores clears up potential misinformation, while addressing potentially controversial issues such as individual responsibility, alcohol and assault, the rights of the survivor, and the rights of the accused. The strongest show of support, Flores tells readers, is to stand by survivors with three powerful words: I believe you.[2]

Chapter 25 takes up an issue that, while lacking the high stakes and potential trauma of sexual violence, nonetheless contributes to problems regarding how we talk about sexuality—and who we talk about. It is no surprise that when it comes to media headlines, sex sells. When we turn on the news, or read a magazine, we are captivated by stories of public figures' sex tapes and sexting, or politicians' extramarital affairs. But if we look closer at who is being asked to tell their stories, a clear pattern emerges: Young, twentysomething white women are increasingly publishing their true-life accounts of sexual escapades in mainstream online venues such as *Nerve*, *Salon*, the *Atlantic*, and *Slate*. Editors love the increased page views and hit counts that result from the sex-based headlines, but what are the consequences for young female writers and the men who read them? In "Kiss and Sell: When Young Lady Authors Write About Our Sex Lives," Allison McCarthy features interviews from feminist scholars, as well as the writers and editors of these popular articles, examining the politics behind the salacious details, and how this work has impacted the careers and safety of professional reputations of its writers.

With the threat of sexual danger so rampant, Charlie Glickman hopes for a safer and more pleasurable world. This, he argues, can be accomplished through one simple act. As chapter 26 by Glickman states: "The World Will Be a Better Place When More Men Take It Up the Ass." While Glickman certainly knows that anal sex will not eradicate hunger or create world peace, his point is that hegemonic, cisgender, heterosexual masculinity stands to be improved. And, in a world where more people than ever before are learning to have sex from watching porn, being on the receiving side of penetrative sex creates a "better understanding of how you can be turned on, be really into your partner, and still need lots of warm up before anything goes inside of you." As a sex educator, Glickman has spoken with enough men and their partners to really believe that anal penetration among men can make a difference. This has a lot of potential to improve our relationships, Glickman writes. And, he explains, "I think that anyone who wants to be on the giving side of anal sex should try receiving it."

Chapter 27 in this anthology ends the collection on an encouraging note. "In Defense of Going Wild or: How I Stopped Worrying and Learned to Love Pleasure (and How You Can, Too)," by Jaclyn Friedman, acknowledges that sexual exploration—and life itself—involves an element of risk. We are entitled to safety, and we are smart to minimize risk, prevent harm, and learn to protect ourselves. We are also entitled to enthusiastically claim the pleasure that is our birthright.

NOTES

1. Julia Lurie, "40 Percent of Colleges Haven't Investigated a Single Sexual Assault Case in 5 Years," July 10, 2014, http://m.motherjones.com/mojo/2014/07/college-campus-sexual-assault. Also see Caroline Heldman and Danielle Dirks, "Blowing the Whistle on Campus Rape," *Ms.* 24, no. 1 (Winter 2014): 32–37.

2. Many resources are available to provide further information about sexual violence. Examples include Lisa Factora-Borchers, ed., *Dear Sister: Letters from Survivors of Sexual Violence* (Oakland, CA: AK Press, 2014); *No! The Rape Documentary*, dir. Aishah Shahidah Simmons, 2006; *The Hunting Ground*, dir. Kirby Dick, 2015; Know Your IX: Empowering Students to Stop Sexual Violence, http://knowyourix.org/; and https://1in6.org/, an online resource for male survivors of sexual abuse and assault.

PLEASURE, PAIN, AND THE FEMINIST POLITICS OF ROUGH SEX

Marjorie Jolles[1]

INTRODUCTION: WHAT IS BDSM?

Pleasure and pain. The two seem like obvious opposites: Pleasure feels good and pain really hurts. How, then, do we understand sexual activity that is simultaneously pleasurable and painful—sex where pleasure is directly linked to the presence, not absence, of pain? What do such activities look and feel like, and how ought we feel *about* them?

Sometimes called "kink," this type of pain-for-the-sake-of-pleasure sex is less judgmentally known as BDSM, a catch-all term used to describe sexual practices that include bondage, discipline, dominance, submission, sadism, and masochism. The word "sadism" describes a psychological state in which intense pleasure is derived from inflicting pain; the word "masochism" describes the experience of intense pleasure when receiving pain (and "sadomasochism" refers to erotic encounters between sadists and masochists). There is no singular style, script, or necessary choreography of BDSM, but there are some elements and accoutrements that have come to be associated with this particular genre of sex: bondage gear involving leather, rope, gags, and blindfolds; whips, chains, belts, and devices for inflicting pain; fictionalized scenes of punishment, captivity, and torture; and dramatized confrontations between harsh authority and docile obedience typical of master-slave dynamics. (For better or worse, readers of E.L. James's controversial blockbuster, *Fifty Shades of Grey*, will recognize this description.) BDSM can take place in a dungeon designed for sexually infused power rituals, in private or before a live audience, at kink parties organized by BDSM communities, in suburban bedrooms, and in any type of venue in between. BDSM can involve straight couples, queer couples, intimate and anonymous pairings, groups, and may be acted out in any type of arrangement: from conventional marriages to sex work, wherein customers pay to be dominated or to dominate, and sex workers specialize in playing the roles of sadist or masochist.

What distinguishes BDSM from actual torture or abuse is that BDSM is a form of consensual play, undertaken for the goal of experiencing pleasure. Practitioners rely on a high degree of trust among each other, radically unlike the total lack of trust or consent among actual torturers and victims. Think of BDSM as a kind of sexual theatre, in which the fictional scenes acted out, the roles (of sadist and masochist, also known as dominant and submissive, or "dom" and "sub"), the dialogue, and the "safe words" (words that can, once uttered, bring an immediate end to the action), are all agreed to in advance. "Safe, sane, and consensual" is a slogan commonly cited among BDSM enthusiasts to highlight the ways in which BDSM differs diametrically from actual and unwanted acts of violence.[2]

THE DEBATE

So what's the problem? Where's the controversy here? BDSM is a subject of fierce debate among BDSM practitioners and their opponents, as well as scholars interested in sexuality, power, and freedom, because it forces us to confront the intersection of two cherished values: sexual freedom and freedom from harm. Pleasurable sex that centers on degrading behavior seems to be at once both (a) protected by our rights to pursue happiness however we please, and (b) a violation of our rights to be protected from physical and verbal injury. Philosophers and political theorists have raised concerns about the ethics and politics of engaging in acts that appear to mimic the most vicious, unrelenting, degrading, and harmful human practices, such as slavery, abuse, and torture. Those interested in sexual freedom champion the way BDSM lets us explore our impulses and curiosity in a context of play and safety, so uncommon in a culture that typically casts shame on sexual desire. Those who think about the way sexual life informs social and political life (and vice-versa) ask what greater good and/or social ills can come of these enactments. By rehearsing these scenes in the context of sexual pleasure, are BDSM practitioners eroticizing horror, possibly serving to redefine violence from awful to sexy? On the other hand, why should we care if someone finds degrading others—or one's own degradation—arousing? Doesn't it make sense to argue that what consenting adults do in their own bedrooms really isn't our business?

Feminists have been among the most vocal in both sides of this debate,[3] as sexual freedom—and freedom from oppression—are two primary feminist commitments. Some feminists oppose BDSM because it exaggerates the patriarchal assumption of male domination and female subordination already embedded in heterosexual sexuality. These feminist critics claim that sexuality is a sphere in which women have been subordinated and violated for millennia, in which female pleasure has been not only neglected but actively repressed, and in which women suffer all manner of violence that has only recently become criminalized.[4] BDSM appears to these critics as a glorification of the worst elements of patriarchal culture: someone giving orders, someone obeying fearfully, and claiming that everyone is having a great time. To such critics, eroticizing dynamics of power is nothing new or revolutionary but instead an endorsement of the oppressive sexual status quo. Furthermore, this view holds that the abject pain and suffering that accompanies domination and submission ought to outrage us, not arouse us.

But there is not a uniform feminist position on BDSM, and many feminists are passionate champions for BDSM as an enlightening and empowering mode of sexual experience. This argument takes (at least) two forms. The first is that we should accept BDSM on the grounds of sexual freedom. That is, making distinctions between politically correct and incorrect sex is not liberating; it is additional moralizing about the proper uses of women's sexuality. This has the effect not of expanding women's sexual agency but constraining it. The second related argument in favor of BDSM from a feminist perspective is that BDSM enables profound emotional and physical transformations by inviting practitioners to explore their sexual fantasies (including fantasies to be dominated) without shame and to take more engaged ownership of their erotic lives. Some BDSM enthusiasts describe the revitalizing power of reenacting memories of domination and subordination in order to master them, thereby redefining formerly vulnerable states into powerful ones.

Thus, the BDSM feminist debate hinges on ethical questions concerning inflicting pain and eroticizing dominance, and championing sexual freedom and personal transformation. Let's work our way through the debate by examining each of these issues in turn.

ON PAIN

It is tempting to argue against BDSM on the simple basis that it involves pain, and it is immoral to inflict pain and unjust to experience it—even if, in the case of BDSM, pain is the path to pleasure. The problem with rejecting BDSM because of the pain involved is that in this view, anything involving pain is de facto morally wrong. But pain has a much more complex history and cultural life, and BDSM practitioners are not the only people conducting experiments with bodily pain or achieving pleasure from it. There is a long tradition in religious cultures of sustaining bodily pain as a way to achieve spiritual transcendence: fasting, flagellation, wearing clothing specifically designed to cause discomfort, and numerous other pain-inducing practices are all intended to enhance one's piety. Body modifying activities such as piercing and tattooing also involve significant pain, and many of us happily submit our bodies to the pain of modifying our bodies, often finding it pleasurable not only after, but during the modification. Indeed, many people report experiencing heightened spiritual attunement and passion while in the throes of physical pain.[5] These examples suggest that voluntary, self-inflicted pain may have a productive role to play in the myriad ways we explore the limits of embodiment.

Still, some might argue that pain happens in these other aspects of life, but it shouldn't happen in sex, where we ought to feel only good and safe. But when it comes to sex, pain is in fact quite common, and pain is certainly not unique to BDSM-style sex. For many women, the vaginal penetration essential to heterosexual intercourse is painful, and that pain has been romanticized so effectively (particularly as a rite of passage if the pain occurs when one has intercourse for the first time) that it is rarely raised as a topic of concern. Many women endure pain for their entire sexual lives because of a misguided belief that only men experience pleasure in sex, and that women are largely asexual, or at the very least, sexually passive by nature.[6] Thus, to single out BDSM as the only kind of painful sex is to make the same type of category mistake we make when we single out BDSM as the only kind of sex that engages a choreography of domination and submission—as noted earlier, feminist critics have argued that normative heterosexual intercourse is rife with its own, if sometimes more subtle, dom and sub dynamics.

But what about other forms of pain that may be more serious than a temporary bruise? The pain sought after in BDSM may also include the psychic pain of verbal abuse. A sadist practicing BDSM may find deep pleasure in calling her masochist partner a humiliating name as part of the ritual they are acting out, and the masochist may be highly aroused in that verbal exchange. As numerous scholars have shown,[7] the ethics of name-calling are not straightforward: For example, does the use of the word "bitch" simply strengthen the word's power to degrade women, or does the word's meaning and impact change when used by different speakers in new contexts? Or does a blanket prohibition of the word unintentionally strengthen its power? Or, more to the point for our purposes, how do we distinguish between the impact of a stranger calling a woman a bitch and a sexual partner doing the same in a consensual and arousing context?

Now imagine how complex the ethics of name-calling is in the case of BDSM that includes "race play." Race play, as described by feminist writer Daisy Hernandez, is sexual activity that uses "racial epithets like the word 'nigger' or racist scenarios like a slave auction . . . [or] 'playing out' Nazi interrogations of Jews or Latino-on-black racism."[8] If confrontations with authority are sexually arousing for some, or if sexual arousal is heightened for some by adding an authoritarian element to their encounters, then it follows that their sexual fantasies and role-playing games may include references to political images that circulate in our shared culture—even ones we find horrific and categorically immoral. But we cannot assume that simply because slavery is immoral, a fictional reenactment of slavery is also immoral. (Quite the contrary—in fact, fictional reenactments of slavery are often used to educate and sensitize Americans to their troubled history of white supremacy.) Then again, even if it's all make believe, symbolic imagery and language can trigger real trauma and persistent, oppressive feelings of terror.

ON EROTICIZING DOMINANCE

Let's examine the claim that BDSM eroticizes dominance. Some feminists argue that BDSM makes oppression and abuse sexy.[9] Such an accusation implies that dominance is not itself erotic but *becomes* erotic in patriarchal culture, in order to serve the agendas of those in charge—if the people being subjugated are taught to get turned on by dominance, then political and inter-personal dominance becomes even easier. Patriarchy is fundamentally a system of domination and submission, enforced through the naturalization of hierarchical gender roles such that masculinity comes to be defined as domination and femininity comes to be defined as submission.[10] These gender roles play out everywhere, especially in sexual activity. Feminist critics of patriarchy seek to eradicate these domination/submission dynamics, and some feminists find BDSM's exaggeration of them morally problematic because they appear as a continuation of patriarchy.

But is all power equivalent to dominance? And is all domination ethically wrong? Sexual life is about desire. How we go about fulfilling desire for another person requires some use of power or managing the dynamics of agency and control. Philosopher Jean Grimshaw argues that eroticism at its base involves power: "the power to give pleasure, to dominate the senses of the other, temporarily obliterate the rest of the world; the power involved in being the person who is desired, the power to demand one's own pleasure." Eroticism also inherently involves submission. Grimshaw continues: "along with this power go forms of 'submission' (of surrendering, letting go, receiving), or of self-abnegation, of focusing entirely for a while on the pleasure of the other."[11] If you aren't convinced, try imagining an erotic scenario in which these states of being are absent. BDSM thus has no exclusive claim on power and submission—*all* sexual activity requires it. Even a feminist vision of an erotic encounter that emphasizes mutual agency, mutual pleasure, and women's liberation from oppressive sexual norms would include exercises of power and phases of submission.

Grimshaw's point is that power is not an inherent moral evil, and submission is not inherently a state of inferiority. These phenomena—power and submission—become morally relevant when they are used in the service of political or social control, such as when they are mobilized to support gender or racial domination. So, which category does BDSM fall into? Is it a continuation of morally abhorrent politics, or is it erotic activity that—like any other—resembles a dance among dom and sub?

ON SEXUAL FREEDOM

Let's say BDSM *is* harmful. So what? Why should the harm of BDSM matter if we believe in sexual freedom among consenting adults? The pro-BDSM feminist Gayle Rubin sees arguments against BDSM as extensions of "extensive and successful morality campaigns" around sexuality, linked to "movements against prostitution, obscenity, contraception, abortion, and masturbation [that] were able to establish state policies, social practices, and deeply entrenched ideologies which still affect the shape of our sexual experience and our ability to think about it."[12] According to Rubin, stigmatizing BDSM as perverse—and BDSM devotees as perverts—cannot be consistent with feminist politics. Instead, feminism must work to make sexual freedom a reality for all consenting adults. Moreover, feminists ought to be skeptical of the impulse to single out certain sexual subcultures for shame and repression. Although sometimes sexual prohibitions are intended to protect the vulnerable from harm (such as laws against pedophilia), oftentimes sexual prohibitions are not meant to protect us from harm but are instead used to maintain social control. This is true of taboos against miscegenation and queerness, and it is true of sexual practices that defy the conventional construction of female desire as bland and dispassionate. For sex radicals who believe that norms of sexuality often function as mechanisms for social control, BDSM is inherently valuable for its experimental and liberatory ethos, and based on a commitment to sexual freedom, those who enjoy it should be able to engage in it without stigma.

Not so fast. The problem with embracing BDSM on the grounds of sexual freedom is that it proposes to make sexuality immune from critique, shielding our erotic behaviors from ethical investigation behind a veil of privacy. Yet the feminist slogan, "the personal is political," challenges a division between public and private spheres. "The personal is political" means that power dynamics do not exist only in public contexts like party politics or direct encounters with the law; in fact, our personal lives are shot through with engagements with power. This slogan took hold when feminists discovered that gender-based oppression was not only something that goes on in public life—in the workplace, on the streets, in our legal codes—but in private life as well—in our bedrooms and at our kitchen tables. We get a woefully incomplete picture of how gender-based power struggles work if we limit our analysis to what goes on in public life only. It is not a violation of freedom to take a good look at how we behave in our private lives, behind closed doors. Therefore, defending BDSM on privacy grounds will not do, since sexuality is not cut off from the "real world" but shaped *in relation to it*. If immoral social ideologies circulate in the world, we can expect them to circulate in our sexual lives, too.

Maybe the best argument in defense of BDSM is that the people practicing it have consented to it. The concept of consent tends to be the logical bedrock we hit when we strip away these other layers of the argument for sexual freedom. The basic meaning of consent is to agree, without force and freely, to whatever one is about to do. Consent is saying "yes," and—importantly—knowing what you're saying yes to. If people consent to BDSM, then what more is there to debate?

It turns out that consent alone cannot resolve the argument either, because merely consenting to something does not make it ethical. Nor should we assume that consent is always free of influence. Philosopher Judith Butler argues that just because BDSM "requires consent does not mean that it has overcome heterosexual power dynamics. Women have been consenting to heterosexual power dynamics for thousands of years."[13] Putting it even more bluntly is journalist Megan Lieff, who observes: "one thing the BDSM community has always been great at is having frank conversations about consent," but, to feminists who find BDSM inherently harmful no matter how much a woman likes it, "the idea of women consenting to this violence smacks of patriarchal brainwashing."[14] This suggests that the contexts—patriarchal ones especially—in which consent is given must be examined as rigorously as the consent itself.

The emphasis on individual consent tends to dominate the BDSM debate, but an exclusive focus on consent misses the larger and more compelling point that anti-BDSM feminists make: Even if BDSM does not harm the individual practitioner, it has negative social consequences that reverberate on a mass scale. This argument is articulated well by feminist scholar Kathleen Barry, who believes that humans are fundamentally relational beings, and that our actions reverberate beyond our own immediate lives. For Barry, "BDSM, bondage and discipline, these originate in slavery. . . .To the extent that we take social institutions such as slavery—that are criminal and violating of the human being—and adore them . . . we are engaged in perpetuating them."[15]

If this sounds far-fetched, let's return to the topic of BDSM race play. Daisy Hernandez observes that although "the players can be of any racial background and paired up in a number of ways (including a black man calling his black girlfriend a 'nigger bitch')" during race play, "white master seeking black slave, however, seems the more popular of the combinations."[16] How can we say there is no social context, or social effect, of these allegedly private activities? In addition to the individual psychic pain risked, repeated racist utterances and enactments of terror have social resonances, precisely because they come from social reality. They draw on shared historical legacies and possibly even extend the life of them, thereby extending their power to harm. A BDSM scene involving race play provides a context in which racial hatred can express itself and thrive. Yes, there are crucial ethical differences between fantasy and reality, but as race play shows, the scripts and plotlines of fantasy are derived from and likely feed right back into reality. It seems reasonable to wonder whether the person who likes to play white male master to his female black slave in the dungeon carries those racist and sexist fascinations with him into his everyday life.

ON PERSONAL TRANSFORMATION

Champions of BDSM argue that it brings about powerful physical and emotional benefits. Physically, BDSM may offer novel sexual pleasures, in that it highlights parts of the body not considered "typical" erogenous zones: Instead of an exclusive focus on genitals and genital pleasure, BDSM may eroticize the handcuffed wrist, the bound ankle, the blindfolded face, or the fist (which may become a fetishized object when used for vaginal or anal penetration). In these important ways, BDSM is celebrated by its feminist practitioners for the way it can open up new modes of sexual experience and help us move beyond the constraints of conventional sexual practice, which—with its predictable scripts, positions, and primary focus on male pleasure—fails to satisfy so many of us.

BDSM practitioners claim that it does more than simply bring fantasies of domination and submission to life: it allows us to question and explore our relationships to authority. BDSM lets women and men design their own sexual scenarios, have uncommonly detailed discussions about consent, and step into roles of power and experiment with them. Some have claimed that because BDSM involves probing the limits of pain and desire, BDSM practitioners become more skilled in articulating desire and listening carefully and empathically to their partners. This is one way BDSM affords opportunities for personal growth that is clearly aligned with feminist principles.

In her study of sixty-six professional dominatrices—female sex workers who specialize in playing the dominating role during BDSM—researcher Danielle Lindemann observed the way these women repeatedly used the word "therapy" to describe their work. This BDSM-as-therapy discourse was apparent in the sex workers' descriptions of what goes on in their dungeons, described by Lindemann as "healthful alternatives to sexual repression, as atonement rituals, as mechanisms for gaining control over prior trauma, and (in the case of 'humiliation sessions') as processes through which clients experience psychological revitalization through shame."[17] These sex workers described clients who pay to have past traumatic experiences staged so that they might relive painful memories of humiliation, punishment, or harsh discipline with a more positive outcome that could lead to a healing of old wounds. This suggests that working through shame (often gender or sex-related shame) may have some positive impact not only on the individual but also on our larger social world, in that individuals may go on to inhabit roles of power and subordination with greater consciousness and sensitivity. In this way, BDSM has the potential to advance progressive social change, should the BDSM practitioner use it in this way.

TAKING SIDES

Is BDSM enlightening or damaging? Does BDSM position the practitioner to be more sensitive to issues of power and gender outside the bedroom, or does it simply tighten the knot between sex and aggression that some feminists claim is central to sexual life under patriarchy?

This is the crucial question.

Alas, we cannot answer this question in any absolute way. This is for two reasons. First, as the above analysis has shown, BDSM is not categorically unlike any other kinds of sexual activity. Pain, power, and submission are inherent—and not inherently negative—elements of sexual experience, not the exclusive province of BDSM. Racism and sexism are not limited to BDSM's race play; we see racism and sexism throughout our culture. And BDSM's potential to enable emotional healing is also not unique to BDSM, as many types of erotic experiments with vulnerability have this potential. BDSM may afford thrilling physical pleasure and profound emotional growth opportunities, and so may non-BDSM sex. Under these terms, feminist-informed BDSM and feminist-informed non-BDSM sex (often disparagingly called "vanilla" sex) are in the same ethical category, in that both practices have explicit elements of political consciousness.

Furthermore, the debate over BDSM is challenged by the fact that the boundaries of BDSM are hard to define. What counts as BDSM, and who gets to decide? Whipping, handcuffing, and blindfolding may seem like obvious BDSM activities, but if we crave a bit of hair-pulling or a gentle spanking during sex, have we entered BDSM's realm? (And what if our partner gets pleasure from lovingly giving that spank?) Let's say a person has a sexual fantasy of seduction by an authority figure: Does role-playing that fantasy with a partner constitute eroticizing violence? What if one partner in an erotic encounter can't be aroused unless he assumes a physically submissive position, would we say that we are in BDSM territory? Does dirty talk constitute BDSM, if dirty talk includes some (debatably degrading) slang? These questions serve the rhetorical function of pointing out that defining BDSM may be hard to do precisely because BDSM is not wholly unlike other genres of sex.

The second reason why we cannot make any final judgment on the value of BDSM is that we cannot assume a universal motivation or ethic among BDSM practitioners. Not all BDSM practitioners have a political consciousness or care about eradicating patriarchy. For many people practicing BDSM, there is not a set of political questions to be actively explored, but rather a situation of power—sadism or masochism—to be simply enjoyed. In this case, patriarchy is not a problem but instead an erotic fetish. When feminists practice BDSM, they may do so with quite different goals. It seems one must make a choice in BDSM: to fetishize brutality or to engage it critically. I take feminist BDSM practitioners at their word when they describe their profound pleasure and personal transformation. I find persuasive the argument that playing these roles with a politically engaged consciousness may heighten our sensitivity to power and even neutralize our unconscious patterns around it.

In light of this, asking whether BDSM is good or bad is the wrong question. The question should instead ask, *Is BDSM politically engaged or politically disengaged sex?* as this is the fulcrum on which this entire debate rests. If greater knowledge of power's cultural and psychic life is valuable, then sexual experience that enhances one's awareness of how power is used and experienced has moral value. If, in BDSM play, I come to better understand situations of authority and obedience that were once baffling to me, and if I gain a clearer awareness of the myriad ways power may be used to control and equip me as well as others, then I can be said to have a raised political consciousness as a result of that experience. On the other hand, BDSM that includes no exploration whatsoever into what power is, and how we exist in it, is not enlightening or politically progressive. But neither is any other kind of sex that runs from political questions.

The debate over BDSM is misguided, because BDSM is not the problem. Political ignorance or avoidance is the problem. In advocating a politically conscious sexuality, I am not suggesting we are always required to insert politics into sexuality, but instead that we ought to attend to the politics already existing in our bedrooms. Sexuality is above all a social and political phenomenon, even though much of our sexual activity goes on in private. Its norms and scripts mirror the ideologies regulating our social world. In making erotic life a context for experimenting with risk and desire, we can critically reflect on how we use, share, and are subjected to power. How we respond to these workings of power, in our intimacies and vulnerabilities, will determine the ethical value of our actions.

DISCUSSION QUESTIONS

• Have you ever experienced a conflict between your political views and your erotic tastes? If so, what was the nature of the conflict, and how did you respond to it?
• Can you imagine a situation in which you consent to be harmed, but still find the harm unethical?
• Do you believe that private sexual activities can have a social or political impact?
• What are some feminist critiques of BDSM? What is your position on this issue?
• Do you agree with the author that pain, power, and submission are not inherently negative? What has been your experience with any of these three?

NOTES

1. I am grateful to my research assistant, Ashley Grace, for her close readings, smart insights, and innovative criticisms.

2. Claims distinguishing "play" violence in BDSM from "real world" violence do not hold up in cases of actual unwanted assault in BDSM contexts. Yes, sexual assault occurs in BDSM, not because BDSM is more likely to provoke assault but because, unfortunately, sexual assault happens everywhere. For more on sexual assault in BDSM, see Megan Lieff, "Safe Words: The History of Anti-abuse Activism in BDSM," *Bitch* 60 (Fall 2013): 20–22.

3. Non-feminists have also criticized BDSM, but for entirely different reasons. Some non-feminist critics of BDSM oppose it because it deviates from reproductive sex (that centers on penis-to-vagina intercourse that begins with male erection and ends with male ejaculation). For these critics, procreative heterosexual mating is the single "right" way to have sex, and anything that deviates from this norm is to be morally opposed. Such moral opposition was long codified as legal opposition: until the Supreme Court's landmark 2003 *Lawrence v. Kansas* ruling striking down a Texas sodomy law and declaring such laws unconstitutional, it was legal to criminalize sexual acts (such as anal sex) that deviate from penis-to-vagina intercourse. If we value sex for reasons other than procreation—for instance, if we value sex for pleasure's sake among consenting adults—then this anti-BDSM rationale cannot be sufficient for condemning BDSM, for such a position would render *any* kind of sexual behavior unacceptable if it does not center on procreative intercourse. For this reason, this view is irrelevant to the BDSM debate explored in this chapter.

4. Marital rape, for instance, is a relatively new legal concept. The notion that a husband does not have full-time access to his wife's body—irrespective of her consent—would confound earlier conceptions of marriage. A husband's ownership of access to his wife's body had been built into the very meaning of marriage for much of the history of marriage, and women had no bodily or sexual sovereignty that was protected by law. It was not until 1993, thanks to feminist organizing on the matter, that rape in the context of marriage became criminal throughout the United States.

5. For more on subcultures that explore the pleasures of painful body modification, see Victoria L. Pitts, *In the Flesh: The Cultural Politics of Body Modification* (New York: Palgrave Macmillan, 2003).

6. From the Bible to Freud and beyond, the belief that passivity and dispassion are signs of proper female sexuality is widespread in Western culture. Scholars often point to the public outrage generated by sexuality researcher Alfred Kinsey's data describing female sexuality as active and passionate as proof of a cultural attachment to the notion that women are largely asexual. See Vern L. Bullough, "Alfred Kinsey and the Kinsey Report," in Mindy Stombler, Dawn M. Baunach, Elisabeth O. Burgess, Denise Donnelly, and Wendy Simonds, eds., *Sex Matters: The Sexuality and Society Reader* (Boston, MA: Pearson, 2004), 34–40.

7. Feminist philosopher Judith Butler's book, *Excitable Speech*, remains one of the most compelling in its analysis of how uses and prohibitions of so-called hate speech influence the construction identity. See Judith Butler, *Excitable Speech: A Politics of the Performative* (New York: Routledge, 1997).

8. Daisy Hernandez, "Playing with Race," *Colorlines*, December 21, 2004, http://colorlines.com/archives/2004/12/playing_with_race.html.

9. See Kathleen Barry, "On the History of Cultural Sadism," in Robin Ruth Linden, Darlene R. Pagano, Diana E.H. Russell, and Susan Leigh Star, eds., *Against Sadomasochism: A Radical Feminist Analysis* (East Palo Alto, CA: Frog in the Well, 1982), 51–65.

10. The argument that femininity is equated with submission is persuasively made by numerous feminist scholars. See Susan Bordo, *Unbearable Weight: Feminism, Western Culture, and the Body* (Berkeley: University of California Press, 1993) and Sandra Lee Bartky, *Femininity and Domination: Studies in the Phenomenology of Oppression* (New York: Routledge, 1990).

11. Jean Grimshaw, "Ethics, Fantasy, and Self-Transformation" in A. Phillips Griffiths, ed., *Ethics* (New York: Cambridge University Press, 1993), 152–153.

12. Gayle Rubin, "The Leather Menace: Comments on Politics and S/M," in Samois, ed., *Coming to Power: Writings and Graphics on Lesbian S/M*, 3rd ed. (Boston: Alyson, 1987), 194. Samois was a lesbian-feminist BDSM organization based in San Francisco and active from 1978 to 1983.

13. Judith Butler, "Lesbian S&M: The Politics of Dis-Illusion" in Robin Ruth Linden, Darlene R. Pagano, Diana E.H. Russell, and Susan Leigh Star, eds., *Against Sadomasochism: A Radical Feminist Analysis* (East Palo Alto, CA: Frog in the Well, 1982), 172.

14. Lieff, "Safe Words," 21.

15. Kathleen Barry, quoted in Meghan Murphy, "Part Two in a Two-Part Series on BDSM & Feminism—An Interview with Kathleen Barry," *Feminist Current*, July 22, 2012, http://feministcurrent.com/5698/episode-004-part-two-in-a-two-part-series-on-bdsm-feminism-an-interview-with-kathleen-barry/.

16. Hernandez, "Playing with Race."

17. Danielle Lindemann, "BDSM as Therapy?" *Sexualities* 14, no. 2 (2011): 157.

TRUE LOVE WAITS—DO TEENS?

The Importance of Sexual Honesty[1]

Janet Rosenbaum

Memory says, "I did that."
Pride replies, "I could not have done that." Eventually, memory yields.
—Friedrich Nietzsche, *Beyond Good and Evil*

Sex can be such a taboo topic that sometimes people don't tell the truth about their sexual behavior, not even to themselves. This chapter examines when people tell the truth about sex and when they seem not to, and whether people seem most interested in lying to themselves or to others. I discuss this topic in four contexts: my studies of virginity pledgers in the United States; a study of premarital sex among Southern Baptists in Texas; laboratory tests for showing when people have been exposed to semen in the recent past; and whether parents deceive themselves about how much they teach their adolescents about sex.

Misreporting is not the same as hypocrisy. American society certainly provides many examples of conservative hypocrisy towards sexuality. One instance of this includes legislators who champion what they call traditional morality, depriving sexual minorities and women of equal rights, yet have committed adultery, had furtive same-sex encounters, or profited financially from abortion. My grandfather, a pediatrician and abortion advocate pre-*Roe*, had such an experience with a legislator who blocked his state's abortion bill, which my grandfather had supported. Several months later, this same anti-abortion politician came to my grandfather's office seeking an abortion for his pregnant teenage daughter in a state where abortion was not available legally. My grandfather told him how his daughter could obtain a safe abortion, but it's tragic that less privileged women and girls in Indiana lacked the same access partially due to this legislator's actions.

As you will see in some of the examples that follow, sometimes people don't report about sex honestly—not because they are hypocrites who want to deceive others but because they have deceived themselves.

ABSTINENCE-ONLY SEX EDUCATION AND VIRGINITY PLEDGES

In 1992, the Southern Baptist Conference created a pledge program to encourage teenagers to wait to have sex until marriage. They called the program True Love Waits. Teenagers were asked to sign a card with the following text, "Believing that true love waits, I make a commitment to God, myself, my family, my friends, my future mate, and my future children to a lifetime of purity including sexual abstinence from this day until marriage." After Massachusetts legalized same-sex marriage in 2004, the text of the pledge was changed to clarify that they meant Biblical marriage, rather than Massachusetts marriage.

To promote the pledge, the Southern Baptists held pledge drives centered around major events. They displayed 210,000 virginity pledge cards at the Youth for Christ rally in July 1994, and 460,000 pledge cards at the 2004 Athens Olympics. Dozens of other organizations—mostly Evangelical, but some Catholic—created their own sexual abstinence pledges modeled after True Love Waits.

Media featured the virginity pledge prominently: The front page of a Sunday *Washington Post* declared "Virginity Is New Counterculture Among Area Teens"[2] and the front page of the *New York Times* Sunday Style section featured "Proud to Be a Virgin: Nowadays You Can Be Respected Even if You Don't Do It."[3] The virginity pledge movement was a sexual Astroturf movement—created by adults but appearing to come from adolescents—but the media seemed to cover the movement uncritically as coming from youth, even if some youth were parroting lines they were taught in the programs.[4]

Shortly after the 1992 emergence of the virginity pledge, in 1996 the federal government started funding abstinence-only sex education. Abstinence-only sex education is defined by statute as having the "exclusive purpose [of] teaching the social, psychological, and health gains [of] abstaining from sexual activity." Birth control may only be mentioned in terms of failure rates. In most years since 1996, the federal government has given states $50 million per year for abstinence-only sex education, which by definition may not teach contraceptive effectiveness. Additional funds were added for community-based abstinence education, so that by the end of the Bush administration, the funding reached $204 million, higher than that year's funding for the National Endowment for the Arts ($145 million) and only slightly lower than the Title X family planning program providing needed health care to 5 million women. President Obama eliminated funding for abstinence-only sex education when he entered office (it expired June 30, 2009), but the funding for abstinence was reinstated for 2010–2014 as a legislative deal made in order to get the Affordable Care Act passed.[5]

The virginity pledge movement became linked to abstinence-only sex education by the 2001 publication in the *American Journal of Sociology* of a study finding that virginity pledgers delay sex an average of eighteen months.

The federal government allowed abstinence-only programs to evaluate themselves using the number of virginity pledges signed instead of participants' actual reports of their behavior. I used the same data to study virginity pledges, but I used a more rigorous statistical method.

I conducted two studies of virginity pledges: one on whether adolescents reported their sexual histories and virginity pledges reliably, and the other on whether adolescents who took virginity pledges were more likely to delay sex than similar non-pledgers.

In one study, I used a nationally representative sample of 14,000 adolescents who answered the same questions one year apart in 1995 and 1996 for the National Longitudinal Study of Adolescent Health.[6] One year after the original survey, some respondents retracted their earlier reports. Among those who said initially that they had taken a virginity pledge, 52 percent said the following year that they had never taken a virginity pledge. Among those who initially said that they had had vaginal intercourse (described specifically on the survey as "where a man puts his penis in a woman's vagina" to eliminate any uncertainty about which act we're talking about), the following year, 11 percent said that they had never had sex.

Previous researchers had found associations with demographic factors, such as being male. But I found that retraction was associated with changed social context.

Virginity pledgers who reported having had vaginal sex, or having left born-again Christianity in the year since reporting their pledge, had three times the odds of retracting their report of having ever taken a virginity pledge. Meanwhile, non-virgins who reported having taken a virginity pledge, or who became a born-again Christian in the year since reporting having had sex, had three times the odds of retracting their report of having ever had sex. We have no way to know which report is true: Some of the respondents who retracted their reports of having had sex may not have actually had sex. The two demographics that retracted their reports of sex were males ages 12 to 14 and females ages 17 to 18. It could be that younger male virgins lied on the first survey and reported having had sex when they hadn't, and after they took a virginity pledge or became born again, they lost interest in fabricating a sexual history on a survey.

Misreporting isn't limited to sex, but it does appear limited to deviant behaviors. I also found that among teens who reported other stigmatized or illegal behaviors—under-aged driving, pierced ears for boys, permanent tattoos, pregnancy history, or having first had sex prior to age 13—more than 10 percent retracted their earlier reports. There was virtually no inconsistent reporting about non-deviant states, such as girls with pierced ears or teens over age 15 who reported having ever driven a car.

One explanation for the changed reports is that the concept of being "born again" in Christianity includes the idea that people literally become new people when they become "born again," and this changed identity impacts their survey responses. It may also be that teens change so much over the course of their adolescence, and they may truly feel like new people. Tattoos have little policy relevance, but the finding that more than 10 percent of adolescents who initially reported having a tattoo is particularly interesting given its physical reality. Unlike a sexual history, a permanent tattoo is literally visible on the person. Not that many adolescents can afford to have a tattoo removed, and although some teens may have lied about a tattoo on the first survey, it's unlikely that many teens failed to tell the truth about their tattoos. The fact that some teenagers with tattoos report that they don't have any suggests that misreporting on surveys has more to do with how teens (want to) see themselves or present themselves to others, rather than precisely recounting their actual histories.

The second study of virginity pledges used a statistical method called "matched sampling." This identified virginity pledgers who were similar to non-pledgers on factors that might otherwise confound the relationship between taking a virginity pledge and having sex. The reason for the matched sampling statistical method is that teens who take virginity pledges are already different from the general teenage population in many ways that make them more likely to delay sex: They go more frequently to church and religious youth groups; they are more likely to report attitudes such as "anticipate feeling guilty" and "losing their partner's respect" if they had sex; they tend to be less sexually experienced, and less likely to anticipate pleasure from sex. These qualities are very different from most teenagers! Comparing such teens with the general population is like comparing apples and oranges, and it certainly doesn't answer the question of whether virginity pledges delay sex.

A straight-out comparison between pledgers and non-pledgers is likely to be confounded by all of the ways in which the two groups differ, so it wouldn't be possible to know what effect the pledge would have setting aside all the pre-pledge differences.

Our study of 934 socially conservative teenagers (289 pledgers and 645 non-pledgers) found that five years after some of them took a virginity pledge, pledgers and nonpledgers had sex at the same rates. But 54 percent of non-pledgers used condoms most of the time, whereas only 42 percent of pledgers did so—even though the two groups had similar views about birth control before the virginity pledge.

I compared the pledgers and non-pledgers on twenty-seven sexual behaviors, and the only differences between pledgers and the similar non-pledgers were minimal. First, pledgers had 0.11 fewer sexual partners in the past year than non-pledgers, but did not differ in number of lifetime sexual partners. Second, pledgers were 2.3 percentage points less likely to have ever been paid for sex. And third, pledgers were less likely to have used condoms in the past year and less likely to have used birth control both in the past year and at last sex. That's it.

After this study was published, a Republican speechwriter criticized the study in a *Wall Street Journal* op-ed precisely for the reasons that the statistical analysis was strong: it limited inference to virginity pledges, rather than the likely confounders. It's fascinating to see a cutting-edge statistical technique that reaches appropriate statistical inference described as a tool of the liberal elite. Author William McGurn's bias against the research is revealed in his *WSJ* quote: "The only way the study's author, Janet Elise Rosenbaum of Johns Hopkins University, could reach such results was by comparing teens who take a virginity pledge with a very small subset of other teens: those who are just as religious and conservative as the pledge-takers."[7] McGurn apparently wanted studies of virginity pledges to be a verdict about two approaches to sexuality: Is it better for teens if they anticipate guilt from sex or not? For better or worse, such a broad-based study is probably not possible. Some individuals in my study may have been on the border about whether to take a virginity pledge or not. Or it's possible they didn't take a virginity pledge for arbitrary reasons. (Maybe they simply missed that day of religious youth group.)

What is clear, however, is that we can learn a few things from our country's experience with abstinence-only sex education. First, teenagers don't listen to one-sided information (i.e., propaganda). In peer-reviewed studies, more than a dozen programs have been shown to delay teen sex. All of these successful programs involve comprehensive sex education that teach both contraception and abstinence. For example, the Becoming a Responsible Teen program helped low-income African-American teenagers in Mississippi both to delay sex and to have safer sex, and its effects were visible one year later: Only 12 percent of sexually inexperienced participants became sexually active, compared with 31 percent in the comparison group. Moreover, 83 percent of sexually active participants used condoms, versus 61 percent in the comparison group.

Second, the same laws that create ineffective programs sometimes also mandate that the programs be evaluated. Congress mandated an evaluation of abstinence-only sex education. Conducted by Chris Trenholm and Barbara Devaney at Mathematica Policy Research, the evaluation used a randomized experiment to compare abstinence-only sex education with comprehensive sex education, and it found no differences.[8]

Finally, statistics matter. Peter Bearman and Hannah Bruckner's study in the *American Journal of Sociology* elevated the virginity pledge from a social trend to a tool for policy evaluation, used for determining the distribution of millions of dollars in federal funds. Their study found that virginity pledgers delayed sex.[9] I replicated their study using the same data but more rigorous statistics accounting for the fact that people who take virginity pledges are more likely to delay sex for reasons other than the pledge. These reasons include their religious affiliation and the sense that if they had sex they would feel guilty. I found that pledgers were not more likely to delay sex, but they were less likely to use condoms.

HOW TO LOSE YOUR VIRGINITY

Interview With Documentary Filmmaker Therese Shechter

Amber Melvin

Like many young people today, I wore a purity ring as a teenager. My born-again aunt offered to get me one when she was buying them for my cousins, and, while I was absolutely certain that I was going to keep my virginity until marriage, I mostly accepted her offer because I like the idea of getting special jewelry. I have long since lost the ring. (Sorry, not sorry, Aunt D.) But while my purity ring is long gone, young people today are still receiving messages that maintaining their virginity and avoiding sex until marriage is the expectation. There is still no national standard for sex education in the United States, and many states still provide abstinence-only sex education for their students. When I heard that there was a new film on these topics, I had to check it out. I caught up with Therese Shechter, director of the film *How to Lose Your Virginity*—a witty documentary about the notion of virginity—to learn more about her work.

Amber Melvin: So tell us why you were curious about virginity and what prompted you to create a documentary about the topic.

Therese Shechter: In the mid-2000s when abstinence-until-marriage sex education programs were at their full glory, I began looking more critically at how we talk to young people about sex and noticing the inherent shame and judgment especially for women's sexual choices. I had thought virginity was a very simple concept, as I think most people do. But it turned out to be related to so many things like history, politics, religion, pop culture. . . . This idea of losing your virginity is something that most people really obsess about at a certain part of their lives. There's a lot of shame and fear and awkwardness around it.

AM: The film explains that there is no clear way to tell if a person is a virgin and people don't even agree about what losing one's virginity means. Yet virginity is such a big deal in our culture.

TS: Exactly. While I was filming the documentary I realized there is a common belief that when a woman is first vaginally penetrated by a penis it will change you. Everything about your life and your value is supposedly different after that split second it goes in. It's completely absurd and yet our entire civilization seems built around that idea. Not only are our beliefs about virginity very gendered, but they are also very limiting. This obsession with virginity dictates who is considered sexual and creates stigma for people who, for whatever reason, have not had intercourse. For example, if you are an older virgin, people wonder what is wrong with you. Or if you are a lesbian and neither partner has a penis to have intercourse with, some people question whether you are even having "real" sex.

This notion about virginity underlies how women are categorized, judged, and punished for their sexual choices. The effects encompass everything from abstinence movements which teach that women become "used" as soon as they have sex outside marriage (in my film, Shelby Knox says she was told she was like a dirty toothbrush); to fetishizing virginity in porn (where women go from pure to slutty thanks to one penetrating penis); to the reality that a young woman who accuses someone of rape gets re-attacked by the legal system if there's even a hint of past sexual experience. The presumption is, *How could she not consent if she's already turned into a slut through sexual activity?* Oh, that magic penis's transformative powers!

AM: If you had to narrow it down, how would you describe the main point of *How to Lose Your Virginity*?

TS: The film's main point is that if you get all of your information from pop culture, porn, or abstinence classes, you get a pretty narrow view of sex and virginity. In fact, there is a whole wide world of experience out there. The first time that a person has intercourse is often not the most important and usually not the greatest sexual milestone in a person's life. We all have various sexual milestones and appreciating them requires a cultural shift away from our obsession with a narrow concept of virginity.

Shechter has turned her blog about the film into an online project called the V-Card Diaries, where you can map other people's "tales of sexual debuts and deferrals." These real-life stories are models that demonstrate how not all first times are life changing and that losing your virginity is not the quintessential life experience that our culture might have us believe.

You can purchase *How to Lose Your Virginity*, find or schedule a screening near you, read the V-Card Diaries, and contact Therese Shechter at virginitymovie.com.

EVANGELICAL ATTITUDES ABOUT SEX

Evangelical Christianity is an important social movement in the United States, but Evangelical Christians and liberals often misunderstand each other. Many religious people are open about sexuality, as I found in a study of Southern Baptists who were surveyed in their Sunday schools. For his doctorate at a seminary in Texas, a Southern Baptist minister conducted a survey of 151 married Southern Baptists in nine Texas church Sunday schools. Southern Baptists are the largest Protestant denomination in the country, comprising 13 percent of American Protestants. Southern Baptists originated the virginity pledge, and they have had an important influence on American society. With the minister's permission, I reanalyzed his data and found three surprising findings.

First, these Southern Baptists participated in premarital sex: More than 70 percent of those surveyed reported having had premarital oral or vaginal sex, although 80 percent claimed they regretted it. Cynics might be surprised to see such high numbers reported on a survey conducted by a member of the clergy in Sunday School. Given the high prevalence of reported regret, it is remarkable that so many nonetheless reported a past behavior that they were uncomfortable with. The sample was not randomly selected from all Southern Baptists in Texas, but there is no reason to expect that the respondents were particularly open-minded: ten out of fourteen churches agreed to participate (one church didn't have enough newly married congregants), so the respondents were unlikely to be unusually liberal or open. Even if the most conservative quartile of respondents were the ones who decline to participate, the most liberal three-quarters of Southern Baptists is hardly libertine. These numbers are similar to those reported on nationally representative studies: About 80 percent of Protestant Christians who attend church monthly report having had premarital sex; about 80 percent of born-again Christians also report having had premarital sex.

Second, most of the Southern Baptists in this study who reported waiting until marriage to have sex . . . got married young. The most common marriage age in this sample was 21 to 24 years old for women and 22 to 26 years old for men. The women who married when they were between 21 and 24 were the least likely to report premarital sex: half reported vaginal sex and 60 percent reported oral sex before marriage. Women who married before age 20 or after age 24 were most likely to report premarital sex: 92 percent of the women who married before age 20 reported premarital sex (potentially some were shotgun weddings), and 85 percent of women who married after age 24 had premarital sex (they were possibly tired of waiting).

Nearly 61 percent of men who married at the most common marriage ages (22 to 26 years old) reported participating in vaginal sex. About 63 percent of these men reported engaging in oral sex. Men were also more likely to have premarital sex the older their marriage age: 78 percent of men who married after 26 had premarital sex, and 86 percent of men who married after 29.

Of course it's impossible to differentiate between two competing reasons for these numbers: whether those who differed from the social norm in marriage age also differed from the religious norm in decisions about premarital sex, or whether they just got tired of waiting for Mr./Ms. Right.

Notice that there is no sexual double standard in these figures: Men and women report having premarital sex in equal numbers, despite the stereotype that religion values female virginity more than male virginity, and thus we might expect women either to conceal their sexual activity more than men or engage in less of it. Women in this sample had premarital sex earlier than men did in chronological age, and in similar numbers relative to the usual age of marriage. The only evidence for a sexual double standard is in reporting of oral versus vaginal sex: Similar numbers of men who married at normative ages (22 to 26) reported vaginal and oral sex, whereas women reported oral sex at a 10 percent higher rate than vaginal sex.

There is some evidence for substitution of oral for vaginal sex in this sample. White young adults in the United States seem to regard oral sex as less intimate than vaginal sex and have a lower threshold for engaging in oral sex than vaginal sex. This study found that young adults with the most religious upbringings or normative marriage age did not differ from their less traditional counterparts in their rate of oral sex, but they were less likely to have vaginal sex. A quarter of those who remained technical virgins had premarital oral sex. Those who attended church more frequently during childhood were slightly less likely to have vaginal sex (58 percent versus 64 percent) but did not differ in premarital oral sex (64 percent versus 67 percent, not statistically significant). Those who married between the ages of 21 and 24 were also less likely to have vaginal but not oral sex.

Third, many Evangelical laypeople favor comprehensive sex education: that is, sex education that teaches contraception. A random phone survey of American parents found that 89 percent of all American parents favor comprehensive sex education, as do 83 percent of born-again Christian parents, and 51 percent of parents who refer to themselves as politically "very conservative."[10] As in the nationally representative sample, 65 percent of this evangelical sample favored secular sex education. People who reported having received the strongest sex education in school supported secular sex education by 29 percentage points more than those who reported the weakest school sex education. Even Sarah Palin was quoted in the 2006 Alaska gubernatorial debate as favoring teaching birth control in addition to abstinence. Despite her conservative evangelical roots, former Governor Palin acknowledged that most teenagers are having sex—even religious teens—so of course they should know about birth control.

BIOMARKERS FOR SEMEN EXPOSURE

Having discussed how people misreport sexual behavior, I can discuss scientific developments that enable researchers to avoid misreports by using a laboratory procedure to assess whether respondents have been exposed to semen in the recent past.

The background of this biomarker goes back to HIV researcher Jonathan Zenilman who was frustrated by survey respondents misreporting about their use of condoms. Among respondents who reported 100 percent perfect condom use, many nonetheless had sexually transmitted infections (STIs), such as chlamydia, that could have been prevented with condoms. This difference between report and reality was termed the "Zenilman effect."

Although testing positive for STIs is a marker for unprotected sex, Ralph DiClemente and his colleagues found that 10 percent of those who are STI-positive claim to have been abstinent for the past 12 months.[11]

Researchers began looking for substances present in semen that remain in the body for days or weeks post-coitus. Prostate Specific Antigen (PSA) is detectable in the vagina for 24 to 48 hours post-coitus, and its presence predicts pregnancy.[12] Due to these properties, PSA is used in condom efficacy trials as an indicator for condom failure because it is more accurate than self-reported data.[13] PSA is currently being evaluated for whether it is an indicator for unprotected rectal sex and, if so, for how long PSA is detectable in the rectum.

Semen Y-chromosome (Yc) DNA is detectable in the vagina for as long as 14 days. The method uses polymerase chain reaction (PCR), which amplifies DNA to enable specific DNA sequences to be identified. The method is also used for forensic DNA analysis, paternity tests, and disease diagnosis (e.g., to find out whether an oral cancer is related to human papillomavirus (HPV)). To avoid contamination, the sample is processed by female lab technicians who also remove epithelial cells to avoid possibility that the Y-chromosome came from non-semen sources such as digital penetration ("fingering"). Among women using condoms with partners, 92 percent tested negative for Y-chromosome. Research methods have improved since then, so the test is likely to be even more accurate.

The Yc test is not yet widely used, but it has been applied in a few contexts. Among archived samples from Baltimore STI clinic patients reporting perfect condom use ($n = 141$), 55 percent tested positive for Yc. Past research with the semen Y-chromosome test in a group of women found that respondents who under-reported semen exposure are disproportionately those with a history of STIs[14] and are thus likely aware that they "should" use condoms. Because of this, they may have reported perfect condom use regardless of their *actual* condom use. My analysis of this data found that women who over-reported condom use—that is, they reported perfect condom use but tested positive for semen Y-chromosome—were more likely to get pregnant than every other category of contraception users, even women who reported never using any type of contraception at all.

PARENT–ADOLESCENT COMMUNICATION ABOUT SEX

The importance of honesty regarding sex isn't limited to sexual behavior; it also extends to sex education. Parents overestimate how much sex education they have given to their children.

Many states' sex education policies are formulated to give parents a primary role in their children's sex education. Thirty-two states do not include contraception in school-based sex education, and few teachers will cover a topic such as contraception because it might put their jobs at risk. It seems that parents have not filled in the gaps in school sex education: Almost no parents discuss concrete topics such as condoms with their teenagers. Past research has found that parents can be effective sex educators, but parents seem to overestimate how much information they give to their children.

The RAND Corporation conducted a study called Talking Parents, Healthy Teens with the goal of teaching parents how to communicate most effectively with their teens about sex. They enrolled 569 parents employed by thirteen large employers in Southern California. These parents had generally permissive attitudes about adolescents and premarital sex. Few parents, however, said that they approved if their adolescents had premarital sex now—understandable, given that their kids were in sixth to tenth grade. But nearly all parents approved of their adolescents having premarital sex once they turned 18. The researchers posed the same questions to both parents and adolescents, giving a unique opportunity to compare the two views.

Even among parents who don't oppose premarital sex, parent-adolescent communication about sex was marred by a few problems in communication style:

• Many adolescents feared questions about sex would cause their parent to leap to conclusions and assume that they were having sex. Only 16 percent of parents said that they would leap to conclusions, but 29 percent of adolescents thought that their parent would leap to conclusions.
• Both parents and adolescents were aware that adolescents may not be comfortable asking questions about sex, which was reported by 53 percent of parents and 42 percent of teens.
• Most adolescents realize that they don't know everything, but still only 76 percent of adolescents say that they know less than their parents about sex.
• 81 percent of parents claim to have spoken with their adolescents about homosexuality, but only 54 percent of teens agree.

- In terms of discussions about male and female sexual development, 63 percent of parents reported that they talked with their kids about menstruation but only 49 percent of teens thought they had.
- Even information about pregnancy and childbirth—a core topic of sex education that many children learn when young—had a gap with 72 percent of parents reporting that they discussed this and only 63 percent of teens agreeing.
- For several crucial topics, parents and adolescents agreed they did not discuss the topics: Fewer than 15 percent reported discussing how to choose birth control methods or how to use a condom; fewer than 20 percent report discussing STI symptoms or how to negotiate condom use with a partner; fewer than 25 percent report discussing why people like sex; fewer than 30 percent report discussing birth control and pregnancy and the importance of not pressuring a partner for sex.

Even parents eager to discuss sex with their teens overestimate the quality of the sex education that they provide. Parents who are realistic about how well they communicate with their teens may be more effective sex educators for their adolescents. Even the most well-meaning parents may benefit from outside assistance in breaching important topics such as contraception, contraception choices, and the prevention of pregnancy and STIs.

CONCLUSIONS

Premarital sex is common but not universal. Some adolescents and young adults wait until marriage or until they are older, but even among the Southern Baptists who married at normative ages, about half have premarital sex.

Many survey respondents report past sexual behavior they are uneasy about, as with the Southern Baptists who reported premarital sex that they regretted. But others conceal past behavior that is at odds with their current identity, as did the adolescents who changed their answers about their sexual or virginity pledge histories. Having had premarital sex does not, in and of itself, put someone at odds with their religious identity: If their religion acknowledges that everyone makes mistakes, married young adult Southern Baptists may be able to reconcile their premarital sex as part of a flawed past that they can repent for without pretending that it never happened. Of course we don't know how many Southern Baptists concealed their sexual behavior in their survey responses. These figures could be similar to the nationally representative sample of adolescents.

In some cases misreporting about sex has severe consequences. Virginity pledgers who have sex are less likely to use condoms, possibly because of negative and inaccurate information taught in abstinence-only sex education programs, and may eventually have unplanned pregnancies and STIs. Adolescents who report having used condoms 100 percent of the time but test positive for semen exposure have a greater risk for pregnancy than even adolescents who admit to unprotected sex, and we don't understand why. Parents who believe that they provide comprehensive sex education to their adolescents but their adolescents don't agree are missing out on an opportunity for honest conversation with their teens and the opportunity to influence their teen's behavior at a formative period.

Fortunately we have good solutions. More than a dozen comprehensive sex education programs have been found to be effective in promoting both safer sex and delaying sex among adolescents. The Obama administration passed legislation allocating $185 million to evidence-based sex education—an amount similar to the funding for abstinence-only sex education during much of the Bush administration. At the same time, however, the Obama administration provided $50 million for abstinence-only sex education in states as part of a likely misguided compromise.

DISCUSSION QUESTIONS

• When people misreport their past behaviors, do you think that they are lying or just not being accurate? What is the difference, if any?
• Have you misreported your past behavior because you think that your misreport represented your actual behavior better than the answer that was strictly true? What happened?
• What are the advantages and disadvantages of using biomarkers instead of survey questions? Some areas that you may want to consider: measurement accuracy, cost, logistics, and ethical concerns.
• Do you think that it's invasive to verify someone's survey responses using biomarkers?
• Do you think school-based sex education should take a bigger role in children's sex education instead of their parents—especially since parents overestimate how much sex education they provide?

NOTES

1. This chapter is based on a talk given at the Science for Sinners event at the MIT Museum on April 26, 2012.
2. DeNeen L. Brown, "Virginity Is New Counterculture among Area Teens," *Washington Post*, November 21, 1993, p. A1.
3. Judith Newman, "Proud to Be a Virgin: Nowadays You Can Be Respected Even if You Don't Do It," *New York Times*, June 19, 1994, http://www.nytimes.com/1994/06/19/style/proud-to-be-a-virgin.html.
4. The term "Astroturf" used in this context comes from political campaigns created by corporations to appear to be grassroots. These are called Astroturf movements.

5. A similar deal was arranged when major abstinence-only funding was added to President Clinton's welfare-reform initiative. A smaller amount of funding to promote abstinence has been allocated since the early Reagan administration.

6. Janet Rosenbaum, "Reborn a Virgin: Adolescents' Retracting of Virginity Pledges and Sexual Histories," *American Journal of Public Health* 96, no. 6 (2006): 1098–1103.

7. William McGurn, "Like a Virgin: The Press Take on Teenage Sex," *Wall Street Journal*, January 6, 2009, http://online.wsj.com/news/articles/SB123120095259855597.

8. C. Trenholm, B. Devaney, K. Fortson, M. Clark, L.Q. Bridgespan, and J. Wheeler, "Impacts of Abstinence Education on Teen Sexual Activity, Risk of Pregnancy, and Risk of Sexually Transmitted Diseases," *Journal of Policy Analysis and Management* 27, no. 2 (Spring 2008): 255–276.

9. Peter Bearman and Hannah Bruckner, "Promising the Future: Virginity Pledges and First Intercourse," *American Journal of Sociology* 106, no. 4 (2001): 859–912.

10. M.E. Eisenberg, D.H. Bernat, L.H. Beringer, and M.D. Resnick. "Support for Comprehensive Sexuality Education: Perspectives From Parents of School-Age Youth," *Journal of Adolescent Health* 42, no. 4 (2008): 352–359.

11. R.J. DiClemente, J.M. Sales, F. Danner, and R.A. Crosby, "Association Between Sexually Transmitted Diseases and Young Adults' Self-Reported Abstinence," *Pediatrics* 127, no. 2 (February 2011): 208–213.

12. T.L. Walsh, R.G. Frezieres, K. Peacock, A.L. Nelson, V.A. Clark, L. Bernstein, and B.G. Wraxall, "Use of Prostate-Specific Antigen (PSA) to Measure Semen Exposure Resulting from Male Condom Failures: Implications for Contraceptive Efficacy and the Prevention of Sexually Transmitted Disease," *Contraception* 67, no. 2 (2003): 139–150.

13. Terri Walsh, Lee Warner, Mauricio Macaluso, Ron Frezieres, Margaret Snead, and Brian Wraxall, "Prostate-Specific Antigen as a Biomarker of Condom Failure: Comparison of Three Laboratory Assays and Self-Reported Condom Use Problems in a Randomized Trial of Female Condom Performance," *Contraception* 86, no. 1 (July 2012): 55–61.

14. E. Rose, R. DiClemente, G. Wingood, J. Sales, T. Latham, R. Crosby, J. Zenilman, J. Melendez, and J. Hardin, "The Validity of Teens' and Young Adults' Self-Reported Condom Use," *Archives of Pediatric Adolescent Medicine* 163, no. 1 (2009): 61–64.

CAMPUS SEXUAL ASSAULT

Myths, Facts, and Controversies

Nina M. Flores

"What was she wearing?"
"Why was she there by herself?"
"What did she expect if she was drinking so much?"
"Wasn't she was asking for it?"

These questions are based on rape myths and we hear them all the time. But the question I'm frequently asked is: *How did you get interested in sexual assault?*

I am an activist, scholar, and a writer. I publish political articles on a range of issues and people generally don't wonder if I have a personal connection to the topic. Yet when I write about sexual assault on college campuses, people often expect me to divulge a highly personal story. There is frequently an assumption that authors only write about rape if they've been assaulted. My story is the same as many women across the country: I am not a sexual assault survivor, but I live my day-to-day life with the deep and palpable fear that I will be assaulted. And that it will be my fault.

I cling to my keys in parking garages, take up a brisk and determined pace as the sun goes down, and keep my eyes alert to patches of thick foliage and darkened alleyways, anywhere someone could hide. I wear thick sweatshirts and jackets when walking home so I don't appear too provocative. Given warnings about being drugged at parties and bars, I never let a drink out of my sight and I don't accept beverages from strangers. I self-scrutinize every situation to make sure I am making the safest decisions possible.

I am, like so many women, carefully attuned to how I can avoid assault—and this is no accident. From a young age girls are taught to take responsibility for their safety, and this mindset continues through adulthood. Sexual assault is framed as a women's issue, a set-up that shifts our focus away from the men who rape—and from male rape survivors—and instead draws our attention to the actions of women. At colleges and universities across the country, young women are blamed for sexual crimes committed against them. The fact is that women on college campuses face sexual assault every year and none of them asks for it. I am interested in the intensely contested perspectives emerging as this issue gains increasing attention across the country.[1]

This chapter provides an overview of key issues regarding sexual assault. These issues include legal foundations, myths about sexual assault, the language we use to talk about assault, debates about alcohol and personal responsibility, and current legal controversies such as the rights of the accused. This chapter ends by suggesting ideas for what each of us can do to be part of the solution.

LANGUAGE MATTERS

There are many debates about the language we use in referring to someone who has been sexually assaulted. Some prefer the term "victim" because this emphasizes the serious impact of rape and sexual assault. Others interchangeably use the terms "victim" and "survivor," because while some people accentuate the strength of moving forward, there are those who do not survive assault.

In this chapter you may notice I intentionally use the term survivor instead of victim. The language we use to discuss sexual assault matters because time and again we see that sexual assault is not about sex: It's about power. Assaults happen because a perpetrator uses power over another person, whether through physical restraint, emotional manipulation, or incapacitation. The term victim is a limiting label, so I use the term survivor because it returns strength and agency to the person who has been assaulted, and recognizes the ability to move past defining one's life by the assault.

LEGAL FOUNDATIONS AND CAMPUS SEXUAL ASSAULT

As the number of reported sexual assaults increases on campuses across the country, conversations about the due process rights of the survivor and the rights of the accused are front and center. This section summarizes the basic legal issues and the reporting measures each school must follow.

Colleges and universities follow regulations at many levels. There are basic health and safety standards mandated by building codes, the fire marshal, or the county health department. Campus administrators are also tasked with enforcing their own set of safety and disciplinary measures. Campuses have built-in procedures for handling student grievances, and schools may even have their own police department that exists separately from local law enforcement. Although colleges and universities may define sexual assault under their sexual misconduct or sexual violence and prevention policies, the FBI's Uniform Crime Report establishes a national standard for defining rape. When sexual violence occurs, campuses also follow two national laws: Title IX and the Clery Act.

Defining Rape

In January 2012, the FBI announced that it was finally revising its archaic definition of rape. Until then, the FBI only counted rape that included penetration of a penis into a vagina by force. That meant that coerced rape, men's rape, drugged rape, anal or oral rape, and rape by objects or fingers did not officially count as rape to the FBI. This revised FBI definition of rape includes any penetration, no matter how slight, of the vagina or anus with any body part or object, or penetration of the mouth by a sex organ of another person, without the consent of the victim.[2]

The previous FBI Uniform Crime Report defined rape as "forced carnal knowledge." Professors Caroline Heldman and Danielle Dirks point out that because "forcible" is difficult to define, that term led to a vast underreporting of the crime.[3]

Title IX

Title IX (1972) is frequently assumed to be the law mandating equal athletics funding for women and men. However, the brief thirty-seven-word law specifies the following:

> No person in the United States shall, on the basis of sex, be excluded from participation in, be denied the benefits of, or be subjected to discrimination under any education program or activity receiving federal financial assistance.[4]

Clearly Title IX applies to much more than sports. It also requires colleges and universities to offer equal educational opportunities to female, male, trans, and genderqueer students.

Since the inception of Title IX, court cases have confirmed that it applies beyond sports to harassment and sexual assault. As feminist legal scholar Catharine MacKinnon explains, sexual crimes against women pose a limitation to equal educational opportunities, triggering Title IX attention. Since 2011, the Department of Education (DOE) released several policy updates, called Dear Colleague Letters,[5] reminding campuses about the reach of Title IX. As the issue continues gaining national attention, an unprecedented number of survivors have come forward to file complaints about mishandled sexual assault cases. At the time of this printing Title IX investigations were open at more than 60 campuses across the country. When a school is found in violation of Title IX the Department of Education can cut their federal funding, but despite many proven violations in the past few decades, they have not used this punishment in a single case.

If you have questions about Title IX, there are several options available. First, a Dear Colleague Letter (DCL) released by the Department of Education mandated that each school appoint a Title IX coordinator.[6] To find the Title IX coordinator on your campus, ask someone you trust on campus or run a quick web search to locate their office or email address. Second, a website called Know Your IX (knowyourix.org) was developed by a collective of survivor activists to empower students to stop sexual violence. The site contains information on Title IX, the Clery Act, how to file complaints, and how to deal with reporting violence, among other resources.

The Clery Act

The Clery Act[7] is a federal law that requires campuses to maintain and share an annual public report containing statistics on seven categories of crime, including homicide, sex offenses, robbery, aggravated assault, burglary, motor vehicle theft, and arson. The law also requires schools to have a public crime log, and to give students timely crime warnings when there is a threat to safety. Many campuses use email or text messages to alert students about crimes. The Clery Act is named for Jeanne Clery, a 19-year-old student at Lehigh University who in 1986 was found raped and murdered in her dorm room.

Although the law was meant to require campuses to track crime statistics, it is not without criticism. For instance, there is no uniform approach to the Clery Act. Depending on how a school interprets which crimes to track, it is easy to keep up the appearance of a low campus crime rate. For instance, some schools may only track crimes reported to their campus police, or only crimes in which the perpetrator is convicted. Others may report every complaint. Additionally, there is no agreement on which crimes should merit warnings to students. There are arguments on both sides about whether warnings should be issued for sexual assaults. On one hand, schools create a de facto hierarchy of crime if they send warnings about robberies and not sexual assaults. On the other hand, including too many details in the warning, such as location information, may draw attention to the survivor.

THE REPORTING PROCESS

The process for reporting an assault varies by campus. Some students choose not to report, instead confiding their story confidentially with counseling staff. Other students may share their experience with a resident assistant in their dorm or another employee who is a mandatory reporter. When a campus employee is a mandatory reporter, it means that speaking to them about an assault may automatically trigger another step of the reporting process. In many cases students welcome taking the next step in the reporting process, but some students express surprise or are upset that mandatory reporting happens on campus. It is important to know to whom you are talking, and whether they are required to report your story to administrators. The reporting process can be long and drawn out, and it can also be emotionally difficult. If you or someone you know is engaging in this process, be sure to take advantage of counseling and support services on campus.

However, if you are considering filing a report, there are few things to consider. First, filing a report with your campus or the campus security is not the same thing as filing charges with local authorities. On one hand, reporting assault to the campus means the investigation and judicial process will be handled through what is called a campus tribunal. If the perpetrator is convicted, punishments will be limited to the discretion of administrators. On the other hand, reporting assault and pressing changes with the local authorities means engaging in a legal system where rape is a criminal offense involving potential jail time. It is important to note that it is much more difficult to get a sexual assault conviction when pressing formal charges in the courts. Second, Title IX coordinators are employees of the university tasked with maintaining up-to-date expertise on the relationship between Title IX and the campus. This also means that it is unlikely they are neutral parties in grievances between students and campuses. Additionally, their priorities may lie with upholding Title IX in conjunction with university policies, not with advocating on behalf of students.

Rights of the Accuser

As a sexual assault survivor, what are your rights? A basic human right of survivors is to be believed, and to have their assault acknowledged by the college. The specific legal rights of survivors are detailed in The Federal Campus Sexual Assault Victims' Bill of Rights—this was signed into law in 1992 and is now part of the campus security reporting requirements. Among these rights:

* Survivors shall be notified of their options to notify law enforcement.
* The accuser and accused must have the same opportunity to have others present.

- Both parties shall be informed of the outcome of any disciplinary proceeding.
- Survivors shall be notified of counseling services.
- Survivors shall be notified of options for changing academic and living situations.

Survivors also have the right to a fair judicial process, to engage with personnel trained to hear about their experience, and to know the ins and outs of their decision to report.

THE LOWDOWN ON ANNUAL CAMPUS SAFETY REPORTS

Annual Clery Act reports containing campus safety statistics are public information meaning anyone can access the data. In addition to safety concerns, what impact does campus crime have on colleges and universities? Why might a university want to keep the number of reported assaults to a minimum? The following are three points to consider:

1. *Campus Reputation.* A high number of sexual assaults can tarnish a school's reputation among current students, their families, and the community.
2. *Potential Applicants.* As sexual assault receives more attention, students and parents are beginning to consider campus assault prevention and response in their decisions about where to apply to college.
3. *Alumni Donations.* Alumni donations provide crucial funding for many campuses. Alumni may withhold donations from campuses with continuing high rates of sexual assault.

Rights of the Accused

In the twenty-first century, information spreads at lightning speed thanks to the widespread availability of technology, handheld devices, and social media. Although due process guarantees innocence until proven guilty, for the accused, online media can mean facing an immediate avalanche of public judgment ranging from personal attacks to mounting pressure on campus administrators to take action, all without regard to the idea of innocent until proven guilty. Media outlets often contribute to the flurry of attention, with major news publications quick to assume guilt once slivers of evidence appear. One infamous story involved three members of the Duke lacrosse team who were brought up on charges of rape in 2006. The scandal that followed revealed inconsistencies in the accuser's story, tampered DNA results, and resulted in an ethics-based disbarring of the lead prosecutor.[8] In this case both the prosecutor and the media were heavily criticized for rushing to judgment.

As the number of sexual misconduct cases increases, men's rights advocates across the country argue that the trend in assuming guilt comes at the price of due process, meaning the legal rights a person has when accused of a crime. For instance, if charged with a crime you have the right to an attorney, a speedy and fair trial, and a jury of your peers. At several colleges male students are suing their schools, complaining that new sexual misconduct policies and campus judiciary processes violate their right to a fair hearing.[9] The Foundation for Individual Rights in Education (FIRE) encourages students to come forward with campus-based due process cases. On the FIRE website, text explains that the organization has "concerns about campus civil liberties and the reliability, impartiality, and fundamental fairness of campus judicial proceedings for students accused of sexual harassment and assault."[10]

The increasing number of reported campus assault cases has even led some groups to flip Title IX on its head, arguing that male students are unfairly charged at higher rates than female students. In these cases attorneys are using competing interpretations of Title IX. Typically, the sex-based discrimination prohibited by Title IX is used to show how assaults against women limit their educational opportunities as compared to men. However, when Title IX complaints are filed on behalf of accused male clients, there are generally two types of claims: (1) men face a higher risk of being accused of assault than women; and (2) campus judicial systems are biased against men by working in favor of accusers who are most often women. Others argue that when college administrators rush to judgment, male students are branded as rapists before any investigation occurs.[11] The main force driving these complaints is the idea that men are falsely accused of rape.

"IT WAS JUST A MISUNDERSTANDING," "SHE LIED," "MEN CAN'T BE RAPED," AND OTHER MYTHS ABOUT SEXUAL ASSAULT

Myth #1: The Sex and Gender Issue

One myth about sexual assault is that only women are assaulted and that men never are. Based on the evidence, this is untrue. However, there is a serious disparity in regard to the sex and gender of perpetrators and survivors (or victims).

According to anti-violence educator Jackson Katz, men commit more than 95 percent of rapes.[12] According to the National Intimate Partner and Sexual Violence Survey, a man was the perpetrator in 98.1 percent of rapes against female survivors. For male rape survivors, 93 percent of the time a man was the perpetrator.[13] This means that men perpetrate almost all rapes, whether the survivor is male or female. Nearly 6.5 percent of college men admit they have committed rape or attempted rape; 6.3 percent of these men admit they have committed multiple offenses; and these multiple offenders each commit an average of six rapes.[14]

Department of Justice statistics show that one in five women will experience a rape or an attempted rape while in college. That means that statistically speaking, one in five of your roommates, friends, or classmates may be assaulted. Do you share a dorm suite with five other women? It is likely that at least one of them will experience sexual assault while in college.[15] Are there fifty women in your sorority, student government, or campus organization? Researchers suggest that during college ten of these women will be sexually assaulted. Taking this to the campus scale, a National Institute of Justice report suggests that at a school with 10,000 students there could be as many as 350 rapes per year.[16] Ninety percent of these rapes will be perpetrated by acquaintances while only 12 percent "of college rape survivors will report their experience to law enforcement authorities."[17]

However, women are not the only survivors, and framing assault as a women's issue fails to recognize the experiences of male survivors. Men are assaulted at a lower rate than women; however, ignoring their stories marginalizes their struggles, may impact men's decision to file a report, and contributes to the silence around this issue by adding to the stigma. A study of 5,000 college students at more than 100 campuses revealed that 4 percent of male respondents had already experienced forced sexual intercourse in their lives to that point.[18] This means that one out of every twenty-five male students has been sexually assaulted by the time they get to college. According to the Campus Advocacy Network (CAN), one in ten men will be sexually assaulted during adulthood.[19]

In addition to concerns about being believed, male survivors may also face shame about reporting their assault because of society's expectations about masculinity, sexuality, and what it is to be a man. It can be hard for male survivors to name their experience as sexual assault because "gender roles dictate that males are expected to be strong and self-reliant" combined with the misconception that men always want sex.[20] As B. Loewe recounts in describing his own sexual assault, "I never classified my experience as sexual assault because it never fit my definition of abuse . . . I was a man-boy and they were women. I knew that as a 'red-blooded American teenage boy' I was supposed to want sex and the time and welcome any chance at it."[21]

Just as there are rape myths aimed at women, there are also many myths about male sexual assault. For instance, some people believe that an erection means that a man wanted or liked it. This is not true: Erections are a physiological response and not an indicator that an assault is desired or pleasurable. A related myth is that a male-on-male attack means that the survivor is gay. As the research attests, these myths are dangerous because they interfere with preventing, understanding, responding to, and healing from abusive sexual contact.

DID YOU KNOW?... WOMEN OF COLOR, JUSTICE, AND SEXUAL ASSAULT

Nia Pines

Though understudied in research on sexual assault and rape, race is a salient component that can contribute to a culture of victim blaming, the silencing of survivor's stories, and the attainment of justice. Because women of color are overrepresented in lower socioeconomic categories, understanding the intersections between race, poverty, and sexual assault is imperative when demanding accountability. The criminal justice system's low conviction rates for sexual assaults against black and brown women demonstrate the problems of systemic racism and the resulting disparities in justice.

The Women of Color Network is a national advocacy organization whose mission is to enhance the leadership capacity and resources for women of color in the United States. In their Sexual Violence Factsheet, the following was reported:

• Stereotypes regarding African American women's sexuality, including terms like "jezebel," "promiscuous," and "exotic," perpetuate the notion that African American women are willing participants in their own victimization. However, these myths only serve to demean, obstruct appropriate legal remedies, and minimize the seriousness of sexual violence perpetrated against African American women.

Myths and stereotypes that all Hispanics/Latinas speak the same language or are in the U.S. illegally, preclude victim service providers and law enforcement from providing appropriate assistance. Stereotypes also deter victims from reporting their abuse or seeking help.[22]

This information reported by the Women of Color Network helps to contextualize some of the staggering data found in the following publications.

The Black Women's Health Imperative found that:

• One in five African American women report that they have been raped in their lifetime.
• By age 18, 41 percent of black women have experienced sexual coercion and other unwanted forms of sexual contact.

Given that 41 percent of black women report that they have experienced unwanted sexual contact in their adulthood, it is evident that sexual violence cuts across socioeconomic status. However, there is also a complex interconnection between poverty and sexual violence. This is particularly important for understanding rape in the lives of black women because 27.7 percent (10.9 million) of black households live below the poverty level ($23,050 yearly income for a family of four).[23]

Finally, according to a 2009 Bureau of Justice Statistics Report and The National Intimate Partner and Sexual Violence Survey of 2013:

• Black females experienced higher rates of rape or sexual assault in 2008 than white females or females of other races.
• Black females were four times more likely than white females to be murdered by a boyfriend or girlfriend.

Approximately 7.9 percent of Latinas will be raped by a spouse, boyfriend, or ex-boyfriend during their lifetime.[24]

Myth #2: Beware of Strangers

A common assumption about campus assaults is that they occur at the hands of strangers. Like so many women, I am careful to reduce my risk in public places by looking out for lurking strangers in parking garages, on streets, or in bars. But what's wrong with this picture is one significant fact: The vast majority of sexual assaults on college campuses are not perpetrated by strangers. Instead, perpetrators are most often acquaintances, someone the survivor knows. Research shows that nine out of ten campus assaults are committed by an acquaintance,[25] meaning that 90 percent of sexual assault survivors know their attacker.

The idea that strangers commit sexual assaults is deeply embedded in college safety policies across the country. Think about your campus: Are there strategically located poles with blue lights that connect to emergency personnel with the push of a button? Is there a program for escorting you to your car or dorm at night? Are there areas of campus with bright flood lighting? Although these measures may be intended to dissuade perpetrators from carrying out nighttime attacks in the public space of campuses, they are also examples of security theater. The term "security theater" is used to describe measures intended to produce a sense of safety and security without actually doing much to prevent crime. Measures such as installing emergency poles assume that potential attackers are hiding behind bushes, in doorways, or following you to your car after class. Security theater can create an increased sense of safety among students (and parents), but there is a clear mismatch between policies focused on preventing stranger attacks in public and the acquaintance assaults that make up the majority of attacks on college campuses.

Myth #3: Learning Self-Defense Will Solve the Problem

Many of my students have expressed a fear of assault. This is the case whether the person speaking is male, female, trans, or genderqueer. As our conversations shift from issues of personal safety to sexual assault prevention programs to campus response policies, a familiar theme emerges that pits the responsibility of the individual against the responsibility of the college or university. A common question looms: Where does a school's responsibility end, and where does the responsibility of the student begin in preventing sexual assault?

In fact, safety-based actions on the part of individuals and institutions are not mutually exclusive. Responsible action on the part of individuals and institutions can and should happen at the same time. Yet, when it comes to campus assaults, discussions about individual responsibility frequently dwell on the actions of survivors. Was she drinking? Why was she there? This emphasis places sole blame on survivors and shifts our attention away from the perpetrators who are committing assaults. More constructive questions would include asking: (a) What are campuses doing to prevent sexual assault? (b) How are institutions dealing with perpetrators? (c) What programs are in place to address bystander issues?

Bystanders can be friends or strangers, and may include someone such as a fellow party guest or a roommate. While individuals should know how to keep themselves safer, and institutions must have appropriate policies and procedures, bystanders have an obligation to help prevent or stop assaults. Proponents of educating students about the role of bystanders argue that when people see the signs of an inappropriate situation unfolding—for instance, trying to take someone home after they've had a few too many drinks—they can step in and potentially prevent an assault. In this instance the bystander could stop his friend by saying, "No, buddy, this isn't a good idea," or the bystander could be a roommate who assesses the situation and intervenes by saying, "It's time to go home—I'll call you a taxi."

Myth #4: Women Lie about Rape

During the past few years Men's Rights Activists (MRAs) have launched an aggressive campaign against women and feminism, with one branch of the movement focused on derailing discussions about campus assault. The movement attempts to draw attention to what they view as overinflated sexual assault statistics. MRAs insist that false rape claims are the real issue, and use dangerous rhetoric to shift the conversation away from sexual assault to blame women who simply regret one-night stands. Media pundits also contribute to this misleading perception. For instance, award-winning columnist George Will uses quotes around the words sexual assault in his writing,[26] implying that reports of assaults are bogus, or that an assault didn't actually happen.

Survey results show that male and female college students share the belief that 50 percent of all rape claims are false.[27] In other words, this study suggests that college students believe half of the reported rapes on campus didn't actually happen, and the survivor made up a story. This assumption is not only detrimental to rape survivors, but is also wildly incorrect.

It is imperative that we distinguish between two concepts: false rape reports and unfounded claims. A false rape report is when the accuser has fabricated a story about a rape that did not occur. However, an unfounded claim is quite different. A claim can be labeled as unfounded for any number of reasons. For instance, if a survivor decides not to continue an investigation, or recants their story as a measure to stop invasive questioning, the claim may be classified as unfounded. If a District Attorney does not think a jury will believe the accuser they may set aside the claim as unfounded—not because the assault didn't happen but because the District Attorney may be concerned about losing the case in court.

An unfounded claim is not the same as a false claim. Research shows that between 2 percent and 8 percent of cases involve false claims.[28] In fact, the rate of false rape reports is about the same as any other crime.[29]

Myth #5: They Were Drinking So It Wasn't Rape

Studies show that alcohol can increase the likelihood of campus sexual assaults. According to research supported by the National Institute on Alcohol Abuse and Alcoholism, the effects of alcohol are apparent in several ways, for instance altering perceptions of responsibility and assessing risk, increasing a man's willingness to behave aggressively, and limiting a woman's physical ability to resist assault.[30] This understanding has led some journalists to opine that the problem of campus sexual assault is in reality a problem of reckless drinking.[31]

However, it is critical to untangle sexual assault from alcohol use. At many schools, students are warned during orientation or safety presentations that sexual assault can happen when you've had too much to drink. This immediately ties sexual crimes to the alleged poor decisions of the survivor rather than the criminal actions of the perpetrator. Although alcohol may affect actions, the fact is that assault and rape are serious crimes that warrant investigation and punishment.

Photo 24.1 Circle of 6

THE THREE MOST IMPORTANT WORDS: "I BELIEVE YOU"

Student- and faculty-driven activism across the country has led to mounting pressure on campus administrators and the federal government to improve campus safety. The term "campus community" is often used in conversations about safety, but what does it mean? What do you consider part of your campus community? Is the community limited to the borders of the campus, or does it also include off-campus housing? Or is the community simply wherever campus students are? For instance, if students are on spring break, are they still members of the campus community?

Thinking about what counts as the campus community is important when thinking about sexual assault and safety. According to research conducted for the National Institute of Justice, more than 60 percent of assaults happen between students while they are off campus. Therefore, what a campus considers within the bounds of its student community can affect sexual assault statistics and response, particularly if these boundaries are meant to exclude off-campus housing or other areas where assaults may occur.

Another important consideration is online activity. In a time when social media plays such an integral part of our lives we are seeing more cases of students bragging about assaults on Twitter, posting derogatory photos to Facebook, or sharing incriminating videos on YouTube. Social media sharing can implicate perpetrators in several ways. Someone may admit to their actions online, or a witness might post photos or information that implicates other students.

Likewise, survivors may post their experiences and name their attackers online. Campus groups across the country have organized anonymous forums for sharing stories, such as the Survivor Stories blog at Occidental College in Los Angeles.[32] Virtual data can provide crucial evidence of assault, begging the question of where the virtual activity of students fits within the campus community.

According to the Justice Department, survivors report fewer than 5 percent of attempted and completed rapes.[33] Many reasons contribute to the low number of disclosures such as not knowing who to report to or feeling uncomfortable or afraid about filing criminal charges against a friend or acquaintance. A common concern among survivors is that no one will believe them. Even when reports are filed and perpetrators are held accountable, disciplinary actions during the past few years range from ineffectual—slap on the wrist warnings coupled with promises to do better—to downright appalling—stories of colleges assigning book reports to admitted rapists as punishment.[34]

Student activism around this issue occurs in many ways: hosting on-campus rallies, sharing stories and encouraging others to do the same, using social media to spread the word about recent news and events, and connecting with survivors and allies at other schools. Allies are friends, students, faculty, and staff who support survivors, and may or may not be survivors themselves. For instance, I am an ally. In that role I attend rallies, lend an ear when someone needs to talk, remain up to date about campus resources, write about sexual assault prevention and response, and use my social media accounts to share articles and information about campus assault.

As the movement to increase campus safety grows, there are several ways you can be part of the solution. First, speaking out when you hear a rape myth. You now have the information you need to refute rape myths when you hear them in conversation or read them on-line. Second, find out what your campus is doing to improve sexual assault prevention and response policies. Consider joining a campus student organization that focuses on this issue. Third, use your social media accounts to voice your questions and concerns directly to your campus. Remember, someone at your school is paying attention to the official campus social media accounts. Lastly, simply saying, "I believe you" can be a powerful way to show support for a survivor. Those three small words may lend someone just the courage and support they need to keep moving forward.

DISCUSSION QUESTIONS

• Do you know where to find your campus sexual assault policies? What do you think is the best way to teach students about sexual assault prevention? Can you think of a scenario where the bystander approach could be helpful?

• Where do you think the line should be drawn between the rights of the survivor and the rights of the accused? How do your campus policies measure up?

• How would you respond to someone who is misinformed about false rape claims?

• Where does the campus community begin and end? Should we include the virtual world? How should we think about the on-line actions of students who post or are incriminated by photos or video footage on social media?

• In what ways can you be an ally to survivors? How can you work to prevent sexual assault? What are students at your school doing to fight back against campus-based sexual assault?

NOTES

1. For examples of national attention to campus sexual assault see Eliza Gray, "The Sexual Assault Crisis on American Campuses," *Time*, May 26, 2014, pp. 20–29; Katie McDonough, "The Good, the Bad and the Ugly in that Time Magazine Feature on Campus Sexual Assault," *Salon*, May 15, 2014, http://www.salon.com/2014/05/15/the_good_the_bad_and_the_ugly_in_that_time_magazine_feature_on_campus_sexual_assault/; The White House, "Not Alone: The First Report of the White House Task Force to Protect Students from Sexual Assault," http://www.whitehouse.gov/sites/default/files/docs/report_0.pdf.

2. Shira Tarrant, "Wardrobe Choices Are Not an Invitation to Date Rape," in *Date Rape (Issues That Concern You)*, ed. Norah Piehl (Detroit, MI: Greenhaven Press, 2012): 55–60.

3. Caroline Heldman and Danielle Dirks, "Blowing the Whistle on Campus Rape," *Ms.* Winter/Spring (2014): 35.

4. "Know Your IX," www.knowyourix.org.

5. The Department of Education Office for Civil Rights, "Dear Colleague Letter," April 2011, http://www.whitehouse.gov/sites/default/files/dear_colleague_sexual_violence.pdf.

6. Ibid.

7. Clery Center. For more information on the Clery Act visit http://clerycenter.org/summary-jeanne-clery-act.

8. Laura Miller, "The Duke Lacrosse Rape Scandal: The Definitive Account," *Salon*, April 6, 2014, http://www.salon.com/2014/04/06/the_duke_lacrosse_rape_scandal_the_definitive_account/.

9. Teresa Watanabe, "More College Men Are Fighting Back Against Sexual Misconduct Cases," *Los Angeles Times*, June 7, 2014, http://www.latimes.com/local/la-me-sexual-assault-legal-20140608-story.html#page=1.

10. The FIRE, "National: White House Task Force on Sexual Assault Jeopardizes Student Due Process," http://www.thefire.org/cases/national-white-house-task-force-on-campus-sexual-assault-jeopardizes-student-due-process/.

11. John Lauerman, "College Men Accused of Sexual Assault Say Their Rights Violated," Bloomberg.com, December 16, 2013, http://www.bloomberg.com/news/2013-12-16/college-men-accused-of-sexual-assault-say-their-rights-violated.html.

12. Cited in T.M. Lindsey, "Jackson Katz: Violence against Women Is a Men's Issue," *RH Reality Check*, June 3, 2008, http://rhrealitycheck.org/article/2008/06/03/jackson-katz-violence-against-women-is-a-mens-issue/.

13. M.C. Black, K.C. Basile, M.J. Breiding, S.G. Smith, M.I. Walters, M.T. Merrick, J. Chen, and M.R. Stevens, "The National Intimate Partner and Sexual Violence Survey (NISVS): 2010 Summary Report" (Atlanta: National Center for Injury Prevention and Control, Centers for Disease Control and Prevention, 2011).

14. Heldman and Dirks, "Blowing the Whistle on Campus Rape," 36.

15. Data cited in Caroline Heldman and Danielle Dirks, "Blowing the Whistle on Campus Rape," 35. It is important to note the controversy over these research findings. As more organizations cite the one-in-five statistic, critics claim that the study generating this number is not generalizable to the entire country because it only included responses from a single study of women at two campuses (see Christopher P. Krebs, Christine H. Lindquist, Tara D. Warner, Bonnie S. Fisher, and Sandra L. Martin, "The Campus Sexual Assault (CSA) Study: Final Report," Washington, DC: National Institute of Justice, US Department of Justice [2007], https://www.ncjrs.gov/pdffiles1/nij/grants/221153.pdf). However, the survey included more than 5,000 responses leading others to argue that the study is adequately representative. A 2009 review of the same data revealed that among college seniors, 287 of 1,402 women had experienced sexual assault, or roughly one in five. For more information on the data and debates, see Glenn Kessler, "One in Five Women in College Sexually Assaulted: The Source of This Statistic," *Washington Post*, May 1, 2014, http://www.washingtonpost.com/blogs/fact-checker/wp/2014/05/01/one-in-five-women-in-college-sexually-assaulted-the-source-of-this-statistic/.

16. Bonnie S. Fischer, Francis T. Cullen, and Michael G. Turner, "Sexual Victimization of College Women," National Institute of Justice (2001), http://www.nij.gov/publications/pages/publication-detail.aspx?ncjnumber=182369.

17. Heldman and Dirks, "Blowing the Whistle on Campus Rape," 35.

18. Patricia Tjaden and Nancy Thoennes, "Prevalence, Incidence, and Consequences of Violence against Women: Findings from the National Violence against Women Survey. Research in Brief" (1998), http://files.eric.ed.gov/fulltext/ED434980.pdf.

19. Campus Advocacy Network, http://www.uic.edu/depts/owa/sa_male_survivors.html.

20. Sarah LeTrent, "Against His Will: Female-on-Male Rape," *CNN*, October 10, 2013, http://www.cnn.com/2013/10/09/living/chris-brown-female-on-male-rape/.

For further resources and more on myths about male sexual assault see Shira Tarrant, ed., *Men Speak Out: Views on Gender, Sex, and Power*, 2nd ed. (New York: Routledge, 2013), 113–164; and "Myths & Facts," 1in6, https://1in6.org/men/myths.

21. B. Loewe, "How We Enter: Men, Gender, and Sexual Assault," in Shira Tarrant, ed., *Men Speak Out: Views on Gender, Sex, and Power* (New York: Routledge, 2013), 125.

22. "Facts and Stats Collection," *Women of Color Network*, http://womenofcolornetwork.org/docs/factsheets/fs_sexual-violence.pdf.

23. Carolyn M. West and Kalimah Johnson, "Sexual Violence in the Lives of African American Women," *Black Women's Health Imperative*, April 16, 2013, http://www.bwhi.org/news/2013/04/16/women-health-news/sexual-violence-in-the-lives-of-african-american-women/.

24. Shannan Catalano, Erica Smith, Howard Snyder, and Michael Rand, "Female Victims of Violence," *Bureau of Justice Statistics*, U.S. Department of Justice, October 23, 2009, http://www.bjs.gov/content/pub/pdf/fvv.pdf; "An Overview of Intimate Partner Violence," *The National Intimate Partner and Sexual Violence Survey*, Centers for Disease Control, http://www.cdc.gov/violenceprevention/pdf/ipv-nisvs-factsheet-v5-a.pdf.

25. Krebs et al., "The Campus Sexual Assault (CSA) Study."

26. George Will, "Colleges Become the Victims of Progressivism," *Washington Post*, June 6, 2014, http://www.washingtonpost.com/opinions/george-will-college-become-the-victims-of-progressivism/2014/06/06/e90e73b4-eb50–11e3–9f5c-9075d5508f0a_story.html.

27. Soraya Chemaly, "50 Actual Facts about Rape," *Huffington Post*, October 26, 2012, http://www.huffingtonpost.com/soraya-chemaly/50-facts-rape_b_2019338.html.

28. David Lisak, "False Reports: Moving beyond the Issue to Successfully Investigate and Prosecute Non-Stranger Sexual Assault," *Voice*, 3, no. 1 (2009): 1–11, http://www.ndaa.org/pdf/the_voice_vol_3_no_1_2009.pdf.

29. Mark Potok and Evelyn Schlatter, "Men's Rights Movement Spreads False Claims about Women," *Southern Poverty Law Center, Intelligence Report*, Issue 145 (Spring 2012); David Lisak, "False Reports," 3; Joanne Belknap, "Rape: Too Hard to Report and Too Easy to Discredit Victims," *Violence Against Women* 16, no. 12 (2010): 1335–1344, http://vaw.sagepub.com/content/16/12/1335.full.pdf.

30. Antonia Abbey, "Alcohol-Related Sexual Assault: A Common Problem among College Students," *Journal of Studies on Alcohol and Drugs* 14 (2002): 118.

31. James Taranto, "Drunkenness and Double Standards: A Balanced Look at College Sex Offenses," *Wall Street Journal*, February 10, 2014, http://online.wsj.com/news/articles/SB10001424052702304558804579374844067975558.

32. "Survivor Stories," *Oxy Sexual Assault Coalition*, http://oxysexualassaultcoalition.wordpress.com/survivor-stories-2/.

33. Bonnie S. Fischer, Francis T. Cullen, and Michael G. Turner, "Sexual Victimization of College Women," National Institute of Justice (2001), http://www.nij.gov/publications/pages/publication-detail.aspx?ncjnumber=182369.

34. Tyler Kingkade, "Occidental College Sexual Assault Response Subject of Federal Complaints," *Huffington Post*, January 1, 2014, http://www.huffingtonpost.com/2013/04/19/occidental-sexual-assault_n_3118563.html.

KISS AND SELL

When Young Lady Authors Write About Our Sex Lives

Allison McCarthy

Journalists are fully aware that when it comes to headlines, sex sells. When we tune into the news, we are captivated by reports about former congressman Anthony Weiner's sexting, former CIA director David Petraeus's extramarital affair, and more leaked celebrity sex tapes than viewers may ever have time to fully watch. The salacious details of these events are fodder for everything from front-page investigative news to editorials and in-depth profiles, analyzed and scrutinized by the public until the next controversy appears on the horizon.

Waiting for a political or celebrity scandal to break, however, isn't always necessary in order to garner attention from an international audience. Mainstream media such as the *New York Times*, *Slate*, the *Village Voice*, *Huffington Post*, and other outlets prominently feature non-fiction, first-person essays on sex. Often marketed under the categories of lifestyle or women's interest, these works do not fit the definition of smut or erotica; instead, they are personal reflections on diverse social experiences ranging from rite of passage (such as loss of virginity or a relationship break-up) to societal transgression (non-monogamy or an interest in kink)—or sometimes even both. Many writers are discovering that chronicling their sexual escapades can be provocative, challenging and—perhaps most importantly—a stepping stone between relative obscurity and a prestigious byline.

But if we look closer, we start to notice race and gender-specific patterns regarding who is being asked to tell their stories and why. Several years ago, as a twenty-five-year-old freelance writer, I came to this crossroads as I considered the ramifications of publishing an explicitly sexual feature essay with the online section of *GOOD* magazine. I had pitched to a column called "Dealbreakers," a term popularized by writer and actress Tina Fey on the television series "30 Rock," that refers to a romantic partner's subjectively unacceptable behaviors or idiosyncrasies that ultimately precipitate a relationship's demise.[1] I emailed the column's editor, Amanda Hess, with the story of my break-up with an ex-boyfriend because he refused to perform cunnilingus. This was not a story I previously felt comfortable sharing with anyone except my closest friends, but in the context of the magazine's "Dealbreakers" column, I saw an opportunity to share an excruciating experience I had never seen described in print. I thought this was a good chance to write about oral sex through a feminist lens—as well as a chance to bolster my readership. Hess's response was favorable: She liked the idea and encouraged me to submit the essay for publication.

As my Dealbreakers deadline approached, I began to question the wisdom of revealing so many details from a sexual relationship with the public. I sought advice from other professional writers and editors. One warned me not to be pigeon-holed in the genre of sex writing; another suggested using a pseudonym in order to protect my privacy. I considered their advice carefully and wondered what impact publishing this essay would have on my career.

Would going public with this essay cause me to be stigmatized as a tell-all confessional writer? Would I be deemed too risqué for other publishers to consider working with in the future? The answers were unknown, but I realized that I could look at the paths that other writers like me had taken—writers who were young, educated, and female, those who recounted their sexual experiences in the context of self-reflective commentary for their audience. I could identify the common traits and patterns, follow the various print and digital trails of their archived work and then make my publishing decisions accordingly. In analyzing the realm of female sex writers, their editors and their audience, I could weigh the risks and then move forward in blazing my own literary trail.

WHO GETS THE BYLINES . . . AND WHY

Sex writing's shift from underground to the mainstream is analogous to the shift from print to digital media. Before the Internet, sex writing was typically restricted to what could be found in adult entertainment stores or mail-order catalogs. Independent presses provided a variety of opportunities to read the titillating truths about the sex lives of its writers, but access to such material was limited to what could be either physically bought in person or borrowed from someone else.

But unlike walking into a store or signing up for a mailing list, reading a Website is a fundamentally different experience, at once both more discrete and interactive: Audiences can browse through intimate personal essays on sex from the privacy of their computers, laptops, tablets or smartphones, flipping through Web pages with the speed of a wireless connection while leaving their reactions to the material as a comment. If a reader wants to share the essay with others, they can merely click on the pictorial icon for their preferred social media platform and the essay is cross-posted on sites such as Facebook and Twitter.

Editors of online media have a vested interest in work that will generate a high amount of traffic for their publication. Hit counts reflect the number of browser requests transmitted through a server to a Web page. However, these requests may be a result of searches for a page's images, graphics, or files unrelated to the content of the Web page. Most major Websites measure their readership through page views, which reflect the number of times a Web page is seen by distinguishable visitors. Editors can even track returning visitors, showing readers who view a Web page repeatedly within a timeframe of twenty-four hours or more in between visits.[2] Expectations for robust hit counts, page views, and returning visitors will motivate savvy editors to publish content that will draw the highest quantity of readers and commenters to their sections, thus ensuring the popularity of the Website and its continued funding through both advertisers and investors.

Sarah Hepola is the Personal Essays editor of the Life section for popular news site *Salon*. In her round-up of the site's top ten personal essays for 2013, she claims to have read (at a minimum) twenty pitches per week, all of which are confessional and intended to highlight the lived experience of the writer. Yet as she goes on to describe the selection process, Hepola's description of her work turns amorous. "I know I've stumbled on a winner the same way I know I have a crush on someone. My heartbeat quickens, and I get that nervous fluttering in the belly . . . Like great romances, these stories instruct me, challenge me, beguile me. Most of all, they stay with me."[3]

But whose stories have staying power? The erotic experiences of white women writers, as it turns out, overwhelmingly dominate the list. Her romance and sex-focused selections for *Salon*'s top essays of 2013 include Anne Lamott's "My Year on Match.com," Jillian Lauren's "My Inappropriate Relationship," Clara Bensen's "My Craziest OK Cupid Date Ever," Emily DePrang's "The Tell-All Memoir I Decided Not to Tell," and Angi Becker Stevens's "My Two Husbands."[4]

Hepola's eroticization of the editorial process is far from accidental; her writing at *Salon* frequently relies on first-person sexual details to lure in readers. Her article "Never Show Them Your Back" is ostensibly about body image issues, but leads with the lines "I used to flash my bra when I was good and drunk. I didn't really care."[5] The use of titillating details inevitably brings in readers, who may choose to slut-shame or praise Hepola in the article's comments and on various social media forums. Writers who garner a high volume of comments and social media accolades are more likely to have their work promoted than those who otherwise toil in obscurity—or those who never even get the chance to share their stories.

If sex is always an interesting story, it is usually race and gender that control the message. The sexual experiences of women of color are not as frequently published as those written by white women. Noted hip-hop feminist Tricia Rose explains this phenomenon in the introduction to her anthology *Longing to Tell: Black Women Talk About Sexuality and Intimacy*: "The sexual stories that black women long to tell are being told in beauty parlors, kitchens, health clubs, restaurants, malls, and laundry rooms, but a larger, more accessible conversation for all women to share and from which to learn has not yet begun."[6] While *Longing to Tell* provides a space for black women to discuss their sexual experiences in print, editor Rose changed all of the names and many identifying details of her contributors. Unlike the bylines found in *Salon* and the *New York Times*, the women of color who describe their real-life sexual experiences within *Longing to Tell* are not credited and therefore cannot use the book as a stepping stone to other paid and professional writing gigs.

Even if a woman of color is credited for her sex writing under her legal name, this does not guarantee that other media outlets will view her writing identity as legitimate or respectable. In a May 2008, *New York Times* article covering sex writers in Ivy League institutions, popular blogger Lena Chen was tellingly typecast as "a small Asian woman in a miniskirt and stilettos," even though no other blogger in the article was racially identified.[7] Her blog "Sex and the Ivy" faced a brutal backlash online in response to her writing. An ex-boyfriend published nude photos of Chen without her consent; the names of her family and friends were also posted online and used as fodder for racist commentary.[8]

As a result of being viciously trolled and threatened by anonymous readers, Chen suffered from a self-described "nervous breakdown" and ceased writing "Sex and the Ivy," eventually shifting her focus in writing to topics related to gender equality and her domestic life with a boyfriend and dog. In her personal essay "I Was the Harvard Harlot," Chen laments her retirement from sex blogging: "I frequently mention the importance of truth-telling as consciousness-raising in my feminist work, while ignoring the fact that I hold back from telling my own truth every day. I talk of gender liberation and social justice, things I truly believe in . . . [b]ut because I'm not interested in spending more of my young adulthood deflecting misogynistic slurs and shielding loved ones from incrimination by association, I've simply stopped writing about the many things that continue to scare and confuse me."[9]

Women of color who also identify as trans (an umbrella term popularized by Sam Killerman that signifies "all of the identities within the gender identity spectrum") are frequently under-represented in popular narratives of sex writing featured in mainstream media.[10] In her blog's coverage of the small press memoir *Trauma Queen*, Janet Mock reflects on the inequities faced in traditional spheres of publishing by trans women of color. "I, a young, poor-raised, multi-racial trans women [sic] did not have access to stories because the stories I craved did not exist, and the ones that did exist are consistently being erased," she writes. "And because I didn't have examples of women like me who made it through it was difficult to imagine a future beyond what I was living. When we discuss resources (sitting space and time, pen, paper, computers, wifi [sic], internet, editors, publishers), we must realize that everyone doesn't have equal access to those resources."[11]

Personal essays on sex from LGBT writers are also frequently marginalized in mainstream outlets. Currently a staff writer at *Slate.com*, Amanda Hess feels that the commercialization of popular media prohibits queer female writers from gaining admission to the prolific and well-paid sites for publishing frequented by young, straight white women writers. In an interview for this essay, Hess argued, "I think straight women—no matter what aspect of sexuality they're reporting on or writing about—are marketed as 'sexy' to mainstream audiences . . . One of the frustrations of writing about sex is that it's often perceived as salacious in some way and not taken seriously as another part of the human experience or as a way of looking at legitimate social problems."[12]

Hess's observations present another question: Who are the true-account sex writers that are being taken seriously in mainstream media? In profiling the careers of several female writers who have bared their sexual experiences for bylines, one common fact emerges: It takes more than talent and a great story to achieve high-profile professional advancement.

WHAT THEY WRITE

By her own account, Mandy Stadtmiller did not launch her writing career by specializing in topics on dating and sex. Prior to her stint as a dating columnist for the *New York Post*, Stadtmiller was an intern for the *Washington Post* and then moved onto work as a reporter for the *Des Moines Register*.[13] Though she found success in both comedy writing and celebrity interviews, her dating column soon attracted the attention of the highly trafficked gossip website *Gawker*, which came up with its own derisively named column to critique Stadtmiller's work: "Oh, Mandy."[14] Her most popular piece, "My night with a prosti-dude," ranked in the Top 10 most-read articles on *nypost.com* from February 2 to 6, 2010 and was covered by television programs such as "The Colbert Report" and "The Joy Behar Show."[15]

Stadtmiller is highly conscious of the role social media plays in enhancing her public profile. In an interview with online literary magazine *The Rumpus*, Stadtmiller claimed, "Honestly, no one gets hired because of résumés anymore. They get hired because of a Google search. They get hired because of a Twitter feed."[16] After leaving the *New York Post*, Stadtmiller parlayed her success as a dating columnist into accepting an editorial position at the widely read women's website, *XOJane*. Many of Stadtmiller's articles seem intentionally designed to capitalize on the interest generated by her sexual activities. Some of her more recent headlines—which have drawn high traffic to *XOJane*—include "Should I Be Offended That One of the Guys I'm Dating Refused a

Blow Job Because He Said His Penis is 'On Vacation'?" (212 comments) and "It Is a Jerk Move Not to Call or Text a Woman Within 24–72 Hours After Having Sex For The First Time" (418 comments).[17]

Stadtmiller is far from the only straight white female reporter-turned-dating columnist. Melanie Boyer's writing experience started as a beat reporter at her college town's newspaper, the *Arizona Daily Sun*, but after pursuing other potential career paths—including a stint in the Peace Corps and teaching English as a second language at the high school level—Boyer accepted an administrative role at USAID in Washington, DC. However, Boyer confessed in an interview for this essay that "The job could not have been a worse fit . . . I finally had to admit that if I didn't start writing again, my fingers were going to fall off." In December 2005, Boyer responded to an ad in the *Washington City Paper* for a dating blogger, a position which required new blog posts five days per week.

After being hired, Boyer says, "I started out with a post about the female orgasm. I was petrified that the blog would be a flop and that readers would figure out I wasn't an edgy, hot-sex-having *Hustler* model, so I started with something big." However, Boyer eventually switched gears to less provocative topics, including writing about the death of her father. After eighteen months of blogging, Boyer left the site to join a private public relations firm, in part because she felt the market for dating blogs had become "oversaturated . . . Because it's easy. And it gives the writer a sense of being edgy, of being 'that girl' who is desired and wanted. It's an easy way to garner a following, if that's what you want as a writer, and of getting a bit of an ego boost." Though Boyer is proud of her column, she wishes she could rewrite "the posts where I was trying to be edgy. They never got a good response, I think, because I was working so hard to be edgy that it wasn't sincere."

Though much of this essay has focused on writers whose profiles rose through writing about their sex lives, Lisa Jervis was already an established writer and the co-founder/editor of *Bitch* magazine when she began writing about her sexual experiences in 1996. In an interview for this essay, Jervis said, "I felt like it was part of my editorial politics to write more frankly about sexuality, to bring a very intentional strategy to counter all of those messages about what female sexuality was supposed to be. If I wanted to normalize these flavors of female sexuality, I had to be willing to come out about it—even if it meant my parents were going to read about some things I did in the shower with this dude I didn't know very well. If I wanted the culture to recognize the broad range of female sexuality, I was going to have to be out." Over the next decade, Jervis published multiple essays in magazines and anthologies. While many were under her professional name, Jervis notes that "Sometimes I would publish under a pseudonym. It wasn't about shame, but about realizing that some things I want to keep private. It's not about protecting someone else or feeling shame about my behavior or my choices, but having a healthy boundary." Eventually, Jervis left personal sex essays behind in order to focus on other writing, including publishing a cookbook with PM Press. "I'm not interested in being one of those privileged white girls who gets to write about certain stigmatized sexual experiences and make money/get positive attention," she says, "while people with less privilege of every kind—genderqueer folks, people of color, folks with less class privilege—get punished" for writing about the same topics.

PERIL AND PLEASURE

In the search for safety and professional advancement, not all female writers with racial and heterosexual privilege feel comfortable with revealing personally identifying details in their work. As a panelist for the FEMINISM/S "Sex in Journalism" talk at the Kelly Writer's House in Philadelphia, online editor Kelsey McKinney discussed her experiences as both an editor and contributor to several sex columns written by pseudonymous student writers for *The Daily Texan*, a student newspaper affiliated with the University of Texas-Austin.[18] The columns penned by straight women included "Sexy Sally," "Virgin Veronica," and "Committed Caroline." In defending her decision to use a pseudonym to *The Daily Beast*, "Sexy Sally" cited a repressive sexual politics as motivation to write under the cover of anonymity: "For the most part, people who grew up in Texas—we didn't have a very good sex education and it's not typically something parents are super open [about] with their kids and I think that's why it's made some people feel kind of uncomfortable."[19] McKinney largely agrees with this assessment. She told the *Yale Herald* that "UT-Austin is a tiny blue dot in a massive red ocean, and we have a mostly conservative student body. People here still aren't really having open conversations about sex, and so this is still relatively shocking to people here."[20]

Though I never seriously considered using a pseudonym, I certainly had my own fears about writing the article for *GOOD* magazine's "Dealbreakers" column. I published the piece as "A. McCarthy" because I knew that would make it less likely for readers to connect my other writing to this piece. I also thought that if there was any controversy over the article, I could still maintain some distance from any potential backlash by keeping my full name under wraps. When I was asked by Hess to provide an author photo for the piece, I chose a shot that framed my torso from the neck down; my face was not visible. This choice enhanced my sense of privacy as I moved forward in going public with the essay.

As it turned out, my instincts for self-protection were correct. After the essay was published, commenters lambasted me for the article's content and tone. I was criticized for writing about the decision to break-up with my former partner over his refusal to perform cunnilingus. I was deemed selfish, manipulative, and many other unpleasant (and often unprintable) terms that were loaded with condescension and misogyny. I felt fortunate to have some support from other prominent womanist and feminist writers, including Jill Filipovic,[21] Renee Martin,[22] and Amanda Marcotte.[23] Their support of my work gave me solace at a time in which I felt exposed and vulnerable to the judgment of others.

Still, the byline at *GOOD* magazine was the highest-paid essay of my career at that time. I leveraged the new writing credit into pitching other major media publications, including articles for *AlterNet* and the *Guardian* (UK). By the end of the year, my "Dealbreaker" essay was selected by Hess as an Editor's Favorite.[24]

In looking back on the experience of writing about my intimate relationship for a major media publication, it's hard not to imagine how a slightly different story would have been perceived, for instance if I had written instead about my bisexuality and some of the sexual frustrations I've experienced with women as opposed to the frustration I experienced with this particular man. I wonder if my explicitly stated affinity for cunnilingus would have led to me being stereotyped as hypersexual or even dismissed altogether if my race were not white. I still worry even now that someone might go looking for the connection between the *GOOD* article and my current work, using this information to harass or troll me.

I knew that writing about my sex life was a dicey proposition, but the rewards of support from other writers, as well as opportunities for future writing credits, ultimately outweighed the risks in publishing a story from my personal experience. I am pleased that my article launched online conversations about the importance of mutually fulfilling sexual relationships; writing about those years of sexual deprivation allowed me to let go of a lot of the resentment and frustration that I had felt both during and after my relationship. Though factors of social privilege cannot be denied, it is my hope that in describing the perils and pleasures of sex writing, other marginalized writers—of all backgrounds and orientations—will feel similarly emboldened to document their own idiosyncratic true-life tales of love and sex.

DISCUSSION QUESTIONS

• What are the main issues the author raises about the media's tendency to publish first-person sex stories by straight white women?

• Why do you think men are not experiencing the same consequences that women writers deal with? Is there a market for men's stories?

• Would you publish a story about your sex life? Would you read other people's sex stories?

• What are some of the risks involved for women in publishing non-fiction material on their sexuality? Does the backlash that women writers receive seem worth publishing these stories?

- What are some personal and professional boundaries worth considering in memoir-style writing?

NOTES

1. Aisha Harris, "Blergh! The Linguistic Legacy of *30 Rock!*" Slate.com, January 30, 2013, http://www.slate.com/blogs/browbeat/2013/01/30/_30_rock_catchphrases_that_will_survive_blergh_dealbreaker_egot_and_more.html.
2. Opentracker, "Hits or Pageviews?" *Opentracker*, http://www.opentracker.net/article/hits-or-pageviews.
3. Sarah Hepola, "Sex, Drugs and Superheroes: Our 10 Best Personal Essays," Salon.com, December 31, 2013, http://www.salon.com/2013/12/31/salons_10_best_personal_essays_of_2013/.
4. Ibid.
5. Sarah Hepola, "Never Show Them Your Back," Salon.com, November 23, 2012, http://www.salon.com/2012/11/24/never_show_them_your_back/.
6. Tricia Rose, *Longing to Tell: Black Women Talk about Sexuality and Intimacy* (New York: Picador, 2004), 4.
7. Randall Patterson, "Students of Virginity," *New York Times*, March 30, 2008, http://www.nytimes.com/2008/03/30/magazine/30Chastity-t.html.
8. Claire Gordon, "Sex, Lies and the Internet: The Tale of Lena Chen," *Al Jazeera America*, December 12, 2013, http://america.aljazeera.com/watch/shows/america-tonight/america-tonight-blog/2013/12/9/lena-chen-onlineharassment.html.
9. Lena Chen, "I Was the Harvard Harlot," *Salon*, May 23, 2011, http://www.salon.com/2011/05/24/harvard_harlot_sexual_shame/.
10. Sam Killerman, "What Does the Asterisk in "Trans*" Stand For?" *It's Pronounced Metrosexual*, May 2012, http://itspronouncedmetrosexual.com/2012/05/what-does-the-asterisk-in-trans-stand-for/.
11. Janet Mock, "Not All Memoirs Are Created Equal: The Gatekeeping of Trans Women of Color's Stories," *Janet Mock*, June 5, 2013, http://janetmock.com/2013/06/05/memoir-trans-women-of-color/.
12. Amanda Hess, online interview by Allison McCarthy, January 15, 2014.
13. Kara Bloomgarden-Smoke, "Gross Encounters of the Mandy Stadtmiller Kind," *New York Observer*, April 30, 2013, http://observer.com/2013/04/gross-encounters-of-the-mandy-stadtmiller-kind/.
14. Gawker Media, http://gawker.com/tag/oh-mandy.
15. Mandy Stadtmiller, "About," http://mandystadtmiller.com/about.
16. Abigail Walehouse, "The *Rumpus* Interview with Mandy Stadtmiller," *Rumpus*, November 15, 2013, http://therumpus.net/2013/11/the-rumpus-interview-with-mandy-stadtmiller/.
17. XOJane.com, "Mandy's Posts," http://www.xojane.com/author/mandy/allArticles?query=date.

18. Deepa Lakshmin, "Journalists Sound Off on Writing about Sex," *Daily Pennsylvanian*, February 5, 2014, http://www.thedp.com/article/2014/02/sex-in-journalism.

19. Caroline Linton, "Let's Talk about Sex, Texas," *Daily Beast*, October 21, 2013, http://www.thedailybeast.com/witw/articles/2013/10/21/ut-austin-student-sex-columnist-s-masturbation-how-to-causes-conservative-firestorm.html.

20. Sophie Haigney, "The College Sex Column, from Top to Bottom," *Yale Herald*, February 14, 2014, http://yaleherald.com/culture/the-college-sex-column-from-top-to-bottom/.

21. Jill Filipovic, "Dealbreaker, Indeed," *Feministe*, August 8, 2011, http://www.feministe.us/blog/archives/2011/08/08/dealbreaker-indeed/.

22. Renee Martin, "Oral Sex and Dealbreakers," *Womanist Musings*, August 9, 2011, http://www.womanist-musings.com/2011/08/oral-sex-and-dealbreakers.html.

23. Amanda Marcotte, "The Feminist Wisdom of the Ramones," *Pandagon*, August 8, 2011, http://www.rawstory.com/rs/2011/08/08/pandagon-the_feminist_wisdom_of_the_ramones/.

24. Amanda Hess, "The Year in Dealbreakers," GOOD, December 19, 2011, http://www.good.is/posts/the-year-in-dealbreakers.

THE WORLD WILL BE A BETTER PLACE WHEN MORE MEN TAKE IT UP THE ASS

Charlie Glickman

There are lots of things we can do to make the world a better place. We can reduce our consumption of irreplaceable resources, we can develop our capacity to bring compassion to our relationships, we can support people in crisis or in need—there's plenty to be done. And there's one thing that I think has an unrealized potential to improve things: The world will be a better place when more men take it up the ass.

Before you get all worked up over that, I want to be clear about something. I don't think that *every* man needs to explore anal play and prostate pleasure. There are many reasons why someone might not, ranging from it simply not being their cup of tea to being a survivor of sexual assault and finding it too triggering. I will never say that everyone should do anything, especially when it comes to sex, since there are so many different experiences and histories.

I also want to make it clear that I'm talking about cisgender men. Some of this will apply to many trans men as well, but not all of it. The experiences of trans men with respect to gender, sex, and bodies vary in different ways than the experiences of cisgender men, and I don't want to sound like I'm oversimplifying those complexities. Having said that, anal play has the potential to offer cisgender men (and their partners of any gender) insights that nothing else can.

WALKING A MILE IN THEIR SHOES

As a sex and relationship coach, I can attest that one of the common challenges in heterosexual relationships is that men often want to rush to intercourse and see foreplay as a chore they need to get through in order to "get their partner ready." I know what that's like—I've certainly had the urge to skip ahead in my excitement, though fortunately, that's something I've mostly outgrown over the years. But even the word "foreplay" assumes that the goal is intercourse, as if the destination is more important than the getting there.

This situation is the source of a lot of frustration between partners and it's partly due to the physical way that sex often works for cisgender men. Unless we've explored receiving anal penetration, sex happens outside our bodies. It's a lot easier to do that when you have a headache or you're in the mood for a quickie or you just want to fuck. That's especially true for younger men, since older guys are more likely to need direct stimulation in order to have erections, and because the relative novelty of sex when we're younger often makes us so excited that we rush into it.

But when sex is something that happens inside your body, whether vaginally or anally, you often need a bit more warm-up. Taking things more slowly and attending to your arousal makes a big difference because how you feel physically, emotionally, relationally, and mentally can have a much bigger influence when sex happens inside your body.

Of course, plenty of men do understand this, at least intellectually. But receiving anal penetration gives us an opportunity to learn it on an embodied level. Once you've explained to a partner that you really do need them to go slower or that you need more warm-up or lubricant before hard, pounding sex, it becomes much easier to remember that when you're on the giving side. That makes you a far better lover than any amount of reading can do.

In fact, I think that anyone who wants to be on the giving side of anal sex should try receiving it. Who would be a better massage therapist? Someone who has received bodywork and knows how it feels, or someone who has read about it and given massages but has never received one? The somatic experience of receiving a massage will teach you how to be a better giver, no matter how much you think you know. It works the same way for anal sex.

That's especially relevant in a world where more people than ever before are learning to have sex from watching porn. Sex in porn is a lot like cooking shows. In a cooking show, the chef says something like, "Half a half-cup of chopped onion," and there it is, like magic. There's no cutting board to clean or onion skins to throw out, and everything is ready to go. The same thing happens in most porn. When it's time to get to the intercourse, there's no need for warm-up, for figuring out which positions will be fun, for lubricant, or for talking with each other to make it feel good. It's a lot like that cooking show, where everything just sort of happens perfectly.

The difference, of course, is that anyone who has ever cooked knows that real-life kitchens don't work like the fantasy shown on the screen. But I've worked with a lot of people who think that their sex is supposed to look like what they see in porn. There's plenty that could be said about that, but what I'd like to focus on for the moment is that intercourse in porn usually dives right into hard, deep pounding sex. There's certainly nothing wrong with enjoying that kind of pleasure, but the problem is that a lot of men don't seem to realize that in real life, lots of people need a lot more arousal, warm-up, and attention before going there. And even the men who think they understand that might still get impatient or want to move things along faster than their partners can accommodate.

But once you've been on the receiving side of penetrative sex, you have a much better understanding of how you can be turned on, be really into your partner, and still need lots of warm up before anything goes inside of you. When you've had the experience of telling a partner to slow down, or asking for more lubricant, or suggesting a different position in order to be more comfortable, it becomes much easier to hear someone else say those same things without getting frustrated or impatient. I've spoken with enough men and their partners who have shared similar stories for me to really believe that it can make a difference. That has a lot of potential to improve our relationships.

On the flip side, quite a few women have told me that once they started exploring giving anal pleasure to a man, whether with their hands or with toys, they finally understood how excitement and arousal can make you speed things up more than your partner wants. It's easy to get so caught up in your enjoyment of the experience that you forget to pay attention to your partner. That doesn't mean that you are inconsiderate or selfish, though some people definitely are. It can simply be the result of your attention drifting. Learning to stay focused on your partner and present in the moment when you're turned on takes practice, and many of the women I've spoken with about their experience in giving anal pleasure have been amazed to discover just how challenging that can be.

There can also be a tendency to fall into the trap that if something feels good, then doing it faster or harder will make it feel even better. Even if this seems to make sense, very few things actually work that way when it comes to sex. Sensations that feel good at one level of intensity can become over-stimulating or painful if done too much. It's sometimes hard to tell where the line is, especially if your partner doesn't give you direct, verbal feedback. Quite a few women have told me that their exploration giving anal pleasure has shown them the importance of clear communication during sex, and it has inspired them to be more clear with their partners when they're on the receiving side.

So, just as a lot of men who explore receiving anal stimulation gain new insight into what it's like to be penetrated, many women get new perspectives on what it's like to give that kind of pleasure. Even when they might know these things intellectually, the somatic experience that comes from switching things up has a much deeper and long-lasting impact. Think of it as walking a mile in the other person's shoes. It's one thing to intellectually know this stuff. It's a very different thing to experience it on an embodied level. And one way to gain that experience is for male/female couples to explore anal play for men.

YOU CAN'T BE FULLY PRESENT IN YOUR BODY IF YOU AREN'T PRESENT IN YOUR ASS

How does your ass feel? Not your buttcheeks. Your ass. Your anus. What sensations are you feeling there, in this moment?

We live in a world that is very anal-phobic, especially for men. Most people learn to tune that part of their bodies out, to not pay attention to it, to ignore it. It's a no-go zone, full of tension and shame. A lot of men never touch themselves there at all.

There's a reason that people who are stressed out all of the time are sometimes called "tight asses." Think about how a dog tucks his tail when he's done something bad and is being punished. People have very similar responses, but lacking a tail and standing upright makes it less visible. When we're scared or angry or embarrassed, the pelvic floor clenches. If you're tuned into your body and can relax, your muscles probably calm down on their own. But for people who are chronically stressed out, the pelvic floor doesn't relax when the stress goes away because it's so used to holding tightly. As a result of that tension and the discomfort it causes, a lot of people simply tune out of that part of their bodies. Their asses become numb zones that they don't even notice anymore.

There are a lot of reasons why that can happen. It can result from early shaming as part of toilet training. It can be due to sexual injury or trauma. It can be caused by long-term toxic shaming and lack of shame resilience. It can be a result of sitting in chairs and car seats so much that the muscles numb out. It can be caused by the pressure that pregnancy places on the pelvic floor.

While people of any gender can learn to dissociate from their asses, heterosexual men are especially prone to it because of the cultural and personal associations they commonly have around the pelvis and the anus. Plenty of men believe that moving one's hips while walking makes one look unmanly. Go to a busy street or mall sometime and watch how men move. Many of them are so out of touch with their pelvises that they hardly move them when they walk. Or go out to a bar or club and pay attention to how men dance. You'll probably see a lot of guys who dance from their shoulders and knees, rather than their hips.

A tight ass isn't just the result of tension; it also causes it. All of the muscles of the pelvic floor are interconnected with each other and with the muscles of your hips, lower back, and abdomen. You can think of the anus as the center of a web. When it can't relax, it can pull all of the other strands of the web out of alignment. So even if you don't notice how your ass feels, you might be feeling it in your hips or somewhere else and that discomfort makes it difficult to be present in your body.

Pleasurable anal play is all about learning to relax the anus and pelvic floor, rather than forcing it to do something it doesn't really want to do. Contrary to what you'll see in the vast majority of porn, anal play is not about forcing anything: It's about relaxing into receptivity. Receiving caring, loving anal touch (whether it includes penetration or not) can help us calm down, pay attention to how we feel, and tune into that part of our bodies to re-inhabit it. It's only when we can do that that we can be fully present in our bodies.

The more we can do be fully present in our bodies, the more we can open our hearts to the people around us. It is hard to be caring and loving when we're dissociated or in discomfort, especially when we don't even notice that it's happening. Anal pleasure makes it easier to stop being a tight-ass and to expand our capacity for joyful, caring connections with others.

Part of the difficulty is that there's a learning curve. There's a span of time between when we start to notice our discomfort and before we can reliably sustain relaxation, pleasure, and health. That can be a disincentive to doing this work, but it's well worth the effort. Once you get over the learning curve, the payoff is that you become more comfortable in your body and more open-hearted to the people around you. I think it's easy to see how that has the potential to make the world a better place.

TAKE IT LIKE A MAN

When Aislinn Emirzian and I wrote *The Ultimate Guide to Prostate Pleasure*,[1] we surveyed over 200 people of different genders and sexual orientations about their experiences with prostate play. When we asked them about their worries and concerns with this kind of pleasure, we heard three things:

- Will it hurt?
- Will it be messy?
- Will it make me gay?

The first two questions are technical: How do we do this safely and pleasurably? These are important topics to explore, though I also notice that these concerns tend to be much louder in volume when we're talking about men receiving anal play than when women are on the receiving end. I wonder if that's because of the third worry we heard: What does this mean for my masculinity?

There are a lot of reasons that people believe that enjoying anal and prostate pleasure somehow takes away from one's masculinity. Many people see being penetrated as being dominated or taking on "the woman's role," or think that getting fucked means that men lose masculine status. That seems deeply unfortunate to me, especially in light of the ways that sexism and homophobia intertwine to reinforce the performance of masculinity. Even the use of slang like "I'm so fucked" or "fuck you" or "that sucks" rests on the idea that being penetrated is demeaning.

One of the things I've learned from anal and prostate play is that there's something incredibly powerful about being fully present in your masculinity while also being receptive. When we learn that we can be strongly rooted in our masculinity while also opening up to penetration—and when we discover how to hold onto both of those experiences simultaneously—there are amazing new territories we can explore. We can learn that we don't need to see gender or masculinity as an all-or-nothing experience. We can re-envision penetration as simply one way to experience pleasure, without making it a marker of being less-than. Learning to "take it like a man" can make us stronger and more resilient. When more men discover how to do that, the world will be a much better place.

A lot of the heterosexual men who have read our book on prostate play have contacted me to tell me how amazed they are that they can enjoy the wonderful pleasures of this kind of erotic contact. I always tell them that what feels good to you is about how your body is wired, while your sexual orientation is about who you want to do those things with. They are separate questions and we don't need to keep thinking that one has to imply anything about the other.

It is also worth mentioning that some gay and bisexual men who are exclusively tops (the ones who do the fucking) have some similar concerns around their identity. In many parts of the gay community, there's a privilege or status that accrues to tops that parallels the male privilege in the larger heterosexual world. These men sometimes struggle with fears around what it means about them if they enjoy anal or prostate stimulation. So it's important to recognize that someone can be gay and still have these kinds of concerns about anal play and masculinity.

Whatever someone's sexual orientation, anal play can create an opportunity to look at some of the attitudes and beliefs about gender and sexuality that many of us carry. Of course, it's certainly possible to examine those without that erotic inspiration. But in my experience, very few things can motivate us to do that work like sexual pleasure. And when we can rethink what sex means, and let go of the belief that what someone finds pleasurable means anything about them as a person, we can finally let go of some of the judgment and shaming we heap upon those whose sexual desires are different from our own.

Just to be clear: There isn't anything wrong if someone has fantasies about domination and submission, or about gender play. A lot of people get a big thrill about those kinds of sex games and there are many ways to make them fun. If you get turned on by them, enjoy! Just remember that enjoying anal play (and various fantasies and other turn-ons) doesn't have to imply anything about who you are in the world.

PLEASURE HEALS

When men start to explore anal pleasure, it shifts the focus away from that limited and limiting definition of sex. It expands our ideas of what sex can be and how to experience it. It gives us more options and makes it easier to let go of the idea that some desires are "normal." And it shows us that sexual pleasure is a buffet and we can choose any combination that makes everyone involved happy. Of course, none of this requires anyone to stop enjoying intercourse. It simply creates more options and takes a lot of the pressure off of one kind of sex.

This is especially important in light of how many people struggle with shame, self-doubt, blame, and anger when they or their partners face medical issues that affect what kinds of sex are available or pleasurable. Whatever the situation, when men and their partners discover anal and prostate pleasure, it often inspires them to rethink what sex means to them. My observation is that people who explore this tend to be less judgmental about the choices that other people make for themselves, which creates much more room for respecting sexual diversity. It is a lot harder to judge people for not fitting into the standard definition of sexual expression when you don't fit into it either.

Do I think that anal sex is going to save the world? Not in and of itself. And as a sex educator and as someone who enjoys giving and receiving anal and prostate pleasure, I know from both professional and personal experience that it can make a huge difference in how cisgender men feel about sex and how we build relationships with other people.

Pleasure can be one of the most healing experiences we have, especially when it comes to our sexuality and sexual identity. Of course, pleasure for its own sake can easily become the sexual equivalent of junk food. But discovering the pleasures that genuinely feed us can be a profoundly transformative experience. When men explore anal play, it can help us gain new insight into our partner's experiences, move into more embodiment and connection with our entire bodies, rethink what masculinity means to us, and examine our relationship to sex. All of those have the potential to foster healing the wounds dealt to us by sex-negativity, shame, fear, homophobia, and sexism. The fact that it can also feel incredibly pleasurable is an amazing bonus. For all of these reasons, I firmly believe that the world will be a better place when more men take it up the ass.

DISCUSSION QUESTIONS

• Where does the message that "sex = intercourse" come from? How does this affect sexual relationships?

• Why do so many people think of men receiving penetration as being demeaned or emasculated? How does that relate to attitudes about gay and bisexual men?

• What are some of the ways that pleasure can support healing and growth? What makes that easier? What are some of the challenges that can arise?

NOTE

1. Charlie Glickman and Aislinn Emirzian, *The Ultimate Guide to Prostate Pleasure: Erotic Exploration for Men and Their Partners* (Berkeley, CA: Cleis Press, 2013)

IN DEFENSE OF GOING WILD OR

How I Stopped Worrying and Learned to Love Pleasure (and How You Can, Too)[1]

Jaclyn Friedman

I am one of Those Girls.

I have taken my shirt (and occasionally more) off for an audience. Sometimes to make a political point. Sometimes just because somebody asked. But almost always for the sheer pleasure of it, for the thrill of sexual power that comes from holding a room in your thrall. I've gone home drunk with someone on the first date—scratch that, the first meeting—and fucked sweaty until 2:00 a.m.

I "lost" my "virginity" at age fifteen and haven't had the decency to regret it yet.

I've gone to a frat party already drunk and wrapped in a toga. I've walked through the city after dark by myself, dressed only in a slip, fishnets, and a leather jacket. I've gotten down and dirty with strangers on a crowded dance floor. I've played quarters with the wrestling team. Once, I had sex with my girlfriend in a barely-hidden doorway.

I'm fully aware that from a safety perspective, these aren't the smartest things I've ever done. Nor do I imagine they demonstrate any kind of glittery Girl Power™. Wild sexual behavior is risky at best, and stupid at worst, right? Right?

No. Of course not. Stupid is nowhere near the worst. If you're a woman, wild sexual behavior is downright fucking dangerous. Not only can you "get yourself" raped, but you're also damn likely to find yourself blamed for it. After all, you should have known better.

I'm over the whole thing. Start to finish. And I hereby declare my right to be wild and still maintain my bodily autonomy.

Look, life is full of "stupid." Bungee jumping is stupid. Playing football is stupid. Running for president (even just student body president) is stupid. Riding a motorcycle is stupid. Public speaking is stupid. Falling in love is stupid. Writing this essay is stupid. They're all likely to end in heartbreak, embarrassment, injury, or all of the above. But nobody except your mother is likely to try to talk you out of doing them, and no one, including your mother, is going to blame you or deny you the assistance you need to recover if, in the course of doing them, another person physically assaults you.

And there's the rub: There are risks inherent to any behavior. Even if you never you leave your house, you risk depression due to lack of sun and social interaction (never mind the risk of fire, gas explosion, electric shock, earthquake, falling down the stairs, cutting yourself on a kitchen knife, or getting a splinter). But rape is not a risk inherent in partying or in "wild" sexual behavior.

I'll repeat that: Rape is *not* a risk inherent in unregulated partying or sexual behavior. Need proof? Consider this: It's not a risk for nearly half the population. I've never met a straight man who worried about being raped as he contemplated a night of debauchery. Vomiting in public? Yes. Getting rejected by sexual prospects? Sure. Getting in a fight? Maybe. Getting raped? Come on.

It's a risk for women because, to put it bluntly, simply being female is a risk factor for rape. Partying wouldn't have anything to do with it if vast swaths of the social order weren't constructed on the foundation of control over women's sexuality. If women were just as free as men to go a little crazy on their own terms, things would fall apart. Entire segments of the corporate porn and entertainment industries would crumble because it would no longer be taboo (and therefore thrilling) to see girls "going wild." Men would have to rethink its indulgence of "boys will be boys" behavior if "girls could be girls," too. Homophobia would lose some of its grip, because it would no longer be a scary, vulnerable thing to be "like a girl."

No wonder it's easier to just tell women to "be careful" and create safe-ride programs. But there are costs to asking women to police our own safety, beyond the basic and profound unfairness of the thing. The first is pleasure. Because I gotta tell you: Indulging your wild side can be pretty fun. That's why we do it. For the ecstasy of merging our bodies with the sweaty, throbbing crowd on the dance floor. For the thrill of meeting someone's eye for the first time and indulging our desire to find out *right now* what their skin feels like. For the dizziness of drunken camaraderie. For the way the night air on our bare arms and legs raises goose flesh, our heart rate, and eyebrows, and reminds us what it feels like to be alive.

Sure, there are plenty of ways drinking and/or sexing can be bad for you— any pleasure can be manipulated or abused for any number of reasons. But there's nothing inherently wrong with either, and when you force women to choose safety over pleasure in ways men never have to (and when you shame them for choosing "wrong"), you teach women that their pleasure is not as important as men's. And that's a slippery slope we all need to stop sliding down.

Beyond that, scaring women into safety simply isn't making women safer—and it never will. Very few people of any age or gender go get drunk thinking it's a responsible thing to do. However true it may be that it's safer not to get drunk (approximately 70 percent of rapes among college students involve alcohol or drug use) or go home with people you don't know very well, it's not like women haven't already heard about the risks ad infinitum from parents, college administrations, the nightly news, or any of the twenty-five *CSI* or *Law and Order* clones on TV.

I know what you're thinking: *Okay, so it's unfair. But the risk is still real. Are we supposed to stop warning women about rape?* Believe me, I get it. Almost every woman I know has been sexually violated in some way. I'm no exception (see "played quarters with the wrestling team" above). But we need to not just indulge our desire to *do something*. We need to think first about what will actually work.

The good news? We already know something that doesn't work: blaming and shaming women. We also know something that does work (although it will take a while): holding rapists responsible.

Let's look a little more closely at that correlation between rape and alcohol, for example. That's not a correlation between female drinking and rape. It's a correlation between *all* drinking and rape. In fact, studies have shown that it's more likely that a male rapist has been drinking than his female victim has. So if we want to raise awareness about the links between drinking and rape, we should start by getting the word out to men (who are, after all, the overwhelming majority of rapists) that alcohol is likely to impair their ability to respond appropriately if a sexual partner says no. (This would, not incidentally, be much easier to do if we taught both women and men to seek enthusiastic consent in their partners, not just the absence of "no.") When was the last time you read about *that* anywhere? When we discuss drinking and rape and neglect to shine the light on men's drinking, we play into the same victim blaming that makes it so easy for men to rape women in the first place.

The silence around men's drinking is, of course, part of a that larger "boys will be boys" culture, one that played a large part in my assault. The party I attended was for a men's sports team; the coaches provided the alcohol.

This is the very culture that supports acquaintance rape to begin with, the very culture feminists have been working to dismantle for decades. And that's the problem. Holding boys and men accountable is no quick fix, and in the meantime, women are still in danger.

So, if we can't just wait until feminism smashes the patriarchy, and blaming/shaming/ frightening women isn't working, where does that leave us?

How about we just get real. Tell women about the real risks of rape while also promoting more sophisticated, pleasure-affirming messages that go beyond advocating "abstinence" from drinking and sexual experimentation. Yes, get the message out that when it comes to preventing sexual violence, not drinking is safer than drinking, and staying with people you trust is safer than playing with people you just met. But stop there, and you're setting up a false and impossible choice between purity and rape. These "risky" behaviors can be a lot of fun, both physically and socially, and most of us will choose immediate pleasure over the abstract risk of violence or death, at least some of the time—and why shouldn't we? Plus, the more society warns against something, the more appealing it can become as an act of rebellion.

What if the cultural message we give to women about rape prevention went something like this:

1.   Whatever you wear, whoever you dance with, however much you drink, whatever way you walk home, however many sex partners you choose to have—none of these behaviors make rape your fault. Nothing makes rape your fault. Rape is not your fault.
2.   Unfortunately, we still live in a culture where women are (unfairly) at risk for rape. Even though it shouldn't be your responsibility to worry about this, there are some things you can do to reduce your risk. The safest thing to do is to not drink at all, and to not be alone with anyone you don't know well and trust.
3.   If you decide to drink, it's safer to do it in moderation and/or in the company of a friend you trust to look out for you (not just someone you know. Nearly 80 percent of rape victims know their attackers).
4.   If you decide to have casual sex, take similar precautions: Tell a friend where you're going and with whom, pay close attention to your instincts, and make sure the person respects your boundaries *before* you go anywhere private with them.
5.   For the times you may choose to get properly sauced, or your friend turns out to be not as reliable as you'd hoped, or things get outta hand in a way you didn't see coming, learn how to defend yourself against sexual coercion and assault.

Yes, I said it: Take self-defense. No, I am not blaming the victim, or putting the responsibility on the woman. I'm living in reality—remember the part about how long it's going to be before we're consistently successful at holding rapists responsible? In the meantime, wouldn't you rather know what to do if and when the shit hits the fan?

I sure wish I had. I never even tried to shove that guy off of me. That's something that I now know I could have done easily, even drunk, even if he was bigger than me, which honestly, he wasn't. But it never occurred to me there was anything I could do physically to protect myself. Why? Not because I was drunk. Because literally no one my whole life had told me that my body could work in my own defense (and many, many messages had told me the opposite).

And yet it's true: Women and girls can keep ourselves safe using our very own bodies. No pepper spray. No whistles. Even women who don't work out, or are "overweight" or are physically impaired. If we spent even a fraction of the time we used to teach girls to fear for their bodies teaching girls to use their bodies for their own protection instead, there'd be a hell of a lot less for any of us to worry about. Because the most practical way to reduce the risk of rape for all women is to create a culture in which the rapist has to worry that he'll get hurt.

Will any of this work 100 percent of the time? Nope. Again: Life is risk. But this kind of complex message gives women real choices. Equipping them with the information and tools they need to protect themselves, and then trusting them to make their own decisions, will work a heck of a lot better than knowing less and living in fear. And it will give every woman a fighting chance at a world where she can go out and get a little crazy sometimes if she wants to. Where she can dance and drink and flirt and fool around because it feels good. A world where her pleasure is actually important. That's the world I'm living in. Care to join me?

DISCUSSION QUESTIONS

• The author says that life is risk and this includes sexuality. What do you think about this statement?

• If wild sexual behavior can be dangerous for all women, do you think it varies across race, class, sexual orientation, etc.? Is wild sexual behavior dangerous for men? Explain your response.

• How and when should we start teaching women to choose pleasure over safety? Should "enthusiastic consent" be incorporated into sex education classes?

• Do you agree with the author that we should spend more time teaching girls to use their bodies for their own protection instead of teaching girls to fear for their bodies? When and how should this conversation start? What should we be teaching boys in regard to sexual pleasure and consent?

NOTE

1. This chapter originally appears in *Yes Means Yes!: Visions of Female Sexual Power and A World Without Rape*, ed. Jaclyn Friedman and Jessica Valenti (Berkeley, CA: Seal Press, 2008). Reprinted with permission from Perseus.

CONTRIBUTORS

Rena Bivens is a Government of Canada Banting Fellow in the School of Journalism and Communication at Carleton University in Ottawa, Ontario. She is a sociologist with expertise in the areas of digital media (particularly social media), gender (including gender-based violence), television news production, citizen journalism, feminist and queer theory, science and technology studies, and Internet research methodologies. She completed her PhD at the University of Glasgow as a member of the Glasgow Media Group. She has previously been an adjunct professor and SSHRC Postdoctoral Fellow in the Pauline Jewett Institute of Women's and Gender Studies at Carleton University, and a lecturer in digital media and mass communication at the University of Nottingham's campus in Ningbo, China. She has also been affiliated with the Simone de Beauvoir Institute at Concordia University as a Research Associate.

Aura Bogado is the news editor for *Colorlines*, where she writes about racial justice, Native rights, and immigration. She's contributed to a variety of publications, including *Mother Jones*, the *Nation*, and *Newsweek Argentina*, and is currently working on a book about immigrant detention in the United States. She's a graduate of Yale University, and also holds a certificate in indigenous peoples' rights and policy from Columbia University. She was born and raised in South America, is of Guarani descent, and currently lives in New York.

Mark Carrigan is a sociologist based in the Centre for Social Ontology at the University of Warwick. He edits the Sociological Imagination and is an assistant editor for Big Data & Society. His research interests include asexuality studies, sociological theory, and digital sociology. He's a regular blogger and podcaster at markcarrigan.net.

Samuel Carter joined the Rockefeller Foundation in December 2013. As associate director for the foundation's Resilience program, he works to increase our knowledge and understanding of resilience, and to identify innovative strategies for putting resilience-based solutions into practice. He helped to establish the Institute for Public Knowledge at New York University, where he served as associate director. He worked as program coordinator for the President's Office of the Social Science Research Council, taught at NYU's Stern School of Business, and served as a researcher for Vice President Joe Biden and political strategist Robert Shrum. He is a co-founder and serves on the board of Hollaback!, a global movement to end street harassment and ensure equal access to public space using mobile technology. He received a master's in public administration in public and nonprofit policy analysis and management from New York University.

Soraya Chemaly is a feminist writer, critic, and activist whose work focuses on the role of gender in politics, religion, and popular culture. She speaks regularly on topics related to sexualized violence and media portrayals of gender. She is a regular contributor to the *Huffington Post*, *RH Reality Check*, *Fem2.0*, and *Role Reboot*. Her writing also appears in *Salon*, the *Guardian*, and CNN, and she is a frequent radio commentator, including on the BBC, NPR's *Talk of the Nation*, and Sirius XM *Progressive Radio*. She was one of the primary organizers of a successful social media campaign asking Facebook to remove sexist and misogynistic content in accordance to its guidelines on bullying, harassment, and safety. The #FBrape campaign, widely covered in media, was described as "an historic turning point in the fight against gender based hate speech." Prior to working several years as an executive with the Gannett Company, she was a writer and editor at multiple publications and a founding principal in an urban monthly magazine in Washington, DC. She graduated from Georgetown University's College of Arts and Sciences, where she founded that school's feminist journal, *The New Press*, and attended Radcliffe College for post-graduate studies. She is the 2013 recipient of the Donna Allen Award for Feminist Journalism.

Lynn Comella, PhD, is a women's studies professor at the University of Nevada, Las Vegas. Her research and teaching interests include media and culture, gender and sexuality, and popular entertainment and consumer culture. Her research explores the intersection of feminist sexual politics and marketplace culture, with a focus on the women's market for sex toys and pornography. Her work has appeared in *The Feminist Porn Book*; *Sex for Sale: Prostitution, Pornography, and the Sex Industry*; *New Sociologies of Sex Work*; *Commodity Activism: Cultural Resistance in Neoliberal Times*; and *Feminist Media Studies*, among other places. She's a frequent media contributor and writes extensively on sexuality and culture for the popular press.

Brittney Cooper, PhD, is Assistant Professor of women's and gender studies and Africana studies at Rutgers University. A scholar of Black women's intellectual history, Black feminist thought, and race and gender in popular culture, she writes extensively about both historic and contemporary iterations of Black feminist theorizing. She is currently completing her first book, *Race Women: Gender and the Making of a Black Public Intellectual Tradition*. She is cofounder of the Crunk Feminist Collective, a feminist of color scholar-activist group that runs a highly successful blog.

Jordan Fairbairn is a PhD candidate in the Department of Sociology and Anthropology at Carleton University in Ottawa, Canada. Her research explores social media, sexual and intimate partner violence, feminist activism, and the relationship between academia and social change. She is a member of the Public Engagement Committee at the Ottawa Coalition to End Violence Against Women (OCTEVAW).

Kimberly Fairchild is an associate professor of psychology at Manhattan College. She earned her PhD in social psychology from Rutgers, the State University of New Jersey. She teaches courses in introductory psychology, social psychology, psychology of women, psychology of sexuality, motivation and emotion, and advanced research methods. Her research focuses on women's experiences of and reactions to street harassment. She became interested in studying street harassment when her female students in the psychology of women course had difficulty relating to examples of sexual harassment in the workplace. Few of the students had experienced workplace sexual harassment, but nearly all had been whistled at, catcalled, and groped in public places. Her research has helped shed light on an experience that is exceedingly common for most women, yet frequently ignored, often to detrimental consequences. She continues to investigate the causes and consequences of street harassment. She strongly supports the work of others to help increase awareness of street harassment (e.g. ihollaback.org and stopstreetharassment.com).

Helen E. Fisher, PhD, is a Biological Anthropologist at Rutgers University and Senior Research Fellow at the Kinsey Institute, Indiana University. She studies the evolution, brain systems (fMRI), and biological patterns of romantic love, mate choice, marriage, adultery and divorce, gender differences in the brain, the biology of personality, and the neuroscience of leadership and business styles. She has written five internationally best-selling books, including *Why Him? Why Her?* (Henry Holt), *Why We Love* (Henry Holt), and *Anatomy of Love* (Ballantine Books) and publishes widely in academic journals. She is currently chief scientific advisor to the Internet dating site Match.com and its subsidiary, Chemistry.com, where she designed the Chemistry.com questionnaire now taken by thirteen million people in forty countries. She lectures worldwide including lectures at TED, The World Economic Forum (Davos), the 2012 international meeting of the G20, National Academy of Sciences, the *Economist*, United Nations, Smithsonian Institution, and the Salk Institute. She appears regularly on TV, radio, and print media. For a full CV, see her website: helenfisher.com.

Nina M. Flores is an educator, scholar, writer, and activist living in Southern California. She is a lecturer in the Social and Cultural Analysis of Education (SCAE) graduate program at California State University, Long Beach, and speaks and writes about feminism, sexual assault prevention, street harassment, and social media. Her writing is featured in popular outlets such as *Ms.* magazine blog, the *Huffington Post*, and *Progressive Planning Magazine*. Her research on women and cities focuses on street harassment, exploring how people use technology to virtually document their experiences in public space, and how community planners and organizers can use this information to better understand and resist harassment. She is the former managing editor of *Critical Planning Journal*, has graduate degrees in both political science and education, and is a PhD candidate in urban planning at the University of California, Los Angeles.

Jaclyn Friedman is a writer, educator, and activist. Her books include *Yes Means Yes: Visions of Female Sexual Power and a World Without Rape* (Seal Press) and *What You Really Really Want: The Smart Girl's Shame-Free Guide to Sex and Safety* (Seal Press). She is a founder of Women, Action, and the Media. She is a popular speaker on campuses and at conferences across the United States and beyond. She has been a guest on the *Melissa Harris-Perry Show*, the BBC, *Democracy Now*, *To the Contrary*, and numerous other radio and television shows, and her commentary has appeared in outlets including CNN, the *Washington Post*, *The Nation*, *Jezebel*, Feministing.com, *The American Prospect*, and the *Huffington Post*.

Justin R. Garcia, PhD, is a member of the Kinsey Institute and holds a postdoctoral fellowship at Indiana University. He is a graduate of Binghamton University (SUNY) in biological sciences, with a master's in biomedical anthropology and doctorate in evolutionary biology. His dissertation is titled "Behavioral Ecology of Contemporary Human Sexual Behavior." His current research interests include evolutionary and biocultural models of human behavior, romantic love and intimate relationships, sexual/social monogamy, and uncommitted sex and hook-up culture in emerging adulthood. Contact Justin Garcia at The Kinsey Institute, Indiana University, 1165 E. Third St., Morrison Hall 313, Bloomington, IN 47405, USA. Email: jusrgarc@indiana.edu.

Charlie Glickman, PhD, is a sex and relationship coach, writer, blogger, educator, and an internationally acclaimed speaker. For over twenty years, he has spoken at academic conferences and community events, taught workshops about sexuality, pleasure, and relationships. He trains sexuality educators, medical and mental health professionals, and clergy to enable them to better serve their clients and communities. He also works with individuals, couples, and groups to help them have great sex. His areas of focus include sex and shame, sex-positivity, queer issues, masculinity, and communities of erotic affiliation. He is co-author of *The Ultimate Guide to Prostate Pleasure: Erotic Exploration for Men and Their Partners* (Cleis Press), the first book that explains the amazing pleasures of the prostate and all of the ways that men and their partners can explore the erotic potential it has to offer. Read more at www.MakeSex-Easy.com and www.CharlieGlickman.com, or follow him on Facebook and Twitter as @CharlieGlickman.

Craig Gross is an author, speaker, pastor, and revolutionary. He shot to prominence in 2002 when he founded the website XXXchurch.com as a response to the hurting he saw both in those addicted to pornography and those who made their living in the porn industry. The XXXchurch website mixes the seedy with the sacred in an effort to raise the often taboo subject of pornography as a problem that needs to be dealt with. In the ten years since it began, XXXchurch.com has had over seventy million visitors to the website and his ministry is the subject of an award-winning documentary. He also spearheaded the development of X3watch, an Internet accountability system that is used by over one million people. He is the author of nine books and has been featured in *GQ* magazine, *Newsweek, Time, Wired,* the *New York Times,* the *Los Angeles Times,* and has appeared on *Good Morning America, Nightline,* CNN, Fox News, and the *Daily Show with Jon Stewart.*

Jamie J. Hagen is a writer and doctoral student of global governance and human security at the University of Massachusetts, Boston, with a focus on gender and feminist security studies. As a freelance writer she has covered queer politics, news, and culture for publications such as RollingStone.com and Autostraddle.com, where she was a contributing editor from 2011 to 2012. She has an MA from CUNY Brooklyn College in political science, where she studied political theory.

Caroline Heldman, PhD, is the chair of the politics department at Occidental College in Los Angeles. Her research specializes in the presidency, systems of power (race, class, gender, and sexuality), and sexual violence. Her work has been featured in the top journals in her field and the edited collection, *Rethinking Madame President: Are We Ready for a Woman in the White House?* (Lynne Rienner Publishers). She has been active in "real world" politics as a professional pollster, campaign manager, and commentator for Fox News, Fox Business News, CNBC, and Al Jazeera America. She splits her time between Los Angeles and New Orleans, where she co-founded the New Orleans

Women's Shelter and the Lower Ninth Ward Living Museum. She also co-founded Faculty Against Rape (FAR), a national organization that assists faculty in advocating for student survivors.

Ned Henry is a kinky queer porn performer, adult web developer, and physicist. His performances and productions have won awards at AVN and Cinekink, and the Feminist Porn Awards. When he isn't behind the camera, he uses his background in experimental physics and online archives to reprogram the porn industry, working to give independent performers the tools to monetize their sexuality on their own terms.

Robert Jensen is a journalism professor at the University of Texas at Austin, is the author of *Getting Off: Pornography and the End of Masculinity* (South End Press), and co-author of *Pornography: The Production and Consumption of Inequality* (Routledge). He can be reached at rjensen@uts.cc.utexas.edu.

Marjorie Jolles, PhD, is Associate Professor of women's and gender studies at Roosevelt University in Chicago. Her research is in the area of Continental philosophy and feminist cultural studies, with emphasis on embodiment, ethics, narrative, and the cultural life of feminism. She is co-editor of *Fashion Talks: Undressing the Power of Style* (SUNY Press), and has published articles in *The Oprah Phenomenon* (University Press of Kentucky) and journals such as *Hypatia*; *Feminist Formations*; *Critical Matrix: The Princeton Journal of Women, Gender, and Culture*; and *Feminist Teacher*. Her current book project is a study of contemporary American postfeminism, tracing its philosophical linkages and breaks with 20th-century American feminism and its uptake in popular culture. She earned a doctorate in philosophy from Temple University.

Elizabeth Juarez is a graduate from the Department of Women's, Gender, and Sexuality Studies at California State University, Long Beach. Her research and activism focuses on issues of abortion, sex education, and reproductive justice. She is a member of the Choice USA chapter at Long Beach.

Lara Karaian, PhD, is assistant professor in the Institute of Criminology and Criminal Justice, Carleton University, Ottawa, Canada. She received a two-year SSHRC research grant entitled "Managing Risky Subjects: Teenage Girls, Digital Technology and Canadian Anti-Sexting Public Education Campaigns." She is a contributor to *Feminist and Queer Legal Theory: Intimate Encounters, Uncomfortable Conversations* (Ashgate Press) and co-editor of the award-winning Canadian Third Wave Feminist anthology, *Turbo Chicks: Talking Young Feminisms* (Sumach Press). The author would like to thank Ummni Khan, Evelyn Maeder, Dawn Moore, and Joe Pert for engaging her in critical dialogue on this topic and providing suggestions on an earlier draft of this chapter.

Noah E. Lewis, Esq. is the founder of Transcend Legal, a New York City-based law practice focused on serving transgender clients throughout the United States. The practice focuses on working collaboratively with institutions to achieve solutions for transgender individuals facing discrimination, with a focus on achieving access to health care. As part of this work, he routinely conducts trainings and presentations on transgender issues. He also founded Trans Pride NYC, which organizes positive, community-building events for transgender people in New York. Previously, he served for five years as the staff attorney for the Transgender Legal Defense and Education Fund. There he worked on high-profile, cutting-edge litigation in areas such as single-sex facilities, employment discrimination, health-care access, and identity document changes. He was the first openly trans student to graduate from Harvard Law School. There he received the Dean's Award for Community Service for his work with the Harvard Transgender Task Force, Lambda, and the Student Animal Legal Defense Fund. His work with Harvard included eliminating exclusions for transgender health care in student and employee health plans and assisting with the campaign that added gender identity to Harvard's nondiscrimination policy. A Pittsburgh native, he graduated magna cum laude from the University of Pittsburgh with a BS in chemistry and a BA in the history and philosophy of science. While at Pitt, he helped lead a successful campaign to get domestic partner health benefits at the university. He previously worked in animal advocacy and is a longtime vegan.

Emily May is an international leader in the movement to end street harassment. In 2005, at the age of 24, she co-founded Hollaback! (iHollaback.org) in New York City, and in 2010 she became the first full-time executive director. She has been named one of twenty women "leading the way" by the *Huffington Post*, a "Hero Among Us" in *People* magazine, and one of *Jezebel*'s "25 kick-ass and amazing women we love." She has a master's degree from the London School of Economics.

Allison McCarthy is a freelance writer with a focus on intersectional feminism and social justice. Her work has been featured or is forthcoming in print and online publications such as the *Guardian*, *AlterNet*, *Ms.* blog, *Bitch*, *make/shift*, *Global Comment*, *Role/Reboot*, the *Feminist Wire*, *ColorsNW*, the *Baltimore Review*, and *Hoax*. Her essays also appear in the anthologies *Robot Hearts: Twisted and True Tales of Seeking Love in the Digital Age* (Pinchback Press) and *Dear Sister: Letters From Survivors of Sexual Violence* (AK Press). Her "Dealbreaker" essay was selected as an Editor's Favorite by *GOOD* magazine in 2011, and she was also a finalist in the 2007 Maryland Writers Association Short Works Contest. A graduate of Goucher College and the Master of Professional Writing program at Chatham University, she currently resides in the greater Washington, DC area.

Amber Melvin received her BA in women's, gender, and sexuality studies from California State University. Her research interests include sexual and reproductive health and education, sexuality and disability, queer theory, and fat studies. She is a lifelong activist and currently dedicates her time to training young activists in her community and throughout California on reproductive justice issues and coalition building. You can find her on Twitter @Amberrrm or amberjeanmelvin@gmail.com.

Nia Pines graduated from California State University, Long Beach, with degrees in women's, gender, and sexuality studies and communication studies. Her interests include women of color activism, fat studies, queer theory, and reproductive justice. She has volunteered for community organizations that provide health, housing, social, legal, and other supportive resources to the LGBTQ community. Her previous research has specifically focused on acceptance and invisibility within the Black community and her future endeavors include using legal and political channels for social justice. As a part of the queer community, she is interested in creating spaces and support for all people to be authentically themselves. As she navigates what this possibility looks like for herself, she aspires to use this passion to change systemic laws, policies, and attitudes that restrict others from living their truths.

Janet Rosenbaum, PhD, studies educational and economic factors in adolescent health. Her methodological expertise is in causal inference methods such as matched sampling. Her current projects include high school suspension (funded by the Spencer Foundation), community colleges (funded by the American Educational Research Association), and coerced unsafe sex and pregnancy. She completed a postdoctoral fellowship at the Johns Hopkins Bloomberg School of Public Health under a sexually transmitted diseases training grant from the Centers for Disease Control and Prevention. She also earned a PhD in health policy and statistics, an MA in statistics, and a BA in physics, all from Harvard University. Her dissertation studied virginity pledges and adolescents' inconsistent reporting of their sexual histories, and was covered by media including the *New York Times*, National Public Radio, and *Weekend Update* on *Saturday Night Live*.

Jessica Ross is a feminist social justice activist and graduate from California State University, Long Beach, with a BA in women's, gender, and sexuality studies. Her main interest is reproductive justice work, and she has been part of the national youth-led reproductive justice group Choice USA for two years while being the co-organizational director of the CSULB chapter for one of those years. She aspires to be many things in life including a comprehensive and inclusive sex educator for K–12 youth in schools and a social and reproductive justice non-profit employee; and she has always seen herself as entering the academic realm in some way. Her mother always tells her she can see her catching babies as a midwife, so she keeps that in the back of her mind, too. After graduating college she plans to travel the world and then pursue her passions. When she isn't thinking about gender justice or taking action to change the world you can find her hiking with her dog Kona, browsing YouTube for awesome feminist and sex-positive videos, snowboarding in the mountains, or having Netflix marathons while cuddling with her two cats Star and Rascal.

Joe Samalin has been addressing gender-based violence for over fifteen years, including as the Training and Technical Assistance Coordinator for Men Can Stop Rape. He is currently the Outreach and Training Manager for the Disaster Distress Helpline and is examining, among other things, gender-based violence in the aftermath of disasters. Follow him on Twitter @joesamalin.

Jennifer Scott is a violence prevention advocate and activist. She is currently serving as Title IX program coordinator at the University of North Carolina Chapel Hill. She has also written for the *Ms.* magazine blog. She is an avid traveler and foodie.

Carrie Tilton-Jones is a writer, activist, and fifth-generation Texan who is completing a dual master's degree through the University of Texas at Austin Center for Women's and Gender Studies and the LBJ School of Public Affairs. She is the president of Austin NOW and a member of NOW's national Combating Racism Committee. Her background includes over a decade of experience in nonprofit, state agency, political campaign, and coalition-building work. An honor graduate of UT, she was a co-director of the UT Women's Resource Center and a founding board member of the UT Gender and Sexuality Center. She lives in Austin, Texas, with her very patient and supportive partner, three extremely silly cats, and an embarrassingly large number of computers.

Alexandra Tweten has been writing news since she was 14 years old. Her writing has been published in *Ms.* magazine, *Jezebel*, the *St. Cloud Times*, and the *Grand Forks Herald*. She served as editor-in-chief and news editor for St. Cloud State University's *University Chronicle*. After graduating from SCSU with a BS in mass communication and a minor in women's studies in 2009, she became lead editorial intern at *Ms.* magazine. Helping to launch the *Ms.* blog became her first foray into online activism. She began writing about online dating in 2010 with her "Feminist Craigslist Dating Experiment," which detailed what straight dating was like while disclosing her status as a feminist. Becoming the subject of the news in 2014, her Instagram account @ByeFelipe calling out hostile messages from men online garnered 250,000 followers within two weeks. @ByeFelipe was featured in the *Atlantic*, the *Guardian*, the *Daily Mail*, *Good Morning America*, *Nightline*, *BuzzFeed*, the *Huffington Post*, and many more. She lives in Los Angeles and, at the time of publication, is still searching for the person who will make her delete her dating apps for good.

Ebony A. Utley is an intimacy expert. Her groundbreaking book *Rap and Religion: Understanding the Gangsta's God* examines rappers' intimate relationships with God. Her next book, *Shades of Infidelity*, explores intimate romantic relationships interrupted by infidelity. In her other research, she investigates beliefs about marriage, studies the relationship between hip hop and love, and scrutinizes the effects of technology on intimacy. Her expertise has been featured on the Oprah Winfrey Network and other radio, print, and online outlets. She lectures at universities across the country and is an associate professor of communication studies at California State University, Long Beach. Her expertise is archived online at theutleyexperience.com.

Lisa Wade is a professor of sociology at Occidental College. She holds a PhD in sociology from the University of Wisconsin–Madison and an MA in human sexuality from New York University. She has published extensively on U.S. discourse about female genital cutting, hook up culture on college campuses, and the social significance of the body. She is also the principal writer for *Sociological Images* and appears frequently in print, radio, and television news and opinion outlets.

INDEX